NEW SURVEY OF JOURNALISM

CO-AUTHORS

REUEL R. BARLOW, A.M.
Professor of Journalism
University of Illinois

MAYNARD W. BROWN, Ph.D.
Late Professor of Journalism
Marquette University

BARBARA D. COCHRAN, A.M.
Formerly Editorial Assistant
American Council on Education

EDWIN H. FORD, M.A., M.S.
Associate Professor of Journalism
University of Minnesota

JAMES L. C. FORD, Ph.D.
Dean, School of Journalism
Montana State University

NORVAL NEIL LUXON, Ph.D.
Professor of Journalism, and
Assistant to the President
Ohio State University

DOUGLASS WOOD MILLER, M.A., Litt.D.
Executive Secretary
Case Institute of Technology

RALPH O. NAFZIGER, Ph.D.
Director of School of Journalism
University of Wisconsin

STEWART ROBERTSON
Formerly Professor of Journalism
North Carolina State College

FRANK THAYER, M.A., J.D.
Professor of Journalism
University of Wisconsin

ELMO SCOTT WATSON, M.S.J.
Director of Department
of Journalism
University of Denver

ROLAND E. WOLSELEY, M.S.J.
Professor of Journalism
School of Journalism, Syracuse University

NEW
SURVEY OF
JOURNALISM

BY

GEORGE FOX MOTT, Ph.D.

EDITOR

and

TWELVE CO-AUTHORS

With a Foreword by

GRANT MILNOR HYDE

Professor of Journalism
Former Director, School of Journalism
University of Wisconsin

New York

BARNES & NOBLE, INC.

1950

Dedicated by the Editor
to
the memory of
SAM L. COCHRAN
genial companion, journalist, friend
throughout and since Stanford days

FOREWORD

By Grant Milnor Hyde*

A glance back over thirty-nine years of teaching journalism in a university—and that means back almost to the beginning of this young college project—recalls the rapid development of textbooks as one of the most interesting aspects of the work. These struggling books brought the means whereby the subject has been standardized and developed, the means whereby teachers have exchanged ideas and experience, the means whereby the project has been brought concretely to the attention of the publishing world.

In 1905 when the University of Wisconsin launched its courses in journalism—being the first university to undertake such a project that has survived without break—there were, of course, no textbooks at all. By 1910, when I began teaching, there were five or six books on the journalism teacher's desk—mainly handbooks by newspapermen. The next ten years saw the laying of a foundation for the journalist's textbook library—at least twenty-five pioneering analyses of newspaper work in general or of newspaper reporting in particular (as well as five on advertising)—almost all of them written by the pioneer teachers—Bleyer, Williams, Flint, Hyde, Martin, Ross, Harrington, Starch, Lee, Thorp, Spencer. The decade after World War I brought a great increase in the number and size of schools of journalism, resulting in the development of many specialized courses. It also brought two new types of teaching projects—the high-school journalistic writing class and the nonprofessional or "journalism consumer" project of smaller colleges. This was reflected in a growing series of specialized books for these newer courses, as well as the beginning of a library for the high-school or small-college teacher of journalism. Now, journalism textbooks have more than come of age and are acquiring a tone of scholarship and thoroughness not seen in the pioneer texts.

The teaching of journalism has come a long way in forty-four years. What we were doing in 1910, or even in 1925, now seems very feeble

---

* Professor of Journalism, former Director, the School of Journalism, University of Wisconsin.

Author of: *Newspaper Reporting and Correspondence* (1912); *Newspaper Editing* (1915; 1925); *Handbook for Newspaper Workers* (1921; 1925); *A Course in Journalistic Writing* (1922); *Journalistic Writing* (1929; 1935; 1946); *Newspaper Handbook* (1941).

compared with the training that is given today by the better university
schools. To some of us, however, it seems evident that the project has
barely started its development and that it is likely to grow more in the
next ten years than in its first forty years—which served largely to get
its roots down to solid foundation soil. Notable is the extension beyond
newspaper work into many other journalistic fields—advertising, radio,
magazine and periodical work, public relations—opening up new opportunities to graduates.

Parallel with this growth has come the ever-increasing recognition by
the newspaper world. Long ago the newspaper world stopped laughing
at the project, and now there are few leaders in the newspaper profession
—or rank and file—who are not eager to lend a hand. In this, the schools
of journalism have come through an evolution similar to that experienced
by the schools of law and of medicine. The development of college training for a profession brings consequent changes in the profession, whatever it may be. In the world of journalism, the changes have been very
great in the last thirty-five years—the great growth of professional con-
sciousness among newspapermen, the great influx of college men into
the profession, the great increase in financial stability of the press, and
the great improvement in the fundamental character of the news and
other services of the newspaper. That there has been such improvement
is questioned by some critics whose vision is not long, but it is not questioned by persons who have studied newspapers of earlier times or of
other countries. Now, because of these things, the newspapermen are
more and more looking upon university training schools as the right of
their profession—just as lawyers or physicians look to their training
schools—and one of the most interesting developments of the future is
likely to be an increasing closeness of co-operation.

This book—comprising a survey of the entire field of journalism—
represents an entirely new project in journalism textbooks. It has been
jointly written by a group of experienced newspapermen and -women,
teachers, and textbook writers, whose competence in the field is unques-
tioned. It has been edited by a man who has an unusual and significant
background of experience in editing, publicity, business, research, teaching, military service, public and educational administration, including
the deanship of three colleges. He has published books and articles in
history, political science, education, and journalism and contributes to the
press as a commentator on the international scene. It is an honor and a
pleasure to me to have had a small part in this new project under his
editorial direction.

—G. M. H.

University of Wisconsin

PREFACE

The business of producing "words and pictures" has been going on for a long time. Combine an idea and the act of transmitting it to others out of range of immediate voice, and journalism exists at its simplest. Like other human activities the communication of ideas and information has become a complicated process with infinite technical and sociological aspects. The press is a full-fledged institution in our modern world, and the various media utilized by the press are generally called by, and now professionally united under, the common name of journalism.

Such principles of free civilization as individual liberty, individual responsibility, and the right to freedom of movement are all dependent for their fulfillment upon conditions which obtain only when there are the right of free expression and the right of access to information—that is, a free press. Such a press, in action, making effective use of all means of communication, has a specific function in a free society. The greatest single factor in solving problems arising in our domestic life and in international affairs—apart from good faith—is a clear and positive correlation between the problems and the measures which are used to deal with them. Many areas—among them political economy, human relations, and education—are not likely to have their problems resolved until they are realistically stated. One or more channels of journalism must carry such statement; therefore, journalism may not be isolated nor considered apart from the growth of the society of which it is a phase.

While the basic obligation of journalism may be thus stated very simply, its technical aspects have reached a diversity and complexity which makes an over-all view of its various media an essential study to those interested in pursuing any one of its several branches. This concept led to the original edition of this book, which stated the editor's conviction—then not generally accepted—that "journalism . . . is best learned, best appreciated, and most adequately understood only when considered as a field of activity made up of many closely interrelated phases rather than when interpreted as a series of largely independent aspects loosely associated under a common name."

Today, twelve years later, the editor remains convinced that while this book in its present enlarged and completely revised state, as in the original and intermediate editions, is not all of journalism, it fulfills a continuing need "for a book which presents a general and comprehensive survey with emphasis upon the most important facts."

ix

This new book—and it is a new book in the sense that it has been brought up-to-date and revitalized by increased editorial and author experience as well as by new material inserted in chapters retained and by several *new* chapters added—like the original edition organizes "each of the various closely interassociated phases of the journalistic craft in an authoritative, concise, clear, and logical manner. By means of 'word pictures' introducing each chapter, by occasional footnotes, and especially by three selected, annotated, and relatively complete lists of references, the book is closely co-ordinated with other material in the field." Further, this new volume of *Survey of Journalism,* like its much used predecessor, "has been planned, organized, and written for practical students whether they are being trained in the classroom or on the job, whether they are being seasoned behind the copy desk, or by 'pounding the pavement' as advertising solicitors, circulation assistants, or cub reporters. The book aims to be a practical approach with enough historical background and theory to give journalism, including the important *How* element of editing, managing, and writing, meaning and significance."

In addition, phases of journalism not generally accepted as appropriate for inclusion twelve years ago, even in a text as broad in scope as the original edition, are described in this new book. Aside from the introduction of much new material into existing chapters, such as the chapters entitled "The Press as an Institution," "The Newspaper Assembled," "The Press and the Sportsman," and "The World's Press Systems," to mention but four out of more than forty affected, three areas of journalism have been integrated into the book as new chapters. These are "Covering the Labor Run," "Publishing the Business Press," and "Radio-Television—A New Journalistic Medium."

The *New Survey of Journalism* begins with an analysis and an appraisal of the press as an institution, gives a brief overview of the vocational opportunities, presents the historical development and explains the newspaper as a functioning organization, deals in turn with each important editorial phase of gathering and writing stories for the press, is concerned with journalistic presentation, slant, headlining, and news placement, explains policy, interpretation, and influence, reviews the magazine and literary phases of the craft, presents the scope, function, and operation of the business press, discusses radio journalism, defines the legal aspects of publishing, and then deals successively with the important commercial aspects including business organization and income, advertising, distribution procedures, and production methods.

The book is organized into forty-five chapter units, an appendix with a style guide, and bibliographies. Each chapter is independent but interrelated with every other phase. The practicing journalist, student, or instructor will find the volume sufficiently elastic, by reason of its organization, to allow complete freedom in its use. The material is so arranged that one may pick and choose as one likes and still have a reasonably good comprehension of the relationship of one thought to another. In style of treatment and organization of material, the principal phases of the journalistic craft are presented in such manner as to be thoroughly understandable and teachable.

The group of associated authors who have co-operated in writing this volume is made up of recognized leaders in journalism holding posts of significance in American educational, commercial, or publishing fields. All are men and women trained in the better institutions of higher learning; experienced in many phases of practical newspaper and magazine production as applied in many diversified publishing organizations; seasoned by extensive, varied, and accumulated professional activities of all types acquired in the villages and hamlets, the middletowns, and the metropolitan areas of the nation; and, recognized as authorities in one or more phases of the profession, each with publications to his credit and other notable service as a craft member of the fourth estate.

In accord with the plan of the book each author must properly be given full credit for the production of his particular chapter units. Therefore, no author assumes either direct or implied responsibility for the content or interpretation of any chapter other than his own. When two authors have collaborated the responsibility is co-equal. Apart from basic responsibility for the book as a whole and production, or co-production, of several of the chapters, the editor has had the particular responsibility of formulating and accomplishing the plan of the book, of organizing and arranging the content, and of co-ordinating and synthesizing the contributions of the associated authors.

As given in this volume, the three-part representative bibliography has, in addition to its value as a means of co-ordination with other books in the field, two major justifications: first, the relatively few satisfactory books—countable in hundreds—that have been produced; second, the limited bibliographical work available, especially of a critical, selective nature. As in all other general phases of the book, the associated authors should not be held responsible as a group for these bibliographies. The selection and the annotations represent the judgment of Mr. Wolseley and the editor.

As accredited in the table of contents and as expanded and explained hereinafter, specific credit should be given the following authors of the chapter units as indicated.

PROFESSOR REUEL R. BARLOW, of the University of Illinois, has written the important chapters entitled "The Newspaper Sets Its Policy," "The Press as a Political and Social Force," and co-authored with the editor, in the present edition, the significant and timely chapter "The World's Press Systems."

Dr. MAYNARD W. BROWN, late professor of journalism at Marquette University, added much to the completeness and value of the original book by contributing six excellent chapters, two in collaboration with the editor. These included "The Civic Project Is News," "The Press and the Sportsman," "The March of Science as News," "The Editor Speaks," "Advertising Copy Informs, Appeals, Impels," and "Advertising Layout Attracts, Displays, Vitalizes." In the present edition the responsibility for revising or rewriting these chapters has been divided among three authors as shown by the table of contents and as developed hereinafter specifically. However, the fact is, Dr. Brown's original writing has withstood the test of time well.

Mrs. BARBARA D. COCHRAN, formerly editorial assistant of the American Council on Education, Washington, D.C., has had varied experiences in both the editorial and circulation phases of journalism and contributed much by writing the three chapters entitled "The Evolution of Journalism," "The Vigorous Voice of Circulation," and "Terminology and Press Jargon." The first-mentioned chapter is an especially fine condensation of the history of American journalism. In addition to contributing these chapters, Mrs. Cochran has rendered, in connection with the present edition, appreciated editorial assistance in a variety of ways.

The chapter "Terminology and Press Jargon," aside from being greatly enlarged, now includes a new section dealing with technical terms peculiar to radio journalism. This chapter thus becomes the most nearly complete selective list of journalistic terms available to students or practitioners of the press.

PROFESSOR EDWIN H. FORD, of the University of Minnesota, has written two chapters in the present edition—namely, "Names Make News" and "The Art and Craft of the Literary Journalist." The last-mentioned chapter is a particularly valuable contribution, for it was the first concrete presentation in a journalism text of this vital and distinctive side of the profession.

Dr. JAMES L. C. FORD, dean of the School of Journalism, Montana State University, joins the associated authors for the first time with this new edition of the book. Dean Ford has completed a variety of assignments with skill and effectiveness, including completely revising and thus co-authoring the chapter "The Press and the Sportsman," and completely redoing, as a new contribution, the chapter on business writing now called "Covering the Business Beat." Further, apart from doing a new chapter entitled "Women 'Arrive' in Journalism," replacing the work of an author no longer associated with the book, he has also done a new companion chapter to the one dealing with the business world called "Covering the Labor Run," which is a definite contribution to a field of newspaper reporting not altogether well handled by either the conservative or the radical press. And, finally, Dean Ford has authored the important chapter entitled "Radio-Television—A New Journalistic Medium," which covers a field, now definitely a significant part of journalism, not presented at all in most books on journalism.

GERALD G. GROSS, editor of *Washington Report on the Medical Sciences*, was science writer on the staff of the *Washington Post* from 1930 until his resignation in June, 1947, to establish and edit his own publication. During World War II he served as public relations officer of the Bureau of Medicine and Surgery, Navy Department, returning to inactive duty with the rank of Commander. Mr. Gross has ably reviewed, materially revised, and thereby co-authored the important chapter "The March of Science as News."

DR. NORVAL NEIL LUXON, assistant to the president and professor of journalism at Ohio State University, has written three valuable chapters entitled "News from Near and Far," "Headlining the News," and "Page-One Make-up." Each chapter is an effective and significant condensation of particularly important phases of journalism.

PROFESSOR DOUGLASS WOOD MILLER, now of the Case Institute of Technology, has produced five authoritative and helpful chapters for those beginning to learn the writer's craft and those interested in knowing more of journalistic style and presentation technique. These chapters are entitled "The Word Pattern of News," "The News Slant and the Reporter," "Building the Story," "The Technique of Leads," and "When Others Come to Town."

DR. RALPH O. NAFZIGER, director of the School of Journalism at the University of Wisconsin, has materially added to the volume by developing three chapters entitled "Political Affairs Create News," "Syndicated Features and Illustrations," and "Mechanics of Publication." Each of these phases benefits by the scholarly, complete, and accurate presentation of Professor Nafziger.

STEWART ROBERTSON, sometime professor of journalism at North Carolina State College, has contributed the chapter entitled "Police-Blotter Stories" and co-authored with the editor the chapter "Journalism as a Vocation." Both chapters benefit by Professor Robertson's practical background.

PROFESSOR FRANK THAYER, of the University of Wisconsin, has produced for this new edition the very valuable chapter "Publishing the Business Press" dealing with an area of journalism which has too often received but passing attention. As in previous editions, he has collaborated with the editor on two other aspects which also have too often suffered by neglect in journalism texts. Professor Thayer is a member of the Illinois bar, holds the J.D. degree, and has long been an authority on newspaper management which enhances the value of the other two chapters entitled "The Law Limits Journalism" and "Making Journalism Pay Dividends."

PROFESSOR ELMO SCOTT WATSON, aside from being one of the most popular and prolific feature writers in the nation, contributing editor to *The Publishers' Auxiliary,* a visiting professor of journalism at Illinois Wesleyan University, chairman of the Chicago division of the Medill School of Journalism of Northwestern University, has been announced, as this book goes to press, as the new director of the Department of Journalism, University of Denver. He has written four chapters which include "The Calendar as News," "The Interview and the Interviewer," "The Human Touch Makes the Feature," "Building the Magazine Article," and, in the present edition shares with the editor the authorship of a fifth, "Columns and Columnists."

PROFESSOR ROLAND E. WOLSELEY, of the School of Journalism of Syracuse University, has contributed five chapters, one in collaboration with the editor, and in addition is co-responsible with the editor for the selection and evaluation of the books given in the three reference bibliographies. The chapters benefiting by his skill include "The Newspaper Assembled," "When the Stylebook Is the Master," "Reviews, Comments, and Opinions," "The Rewrite Man Revamps the Copy," and "The Copy Goes under the Pencil." Since the first edition, he has co-operated above and beyond the requirements of his accepted assignment.

Acknowledgment of encouragement and help received by the editor and certain of the associated authors in the development and production of the original edition was made in the preface thereof. In connection with the present book the editor desires to express his appreciation to his wife, Dorothy Williams Mott, for her material assistance and her co-operation in many times of stress. Mrs. Cochran wishes to thank Miss Gladys Andrews and Delbert M. Nichols for their assistance.

A special word of thanks is extended by the editor to Dr. Roger R. Walterhouse of the editorial department of the publishers for his scholarly and helpful suggestions.

—GEORGE FOX MOTT

Washington, D.C.

TABLE OF CONTENTS

xv

ILLUSTRATIONS, DIAGRAMS, AND CHARTS

TABULATED BIBLIOGRAPHY NO. I
(See Next Two Pages)

This list gives the author, title, publisher, and year of publication of ten general textbooks or volumes on special phases of journalism that nevertheless deal with many of the topics of this book. These volumes are referred to in the tables on the next two pages.

1. Bastian, G. C., and Case, L. D., *Editing the Day's News*. Macmillan. 1943.
   Strong on general copydesk problems, as well as those facing picture editors and deskmen in charge of office routines, this new edition is set in a broad background of big-city newspaper operation. Limited attention is given to problems of handling different types of copy and to make-up of inside pages. Most applicable to large papers, the book gives little consideration to state and suburban copy.

2. Clayton, C. C., *Newspaper Reporting Today*. Odyssey. 1947.
   One of the most recent books on newspaper reporting. Its greatest virtues are its up-to-dateness and attention to several topics neglected or superficially treated by almost all other reporting texts. Content is better than method of presentation, for it is routine in style and drab in appearance.

3. Hall, W. E., *Reporting News*. Heath. 1936.
   Informally and realistically written, this book's value is in its approach rather than in its scope. More than a decade after publication the narrowness of its topics is still more evident. Emphasis, despite the title, is on writing news, an aspect the author presents attractively.

4. MacDougall, C. D., *Interpretative Reporting*. Macmillan. 1948.
   A veritable encyclopedia of newspaper reporting, this widely-used text is elaborately documented and intelligently organized. It is sufficiently concerned with general phases of journalism to serve as a survey that restricts itself to the newspaper and the wire service. First to introduce the interpretative techniques at this level, it is in need of strengthening on this type of news writing as well as on some kinds of news that have become more important since the book first was published, a lack not met by the revisions.

5. MacNeil, Neil, *Without Fear or Favor*. Harcourt, Brace, 1940.
   A survey of the technical and social aspects of the modern metropolitan newspaper; thorough but commonplace in style, it is by a *New York Times* editorial staff executive. It is largely descriptive but does not overlook the impact of the press.

6. Neal, Robert M., *Editing the Small City Daily*. Prentice-Hall. 1946.
   Thorough treatment of all important and many minor phases of the subject is an outstanding feature of this book. Another characteristic is that it is written in a somewhat fictionized style which gives it readability but an unprofessional, unbusinesslike tone.

7. Neal, Robert M., *News Gathering and News Writing*. Prentice-Hall. 1949.
   Newspaper reporting is handled in much the same manner as the author dealt with editing in the book listed above, although the revision has eliminated some of the storyizing; a highly practical manual.

8. Porter, P. W., and Luxon, N. N., *The Reporter and the News*. Appleton-Century. 1935.
   Emphasis in this older book is on reporting rather than on writing the news. Certain chapters—out-of-town correspondence and governmental offices—are unusually thorough and while somewhat outdated are still effective because specific and fundamental.

9. Radder, N. J., and Stempel, John E., *Newspaper Editing, Make-up and Headlines*. McGraw-Hill. 1942.
   A revision of Radder's *Newspaper Make-up and Headlines*, it is a well-arranged and easily-used text, covering deeply and with abundant examples and illustrations the basic techniques but not handling certain aspects, such as reader-interest and readability, to be found in Bastian and Case.

10. Wolseley, Roland E., and Campbell, L. R., *Exploring Journalism*. Prentice-Hall. 1949.
    All phases of journalism are described. Broadly interpretative, this volume, now in its second edition, brings together a presentation of the technical, social, and vocational aspects of newspapers, magazines, advertising, radio, and the other components of modern journalism; newspaper techniques are explained more in detail since they are the core of so much other journalism.

Tabulated bibliographies are fully protected by copyright. For additional lists and tables of special and general books see pages xxiii–xxv and 418–431.

QUICK REFERENCE TABLE TO STANDARD TEXTBOOKS, I

Light italic figures indicate pages.   Heavy roman figures indicate chapters.

Mott, et al., Journalism	Topic	Bastian & Case	Clayton	Hall	Mac-Dougall	MacNeil	Neal (Editing)	Neal (News)	Porter & Luxon	Radder & Stempel	Wolseley & Campbell
I	The Press As An Institution								1		1
II	Journalism As A Vocation	6	1, 2, 4	34	2, 3	4, 6, 7, 8, 9, 21		1, 2	1		5
III	The Evolution Of Journalism					1					1, 3
IV	The Newspaper Assembled	5		35	4	2	1	17-25	2	2, 3	3, 6, 7
V	The Word Pattern Of News	109-122, 198-203		8, 9, 10, 11	10		4		5		11
VI	The News Slant And The Reporter		3	2	5	3	17	6	3	4	14, 15
VII	Building The Story	10	7	5, 6	7			7	5		15
VIII	The Technique Of Leads	9	8	5	8, 9				5		15
IX	When The Stylebook Is The Master	94-108		4	App. A		3, App. II	31-33	App. I	App. B	11, 15, App. II
X	Names Make News		375-376	19	15				3		6, 16
XI	Police-Blotter Stories		15	22	19, 20			18, 19, 20	7		16
XII	When Others Come To Town	168-170	14	24	16		13	8, 9, 10	8		17
XIII	The Civic Project Is News										16
XIV	The Calendar As News										
XV	The Press And The Sportsman	172-173	24	23	28	12	29	24	17		16
XVI	Women "Arrive" In Journalism	167-168	25		2		30	25	9		
XVII	Covering The Business Beat		316-324	18	26	11	32	34	9		
XVIII	Covering The Labor Run		324-327		26				199-206		
XIX	The March Of Science As News		23	362-367	27			33			
XX	Political Affairs Create News		21	18	22, 23	10		32	15		16
XXI	Columns And Columnists							367-370, 396-397			18
XXII	The Interviewer And The Interviewer	171-172	12	16	17		14	15, 16	14		17
XXIII	The Human Touch Makes The Feature	177-180	13	26, 27	30	16		30	8		22, 23

See page xix for list of authors and complete titles.

TABULATED BIBLIOGRAPHY NO. II
(See Next Two Pages)

This list gives the author, title, publisher, and year of publication of ten textbooks on special phases of journalism that nevertheless deal with many of the topics of this book. These volumes are referred to in the tables on the next two pages.

1. Bond, F. F., *Breaking into Print*. McGraw-Hill. 1933.
   Professor Bond has approached news reporting from the standpoint of reader-interest. This original and stimulating study is not for use as a main text but as an auxiliary.

2. Brennecke, E. Jr., and Clark, D. L., *Magazine Article Writing*. Macmillan. 1942.
   A step-by-step description of the procedure of article production is followed by consideration, with well-selected examples, of the types of articles and the special problems of writing them.

3. Campbell, L. R., and Wolseley, Roland E. *Newsmen at Work: Reporting and Writing the News*. Houghton Mifflin. 1949.
   The first journalism text to present the handling of news for all major media of communication, including newspapers, radio, magazines, house publications, and wire services; labor, social welfare, educational, religious and other types of news lightly touched by many texts are thoroughly examined here; the legal, social, and other theoretical aspects of news are integrated with each chapter.

4. Garst, R. E., and Bernstein, T. M., *Headlines and Deadlines*. Columbia, 1940.
   The *New York Times'* editing techniques incorporated in a textbook. The primary material is conventional but complete; the auxiliaries, such as a list of headline words, are extremely helpful.

5. Hyde, G. M., *Newspaper Handbook*. Appleton-Century. 1941.
   A useful compendium of journalistic information serving as a manual of style and newspaper practice.

6. Johnson, S., and Harriss, J., *The Complete Reporter*. Macmillan, 1942.
   A combination newspaper reporting, writing, and editing text, built with such English manual devices as a correction chart for errors keyed to each section. It is intended for general college classes in journalism rather than professional schools but is too narrow for a survey.

7. Lundy, M., Editor, *Writing Up the News*. Dodd, Mead. 1939.
   Nineteen widely-known journalists, including Burns Mantle, Stanley Walker, and John Kieran, spoke on their specialties in newspaper work; Miss Lundy edited them into this readable collection of chapters on as many different aspects of the profession.

8. Merriman, L. M., *Between Deadlines*. Sanborn. 1941.
   Prepared by a California newspaperman, this was aimed at school journalists. It is pleasantly written and well-illustrated, telling the story of newspaperdom attractively and simply, but with not too much knowledge of school needs.

9. Otto, W. N., and Finney, N. S., *Headlines and By-Lines*. Harcourt, Brace. 1946
   Also for high-school use, this book has the qualities of Mr. Merriman's noted above but a thorough understanding of high-school journalism, as proved to us by Mr. Otto's two earlier editions titled *Journalism for High Schools*.

10. Patterson, H. M., *Writing and Selling Feature Articles*. Prentice-Hall. 1949.
    Miss Patterson has for many years been director of a highly successful feature writing course at the University of Wisconsin; this book brings together the material used in that course; it is rich with examples, innumerable hints and short-cuts learned from experience, and sound methods of article research and writing with commercial outlets as the goal.

Tabulated Bibliographies are fully protected by copyright. For additional lists and tables of special and general books see pages xix–xxi and 418–431.

QUICK REFERENCE TABLE TO STANDARD TEXTBOOKS, II

Light italic figures indicate pages.   Heavy roman figures indicate chapters.

Mott, et al., Journalism	Topic	Bond	Brennecke & Clark	Campbell & Wolseley	Garst & Bernstein	Hyde	Johnson & Harriss	Lundy	Merriman	Otto & Finney	Patterson
I	The Press As An Institution										22
II	Journalism As A Vocation		2	1, 2	1		1	3, 4, 18			1
III	The Evolution Of Journalism										
IV	The Newspaper Assembled				1		2		7, 8	2, 3, 6	
V	The Word Pattern Of News			5	5	1, 3, 4	4				
VI	The News Slant And The Reporter	2	12	3		14	3		18	4, 12	9
VII	Building The Story	3, 5	7, 8, 9, 10	6	3	5	8		11	13	
VIII	The Technique Of Leads	1		6	3	5	5, 6, 7			13	
IX	When The Stylebook Is The Master			5, App. II		2, 6, App. II	4				
X	Names Make News			7			12				
XI	Police-Blotter Stories			19			13, 14				
XII	When Others Come To Town	8					17				
XIII	The Civic Project Is News			24							
XIV	The Calendar As News						16				
XV	The Press And The Sportsman			15			25	9, 10	22	16	
XVI	Women "Arrive" In Journalism			10			24	12, 14	29		
XVII	Covering The Business Beat			25			20				
XVIII	Covering The Labor Run			26							
XIX	The March Of Science As News	5		28			22				21
XX	Political Affairs Create News			23			21	5			
XXI	Columns And Columnists			230-240				11, 13	23	18	
XXII	The Interview And The Interviewer	9	16	12, 13			17		14		3
XXIII	The Human Touch Makes The Feature	5, 6, 12	15	16			23	17	12	15	

Ch.	Title										
XXIV	News From Near And Far	1		4				19			13
XXV	The Rewrite Man Revamps The Copy		10				9, 28	19	20		
XXVI	The Copy Goes Under The Pencil				3	10	29	15	20	22	12
XXVII	Headlining The News				Part Two	11	31	15		14	
XXVIII	Page-One Make-Up						32			23	
XXIX	Syndicated Features And Illustrations		5			13	26		25, 27		15
XXX	The Newspaper Sets Its Policy						11				
XXXI	The Editor Speaks						27		24	8, 19	
XXXII	The Press As A Political And Social Force					16					
XXXIII	The World's Press Systems										
XXXIV	Building The Magazine Article	12	7, 8, 9, 10								10, 11
XXXV	Reviews, Comments, And Opinions		18	29			22		28		
XXXVI	The Art And Craft Of The Literary Journalist	4	20					6, 7			
XXXVII	Publishing The Business Press		13								
XXXVIII	Radio-Television—A New Journalistic Medium			6					6		4
XXXIX	The Law Limits Journalism		App. II, III		3	15	10		32		16
XL	Making Journalism Pay Dividends										
XLI	Advertising Copy Informs, Appeals, Impels									10	
XLII	Advertising Layout Attracts, Displays, Vitalizes									25	
XLIII	The Vigorous Voice Of Circulation					12				25	
XLIV	Mechanics Of Publication									24	
XLV	Terminology And Press Jargon		App. I		Glossary		App.			Glossary	

See page xxiii for list of authors and complete titles.

THE FIELD OF JOURNALISM INCLUDES:

Newspapers

Magazines and Reviews

Class, Trade, and Professional Journals

News Magazines

Radio

CHAPTER I

THE PRESS AS AN INSTITUTION

> Communication is a necessary tool of learning, and mass communication is prerequisite to mass education. A public-spirited press is therefore a chief instrument whereby contemporary society orders and changes its ways in the direction of clearly visioned goals of increased human welfare.—HAROLD BENJAMIN.*

> The difficulty in keeping well informed today is not that news is scarce, but that there is so much more "news" each day than the average man can assimilate.—HENRY R. LUCE.**

THE PRESS IS AN INSTITUTION OF SOCIETY

As an institution of society the press is an agency of mass communication. Technological developments gave the press the scope, variety, and immediacy required to make it such an agency. The American press is private industry, public service, and, in a sense, also applied science —that is, the press is an agency of the science of the dissemination of news and opinions. It is the most generally important medium of expression. As such, the press is one of the significant institutions of society and makes its appeal as a vocational opportunity accordingly.

The Press Has An Increasing Responsibility. As the press evolved into an agency of mass communication through technological changes, beginning with the steam-driven press,[1] it assumed a larger degree of responsibility. It also was forced to take unto itself a moral and to some extent a legal accountability for its performance. Although the reader still has the responsibility for selection of what he reads and believes, the press, in England and America at least, has assumed a considerable responsibility for giving the reader an opportunity to maintain this right to select and reject. A free press may not shackle a free people by disseminating only part of the news and opinions of the times. On the other hand, of course, mass communication increases the possibility of mass distortion of information and may serve to spread untruth as well as truth. Mass enlightenment does not necessarily follow improvements in

---

* Professor of education, dean of the College of Education, University of Maryland, and consulting editor, The McGraw-Hill Series in Education.

** Editor, *Time,* The Weekly Newsmagazine.

[1] This early nineteenth-century invention was followed by, among others, the development of the high-speed rotary press, the Linotype, and photoengraving.

mass communications. In fact, the reverse is apt to happen without a vigilant, independent, and freely competitive press.

Under such circumstances, the practicing journalist must have a mature conception of the importance of objectivity in news gathering and writing. This does not mean the absence of the right to slant news or to express opinion when it is easily recognized or frankly labeled as such. This right to personal journalism merely recognizes the inherent right of a free press to choose its editorial position and select news or views accordingly. Whether the publication be a newspaper, magazine, or trade journal its reader-group will be determined at least partially by its reader-appeal, which itself will be conditioned by the editorial position taken. Thus, journalism as a vocation presents at one and the same time the dual need for objectivity and personal conviction.

The Press Is Private Industry And Public Service. In reality the journalist is in private industry. The press is a highly competitive and relatively individualized kind of business. This is true despite the very considerable concentration of ownership of newspapers and magazines in America and in most other countries since the turn of the century. That is, there are fewer newspaper publishers today in America than in 1910.[1] As private business all branches of the press are subject to the economic logic of being successful in accordance with the principles as well as the pressures controlling private enterprise.[2] The competitive nature of free enterprise as applied to a free press provides the sort of genuine incentive essential to continuing improvement in the end-product. This in turn provides a practical challenge to the quality and nature of journalism turned out by members of the fourth estate. A practicing journalist cannot slip into armchair attitudes or continue outmoded methods and long earn a living. As he is in private business, he must produce!

No more important aspect of the press exists than its public-service function. The very complexity of society today requires greater dependency upon agencies of communication of which none is more influential than the press. Consequently, newspapers and magazines, of general circulation at least, must provide the facts which keep the citizen informed. They must also serve as leaders, moderators, and critics of events, ideas, and actions in the public interest. To do so, the press must remain substantially free from compulsions applied from within or

---

[1] In 1910 there were approximately 2500 English-language dailies in America, whereas in 1949 there were only an approximate 1800. The magazine situation is similar in that at the beginning of World War I there were about thirty major women's magazines, whereas now the number is much smaller with six having close to 85 per cent of the total circulation.

[2] For example, most newspapers and magazines seek an ever-increasing audience in order to increase earning capacity.

without except the compulsion of public service. Although freedom from pressure will rarely obtain where a newspaper or magazine accepts its public-service function fully, journalism as a profession demands acceptance of this public-service accountability.

As long as newspapers and other journalistic media are subject to the competitive forces of private industry and public service in nations having a free press, there is opportunity for each—it is only in the absence of one or more of this trilogy that there is danger. No one should be a journalist unless he is willing to serve the public weal.

The Press Applies The Science Of Mass Communication. It has taken the remarkable achievements of the modern dictator states in indoctrinating and instructing whole populations to the purposes of the state to point up the extraordinary predictability and exactitude of results to be gained through applied journalistic techniques.[1]

The American press in its various stages of evolution has well served the changing needs of the public. It is not chance that has made the press in America primarily one of news and information, thus serving a democratic government in its functioning over a vast spread of territory with a nonhomogeneous population. However, American journalistic development along these lines has been the largely unstudied result of supplying a demand.

That specific and exact results can be achieved through manipulation of the press is strikingly evident in today's world picture. That mass communication is a potent instrument of influence on society is also clear. Like the whole field of human psychology the science of propaganda is as yet more exact in its application than in its theoretical premises, but down the ages from Demosthenes through Savonarola to Hitler and Huey Long demagogues have known how best to sway public opinion. Much the same basic technique may be, and has been, applied to the enormously multiplied newspaper audience. Given a free press and a free people the science of mass communication may be a benevolent and constructive institution—in a "controlled" society it may be and is used as one of the principal methods of enslavement.

PUBLICATION OF NEWS AND VIEWS IS JOURNALISM

As chroniclers of timely events, information, and opinion, journalistic media catch and reflect the drama of human performance in response

---

[1] The late liberal British historian, H. A. L. Fisher (*A History of Europe*, published just prior to World War II) observed, for example, "Yet there is this novelty in the Soviet system. A living religion is enforced by the massed large-scale propaganda of a scientific age, by machine guns and airplanes, telephone and telegraph, printing press and film, broadcasting and the regimentation of all the arts. A hundred and sixty million human souls are by a gigantic system of governmental pressure hermetically sealed against the invasion of unwelcome truth. All previous experiments in tyranny recorded in human annals pale beside this colossal achievement."

to a universal demand for the publication of news and views. As such, journalism has the service opportunities and definite responsibilities of a profession; the aptitude requirements and technique qualifications of a trade; and the financial structure and economic procedures of a business.

Journalism May Be A Potent Instrument Of Service. An honest and intelligent journalism is one of the most potent instruments for constructive service. For, if you remove education from the abstractions of theorists, it becomes clear that its objective is simply that of making the members of a community better informed and more skillful in their approach to life. On the basis of this concept, journalism becomes a great educational agency. Journalistic media are more than purveyors of news and comment; they are agencies having policies of their own, responsibilities of far-reaching importance, and worthy missions of great significance. They are both leaders and servants. They are leaders because they help to create public sentiment, formulate the ideas and ideals of millions, and bring carefully conceived messages into the homes and minds of their readers. They are servants because journalistic media, like governments, project and are projected by the people they serve, fairly reflecting public opinion to the extent that they are supported by paid subscriptions and advertisements, and so, permitted to exist. In brief, journalistic media prosper in direct proportion to their own sense of responsibility, which is shared by every member of the editorial staff; and to their own value as journalism, which is gauged and accounted for by the business staff in proportion to its economic support from the public it serves.

Journalism Requires Trade Skills. The art and craft of journalism necessitate individualized training, specialized knowledge, and technical skills, which should be supplemented by interest, aptitude, and ethical character. These trade qualifications may be acquired in many ways. They are sometimes obtained from one or another of the more progressive schools of journalism which provide laboratory work for their students as members of the staffs of news organs and periodicals. They are frequently gained through supervised vocational activities or other actual participation as apprentice members of the fourth estate.

As a trade, journalism generally requires an aptitude and facility for perceiving, ferreting out, comprehending, and reporting the ingredients of major happenings in the lives and surroundings of the humble and the mighty, as well as an aptitude for interpreting and putting into "news shape" the significant ripples of village gossip, middletown chatter, and urban talk because of their news value, human interest, or their weird, strange, or unusual flavor. Furthermore, the practicing journalist must understand the art of headlining and displaying the news as well as all the other ever-important factors in the mechanics of publication.

In addition, he may well need to be fortified by a faculty for becoming an accepted member of the community if he practices his trade on a newspaper in any but the great metropolitan centers.

Quite apart from these requirements, journalism as a profession rendering a service to the needs of the society of which all segments of the press are an integral part demands of a really top-flight journalist a sense of equity which lacks neither courage nor what is frequently referred to as common sense. In order to exercise these characteristics meaningfully, the journalist must have attained a significant appreciation of the factors governing and conditioning the relationships of man to man as applied at all levels of human activity, including today, especially, the international scene. To exercise such special acumen no journalist may be expected to achieve qualification without both a personal philosophy and a mature conception of economic, cultural, and political history, including the current mores, fears, and interests of the principal peoples who inhabit the earth.

Journalism Prospers Only When Conducted On Business Principles. Successful publications must be conducted on business principles with the same ability, energy, and astuteness as other successful enterprises. A newspaper, magazine, or other periodical is free to serve constructively as a disinterested leader and servant of the public only when the publication's financial structure is such that its economic life does not depend upon the whims, caprices, or selfish purposes of vested interests. All journalistic media are manufactured products; they require elaborate equipment which must be operated by qualified tradesmen; they must be turned out in large quantities; and, they must be produced and distributed within a comparatively short period of time—sometimes within a few hours. Whether the publication be a large metropolitan daily, a small nonmetropolitan weekly, a newsmagazine, or a class periodical, it must be at one and the same time a successful business enterprise and a successful purveyor of news and views. Certainly, the editorial room cannot be free unless the "counting room" is well ordered.

THE PRESS INCLUDES VARIOUS MEDIA

The field of journalism may be roughly divided into five categories: (1) newspapers, (2) general magazines and reviews, (3) class, trade, and professional journals, (4) newsmagazines and magazine digests, and (5) radio and television.

Newspapers Are Essentially News Organs. American and British newspapers are essentially news organs in that an event is put into "news shape" and displayed in proportion to its relative value and timeliness. Material having news value comes from the new, the strange, the interesting, the significant.

News may be further divided roughly into several types, for example:

from the geographical or political point of view news may be considered as local, state, national, or international; or from the subject-matter point of view it may be considered as news of crime, finance, sports, society, science, or politics.

General Magazines And Reviews Do Not Depend Upon Timeliness. Magazines specialize in fictional, factual, and discussion material. The general magazine occupies a distinctive place in American journalism. In the strict sense, such magazines do not serve as purveyors of "new" news. The magazine contains articles, stories, essays, sketches, and editorials which convey thoughts, ideas, facts, and fiction, in accord with an established editorial policy.

Magazines may be defined as bound pamphlets, published periodically. They are issued in various sizes with a variety of formats, and contain miscellaneous subject matter which frequently has entertainment as its primary objective.

A review is a distinct type of periodical. All subjects are dealt with from the editorial point of view and the articles included in this kind of publication may be defined as editorial expositions or criticisms. When this type of writing is published in magazine form the resultant periodical is called a review. However, review material can be put into "news shape," and many newspapers and magazines have review sections of one sort or another.

Class, Trade, And Professional Journals Serve Special Groups. Class, trade, and professional journals feature material which is especially gathered, compiled, and written for the benefit of a limited group of individuals, who are banded together for some particular purpose. As such, these specialized magazines, or journals, are concerned with the advancement of the field to which the publication belongs. Each type of publication in this category may be national, sectional, state-wide, or even local in its distribution.

Newsmagazines And Magazine Digests Are Increasingly Important. There is probably no form of journalism which has become so important within recent years as the newsmagazine. It serves to summarize, organize, condense, and disseminate the most important newsworthy facts, which may be published by any of the journalistic media—particularly, the news reported by the metropolitan press. It does so with remarkable accuracy and unusual effectiveness for the millions of readers who like to have their news "predigested," although served somewhat after the "main course." In general style of presentation the news slant and general word pattern with the lead technique are observed. In format, method of distribution, editorial direction, it resembles the general magazine, as well as the review.

Magazine digests are condensations of the most important stories and articles, more especially the latter, appearing in various publications. As such, they purport to be, and sometimes succeed in being, critically selective groups of condensed magazine articles.

Radio Is The Newest Major Medium Of Journalism. In many ways radio journalism is quite different from published journalism. This is true both as to newscasting and as to all other aspects, including radio advertising. Even so, the differences are no greater than those between writing and speaking for public information or entertainment. Radio journalism has come a long way since its embryonic beginning in 1920. For example, news reporting over the air has become routine, and television is carrying news reporting into the visual phase as well.

There are many forms of radio journalism. One of the most important is the commentary, of which there are two general types—namely, the review and the editorial. Commentaries may be created by different types of script material, such as the essay which produces a co-ordinated and smooth broadcast, the outline which permits flexibility of expression, and the topic script which insures naturalness often at the cost of unity and, sometimes, of good taste. Besides the important commentaries, radio news may take the form of the spot newscast, dramatized news of various kinds, and the formal or direct newscast which is reporting as opposed to interpreting and columning. The direct newscast may take different forms, including the bulletin, the straight report, the review, or the human-interest feature. Radio journalism gathers its news in much the same way as do other agencies of journalism.

Writing for radio requires the knowledge of certain techniques of journalism and the understanding of radio as such. In general, whether writing is script for a commentary, a newscast, or a radio commercial, copy is more "condensed, terse, and telegraphic" than newspaper or magazine copy. In addition, such copy is usually conversational by nature. A radio editor must be as skilled in "radio sense" as a city editor is in "news sense."

Apart from the foregoing categories of radio journalism, there are other kinds which are equally important but which in many respects are more closely allied to "show business" or to literary journalism than to newspaper or magazine journalism; and, of course, one of the greatest fields is radio advertising, which is now a major advertising medium.

EACH TYPE OF MEDIUM VARIES WITHIN
ITS OWN CATEGORY

As might be expected, these five general types of journalism vary within their own classes, according to the special reader-audience–group to which each makes its major appeal.

Newspapers May Differ According To The Clientele. Newspapers are apt to vary according to whether they are intended primarily for those living in cities, suburban communities, medium or small towns, or rural sections. Of course, there is great similarity in appearance, but, in general, metropolitan journalism differs from nonmetropolitan journalism to a very considerable degree both in approach and in appeal.

News in the city is not necessarily news in the suburban community; news in the suburban community is infrequently news in the metropolitan centers; and news in the villages or rural areas is rarely news farther away than the county seat.

All persons are interested in other persons. Most people like to imagine themselves doing, or not doing, the things that are news. As a result, newspapers are apt to be read in direct proportion to the success of the editor in enabling his readers to see themselves in the news. Generally, the metropolitan daily is only indirectly personal in appeal, while the nonmetropolitan paper is directly personal in appeal. Thus, although the city daily appeals to a large reader-group, it does not appeal to that class completely. On the other hand, the nonmetropolitan newspaper—dealing in personals and brevities extensively—frequently reaches its comparatively small number of readers completely. Consequently, nonmetropolitan newspapers often have unusually large circulation coverage in proportion to their reader-population.

Each Type Of General Magazine And Review Has An Individual Appeal. The general magazine is a powerful educational agency, as well as the source of much recreation and entertainment for persons of every socio-cultural stratum. With the exception of certain rather general informative magazines, the majority of successful publishers in this field attempt to please a rather definite class, or reader-group, which may be a broad, rather universal one or a somewhat limited and narrow one. The market sought determines the journalistic style, which in turn gives the magazine its appeal and interest. Frequently, the appeal is to the more limited classes, such as: the urban sophisticate, the social and political enthusiast, or the scholar.[1] Other magazines make their appeal more directly to the average citizen. These magazines may be either the smooth-paper publications or the cheaper pulp variety. In general, they deal largely in fiction and articles but may deal exclusively in some particular type of narrative; for example, romance or love stories, success or adventure tales, mystery or detective narratives. Perhaps the largest number of the more wholesome publications are written particularly for the housewife and include those things most interesting to her. Typical of such women's interest magazines are: *Ladies' Home Journal, Good Housekeeping,* and *McCall's Magazine.*

For the domestic or government worker, for the small businessman or millionaire tycoon, there is a magazine to serve his interests, tempera-

---

[1] For example, the *New Yorker,* the *New Republic,* the *Annals* (of the American Academy of Political and Social Science), respectively.

ments, and needs. As such, the monthly and weekly magazine publications give pleasurable recreation and entertainment to every class and occupation. Whatever the reader-group, the publisher's aim and the editor's method of treatment of content help determine the market of the publication.

While few examples of American magazine journalism can rightly claim universal appeal, there are those that come remarkably near. These command circulation more or less national and more or less among all classes. Justified examples of this last group are: the *Saturday Evening Post, Collier's, Cosmopolitan,* and the *American Magazine.*

Reviews appeal to highly specialized groups and aim to please those groups. As a result, even more than in some other types of journalism, reviews are written for relatively small groups of discriminating review magazine buyers, who want to be challenged, or agreed with, or lectured to—in one way or another. Such publications as the *Saturday Review of Literature* and the *American Review* are well-known examples. A newcomer to the field is the *Pacific Spectator,* which is published by the Pacific Coast Committee for the Humanities of the American Council of Learned Societies.

Class, Trade, And Professional Journals Touch The Whole Range Of Human Activity. Thousands of class, trade, and professional journals are issued to fulfill the needs of selected reader-groups. They convey information; stimulate interest, views, versions, and discussions; and report findings of research, trends, and opinions. There is no other field of journalism in which there are such wide differences. And, although all such examples of journalism have certain things in common, they differ widely in aim, appeal, and scope.

Class journals abound in every phase of human activity; trade journals are to be found in every recognized vocation; professional journals exercise much influence within the scope of their particular fields. In fact, no major occupational endeavor, including most of the great industrial organizations and city department stores, is without one or more technical publications. These range all the way from scant bulletins to valuable publishing properties. Regardless of their individual significance, each has to go to press regularly, and each must be filled with its own particular brand of journalism. As would be expected, some are daily, some are semiweekly, more are weekly or semimonthly, and a very large number are monthly or quarterly publications.

Newsmagazines And Magazine Digests Supplement Other Types Of Journalism. In the United States, the newsmagazine and the magazine digest, as supplements of the older forms of journalistic media, have as their principal function the culling from the great quantity of published material the most newsworthy stories and human-interest items, in the first place, and the most informative and entertaining stories, in the second place, for those readers who value the critical, selective service given by the editorial staffs of these publications.

Time, Newsweek, and *U. S. News and World Report* are outstanding examples of the newsmagazine, while the *Reader's Digest*[1] is the best-known example of the magazine digest. The salient point about digests is that, as the name implies, brevity is achieved through critical condensation.

Radio Stations Vary Their Programs To Reach Different Audience-Groups. Although radio stations themselves are less apt to direct their programs to any single or limited audience-group than, for example, are the specialized magazines, stations do, almost invariably, direct their programs at certain hours to specific audience-groups. Radio sponsors also take advantage of this technique. Of course, some programs such as straight newscasting have a nearly universal appeal to adult audiences, However, many programs, such as those sponsored by certain breakfast foods are beamed directly to a juvenile audience. Others generally programed during the morning, frequently sponsored by manufacturers of housekeeping and cooking products, are directly beamed to the housewife.

Program-appeal in itself is a highly specialized business, and competition is keen among sponsors for certain types of programs and certain hours of broadcasting time. The factors to be weighed by station and program sponsor are complex and frequently can be evaluated only on the basis of continuing research.

----

[1] In addition to its English-language circulation (more than 8,500,000 in the United States alone), there are Spanish, Portuguese, Swedish, Arabic, Danish, and Finnish editions which totaled something close to 1,500,000 in 1948.

CHAPTER II

JOURNALISM AS A VOCATION

The practice of journalism is two-fold. On the editorial side, it is an applied art; on the publishing side, an economic or business enterprise. Newspapermen, as a rule, seek to avoid dignifying themselves or the vocation with the term, "profession," but of this we are certain: the equipment of a well-qualified journalist consists of character, native ability, acquired technical skill and a liberal education. His tasks are never easy or simple. The manner in which he bears his public responsibilities, either as publisher or editor, is socially of great importance. If he lives up to the demands put upon him, we should be willing to admit him to professional standing, regardless of how lightly he refers to his job as a craft or even as a "game."—RALPH D. CASEY.*

JOURNALISM PROVIDES MANY OPPORTUNITIES

As a vocation journalism has many facets. A journalist may be a newspaperman, but a newspaperman is only one kind of journalist. No longer is a newspaperman typical of journalists because there are now so many other kinds. Still, when the layman thinks of journalism, he instinctively thinks of the newspaper.

As developed in the preceding chapter, all journalism has certain responsibilities and a great variety of opportunity for constructive service. Further, each of the five categories of the art and craft of journalism has a variety of reader-audience–appeal. Newspapers themselves may be classified into many kinds, as may also magazines, trade journals, reviews, and even radio programs. Consequently, it is hardly appropriate to think of journalism on the basis of the newspaper alone, even though the newspaper is still the most common kind of journalism and one of the most appealing.

Recognition of the truth of the foregoing does not in any way alter the fact that the newspaper is still the "core publication" to which all journalism is related. For example, the editorial as a kind of journalistic writing may find its expression in a magazine of general circulation, a specialized business journal, a review, or in a radio commentary. However, the fact remains that editorial expression is a permanent part of the best newspaper tradition. From another point of view, advertising may be carried

* From a radio address, *Journalism as a Profession*, University of Minnesota Vocational Series, by Dr. Ralph D. Casey, chairman, Department of Journalism, University of Minnesota.

on in all media but perhaps the most vital kind of advertising in the sense of persuading people to act promptly in acquiring some product or service may be found on the pages of the daily newspaper.

As a practical matter then, this chapter, and a large part of this book, concerns itself with the vocational aspects and problems pertaining to newspapering. Even so, much of what is said specifically about newspapers also applies fundamentally to all, or most, other forms of journalistic expression. For example, the qualifications required of a successful magazine writer (fiction writing aside) generally do not differ from those required of a good reporter.

JOURNALISM OFFERS A REAL CHALLENGE

Apart from the challenge of the press as a whole, for one reason or another there has gathered about the newspaperman's job particularly an atmosphere of mystery or romance, a sort of glamour that has an unfailing appeal for youth on the quest for a vocation. In addition, the urge to write has an almost universal attraction for the more mature person seeking an outlet for creative expression.

The Newspaper Attracts Men Of Varied Ability. The American daily as it is generally thought of today is just a little more than one hundred years old, and during this first century of its existence its news and editorial rooms have served as a proving ground for many men of varying character and ability. It has attracted men with great gifts of intelligence, initiative, and resourcefulness, and men of meager endowment and stability. Some of its followers have risen by their own industry and fidelity to commanding positions in the nation. Others, with a flair for politics, have made the easy transition from the editorial desk to the seats of the mighty in public life. Perhaps the greater number, however, have carried on in the less notable roles of newspaper work—growing old, restless, and not infrequently shabby on a well-worn beat or in the routine life of the city room. But all of them, at one time or another, have felt the pulse of power, the throb of life in their work that newspapermen alone seem to feel.

Newspaper Work Has Elements Of Glamour Which Attract Many. The result of the atmosphere of mystery and romance around the life of a newspaperman has been that the newspapers have had difficulty in giving employment to all the young men and women who have flocked to schools that train for newspaper work. Of course, many of the more competent have found equally interesting work in other areas of journalism. However, the facts are that the newspaper office has followed the American tendency for cold-blooded organization, that work on a newspaper is much as it is in other organized commercial activities, and that editors today hire only personable, competent, and well-educated young persons—and not too many of them—who look capable of doing a day's work for a day's pay. Thus the glowing aura that seems to surround the newspaper job fades into the realism of difficult and exacting tasks. Even so, these tasks have a special appeal and are often most rewarding in themselves.

ADEQUATE PREPARATION IS NECESSARY

For the man or woman who is seriously thinking of journalism as a vocation, the first step is to get ready. The newspaper touches life at all points and the active newspaper employee will find occasion to use a diversified store of knowledge.

Graduates Must Have Good Background. The schools of journalism continue to improve, and their graduates are receiving favorable consideration from publishers and editors. Generally, graduates who are well grounded in journalistic techniques and who have a working knowledge of history, political science, economics, English literature, and one or more foreign languages; who are capable of writing English prose simply and naturally; and who have kept up with current events and know most of the names of the men and women in the news, are likely to find favor when they apply for positions on a newspaper or a magazine. A knowledge of foreign languages is not necessary for ordinary newspaper work, but an acquaintance with them tends to improve one's use of his own language and will help to make one available for service as a foreign correspondent. Shorthand is not essential, but the possession of it will enhance a reporter's usefulness in getting exact quotations from public speeches, interviews, and the like. Some knowledge of science is a necessary part of a person's education today, and is an advantage, as is an elementary knowledge of law.

There Is Value In Having Special Training. Courses in the various divisions of the journalism curriculum in the modern college that are devoted to technical instruction, if capably taught, are unquestionably timesavers and serve as useful short cuts to reportorial and editorial work, and editors are becoming more and more aware of this. However, there is no single means of acquiring the combination of abilities needed for successful work in journalism. As developed elsewhere in this text, the exact qualifications are as varied as the individuals who will be found to possess them. Certainly there is no one way to become a journalist, but, as in all areas of human employment, technical knowledge—however acquired—and industry—applied with common sense—will go far toward making a good newspaperman, a competent magazine writer, a successful trade-journal editor, and perhaps an able radio-script or advertising-copy writer.

Investigation As To Qualifications Should Be Made. The person considering newspaper or magazine work as a career should inquire into his own qualifications for such work. A careful reading of this or other books on journalism, together with a visit to the editorial rooms of a daily, should give him some knowledge of what the duties, for example, of a reporter and copyreader are. Still, he should not be content with what he has learned about the job. He should turn the spotlight on himself as well. Is he old enough to know his own mind and young enough to fit readily into a strenuous routine? Has he unusual ability or aptitude for the kinds of tasks involved? For purposes of self-examination, an aptitude for journalism may be described as consisting of (1) an interest in people and in particular an interest in prearranged or accidental happenings that are known in newspaper circles as expected or unexpected news events; (2) a fondness for ferreting out the *who, what, where, when, how,* and *why* of such events as come within his province; (3) a facility for turning out a well-written story; (4) a temperament that will enable the reporter to keep his head, in fact go coolly on with his work, whether it is unearthing the news or writing the story in the face of an onrushing deadline.

Publishers And Editors Are Exacting In Their Demands. Newspaper editors are usually exacting taskmasters, and frequently have minimum patience with cub reporters who fumble unduly at their jobs. However, such qualities of character as determination, eagerness to learn, a capacity for concentration and sustained effort will often win out for a beginner at newspaper work, as indeed it will in most vocations.

OBJECTIVITY AND CREATIVE ABILITY ARE REQUIRED

In a news and information press, objectivity is essential in news reporting. Therefore, the person looking to the city room of a newspaper office as the most interesting place to begin a career should realize at the outset that there is little or no opportunity in the reporting of news for the writer to give rein to his innermost thoughts, however high, or his deep feeling, however subtle. Later, as an editorial writer or literary journalist, he may have a little more latitude.

Reporting Is An Impersonal Job. Reporting the news, even the hot news, is a coldly impersonal job. The editor wants to find the facts in the story and not the writer's personal impressions or emotions. He has learned from long experience that effective news writing must be objective. That any writing for the public press must be scrupulously accurate goes without saying.

News stories are concerned with turns or happenings in the lives of human beings—there is an unfailing quality of newness therein. In the raising of the reporter's work to the level of art, the initial step is to capture that element of freshness, of uniqueness in the human experiences and emotions released by an accident, a happening, an event. The next step is to write it in what Robert Louis Stevenson so well called the "dialect of life." And John Ruskin was getting close to the art of the successful newspaperman when he wrote, underscoring the word *see,* "The greatest thing a human soul ever does in the world is to *see* something, and tell in a plain way what he saw. . . ."

Newspaper Work Is Often A Pathway To Creative Writing. That newspaper work is a pathway to a successful career in the creative or semicreative writing field is attested by the long list of recognized novelists, playwrights, essayists, and the like who have served an apprenticeship in some city room. Reporters undoubtedly profit by their firsthand contacts with real life, their intimate knowledge of human beings whom they see with the masks off. They learn to write by actual daily writing, even if they chafe the while under the restraints of routine news-gathering methods and the restrictions of a well-established news-writing technique. But the best of them learn to make their stories fresh and readable and yet live up to the editor's demands for strict accuracy. They learn what it is to write for a public.

Magazines Offer An Opportunity For Creative Work.[1] Magazine articles have much in common with the signed articles and editorial comment in the daily papers, but there are fundamental differences between them. The center of all newspaper offerings is the day's news, but the magazine is under no such obligation. It frequently does attempt, however, to publish articles that will fit into the thinking produced by the news of the world. Thus, an ability to feel out the public pulse helps in the selection of topics for discussion in magazines. The gathering of this material involves employing the best methods known to newspapermen and to scientific researchers. Facts must be sifted, put in order, illuminated wherever possible, and presented with force and clearness by the best creative ability. There is wide opportunity for magazine journalists to help clarify thought, and all worthy literary devices may be used to that end. When well done, magazine articles are among the very best literary efforts of modern times.

EMPLOYMENT DIFFERS FROM TIME TO TIME

There will doubtless be opportunities for good beginners to get connected with newspapers as long as newspapers are published, but landing a satisfactory job may require patience. The same is true as to opportunities in any of the other fields of journalism.

Individuals today who wish to follow a particular vocation are always faced with the problem of getting a job in the field of their choice. And, it is becoming increasingly difficult to be specific in discussing possible opportunities for almost any kind of employment. Much depends on the

[1] For further information concerning the opportunities for creative writing in journalism, as such, consult such chapters as: I, *The Press as an Institution;* XV, *The Press and the Sportsman;* XXXIV, *Building the Magazine Article;* XXXVI, *The Art and Craft of the Literary Journalist.*

general business conditions at the time. During the past several years relatively few new journalistic enterprises have been launched, and there have been mergers even among the larger dailies and magazines.

Once employed the cub reporter must be prepared to go through a period of self-discipline—insistence on accuracy and expressiveness in all of his work. His concentration on these two objectives will bring him into most immediate usefulness.

By the time a man has become established in the editorial department of a newspaper he has also acquired a certain amount of public notice and prestige. In any event, his advancement will depend in the main on his industry, general competence, and ability to get along with the public he serves. Even in the larger newspaper organizations there is usually considerable shifting from time to time in the personnel of the news and editorial departments. Sometimes men are promoted from the editorial desk to executive positions within the organization. Other men are drawn into allied fields of journalism, to become publicists, advertising specialists, public-relations counsels, and the like. Others leave the newspapers to enter the political or business world. Still others—and the number is increasing—become free-lance writers or literary journalists.

ETHICAL STANDARDS ARE IMPORTANT

As in most other activities, those engaged in newspaper work or any other type of journalism will constantly find arising from their work ethical problems which are not always easy of solution.

A beginner on a newspaper or magazine of the better class will be introduced to the codes or ethical standards followed, and it will be greatly to the journalist's advantage not to deviate very much from these standards. For example, it is a safe rule for a reporter always to conduct himself as a gentleman—that is, to be truthful and straightforward at all times, to honor and protect as far as possible his personal news sources, and in general to conduct himself so as to win full confidence and real respect for the newspaper he serves.

The Code of Ethics adopted by the American Society of Newspaper Editors in 1923 has been generally accepted by editors and publishers throughout the nation as one of the best expressions of the principles of journalism. These *Canons of Journalism* are given on page 17.

NONMETROPOLITAN JOURNALISM IS
ONE WORTHY FIELD

Newspapers published in towns under 15,000 in population are now generally referred to as "nonmetropolitan" [1] and embrace the country weekly and the small-town daily. Both have intimate contact with the

---

[1] Many writers use the term "country newspaper," which is equally correct.

CANONS OF JOURNALISM *

I

Responsibility. The right of a newspaper to attract and hold readers is restricted by nothing but considerations of public welfare. The use a newspaper makes of the share of public attention it gains serves to determine its sense of responsibility, which it shares with every member of its staff. A journalist who uses his power for any selfish or otherwise unworthy purpose is faithless to a high trust.

II

Freedom of the Press. Freedom of the press is to be guarded as a vital right of mankind. It is the unquestionable right to discuss whatever is not explicitly forbidden by law, including the wisdom of any restrictive statute.

III

Independence. Freedom from all obligations except that of fidelity to the public interest is vital.

1. Promotion of any private interest contrary to the general welfare, for whatever reason, is not compatible with honest journalism. So-called news communications from private sources should not be published without public notice of their source or else substantiation of their claims to value as news, both in form and substance.

2. Partisanship in editorial comment which knowingly departs from the truth does violence to the best spirit of American journalism; in the news columns it is subversive of a fundamental principle of the profession.

IV

Sincerity, Truthfulness, Accuracy. Good faith with the reader is the foundation of all journalism worthy of the name.

1. By every consideration of good faith a newspaper is constrained to be truthful. It is not to be excused for lack of thoroughness or accuracy within its control or failure to obtain command of these essential qualities.

2. Headlines should be fully warranted by the contents of the articles which they surmount.

V

Impartiality. Sound practice makes clear distinction between news reports and expressions of opinion. News reports should be free from opinion or bias of any kind.

This rule does not apply to so-called special articles unmistakably devoted to advocacy or characterized by a signature authorizing the writer's own conclusions and interpretations.

VI

Fair Play. A newspaper should not publish unofficial charges affecting reputation or moral character without opportunity given to the accused to be heard; right practice demands the giving of such opportunity in all cases of serious accusation outside judicial proceedings.

1. A newspaper should not invade private rights or feelings without sure warrant of public right as distinguished from public curiosity.

2. It is the privilege, as it is the duty, of a newspaper to make prompt and complete correction of its own serious mistakes of fact or opinion, whatever their origin.

VII

Decency. A newspaper cannot escape conviction of insincerity if while professing high moral purpose it supplies incentives to base conduct, such as are to be found in details of crime and vice, publication of which is not demonstrably for the general good. Lacking authority to enforce its canons, the journalism here represented can but express the hope that deliberate pandering to vicious instincts will encounter effective public disapproval or yield to the influence of a preponderant professional condemnation.

* See Casper S. Yost, *The Principles of Journalism.* D. Appleton & Co., New York, 1924, pp. 161–164.

public they serve. Any journalist will benefit by at least some direct experience on one of these newspapers.

There Are Special Challenges In Nonmetropolitan Journalism. The publishing of a successful weekly, semiweekly, or small-town daily is an honorable vocation, rich in satisfactions, and one to which many city newspapermen look with envious eyes. Although the publisher escapes much of the grind and speed and pressure of city newspaper work, he has his own problems and difficulties. For example, in the handling of news on small papers, strict attention must be given to local items. Such papers are slowly and completely read and errors of omission and commission are quickly noted and long remembered.

The editor soon gets to know his public well and as a consequence he can give them, in addition to the news, much that is valuable—information, entertainment, guidance. To be successful and enjoy the community's wholehearted support, to say nothing of profits from his work, he must publish a paper in which news and advertising matter are well displayed. The dull, unattractive country newspaper has gone the way of the early, shapeless automobile. In its place is a progressive, well-edited news organ. Experience on one of these papers may well prove invaluable to anyone seeking to come to know journalism in a practical way.

Publisher May Do Much Constructive Work For His Community. The operation of a country newspaper may provide the satisfaction which comes from constructive work well done. Apart from a publisher's influence otherwise, he usually is able to take through his columns a real part in maintaining a wholesome community spirit and in promoting civic betterment and general public welfare, and has a clearly implied responsibility to do so. He may not long shirk this obligation if he is to survive.

The publisher of a small newspaper usually has to edit the paper himself and also manage the business and advertising departments. This frequently raises conflicts, for persons or organizations paying large sums of money to a paper sometimes consider they are entitled to a voice in the directing of the news and editorial departments. The shrewd publisher will impress on the community the principles of sound newspaper management, thus securing for himself a free hand in publishing all of the news.

Opportunities Are Available For Those Well Fitted. What are the opportunities for breaking into nonmetropolitan journalism? In the past twenty-five years many qualified persons, including graduates of schools of journalism and men and women once connected with metropolitan newspapers, have taken up the work of publishing country weeklies. To what extent this may be done in the future will depend upon a number of economic and social factors that will have to be examined by the persons interested. As in all other fields of activity, opportunities almost always exist for the able and energetic person in nonmetropolitan journalism in almost any section of the nation. Whether or not all of the specific characteristics required actually will exist for a particular man or woman, with much or little capital, at any given time, is difficult to foresee. Certainly, there is probability of opportunity for the person who is prepared to carry on in the best newspaper tradition.

CHAPTER III

THE EVOLUTION OF JOURNALISM

As modern American jurisprudence is rooted in old English common law, modern American journalism is rooted in early publishing ventures of the English-colonial period. The embryonic stages of journalism gave little indication of the place it was destined to occupy as a means of disseminating news and views, but its evolutionary growth with ever increasing rapidity soon made American journalism a force in the land.

True, an understanding of this journalistic development will not take the place of specific knowledge necessary to succeed in publishing, editing, or writing, but those publishers, editors, reporters, columnists, specialty writers—journalists all—will contribute most, will be better seasoned, will be more alert to future possibilities, and will be more certain of the constructive service which may be rendered if they know something of this rich background. Journalism of the present has been created out of journalism of the past. It is a noble heritage!

—GEORGE FOX MOTT.*

ALTHOUGH HUMBLE, THE BEGINNINGS OF THE PRESS SUGGESTED ITS FUTURE IMPORT

The evolution of journalism has been marked by profound development in size, regularity, and speed of publication; kinds, style, and treatment of news; typographical make-up; editorial influence; mechanical production aids; advertising; and circulation.

American Journalism Had Its Origin In English Journalism. The somewhat drab, ultraconservative English journalism was largely imitated by the colonists, its influence continuing for a long period of time.

Forerunners of English newspapers were the sixteenth-century ballads describing news events, the irregular newssheets and pamphlets containing foreign news, and the written newsletters and printed newsbooks reporting parliamentary proceedings. The era of the newspaper may be said to have been inaugurated with the establishment in 1665 of the *Oxford Gazette,* a semiweekly single sheet, soon renamed the *London Gazette.* Not before 1670, however, did the term "newspaper" come into being.

Strict governmental regulation of printing and repression of discussion doubtless delayed extensive use of the printing press, first set up in England in 1476, and the development of the newspaper. But as restric-

---

* From an address given at a professional meeting in San Diego.

tions diminished, there developed during the latter part of the seventeenth and the beginning of the eighteenth centuries a marked expansion in journalism. The first daily paper, the *Daily Courant,* was established in London in 1702.

The Earliest Colonial Newspaper Was Immediately Suppressed. Although the first printing press was set up in the colonies in the sixteen thirties, it was more than half a century before a newspaper appeared.

Benjamin Harris, whose publishing ventures in England had met with the disfavor of the authorities, attempted to establish in Boston in 1690 the first newspaper in America, *Publick Occurrences Both Forreign and Domestick.* Because the paper incurred the disapproval of the authorities and was not licensed, a practice maintained in the colonies some thirty years after it was abandoned in England, *Publick Occurrences* was immediately suppressed.

The "Boston News-Letter" (1704) Was First Successful Paper. Fourteen years elapsed before the advent of another newspaper, the *Boston News-Letter,* issued in April, 1704, by John Campbell, postmaster of Boston.

The first issue, printed on both sides of a single sheet slightly smaller than a piece of typing paper, contained no advertising and consisted largely of news taken from London papers several months old. Printed by authority and with careful accuracy the paper was never in danger of suppression but, because of its general colorless tone, lacked adequate financial support.

Campbell's refusal to allow William Brooker, who became postmaster of Boston in 1719, to take over the *News-Letter* led to Brooker's establishment of a rival paper, the *Boston Gazette.* This newspaper, the second in America to continue publication, was also published by authority and, like the *News-Letter,* was composed for the most part of foreign news.

The "New-England Courant" (1721) Ushered In A New Phase. A new aspect of journalism appeared with the establishment in 1721 by James Franklin, brother of Benjamin Franklin, of the third paper in Boston, the *New-England Courant.* The *Courant* differed from the other Boston papers in its opposition to constituted authority and in its controversial writing. Essays, verse, and letters were introduced, an indication of continued English influence, further evidenced by imitation of the style of Addison and Steele.

The "American Weekly Mercury" Appeared In Philadelphia In 1719. Outside of Boston the first newspaper to make its appearance was the *American Weekly Mercury,* established in 1719 in Philadelphia by Andrew Bradford. This fourth colonial newspaper devoted somewhat more space to local news than did the early Boston papers.

New York's First Newspaper Was The "New York Gazette" (1725). New York's first newspaper, the *New York Gazette,* was started in 1725 by William Bradford, father of Andrew. Official printer for New York, Bradford made his paper at first little more than a chronicle of news.

The Founding Of The "New York Weekly Journal" In 1733 Was Significant. Established in New York in 1733, the *New York Weekly Journal*, opposing the Crown's authority and openly discussing rights of the people, was particularly significant inasmuch as it was founded as the organ of a political group. In the ensuing controversy between the *Journal* and Bradford's *Gazette*, which upheld the Crown, conflicting ideas of government were first expressed openly in American news organs.

The initial major step in the fight for freedom of the press was taken with the arrest of John Peter Zenger, editor of the *Journal*, whose criticism of the government led to attempted punishment of the editor. The vital underlying issue at stake—liberty of the press—brought Andrew Hamilton, distinguished Philadelphia lawyer, to the defense of Zenger. Hamilton's plea constitutes a significant chapter on the subject of libel and is the beginning of the relative freedom of the press.[1]

Early Publication Efforts Of The Printer-Editor Were Limited. Conditions surrounding and leading to the establishment of newspapers outside of Boston, Philadelphia, and New York were similar to those of the earliest newspapers. The editors were usually printers who established printing businesses before starting weekly newspapers. Publication difficulties were many: subscription lists were small, advertising support limited, paper and ink expensive, printing facilities crude and slow because of hand operation, communication slow among the colonies themselves and between them and England. The papers, small in size, were composed of foreign news taken from English papers, domestic information taken from other colonial papers, private letters and correspondents' letters, and such items of local interest as the printer could obtain easily. Essays and verses were reprinted from English papers and also contributed by local writers, most of whom imitated English writing. Editorial comment was infrequent and usually consisted merely of a sentence or two incorporated with a news item.

DISTINCT CHANGES IN THE CHARACTER OF THE PRESS WERE EVIDENCED EARLY

During the latter half of the eighteenth century the press played an increasingly important part in influencing public opinion and in giving expression to it.

The Press Soon Became An Instrument Of Political Influence. Colonial solidarity was aided in no small degree by the press, a notable example being the publication in 1754 in Benjamin Franklin's *Pennsylvania Gazette* of a cartoon depicting an eight-piece snake, each of whose seg-

---

[1] This subject is discussed in Chapter XXXIX, *The Law Limits Journalism*.

ments was initialed for one of the colonies. Captioned "Join, or Die," this cartoon became the symbol of the need for united action.

American newspapers now became the medium of expression for the controversies between England and the colonies, discussions being carried on largely through letters contributed by those upholding or denouncing British policies. The controversy centered in Boston, where Samuel Adams and other patriots, recognizing the power of journalism, used the *Boston Gazette* as their instrument of influence. The *Boston Chronicle* and the *Boston News-Letter* (the first continuously published American newspaper) were the channels used for opposing the colonial cause, an admission on the part of the Crown that public opinion was now a force to be considered.[1]

After The Revolutionary War News Organs Increased. Following the war there was an increase in the number and the frequency of publication of newspapers and in the amount of advertising, and newspapers became more abusively partisan and important as organs for presenting the contentions of the Federalists and Anti-Federalists.

In 1784 the first daily newspaper in the United States was established in Philadelphia when the triweekly *Pennsylvania Packet or General Advertiser* appeared as the *Pennsylvania Packet or Daily Advertiser.*

Throughout the first third of the nineteenth century the chief purpose of newspapers continued to be that of discussing political and economic questions. Foreign news still remained predominant, domestic news consisting largely of political speeches, reports of governmental proceedings and departments, and information of interest to the mercantile and commercial classes for whom the newspaper was designed. News and editorials commonly appeared on the second and third pages of a four-page paper, the first page containing advertising and reprint materials. The editorial came into being during this period, and newspapers began to be published by editors rather than by printer-journalists. Although there was considerable development in advertising, collections were difficult, and circulations were small, for subscription prices were high, a metropolitan paper, obtainable by subscription only, costing $8 to $10 a year. It was during this period that there developed the popular weekly and semiweekly editions of the metropolitan dailies.

FROM THE PENNY PAPERS DATE THE BEGINNINGS OF MODERN JOURNALISM

The establishment of penny papers marked the beginnings of certain modern newspaper characteristics; namely, low price, wide circulation, financial stability, human-interest news, and wide news coverage.

---

[1] Of the thirty-odd newspapers in the colonies when hostilities began in 1775, few remained neutral.

Human-Interest News Was Introduced. The first permanent penny paper, the *New York Sun,* was established by Benjamin H. Day in 1833, as a small four-page paper which soon demonstrated the appeal of human-interest news. Similar to the *Sun* were the *Transcript* and the *Morning Herald,* brought out in New York within the next two years.[1]

Court News, Sensational Elements, Came To The Fore. The penny papers were generally characterized by police court news (usually treated humorously), detailed accounts of accidents, suicides, murders, trials, and other sensational news, and by their editorials on moral principles. Political news and political editorials were largely ignored.

Editor Day Inaugurated Street Sales. Day practically abandoned the credit system in both circulation and advertising. He also inaugurated the use of street sellers and the "London plan" of selling his papers to newsboys and carriers, who in turn collected from their customers.

Circulation Income Was Subordinate To Advertising Returns. The success of the penny papers was evidenced by their circulation, that of the *Sun* at one time surpassing the circulation of any other paper in the world. Small profit was made on circulation, however, and as the penny papers increased in size production costs were carried more and more by advertising income. The penny papers, however, were often criticized because they carried such a large amount of patent medicine advertising.

THE PERSONALITIES OF JOURNALISM MADE THE PRESS A DYNAMIC FORCE

Developments in journalism during the past hundred years are clearly pictured through the outstanding personalities and organs of the press.

Vigorous, Dynamic, Timely Journalism Began With The Elder Bennett. News emphasis and personal journalism distinguished the *New York Herald,* established by James Gordon Bennett, Sr. (1795–1872), as a penny paper in New York in 1835. It emphasized the importance of timely news of events of the day over political news—a somewhat revolutionary principle.

New news sources, financial, social, sports, religious, theatrical, etc., were sought and developed by Bennett, already an experienced journalist when he founded the *Herald.* He spared no expense and utilized every facility, the *Herald* often being ahead of its competitors in publication date of news. Quick to foresee the value of the telegraph and cable, Bennett made early use of both. As early as 1838 he arranged for foreign correspondents, and during the Civil War he was especially enterprising in maintaining correspondents on the fields of action. Although his unsurpassed enterprise in news collection was recognized, Bennett was often bitterly assailed for his sensationalism and his early exploitation of crime news and scandals.

---

[1] Penny papers were also published later in Boston, Philadelphia, and Baltimore.

The *Herald* was a leader in the development of illustrations and head-lines, the latter becoming prominent shortly before and during the Civil War. Despite his use of illustrations for news purposes, Bennett soon excluded illustrations as well as large display type from advertising and employed the cash-in-advance plan for advertisements. As did other cheap papers, the *Herald* published objectionable advertising relating to patent medicines and quack doctors.

Horace Greeley Has Been Termed "America's Premier Editor." Horace Greeley (1811–1872), founder of the *New York Tribune* in 1841 and "the father of American journalism," was the outstanding example of personal journalism as evidenced through his editorials, the influence of which has never been surpassed.

Believing it an editor's duty to take a decided position, Greeley un-flinchingly proclaimed his convictions of truth without regard to the dis-favor which might ensue. An idealist, ever receptive to new ideas, and in sympathy with the working class, Greeley sought to improve society through his editorials, which were characterized by vigor, sincerity, and simplicity. His influence, for example, in the antislavery cause was tre-mendous.

Nor did Greeley lack enterprise in obtaining news, although the em-phasis thereon differed from that of the other cheap New York papers. Objectionable police court reports were avoided as was questionable ad-vertising.[1] The *Tribune's* remarkably capable writers presented an inter-esting and readable newspaper with a distinct literary quality, instituting the use of travel stories and human-interest stories often dealing with the unfortunate classes, and a regular department for reviews of books and periodicals.

Raymond Recognized The Need For Impersonal Journalism. Through the *New York Times,* established in 1851, Henry J. Raymond (1820–1869) demonstrated the need for and value of impersonal journalism. He sought to provide unsensationally, truthfully, and without bias news of the world that was interesting and important to the public. Desirous of making the *Times* a newspaper fit for the family, Raymond eliminated objectionable news and advertising.

Because of his ability to see both sides of an issue and his distaste for misrepresentation and abuse, Raymond was editorially more conserva-tive and dispassionate than his contemporaries. Although a politician himself, he never utilized his paper to promote personal aspirations and was ever eager to further general public welfare.

Samuel Bowles Made A Small-Town Daily An Outstanding Paper. When Samuel Bowles, Jr. (1826–1877), successfully persuaded his father

---

[1] Greeley was the first editor to show clearly that it was possible to maintain a thoroughly successful paper without depending upon scandal to secure, and retain, a large circulation.

THE "TRIB" EVOLVES
FROM '65 TO '09

Reproduction of the upper half of page one of the *Chicago Tribune* of April 15, 1865, and of the *Chicago Daily Tribune* of September 7, 1909. Used by permission of the publishers.

THE "TIMES" MOVES SEDATELY
FROM '72 TO '96 TO '00

Reproduction of the upper portion of page one of the *New York Times* of July 11, 1872; September 4, 1896; and July 6, 1900. Used by permission of the publishers.

to publish in 1844 a daily edition of the *Springfield* (Massachusetts) *Republican,* he took the first step toward what was to become a model small paper of nation-wide importance and influence.

The *Republican* is an outstanding example of the development of journalism outside of Washington and New York. Growth in communication facilities displaced the monopoly of New York papers on first foreign news and of Washington papers on first governmental news, thus decentralizing American journalism.

Convinced that party success was far less important than public welfare and that support of a just although unpopular cause was more desirable than popularity, Bowles was a pioneer in independent journalism. Ever zealous of the public good, Bowles attempted to expose and combat society's evils, both locally and nationally, taking an active part, for instance, in the antislavery cause. Through the news columns Bowles sought to make the *Republican* a distinctly local paper, although telegraph news became a regular feature.

Godkin Was Able, Gifted, Popular, And Exercised Wide Influence. Edwin Lawrence Godkin (1831–1902) in his association with the *Nation* and the *New York Evening Post* exerted a tremendous influence on the thinking of Americans for more than thirty years.

As the editor of the weekly *Nation,* founded in 1865, Godkin devoted himself to producing a journal for the discussion of important current topics, furtherance of democratic ideals, focusing of attention upon popular education, and criticism of books and art. Fearless, critical, cosmopolitan, dispassionate, idealistic, Godkin presented the truth as he saw it, fought against corruption and sensationalism and for good government, law, order, and honesty. Godkin, an intellectual, believed in democratic principles. It was to the educated class that his *Nation* appealed and through whom he had influence, an influence indirectly transmitted to others by the intellectuals and the journalists, who were the *Nation's* close readers.

When Godkin sold the *Nation* to Henry Villard in 1881, he became identified with Villard's *New York Evening Post,* through which he continued to appeal to the thinking classes with his clear-cut, often ironical, style of writing. Save for curbing sensationalism, Godkin was largely indifferent to what news appeared.

Dana Contributed Much To Journalistic Style. In developing a new style of writing, Charles A. Dana (1819–1897), who became editor of the *New York Sun* in 1868, made a distinct contribution to journalism.

Although the *Sun* was cheaper and smaller than its leading rivals, Dana's emphasis on clarity and condensation enabled the presentation of all important news. Dana encouraged original, clever, concise writing, seeking to develop an American style in contrast to the heavier English news style, the imitation of which had persisted in American newspapers.

Emphasis was placed upon the interest value of news rather than upon the conventional conception of news value, thus making the importance of human-interest stories almost equal to that of informational matter.

An experienced journalist himself, having been Greeley's assistant for several years, Dana secured an able and loyal staff of men, many of whom were college-trained. As a consequence the *Sun* was often regarded as a training school for young journalists.

Editorially, Dana was independent, never hesitating to censor those whom he previously had supported whenever such a course seemed justified. Repetition was, he believed, a potent force in the success of an editorial campaign.

Nelson Built A Great Paper Upon Principle Of Community Service. What can be done by a newspaper to better a community was demonstrated successfully by William Rockhill Nelson (1840–1915). At forty and with little journalistic experience Nelson showed his faith in the principle of service to humanity and in Kansas City's possibilities by establishing the *Kansas City Evening Star* in 1880 when the still unattractive city with a population of but 55,000 already had four newspapers. Nelson not only sought to weed out corruption in city affairs but also to build up the community, especially through the establishment of parks and boulevards and the building of attractive homes.

A fighting but not a writing editor, Nelson expressed his personality through his associates. Nelson believed that it was the duty of reporters not only to write truthfully and entertainingly but also to investigate matters of public concern and thus to promote the best interests of the city and the contiguous territory. Nelson's *Star,* never resorting to sensationalism in either news or make-up (large headlines and colored comics being excluded, for instance), maintained the highest standards of journalism. He ably demonstrated the possibility of a cheap paper of quality.[1]

Pulitzer Built One Of The Greatest Newspapers Of The Century. With the purchase of the *New York World* in 1883 Joseph Pulitzer (1847–1911) renewed the sensationalism of the early penny papers and the editorial aggressiveness of Greeley and injected the element of crusading into both news and editorials. Seeking always to expose abuses and to promote worthy causes for the benefit of the common people, Pulitzer, a sentimentalist at heart, was successful in numerous crusades, important among them being the exposure of mismanagement of life insurance companies in New York City.

To increase circulation in order that he might reach the largest possible number of people through his editorial page, his primary concern,

---

[1] When in 1901 Nelson purchased the *Kansas City Times* and continued it as a morning edition of the *Star,* he furnished his subscribers the morning, afternoon, and Sunday editions of the *Star* for ten cents a week, the *Evening Star's* original price.

Pulitzer emphasized sensational news and introduced political cartoons and striking illustrations, the first colored illustrations appearing in the *Sunday World,* which also initiated the first colored comics. Early headlines were more startling in content than in typography, although page-wide heads were employed during the Spanish-American crisis.

Circulation figures attested to Pulitzer's success: the first year he quadrupled the *World's* circulation; in 1886 the *World* claimed the largest circulation (more than 250,000) of any American newspaper. Pulitzer established the *Evening World* in 1887 shortly after the successful launching of the *Evening Sun.*

Extreme rivalry developed between the *World* and the *Morning Journal,* purchased in 1895 by William Randolph Hearst, who succeeded in enticing many of the best men from the *World.* The war of "Yellow Kid" comics and the sensationalism of both newspapers were responsible for the term "yellow journalism."

An advocate of professional training for journalists, Pulitzer provided a large endowment to be used after his death for a School of Journalism at Columbia University, opened in 1912.

Hearst Has Been A Vigorous Force In Journalism.   William Randolph Hearst (1863–   ), who assumed charge of his father's *San Francisco Examiner* in 1887, entered the New York field by purchasing the *Morning Journal* in 1895. Hearst newspapers have been unequaled in their sensationalism in both news content and make-up. Although it was the *World* and not the *Journal* which first emphasized sensational news, used striking illustrations extensively, employed huge headlines, and campaigned vigorously, it was the *Journal* which exaggerated these devices to an unparalleled extent. Hearst has spared no expense in obtaining the best newspaper workers available and in covering all kinds of news. Because of its success, this type of journalism has been copied, most notably in typography, by other newspapers throughout the country.

Although not the first to establish a chain of newspapers, the Scripps brothers having antedated him in this endeavor, Hearst owned seventeen daily and two separate Sunday newspapers in 1949.

Scripps Brothers Were First To Develop Chain Newspapers.   Chain newspapers were originated by the Scripps brothers in the late seventies and early eighties in the Middle West. In the establishment in 1878 of the *Penny Press,* known later as the *Cleveland Press,* by Edward W., George H., and James E. Scripps, and a cousin, John Scripps Sweeney, was laid the cornerstone of the Scripps-McRae League of Newspapers formed in 1895 and composed of the *Cleveland Press,* the *St. Louis Chronicle,* the *Cincinnati Post,* and the *Kentucky Post.* The Scripps-McRae Press Association (1897) and the Newspaper Enterprise Association (1901) were organized to furnish news and syndicate material, respectively, the first for chain purposes.

When in 1920 Roy W. Howard and Robert P. Scripps, son of Edward W. Scripps, became business manager and editorial director, respectively, of the Scripps-McRae League, there were twelve papers in the League, the name of which was changed in 1922 to the Scripps-Howard Newspapers. One of the notable additions to its present chain of more than twenty newspapers was the *New York World* of Pulitzer fame, purchased in 1931, the morning, evening, and Sunday editions being combined into the *New York World-Telegram*. Editorially the Scripps-Howard papers are independent and liberal.

Publisher Ochs Rehabilitated The "New York Times." Adolph S. Ochs (1858–1935), who became publisher in 1896 of the *New York Times,* revived the then-declining *Times,* making it the outstanding newspaper of the twentieth century. Not entertainment but news—"All the News That's Fit to Print"—was emphasized. During World War I the *Times* gained special prominence because of the completeness of its war news (for example, it was the only paper in the world to print the whole draft of the peace treaty). The pictorial innovation of a rotogravure section in its Sunday edition in 1914 was widely adopted by other newspapers. (The *Times* has since dropped its rotogravure section.)

THE MAGAZINE ENTERED THE FIELD OF JOURNALISM LATER THAN THE NEWSPAPER

While the evolution of the American magazine was less rapid than that of the newspaper, it was no less certain and important.

American Magazines Appeared Near Mid-Eighteenth Century. The first magazines, Andrew Bradford's *American Magazine or A Monthly View* and Benjamin Franklin's *General Magazine and Historical Chronicle,* appeared three days apart in 1741 in Philadelphia. Only three numbers of the former and six of the latter were published. Some eighty magazines were started before the end of the century, but for the most part their lives were brief.

Subscriptions were not only difficult to obtain but also hard to collect, and advertising was undeveloped. Magazines were generally undertaken by printers with a zest for creating a literary interest in America, where few literary books were read or published. Desirous of benefiting and educating their fellow men, the publishers attempted to cover a wide range of subjects—literary, historical, scientific, biographical, religious, etc.—and not only to disseminate information and to popularize literature but also to popularize art by the early use of as many illustrations as could be afforded. Vigorous appeals were made to local and national pride not only in creating an interest in literature but also in stimulating its production. Original contributions were, however, scarce, and reprinting of foreign material was common. In order to print as much material as possible, exceedingly small type was commonly used. Authors generally remained anonymous and unpaid.

The Struggle Continued During The Nineteenth Century. Throughout the first half of the nineteenth century many magazines were introduced, and many went down within a few months or years after their birth. Even in the smallest communities magazine founders attempted to express themselves and attempted to promote a literature within their own circles.

Boston, Philadelphia, and New York became rivals as centers of culture and in the promotion of magazines, and this period witnessed the rise of such writers as Emerson, Hawthorne, Longfellow, Lowell, Poe, Harriet Beecher Stowe, Whittier, and Willis.

Boston's chief contribution in the early nineteenth century to the magazine field was the *North American Review* (1815), a representative of dignity, scholarship, and respectability, which was one of the first journals to secure national circulation and international recognition and to pay its writers.

During this period Philadelphia produced *Godey's Lady's Book* (1830) and *Graham's Magazine* (1840), typical of the lighter magazines and characterized by their display of steel engravings and fashion plates. Philadelphia also brought forth the entertaining weekly, the *Saturday Evening Post* (1821).

Seeking to be politely entertaining and genial, the *Knickerbocker Magazine* (1833) was New York's chief magazine of the period. Lewis Gaylord Clark's "Editor's Table" of friendly chatter was one of its main attractions.

An important magazine of the South was the *Southern Literary Messenger* (1834) of Richmond. Less sectional than the other Southern attempts, this magazine was more successful.

The Latter Half Of The Nineteenth Century Witnessed Advances. Magazines became strong advertising mediums, and circulations increased tremendously during this period.

Harper's New Monthly Magazine was established in Philadelphia in 1850. For a long time it devoted itself chiefly to reprinting English literature, its American articles being those on science, travel, and history. Catering to the general interest appeal in expositions rather than opinions, the magazine was safe, respectable, and a container of high-class illustrations.

Not until 1857 did Boston succeed in a literary magazine, the *Atlantic Monthly,* which even then began its career by attaching itself to the anti-slavery movement. Although the *Atlantic* soon became a national magazine, it was largely contributed to by Bostonians.

Although the original *Putnam's Monthly,* established in New York in the early fifties, was destined to live but a few years, it was one of the first magazines to emphasize original American literature and to devote itself to the discussion of affairs of the day.

Typical of the sense of social responsibility then invading the magazine field was New York's *Nation* (1865), which introduced independent and impersonal judgment in its treatment and appraisal of American life and literature.

Even the dignified *North American* moved to New York early in the last quarter of the nineteenth century and, made a monthly, began to voice opinions and to evidence a lively interest in the affairs of the day.

Scribner's Monthly, established in New York in 1870 and later renamed the *Century*, was a leader in discussion as well as exposition and in the use of first-class illustrations. National in viewpoint, the magazine distinguished itself by encouraging Southern writers whose audience had until then been largely limited to the South.

An era of wide circulation and cheap magazines was ushered in near the close of the century as typified by *McClure's Magazine*, the *Cosmopolitan*, and *Munsey's Magazine*, journals of human-interest and intimate appeal. *McClure's* was exceptional in awakening an interest in public questions through careful and studied histories and expositions of prevailing conditions. This period also saw the rise of the *Ladies' Home Journal*, whose family-circle influence grew during the long editorship of Edward K. Bok, and *Everybody's*, which introduced the fancy magazine cover with a feminine appeal.

Editorial Policies Differed From Modern Practices. The practice of not publishing authors' names persisted for a long time, giving way at first only to the publication of the names of established and recognized writers. Conservatism and the avoidance of new ideas were common magazine characteristics during a large part of the nineteenth century. Editorial privileges of censorship and alterations persisted for some time, and editors freely altered contributions to fit their own views and those of their magazines. Editors also were accustomed to making free use of parts of rejected manuscripts.

Nineteenth Century Marked Changes In The Religious Press. Early religious magazines, the *Christian History* (Boston, 1743) being the first, were commonly devoted to Christianity as a whole, but in the second quarter of the nineteenth century the magazines began to represent church strife. It was during the intervening period between the early magazines and the later controversial ones that there developed a large number of religious newspapers. One of the important religious journals, the *Independent*, established in 1848 in New York, became a power because of its independence, secularity, and personalism. Toward the end of the century the religious press declined, the magazines and papers tending toward church mediums or those of opinions and literature.

TWENTIETH–CENTURY JOURNALISM IS CHARACTERIZED BY FURTHER PROGRESS

Developing into a highly competitive "big business," twentieth-century journalism evidences tremendous mechanical advances, standardization, consolidation, and professional progress.

Mechanical Devices Have Contributed Materially To Growth. Improved mechanical equipment and inventions both within and without the industry are responsible for present-day rapid production of newspapers. The Linotype machine, devised by Ottmar Mergenthaler in the eighties and marvelously improved since, has displaced hand-setting of type save for headlines and display advertisements. Hand-operated until 1812, the printing press has been mechanically perfected so that in an hour's time thousands of papers are now printed on both sides, cut, counted, and folded as one operation. The introduction of stereotype plates in 1860 permitted casting of duplicates for simultaneous printing. Color presses and engraving processes have been greatly improved. Hand-engraved woodcuts used until the seventies were eventually displaced by zinc etchings, with halftones being later adapted to newspapers. Offset printing, a process whereby a page of copy is photographed and the negative is transferred to a zinc plate for printing from an inked rubber roller, may be of prime significance in the newspaper of the future. Also the possibilities of radio-facsimile newspapers delivered on a home receiving set are as yet undeveloped.

The development of both the telephone and the typewriter speeded up newspaper output enormously. The use of telegraph and radio, which now transmit pictorial images as well as news messages, is becoming increasingly important.

Syndicate And News-Agency Materials Have Helped To Standardize The Press. Increased use of syndicate and news-agency materials has tended toward standardization of the press. Since the establishment of the newspaper syndicate of short stories in 1884 by S. S. McClure, the number of syndicates and the variety of material covered by them have grown tremendously. Chief among the news-gathering agencies [1] are the Associated Press, incorporated in Illinois in 1892 and later in 1900 in New York with Melville E. Stone as manager; the United Press, organized in 1907 as a combination of the Scripps-McRae Press Association and the Publishers' Press; and the International News Service, established in 1906 by William Randolph Hearst.

Current Newspapers Reflect Steady Development. Modern newspapers show the effects of the steady development of consolidation, advertising, and circulation, the increased popularity of evening newspapers, and the introduction of tabloid picture papers.

---

[1] These are discussed in detail in Chapter XXIV, *News from Near and Far.*

The tendency to consolidate newspapers, especially evident in the morning field because of the rise of evening newspapers, is exemplified by Frank A. Munsey. By consolidation and reorganization he practically eliminated six newspapers in New York.[1] There is also a tendency to combine under one ownership morning and evening papers in small cities.

Growth of large business enterprises and the national distribution of products have resulted in increased local and national advertising. In order to develop these advertising possibilities it was necessary to enlarge circulation, and this was made possible by growth in population and the wider appeal of newspapers, especially to women. Greater advertising volume and circulation have necessitated an increase in the number of pages per newspaper. As income and costs have become greater, newspaper publishing has become a big business, total revenues in the banner-year 1929, for instance, were more than a billion dollars and the combined daily circulation was nearly forty million. There are now some two thousand daily newspapers and some ten thousand weeklies in the United States. The aggregate circulation of all daily issues (not Sunday) is now some forty-eight million.

Establishment in New York City in 1919 of the *Illustrated Daily News* by Robert R. McCormick and Joseph Medill Patterson, publishers of the *Chicago Tribune,* marked the rise of tabloid picture papers, particularly in New York City. Their popularity with the masses—the *Daily News* having secured within six years of its founding the largest daily circulation in the United States—is due to their condensation of news, to human-interest appeal, to small and convenient size, and especially to the extensive use of pictures.

In recent years, especially because of World War II, there has been a marked increase in the importance of foreign news. National news and science news have been growing in importance for some time. A significant trend toward news interpretation has developed, and there has also been an increase of columns. Newsmagazines, such as *Time* and *Newsweek,* and digests, such as *The Reader's Digest* in the monthly field, and such pictorial magazines as *Life* are especially significant developments in the field of journalism, as are also confidential newsletters. A recent innovation in the newspaper field *PM,* established in New York in 1940 as an adless and highly departmentalized tabloid, failed to make its way. A current tendency in newspaper make-up is that of simplification of headlines by less exactness in count and by a reduction in the number of decks.

Advertising, Standards, Training Are Constantly Improving. Twentieth-century journalism is characterized by efforts within the field to im-

---

[1] Munsey's sale, for instance, in 1924 of the *New York Herald* to the *Tribune* resulted in the *New York Herald-Tribune.*

prove the quality of advertising, to furnish dependable information on circulation, to establish codes of ethics, and to promote professional training.[1]

Individual newspapers and organizations are endeavoring to eliminate dishonest advertising as indicated, for example, by the adoption in 1914 of the Standards of Newspaper Practice by the Newspaper Division of the Associated Advertising Clubs of the World. For the purpose of furnishing reliable circulation data the Audit Bureau of Circulations was established in 1914.[2]

With the development of state and national organizations of newspaper publishers and editors efforts have been made to improve the standards of journalism. The American Society of Newspaper Editors, established in 1922 as an association of large-city newspaper editors, early adopted a code of ethics known as the "Canons of Journalism."[3]

Attempts to improve the profession of journalism have been evidenced in this century in the establishment of college and university schools and courses in journalism. Among the very first courses to be offered in professional journalism were those given at the University of Wisconsin in 1905. The University of Missouri established a School of Journalism as early as 1908; the School of Journalism endowed by Pulitzer opened at Columbia University in 1912.

There Has Been An Advance In The Guild Movement. Recently there has been an advance in the union movement for newspaper employees. The American Newspaper Guild has united more than 25,000 workers in the advertising, business, circulation, and editorial departments in a union affiliated with the Congress of Industrial Organizations. They are organized into units within a particular plant and locals within a city and have obtained recognition or contracts on the majority of the metropolitan papers. This organization is doing much to correct a condition of low pay and long hours but so far has been opposed by publishers' groups, and victories sometimes have been won only through strikes or negotiations of many months' duration.

---

[1] Discussed in Chapters II and XXXII on *Journalism as a Vocation* and *The Press as a Political and Social Force,* and elsewhere throughout the volume.

[2] Discussed in Chapter XLIII on *The Vigorous Voice of Circulation.*

[3] See page 17.

CHAPTER IV

THE NEWSPAPER ASSEMBLED

The newspaper is the servant, the leader and the whipping boy of the community. It is a medium of information, a stimulating force behind public betterment, a source of education and entertainment. It is frequently condemned for the various points of view expressed by its many writers, yet through this condemnation arises clarifying discussion for better understanding.

To survive in a highly competitive field, a newspaper must have competent advertising and circulation management; it must keep abreast of each succeeding mechanical improvement and manufacturing technique; it must be ever alert to obtain the best possible raw materials to produce a workmanlike publication.

Yet the physical product of this high pressured efficiency is of brief duration. Each day's paper is supplanted by to-morrow's—the type and stero plates melted, the paper discarded, the publication remade. The continuity and life of a newspaper is in its spirit, its qualities of leadership and public service.—M. PRESTON GOODFELLOW.*

CITY AND COUNTRY NEWSPAPERS ARE DISSIMILAR

Newspapers are generally classified as either metropolitan or non-metropolitan. These two classes include the large-city daily, the increasingly important smaller-city and community newspaper, as well as that large group traditionally spoken of as the country press. However, the organizational structure of newspapers is not standardized. It is possible to speak of a typical newspaper setup, but not of a general or average structure.

Large And Small Newspaper Structures Vary Distinctly. No two newspapers are exactly alike in organization. The only exceptions are newspapers under chain ownership or management, and even here there are not infrequently many structural differences, especially as to the details of operation.

Local conditions make standardization unlikely. The newspapers of one community need not necessarily provide the services offered by newspapers in another community. The individual nature of the locale which a newspaper serves, including the socio-cultural, economic, and political pressures, condition the particular pattern of even its organization. Quite

---

* Publisher, the *Pocatello Tribune,* and others; former publisher, the *Brooklyn Eagle.* Used by express permission of Colonel Goodfellow.

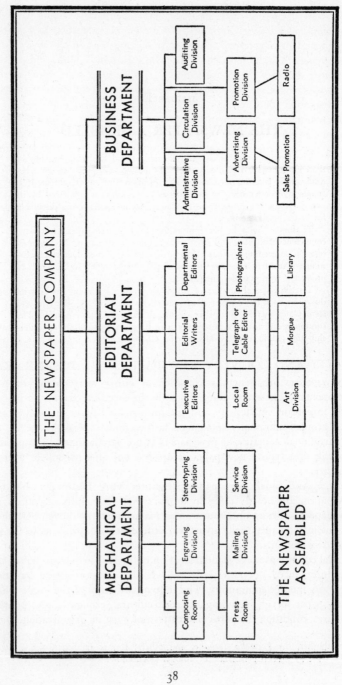

THE NEWSPAPER COMPANY

MECHANICAL DEPARTMENT

EDITORIAL DEPARTMENT

BUSINESS DEPARTMENT

Composing Room

Engraving Division

Stereotyping Division

Press Room

Mailing Division

Service Division

Executive Editors

Editorial Writers

Departmental Editors

Local Room

Telegraph or Cable Editor

Photographers

Art Division

Morgue

Library

Administrative Division

Circulation Division

Auditing Division

Advertising Division

Promotion Division

Sales Promotion

Radio

THE NEWSPAPER ASSEMBLED

apart from these factors, differences in practices, as well as in financial strength and in degrees of efficiency, make for variations.

Differences Are Both In Size And In Function. The metropolitan newspaper includes the entire range of dailies from the largest metropolitan paper with ten editions and a half-million circulation to the small-city paper with but one edition and 10,000 circulation.

The nonmetropolitan, or country, newspaper is the term used to designate smaller news organs. This group includes not only the rural weekly papers, but also the semiweekly, the community, and the suburban papers and newsmagazines.

The chief differences between these groups are their size and function. Although newspaper organization is not standardized, most nonmetropolitan papers are similar in setup, and most metropolitan papers resemble each other somewhat in general structure. The two classes vary chiefly in the degree of complexity.

NEWSPAPERS HAVE THREE MAIN DIVISIONS

In its general organization a newspaper, regardless of class, must have three main divisions—editorial, mechanical, and business.

A newspaper cannot function with fewer than these three. It must have a department to provide news, or it no longer qualifies as a newspaper. It must either own or rent printing services, or the news that is gathered never will reach the public in readable form. It must set up equipment and personnel for taking care of the financial aspects of the paper, including its management, its revenue-bringing divisions, and its distribution.

All newspapers, therefore, are somewhat standardized in having these three departments. The country weekly may have an editorial department consisting of one man, yet he performs all the functions necessary to supply the needs of his department. The city paper may have an editorial department of a hundred employees who collectively function much like the one-man editorial worker.

THE EDITORIAL DEPARTMENT PROVIDES THE COPY

The editorial department provides the reading matter in the newspapers. It commonly includes the news, art, and many other subordinate departments. It is responsible for providing much more material than its personnel supplies directly.

Reading Matter Of Many Kinds Is Prepared. Reporters gather news for the paper in foreign countries, in other parts of the nation, and in the city of publication. Photographers similarly provide pictures; cartoonists supply drawings. Editorial and special writers compose articles, special columns, and other feature matter. From outside firms editors obtain special articles, illustrations, and features. All this must be co-ordinated with the work of reporters and other "home" staff members.

The editorial department, in providing this material, prepares copy for the printer and the engraver. News stories and other written material must be copyread and headlined. Photographs and cartoons must be retouched and mounted.

Records And Information Are Kept Current. The editorial department must act as an information center. It must keep records of happenings, gather reference material, and assemble collections of illustrations. This is done by maintaining extensive files of clippings and photographs, a library, and bound copies of newspapers. Some large papers make arrangements with experts in various fields to draw upon them as sources of information.

The Editorial Department Co-operates With The Advertising Department. The editorial department, in co-operation with the advertising department, must plan the paper. To it fall such tasks as "dummying" each page, replacing old news with fresh news as editions change, and directing the make-up of the paper. Editorial department staffs must set up a system of handling copy which co-ordinates the duties of the various workers and makes for the smooth passage of copy through its various states of preparation into the hands of the printer or engraver.

City Papers Have Elaborate Editorial Staffs. The largest metropolitan newspapers will not infrequently maintain the following positions:

Editor	Special writers	Real-estate editor
Associate editors	Picture editor	Stamp editor
Managing editor	Rotogravure editor	Aviation editor
News editor	Society editor	Garden editor
Sunday editor	Drama editor	Farm editor
City editor	Columnists	Copyreaders
Assistant city editor	Literary editor	Rewriters
Telegraph editor	Music editor	Reporters
Cable editor	Movie editor	Photographers
Make-up editor	Cartoonists	Artists
Sports editor	Art editor	Clerks
Financial editor	Radio editor	Office boys
Labor editor	Automobile editor	Copy boys
Women's editor	Travel editor	Messengers
Editorial writers	Religious editor	Librarian

The small-city daily will combine many of these positions or eliminate some altogether and have an editorial staff of from ten to fifteen persons.

Country Papers Necessarily Have Small Staffs. The editorial department of a country newspaper may have only an editor and a reporter. Between them they will perform the duties of editor, editorial writer, reporter, copyreader, make-up editor, departmental editor, copy boy, photographer, librarian, and the host of other editorial jobs. In addition, it is not uncommon for the editor to carry on many of the business transactions of the paper. This is even the more probable when the editor is also the publisher.

THE MECHANICAL DEPARTMENT PRODUCES
THE NEWSPAPER

The editorial and advertising departments feed copy into the mechanical or printing department. The function of the mechanical department is to produce the newspaper. It must set in type the news, editorial, and advertising matter that arrives in copy form, manufacture several types of engravings from photographic or other art department copy, and perform other mechanical operations relative to issue of a newspaper.[1]

The Mechanical Department Needs To Be Efficient. The mechanical department necessarily works hand in hand with the editorial and advertising departments. This is true not only in speaking of the system whereby copy (photographic, editorial, news, advertising or art copy) is routed to the printing department but of the physical relationship of the departments. Modern newspaper plants seek to have the printing department (familiarly called the composing room) so situated as to be readily accessible to the advertising and editorial groups, usually on a floor between them or in rooms adjacent. The mechanical department is itself subdivided. Its divisions are:

THE COMPOSING ROOM. Here are the Linotypes and other typesetting machines which transform copy into lead columns, set advertising matter, prepare headlines, and assemble this material into forms preparatory to casting into plates for printing. Even so only a portion of the mechanical operations takes place in the composing room.

THE ENGRAVING AND ART DEPARTMENT. Sometimes these are separate or the art department is a close companion or part of the editorial department. In the art division photographs are retouched or improved in other ways; groups of them are mounted to enhance interest or present artistic layouts; cartoons, comic strips, and illustrations are drawn. In the engraving department this copy is converted into metal reproductions so it may be printed.[2]

THE STEREOTYPING DEPARTMENT. Equipped with machinery that permits speedy operations to be carried on, this department transforms the type forms into metal plates, curved to fit a cylinder press (the type used in most large plants) by taking a papier-mâché impression of the form

---

[1] This chapter presumes letterpress, though during emergency periods there has been extensive resort, by the metropolitan newspapers of Chicago and other cities, to engraving processes for printing typed copy. Thus, experiment has been made toward using more offset and other substitutes for the standard letterpress.

[2] See Chapter XLIV, *Mechanics of Publication*.

and reproducing it in lead. The men working in this division also provide casts of mats for use as illustrations in the advertising and reading matter of the paper.

THE PRESSROOM. One or more press units, depending upon the size of the newspaper, are housed here for the final mechanical operation of printing the paper. This equipment, in addition to making many and speedy impressions, also folds and counts the papers.

THE MAILING DEPARTMENT. Sometimes connected with the circulation department, the mailing department also must be correlated with the pressroom; the papers dropping off the press must not be delayed in transmission to the public. Here is equipment to bind, wrap, and address the papers singly or in bundles and to expedite their reaching readers. Distribution equipment consists of trucks, motorboats, motorcycles, airplanes, and similar vehicles.

The Mechanical Department Has A Varied Personnel. Division of labor is characteristic of the department throughout. There is a superintendent over all subdivisions. He is assisted by foremen, for both day and night operation. They in turn have assistants. Working as craftsmen are engravers (whose trade is subdivided into etchers, routers, and other workers), photographers, and artists. Then there are operators of typesetting machines (known as compositors), pressmen, stereotypers, mailers, inkers, binders, proofreaders, make-up men, utility men, casting machine operators, and miscellaneous workers for repairing and servicing machines, cleaning forms, assembling portions of type matter, filing, and performing other duties.

The printing or mechanical department is responsible for paper, ink, and other supplies. Large newspapers require huge storerooms for the rolls of paper used in producing newspaper editions and must have speedy mechanical means of bringing those rolls to the presses and placing them in position. In the small paper the job printing work adds greatly to the kinds of paper stored and to the colors and qualities of ink in reserve and use.

The Plant Of The Country Newspaper Has Varied Uses. The city daily and the country weekly differ sharply in the matter of mechanical department equipment. In the country plant all this equipment and personnel are reduced to a few machines, the principal ones being the typesetting and the printing press, and two or three workers engaged in the production of the paper for a limited time each week, giving most of their time to job printing. The sharpest difference is that the large paper does not use its plant for much more than production of the paper but the small weekly and even the small-city daily depend upon their printing plants for much of their revenue; the publisher may be a printer first of all and issue a newspaper as a matter of pride, political necessity, or to promote his printing plant. The city daily's press is in almost constant operation spewing editions whereas the country weekly is in need of its press but once a week.

THE BUSINESS DEPARTMENT PROVIDES MANAGEMENT AND REVENUE

The business department of a newspaper may be organized in any number of ways but, large or small, performs such functions as administration, circulation, advertising, auditing, and promotion. In reality the newspaper is private business with a social obligation.

Newspapers Are Business Organizations. The uninformed are apt to think of the newspaper as primarily a literary venture. By the very nature of the press as an institution in a free enterprise society, the activities of two-thirds of a newspaper's main departments are no less commercial than those of the corner drugstore. Under the present economic order the newspaper is, and must be, a business. To be successful it must be a well-ordered one. Certainly, the advertising and circulation departments are just as vital to the publishing of a newspaper as the editorial or mechanical departments.

The Administrative Division Is The Center Of Responsibility. A news organ must have a person or group of persons responsible for the operation of the paper, able to decide departmental policies, and authorized to represent it legally. The administrative division commonly gives most attention to the business department. Although the administration of the paper usually contains upon its board or other governing body representatives of all departments, it gives most of its attention to the financial side of the paper. This is more true when owners or publishers are businessmen first and newspapermen second.

At the head of most newspapers is an owner, or a corporation which legally serves as an owner but may be made up of few or many stockholders. The owner may employ a publisher as top-management's representative but very often the owner and publisher are one.

Newspapers are financed by the same methods as are other businesses. The financial provisions of a metropolitan newspaper are the same as those of a city department store or manufacturing plant of similar size. The main difference between the newspaper business and any other is that the newspaper is appropriately regarded somewhat as a public-service organization. However, as large newspapers become million-dollar corporations the newspaper company may, and often does, lose the major significance of that individuality. Still, for the most part, the newspaper as a social institution has been fairly successful in withstanding the more impersonal commercial effects of large corporate enterprise.

Generally the principal business administrative officers on newspapers are: the publisher or owner, business manager, circulation manager, and plant superintendent. If the ownership is vested in a company, the editor may be president and the business manager secretary of the firm. There is no greater standardization in newspaper management in this regard than in other businesses. On a large newspaper these officers are supplemented by numerous assistants, office managers, credit managers, accountants, cashiers, secretaries, stenographers, and other office workers. Chain operation disturbs this setup only at the top. Except in the nature of the commodity handled, the work of the administration of a newspaper varies little from that of any well-run business office.

The Advertising Department Brings In The Principal Revenue. The advertising department's success depends to a large degree upon: (1) whether the editorial department creates the greatest possible amount of reader-interest; (2) whether the mechanical department produces an attractive paper; and (3) whether the circulation department succeeds in maintaining wide distribution for the paper. The advertising department, in one phase of its work, operates much as does the editorial department. It gathers and assembles advertising copy. Advertising staffs obtain copy from the advertiser and submit it to department heads before it is sent to the print shop for setting in type according to contractual agreement and layout and copy plan of the advertiser. A major task added to this basic one is that of merchandising or otherwise aiding the advertiser.

The advertising department staff falls logically into nine groups. On large papers, it not infrequently consists of: (1) an advertising director or manager, (2) head of the classified section or "classified" manager,[1] (3) manager of the national advertising section, (4) local advertising manager, (5) solicitors, (6) copy writers, (7) research and statistical workers, (8) merchandisers, (9) want-ad and telephone clerks and operators.

Copy follows a definite route in the advertising office. When a solicitor obtains a contract for advertising he has completed the first step in a routine something like this: (1) Salesman or solicitor arranges contract for space. (2) Copy is provided by advertiser or prepared by the newspaper in collaboration with the advertiser. (3) It is set in type and proofs are sent to the advertiser. (4) Necessary changes are made. (5) The advertisement is run according to schedule. (6) Checking copies are provided the advertiser or his agency. (7) The accounting department bills the advertiser or his agency or sends a collector authorized to obtain the sum owed for the service. (8) Replies to the advertisement (especially in the case of a classified or "keyed" ad) and promotional work to assure the "pulling power" of the advertisement follow.

Classified advertising is often most important to a newspaper and al-

---

[1] Many newspapers derive a large amount of their revenue from classified advertising. It may be almost as important as display advertising both as to revenue producing and as to value to the reader. Even some radio stations are now beginning to carry classified advertising.

ways to the public. Its use by the public varies somewhat in the same ratio as it is promoted by a newspaper. Much classified advertising is solicited over the telephone. The department does not in this case resort to personal calls upon a potential advertiser. Newspapers keep a close watch on all news for "leads" which may provide classified business. In fact, staffs frequently carefully study the classified advertisements appearing in competitors' papers.

The Circulation Department Is Responsible For Distribution. The editorial, advertising, and mechanical departments do all that men and machines will enable them to do in bringing material into the plant quickly, unrevealingly, and smoothly. They do their best to compress it into newspaper form completely and rapidly. They are dependent upon the circulation department for the distribution of this material to the public. All other departments bring material in; the circulation department takes it out. If reporters dig up amazing news and prepare entertaining features but the circulation department fails to get the papers into readers' hands, the editorial work has gone to waste.

The circulation department must have a relatively large and well–coordinated personnel. Only the small weekly can confine that personnel to a few persons. Even the rather small city daily must have a circulation staff of about seventy-five boys and men. The metropolitan paper, with many editions daily, has a staff mounting into the many hundreds.

This staff has a constant basic personnel. It consists of a circulation manager or director, his assistants—who may be city, county, and state circulation managers—a delivery superintendent, supervisors of carriers, truck drivers, delivery clerks, district managers, carriers, and miscellaneous office help. In some instances airplane and boat pilots are added. Carriers are not always a part of the staff. They may work independently, the circulation department selling the papers to the boys at a price low enough to afford them a profit.

The equipment for the department includes office files for elaborate records of subscribers; one or many autotrucks, bicycles, passenger cars, motorcycles, and possibly boats and airplanes; and receptacles for papers on street corners and on rural routes.

The circulation works on a time schedule. This fact requires the meeting of deadlines by all whose work precedes that of the distribution department. There may be but one train a day to an outlying point and to miss it with the bundle of papers calls for costly trucking or some other special means of distribution. The moving force behind the department is that all readers must get their papers when they are wanted or a competitor will supply the need first.

The Accounting Department Is The Countinghouse Of The Newspaper. A newspaper company must keep records of its business transactions no less carefully than any other business. Hence it operates with a bookkeeping system which accounts for all money received from the circulation department, the advertising department, and (if it is a small paper) the job department. It also records all operating expenditures, such as salaries, purchase of new equipment, materials, and supplies, and must balance the books and keep the administration of the company informed of all financial activities.

The accounting department is standard among such departments. That is to say, this department of a newspaper is no different, except for the nature of some of the items dealt with, than the same department might be for a furniture company or a grocery store. In a large newspaper, the personnel may consist of a manager, cashiers, an office and a credit manager, accountants, general office help, filing clerks, stenographers, mail clerks, credit men, and collectors. Small daily papers and weeklies do not need more than three or four persons for all these operations and generally attempt to have the work carried by one or two.

A Newcomer To The Newspaper Assembled Is The Promotion Department. A half-century ago the promotion department was unheard of among newspapers. A newspaper owner would scoff at a suggestion that he needed such an organization. But today newspapers must meet competition, not only from each other, but also from other attractions to the public and from other commodities.

The main function of a promotion department is to build good-will for the newspaper. This means that the paper must do all in its power to be of service to its readers and advertisers. A man whose hobby is fishing will feel kindly towards a paper that has provided him with a directory of the best fishing spots in his state. His wife will be friendly if the cooking editor helps her with a book of recipes.

Thus, the newspaper, large or small, goes out of its way to be useful to the public. The small paper prides itself on being a reference bureau for the town. Its clerks may do no more than answer questions about train schedules, the correct time, or the weather report. However, as it organizes and prepares itself to do this for the public, just so much is it promoting itself. The large paper may have an entire building or a large suite of offices for promotional use. It will have touring hours for visitors to the plant. It will prepare literature about the paper for public distribution. It will give travel, road, health, cooking, and other advice. It will operate a radio station. It will advertise itself on the screen, on billboards, in other papers, on car cards, and by mail. All these and dozens of other promotional functions will be performed by a staff headed by a promotion manager, clerks, guides, and office workers, all in collaboration with the business, mechanical, and advertising departments.

Other Departments Complete The Newspaper Assembled. Other departments must be operated to make the newspaper complete as an organization. These are: (1) *service department,* which provides janitorial, garage, stockroom, and shipping service; (2) *radio department,* which may be set up as practically a separate company with a staff and equipment almost as elaborate as the paper's; (3) *sales promotion,* which organizes cooking schools, food shows, amateur athletic contests, and other devices to make advertising more effective and to create circulation.

CHAPTER V

THE WORD PATTERN OF NEWS

The qualities most to be desired and striven for in newspaper writing
are accuracy of statement—in small things as well as in great, in par-
ticulars as well as in essentials—simplicity, directness, accuracy, and
point. Never attempt fine writing for the sake of fine writing, never use
big words where small words are possible. Go right to the heart of the
subject without flourish of trumpets or introduction. Stop when the story
is told without conclusion or moral tag.*

READERS DETERMINE NEWS STYLE

The style of news writing is determined by the character of newspaper
readers, conditions under which they read, and mechanics of newspaper
publication.

Stylistic requirements of a good news story are not arbitrarily conventional and traditional. They have been found after centuries of trial-and-
error development to be those qualities best suited to hold the reader's
interest and assure his clear understanding.

For this reason, style varies somewhat between one news publication
and another. A newspaper such as the *New York Times* with considerable circulation among the better educated may employ successfully more
sophisticated diction and heavier sentence structure than would a publication circulating principally among the less well educated.

**The Reader's Capacity For Understanding Limits The Range Of The
News Writer's Style.** A news story must be so written that all of the
paper's readers from college presidents to those possessing least education
and most limited intellectual capacity may understand it with ease. Difficulties this requirement presents are made clearer by the portrait of the
average reader once sketched by Dr. Harry L. Hollingworth in a *New
York Times* interview:

> The average man has a vocabulary of about 7,500 words. Words
> like "dilapidated" and "philanthropy" are just a little beyond his
> mental reach and he cannot put into words the difference be-
> tween "poverty" and "misery."
>
> The average man leaves school at the eighth grade. He has a
> smattering of local geography, a little bit of history, and a few
> elementary facts of physiology.

---

* *Indianapolis News* stylebook during editorship of Charles R. Williams.

He believes that a couple of quinine pills and a stiff drink of whiskey will cure a cold, that a Masonic order goes back to the days of King Solomon, that it is practically fatal to eat lobster and follow it with ice cream, that all Swedes have thick skulls and are stupid, that redheaded people always have quick tempers, that tan shoes are cooler than black for summer wear, that dew falls, that morals were purer twenty years ago, and that the winters were longer, the snow heavier and more frequent when he was a boy.

The news writer, however, must reach the understanding not only of this average man but also of his less fortunate fellows as well.

Newspaper Reading Habits Guide The Telling Of The Story. The newspaper, propped against the coffeepot at the breakfast table or clutched in the free hand of a strap-hanging commuter, is read under conditions far different from those which govern the use of a textbook in the student's room or perusal of a reference volume in the cloistered quiet of the library. In a majority of cases, it is read more hurriedly than any other medium of communication. Its style must be indeed such that "he who runs may read."

A commuter's description of conditions under which newspapers often are read illustrates the test which clarity of news writing must meet in metropolitan areas:

> Some weeks ago I sat cramped in a seat on a packed suburban local that pulled out of the train shed a half hour behind time.
>
> We crawled out into the night, stopped, crawled on again, gathered a little headway, and limped in that fashion from station to station, losing more time at every stop.
>
> The lights on that train were miserable. Two of them in our car were clean out of commission. Some of us stood in the aisles. All of us were uncomfortable and disgruntled. Nearly every mother's son of us was making futile efforts to read a newspaper or some other periodical.
>
> Trying to read newspaper body type in semi-twilight like that is hard on the nerves of men who have worked at high speed all day. Yet there was much we wanted to know in those close-set columns.
>
> We scanned the headlines, elbowed and manoeuvered for better light, strained our eyes and tempers trying to read type that was barely legible. Under such conditions, our optical and psychological mechanism simply refused to tolerate non-essentials.[1]

No leisurely, heavy style will meet requirements created by reading habits such as these. Ease of reading becomes a requisite. Clarity is essential.

---

[1] From *Printers' Ink,* February 28, 1918. Used by permission of the publishers.

Our common reading habits have created a situation also in which the news story is competing for the reader's attention, not merely with other news stories in the paper and advertisements in adjacent columns but with many other attractions to which he might devote his time. The radio is blaring in his ear; lights of a near-by movie theater beckon; his motor waits outside to whisk him away.

The reader amidst this complexity of modern life will not pause over a story he cannot understand immediately. He will not linger over the uninteresting. When clarity fails or interest lags, he is away to the next column or the next page or, perhaps, he discards the paper altogether for golf, bridge, or the latest detective thriller.

Mechanical Requirements Govern Sentence And Paragraph Length. The narrow column width and small type common in newspapers make long sentences and paragraphs difficult for readers. The basis of this difficulty is physiological. A long sentence will fill many lines of type in the newspaper column. To read it, one must continually shift his gaze back and forth across the column. This process is obviously tiring and gives a heavy appearance to a sentence which, set in the greater width and larger type of a book, would not seem difficult.

The short column width has a tendency also to make paragraph lengths seem greater than they are. When a paragraph extends down the column for a distance greater than the column width, the reading matter begins to appear solid and forbidding.

THE NEWS WRITER MUST OBSERVE CERTAIN PRINCIPLES

The style of the news story should be correct, simple, concise, objective, interesting. News writing must observe the rules of rhetoric.

Correctness Is Essential. "Good newspaper writing today must observe rules older than Moses," wrote Stanley Walker. "Newspaper writing at its best seeks to present facts, tersely, logically, completely. The result may be satisfying, amusing, or even beautiful. But first it must respect the ancient precepts." [1]

Correctness of news style is essential to clarity, to ready understanding of a story. Our language is but a conventional set of symbols, a refinement of the sign language of the ancients. We expect and readily understand the conventional use of these symbols. When conventional use is violated, we are surprised; continuity of thought is broken, its meaning uncertain.

What happens when conventional use of symbols is disregarded may be made clearer, perhaps, by illustration from another field of sign language. A motorist is entering a strange city. As he approaches a street intersection, a purple light suddenly flashes before him in the traffic signal. He is confused. Does it mean "Go" or "Stop"? The familiarly understood

---

[1] From *City Editor* by Stanley Walker, p. 152. Copyright 1934. Used by permission of the publishers, Frederick A. Stokes Co.

green and red lights are missing. The unexpected purple light is surprising and meaningless for him. Similar in effect is the incorrect use of language.

Correctness of style in the news story is necessary also to hold the confidence of the educated reader. If the news writer has been inaccurate in his language, the reader may suspect with good reason that he has been equally at fault in handling the facts. The poorly written newspaper can hope for neither the respect nor the confidence of educated readers.

Correctness of news-writing style implies not only accuracy in grammar, spelling, and diction but also conformity to canons of good taste as well.

Simplicity Is Needed. Simple style is needed to attain that clarity and ease of reading which the wide range of the newspaper reading public, its reading habits, and the mechanics of newspaper printing unite to demand in the news story. This necessity for simplicity touches every element of the news story—word, sentence, paragraph.

It implies further that the news tale shall be told plainly with no obvious straining for effects. "Fine writing" as used in newsrooms is a term not of praise but of scorn. Sports writers seem particularly susceptible to this frailty of style. Illustrative are the following paragraphs in the lead of an account of a Notre Dame–Southern California football game:

> SOLDIERS' FIELD, CHICAGO, Nov. 16.—Football of magnificent stature, comparable in every way to the headline position which the game occupied in national affairs was played in this uncompleted, murk filled bowl, laying within earshot of the lapping waters of Lake Michigan here this afternoon.
>
> California, trained and schooled in the sun kissed climate of the Pacific Coast, rode 2500 miles from the shadows of the Sierra Madre mountains to meet an eleven coached by the vital Viking of America's greatest sport. This blue robed band of flitting, beautifully routined young Hoosiers from South Bend, responding to the inspirational presence of this courageous and incapacitated Viking, Knute Rockne, the bald eagle of the plains of Indiana, emerged from an Homeric contest a victor by a score of 13 to 12.

Arthur Brisbane in his once-famous "Today" column defined "fine writing" as "an attempt to make WORDS take the place of IDEAS, and make exaggeration take the place of truth." He wrote further:

> Avoid such writing if you write, avoid such talking when you talk, and avoid such methods if you prepare advertising.
>
> The FINEST writing is the SIMPLEST writing. The most famous passage in the English language, perhaps, is made up of ten words, all very simple.

"To be or not to be; that is the question."

You couldn't make that MUCH simpler.

Another famous line by Shakespeare comes at the end of Hamlet's tragedy. "The rest is silence."

That is powerful because it tells all that is needed, compelling him who reads or hears the words to think and feel ON HIS OWN ACCOUNT.

Powerful, good writing you will find in a hundred writers, and you will notice that all of them write simply and in no case try to do fine writing.

That which is truly fine comes of itself.

USE OF COMMON AND FAMILIAR WORDS. The reporter writes "fire" instead of "conflagration," "dead" instead of "deceased," "steal" instead of "purloin." He selects the short, well-known word rather than its longer, less common synonym. His writing vocabulary abounds in terms of Anglo-Saxon origin. He uses words with prefixes or suffixes sparingly.

Such diction not only helps the reader to understand but contributes to that vigor and liveliness of style essential to good journalistic writing.

NEED FOR SENTENCES THAT ARE COMPACT, DEFINITE IN STRUCTURE, MODERATE IN LENGTH. The oratorical type of sentence with its elaborate structure has no place in the news story. The reporter's sentence goes directly to the point. Periodic and balanced structures rarely are suitable for the news story. Loose sentence structure marked by dangling modifiers and indefinite reference is banned.

The news writer's sentences are, on the average, shorter than those employed in literary publications, texts, and reference works. Many newspapers currently are asking reporters for sentence lengths of less than twenty words. Studies have revealed that sentences of greater length increase the difficulty of reading for the large number of readers who have had little education.

NEED FOR BREVITY IN NEWS-STORY PARAGRAPHS. The news paragraph rarely should exceed a maximum of six standard typewritten lines (approximately twelve lines of newspaper body type). As this maximum is passed, ease of reading is sacrificed.

Conciseness Has Special Value. "A press release should be the length of a woman's skirt—short enough to attract attention and long enough to cover the subject," a woman publicity writer once declared.

American newspaper reading habits are intolerant of long-winded writing. Demands on newspaper white space are too heavy to permit inclusion of stories which fail to move in the telegraphic tempo of modern living. The large-city newspaper is able to print less than one line of copy out of every ten lines available for publication. Such a newspaper sells space to advertisers at rates running to several dollars per column inch. Obviously, space of such great commercial value must not be wasted.

Desired brevity is attained not by omission of details but by tight phrasing, packing fact upon fact. Most wordy stories are the result of lazy writing. The reporter fails to take time to write briefly. He wastes words and saves work.

Especially helpful to conciseness of style are:

OMISSION OF UNNECESSARY ARTICLES.

> *Faulty:* A fire which started at 7 A.M.
> *Better:* Fire which started at 7 A.M.

AVOIDANCE OF REDUNDANCY. Do not write: present incumbent, early pioneer, past experience, stepped into a waiting automobile.

USE OF DIRECT STATEMENT.

> *Faulty:* Changes which are going to affect tomorrow's news-
> paper . . . .
> *Better:* Changes affecting tomorrow's newspaper . . . .

> *Faulty:* Among the speakers were . . . .
> *Better:* Speakers included . . . .

> *Faulty:* He paid a visit to the office . . . .
> *Better:* He visited the office . . . .

Objectivity Is Important. This quality in style is a reflection of the writer's point of view. The journalistic ideal of fair play demands not only that the reporter in gathering and selecting his news shall seek to tell both sides of the story, but also that the phrasing of his account shall not be colored by his opinions.

Direct expression of opinion is barred in all stories except those carrying the writer's by-line. Indirect expression through color words which unconsciously express the writer's bias should be avoided as well. Verbs particularly must be guarded against this violation of the ideal of impartiality. In reporting testimony of a witness, to write that she "admitted" or "conceded" a fact has implications far different from the uncolored tag, "the witness said." A statement in the report of an interview that its subject "hinted at" certain possibilities carries an innuendo not present in the simple declaration that he "suggested" the contingencies.

Interest Must Always Be Present. Word choice and the organization of sentence and paragraph must be determined in view of the ever-present fact that the hurried reader, beset with his multiplicity of competing interests, will read only so long as the story holds his attention.

FRESH, SPECIFIC, VIGOROUS DICTION.

1. Hackneyed words and phrases are among the greatest enemies of interest. News writing on its lower levels is filled with the clichés of slovenly, imitative reporters. In the copy of these writers, failing banks always "crash," increasing casualty lists are ever "mounting," bandits un-

54

failingly escape in "high-powered cars" after using "high explosives" and "high-powered rifles." Disabled ships inevitably "wallow in heavy seas" and "limp into port," and the women, without fail, are "twenty—and pretty." Through them the public meets the man who "glues his eyes on a picture," "flings himself out of the door," "steals a glance from under his hat," and "cannot believe his eyes."

The trite phrase usually includes a timeworn figure of speech or violation of good usage. Words employed in their proper sense may become common but are not trite.

2. Not only is specific phraseology more concise and vigorous than is a general statement, but it also gives the reader something definite to think about immediately.

> *Faulty:* An accident occurred at Main and Second streets when . . . .
> *Better:* A loaded school bus and a 10-ton truck collided . . . .

> *Faulty:* Bad weather greeted opening-day visitors at the fair . . . .
> *Better:* Heavy rain and chilling winds greeted . . . .

3. Use of the active voice increases the pace of the story and the vigor of its style.

INITIAL EMPHASIS AND VARIETY OF BOTH LENGTH AND STRUCTURE IN SENTENCES.

1. The news writer ever is putting his best foot forward in his effort to maintain reader-interest. If the beginning of a sentence is not interesting, the hurrying reader may never take time to read on to that portion of the sentence which contains the essential material. For this reason the news sentence states its most important fact at once, crowding its punch into the opening phrases. Qualifying and explanatory phrases are pushed into the latter part of the sentence.

> *Faulty:* With 2000 spectators in the stands, Skeet's Motors defeated the Home Bakers 5 to 3 today to win the Industrial league championship.
> *Better:* Skeet's Motors won the Industrial league championship today, defeating the Home Bakers 5 to 3 before a crowd of 2000.

> *Faulty:* At 2 P.M. Tuesday in Town hall, Joe Smith will deliver his opening campaign address.
> *Better:* Joe Smith will deliver his opening campaign address Tuesday at 2 P.M. in Town hall.

2. Although news writing must be simple, its sentences should not be uniformly short or simple in structure. Monotony in style can be avoided only by variety in sentence length and structure. Steady use of the short,

simple sentence will create the effect of speed and excitement if confined to an occasional short passage, but continued use soon simulates the staccato drone of the riveting hammer.

INITIAL EMPHASIS AND VARIETY OF LENGTH ALSO IN PARAGRAPHS. The same reasons which dictate these characteristics in the sentence operate to make them desirable in paragraphs. The news paragraph when expository in content is built on the topic-sentence plan. Variety of paragraph length gives the story a more interesting appearance as the reader glances down the column.

Chapter VI

THE NEWS SLANT AND THE REPORTER

NEWS ARITHMETIC

1 ordinary man + 1 ordinary life = 0.
1 ordinary man + 1 extraordinary adventure = NEWS.
1 ordinary husband + 1 ordinary wife = 0.
1 husband + 3 wives = NEWS.
1 bank cashier + 1 wife + 7 children = 0.
1 bank cashier − $10,000 = NEWS.
1 chorus girl + 1 bank president − $100,000 = NEWS.
1 man + 1 auto + 1 gun + 1 quart = NEWS.
1 man + 1 wife + 1 row + 1 lawsuit = NEWS.
1 man + 1 achievement = NEWS.
1 woman + 1 adventure or achievement = NEWS.
1 ordinary man + 1 ordinary life of 79 years = 0.
1 ordinary man + 1 ordinary life of 100 years = NEWS.
—George C. Bastian.*

NEWS SENSE IS ESSENTIAL TO THE REPORTER

Just as the skilled carpenter must be able to select the good boards from a pile of lumber, so must the reporter be able to distinguish between newsy facts and those of little or no news value. They are the raw material with which he works. This selection requires exercise of that sixth sense, sometimes called the "nose for news," which, although utterly lacking in many individuals, can be developed to a degree in others by experience and study and is the natural endowment of the talented.

Knowledge Of News Values Serves The Reporter. In gathering and writing of news, a knowledge and appreciation of news values serve both the cub reporter and the seasoned veteran. They help the reporter to:

1. Know where to go for facts.
2. Recognize news when he encounters it.
3. Select vital phases of his story for emphasis in the lead.
4. Omit irrelevant material.

Trained News Sense Is Always Valuable. Trained news sense will continue to serve the reporter after he has become a copyreader or news executive. It will enable him to:

---

* From *Editing the Day's News* by George C. Bastian and Leland D. Case, p. 19. Copyright 1932. Used by permission of the publishers, The Macmillan Co.

1. Improve the news writing of others.
2. Determine length of stories and size of their headlines.
3. Judge relative value of stories in page make-up.

READER–INTEREST IS THE TOUCHSTONE
OF NEWS VALUE

Although many definitions of news have been attempted, practically all employ the same largely unexplained term. Here are a few:

> News may be defined as any accurate fact or idea that will *interest* a large number of readers.—DEAN M. LYLE SPENCER.[1]

> In actual practice the definition of news for a given newspaper amounts to this: News is anything timely that is selected by the news staff because it is of *interest* and significance to their readers or because it can be made so.—DR. WILLARD G. BLEYER.[2]

> News may be defined as an accurate, unbiased account of the significant facts of a timely happening that is of *interest* to the readers of the newspaper that prints the account.
> —WILLIAM S. MAULSBY.[3]

> News is the first report of significant events which have *interest* for the public.—ERIE C. HOPWOOD.[4]

Varied as they are in many respects, all these definitions include the term *interest*. In common, they say essentially that to be news an item must *interest* the reader.

READER–INTEREST IS DETERMINED BY SEVERAL ITEMS

Reader-interest in any story is determined by its timeliness, its place of origin, its place of publication, and its content.

News Must Be Timely. To attain that reader-interest or appeal essential to news, facts must be fresh. Newspaper history records constant speeding up of production through improved techniques and mechanical facilities. The first report of events recorded by American colonial newspapers was frequently weeks old. Now transmission of like news is a matter of minutes. Not only is yesterday's news stale, but that of a few hours ago is also crowded out by events occurring immediately before

---

[1] From *News Writing* by M. Lyle Spencer, p. 26. Copyright 1917. Used by permission of the publishers, D. C. Heath and Co.

[2] From *Newspaper Writing and Editing* by Willard G. Bleyer, p. 32. Copyright 1932. Used by permission of the publishers, Houghton Mifflin Co.

[3] From *Getting the News* by William S. Maulsby, p. 71. Copyright 1925. Used by permission of the publishers, Harcourt, Brace and Co.

[4] Former editor, *Cleveland Plain Dealer*.

press time. Some metropolitan dailies put out hourly editions in an intense competition to keep their news up to the minute.

The colonial reader was satisfied with month-old news because his whole existence moved at slow pace. It was new to him. Present-day readers, children of a fast-moving age, have radio and television available to

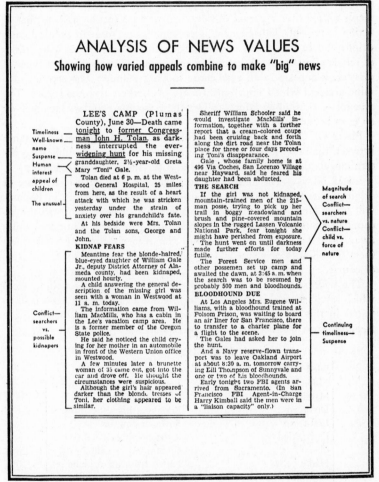

ANALYSIS OF NEWS VALUES
Showing how varied appeals combine to make "big" news

Timeliness —
Well-known —
name
Suspense —
Human
interest
appeal of
children
The unusual —

LEE'S CAMP (Plumas County), June 30—Death came tonight to former Congressman John H. Tolan, as darkness interrupted the ever-widening hunt for his missing granddaughter, 2½-year-old Greta Mary "Toni" Gale.

Tolan died at 6 p. m. at the Westwood General Hospital, 25 miles from here, as the result of a heart attack with which he was stricken yesterday under the strain of anxiety over his grandchild's fate.

At his bedside were Mrs. Tolan and the Tolan sons, George and John.

KIDNAP FEARS

Conflict—
searchers
vs.
possible
kidnapers

Meantime fear the blonde-haired, blue-eyed daughter of William Gale Jr., deputy District Attorney of Alameda county, had been kidnaped, mounted hourly.

A child answering the general description of the missing girl was seen with a woman in Westwood at 11 a. m. today.

The information came from William MacMills, who has a cabin in the Lee's vacation camp area. He is a former member of the Oregon State police.

He said he noticed the child crying for her mother in an automobile in front of the Western Union office in Westwood.

A few minutes later a brunette woman of 35 came out, got into the car and drove off. He thought the circumstances were suspicious.

Although the girl's hair appeared darker than the blonde tresses of Toni, her clothing appeared to be similar.

Sheriff William Schooler said he would investigate MacMills' information, together with a further report that a cream-colored coupe had been cruising back and forth along the dirt road near the Tolan place for three or four days preceding Toni's disappearance.

Gale , whose family home is at 496 Via Coches, San Lorenzo Village near Hayward, said he feared his daughter had been abducted.

THE SEARCH

If the girl was not kidnaped, mountain-trained men of the 215-man posse, trying to pick up her trail in boggy meadowland and brush and pine-covered mountain slopes in the rugged Lassen Volcanic National Park, fear tonight she might have perished from exposure.

The hunt went on until darkness made further efforts for today futile.

The Forest Service men and other possemen set up camp and awaited the dawn, at 3:45 a. m. when the search was to be resumed by probably 500 men and bloodhounds.

BLOODHOUND DUE

At Los Angeles Mrs. Eugene Williams, with a bloodhound trained at Folsom Prison, was waiting to board an air liner for San Francisco, there to transfer to a charter plane for a flight to the scene.

The Gales had asked her to join the hunt.

And a Navy reserve-flown transport was to leave Oakland Airport at about 8:30 a. m. tomorrow carrying Lill Thompson of Sunnyvale and one or two of his bloodhounds.

Early tonight two FBI agents arrived from Sacramento. (In San Francisco FBI Agent-in-Charge Harry Kimball said the men were in a "liaison capacity" only.)

Magnitude
of search
Conflict—
searchers
vs. nature
Conflict—
child vs.
force of
nature

Continuing
timeliness—
Suspense

bring them immediate reports of events direct from the scene of action. They interpret timeliness in terms of minutes rather than of hours.

PREMIUM ON TIMELINESS, FRESHNESS.   This appeal which timeliness possesses is inherent in mankind, observable in many phases of life. The latest songs are those in demand when popular music is played. Recent novels are widely read while those of an earlier year, though often of better quality, gather dust on library shelves. The human mind places a constant premium on timeliness, freshness.

CONTINUING TIMELINESS, SUSPENSE. Continuing timeliness, generally referred to as suspense, is another factor stimulating reader-interest. The serial news story which may run for days or weeks builds a following of readers. When the outcome of a story remains uncertain as its developments unfold over a period of days, a suspense situation akin to that of fiction is present. This element is present in one form in political campaigns and in the period of preparation for athletic contests. In stories of rescue efforts to reach entombed miners and victims of other types of disaster, it appears in an even more moving manner. The account of a mine accident which imprisons a score of workers is a good story. The account of continuing efforts to free these victims five days later will be an even better story.

Places Of Origin And Of Publication Fix Reader-Interest. Distance between the news item's place of origin and its place of publication determines its degree of reader-appeal and the limits of reader-interest.

LOCAL NEWS. The local news item which is published at its place of origin makes a first claim on the reader. The story of a fire in Podunk will prove far more interesting to readers in that town than will the account of a similar happening which occurred in a city a hundred miles away. Proximity of events increases the reader's curiosity concerning them. Familiarity of places and persons involved in these local stories is, of course, an additional factor which stimulates reader-interest.

The wide range of local news in the rural, or nonmetropolitan, field which results from this neighborly feeling and dearth of big news is illustrated in this summary once included by the *Marion* (Illinois) *Daily Republican* in instructions to its correspondents:

HAS ANYONE—

Died	Struck it rich
Eloped	Been arrested
Married	Come to town
Divorced	Bought a home
Left town	Stolen a cow or
Embezzled	the neighbor's wife
Had a fire	Committed suicide
Had a baby	Fallen from an airplane
Broken a leg	Bought an automobile
Had a party	Run away with a handsomer
Sold a farm	man?
Had twins or	That's news.
rheumatism	Phone us at Marion No. 221

Local news appeal is stronger in rural areas and small cities than in larger centers. Less happens in the former; thus added importance is given events. Readers are well acquainted with most of the residents in their communities and, hence, have a personal interest in items which would be utterly without news value if the individuals concerned were strangers. This personal flavor is lacking in the metropolitan news field.

NEWS FROM DISTANT SOURCES. Reader-interest in an item tends to decrease in direct ratio to the increase in distance between its place of origin and place of publication.

Fire in Podunk resulting in $50,000 loss is big local news, for Podunk is not a metropolis. Other papers near-by, in the same county, perhaps, will carry a few paragraphs of the story. In papers at the state capital or other large cities of the state, the Podunk fire probably will be reduced to a mere squib. A similar brief might be carried over the wires in the state services of press associations. Even in this highly condensed form the story would not be placed on the trunk wires of the press associations for transmission to more distant newspapers.

PLACE OF ORIGIN. An item's place of origin may add interest values. Telegraph and cable items carrying date lines of cities which are of interest in themselves or which are in the spotlight because of connection with some timely event of importance get special attention from newspaper readers. Santa Claus, Indiana, is probably the one village which regularly gets into the news solely because of its name. The items which appear under this date line just before Christmas depend for their interest value entirely on the name of the village. Stories from Hollywood have special interest for a large group of readers because of the glamour connected with that name. Lake Success, New York, became of special interest to readers interested in international affairs after it had become the temporary headquarters of United Nations.

ECONOMIC AND CULTURAL INTERESTS. Economic and cultural interests of readers in its place of publication help determine an item's value. A bit of timely information will arouse greater reader-interest in one city than in another. In a railroading center, for example, a story concerning railroads is a bigger piece of news than it would be in cities which do not include many railway employees. Similarly, a story dealing with controversy over miners' wages is of greater interest in cities located in mining regions than in cities outside. Announcements of significant new books are better news in a university town than in an industrial center. The editor and reporter in judging news values must keep such common interests of their reading public in mind.

Content Of A Story Should Stimulate Thought Or Emotions Of Reader. Content of a story to arouse interest must be such as to stir the thought or emotions of the reader. When the mind reacts to a stimulus, unless the reaction is merely that of rejection, it is interested in it. Interest is sustained attention to a stimulus. If the reaction has been intellectual and resulted in thought concerning the stimulus or if it has been emotional because of the fact that the stimulus has made its object angry, or sad, or happy, it has been such as to sustain attention.

The human mind reacts to a large range of subjects but with wide individual variations. Hence, subject matter which appeals to one reader will arouse no reaction in another.

INFORMATION RELATING TO SELF. The human being is selfish. Himself and those things which directly concern him are his first consideration. John M. Siddall when editor of the *American Magazine* expressed this fact well:

> What interests people? One thing only interests all human beings always, and that is the human being himself.
>
> There you have the gist of the matter. No prescription can beat it—if you want to know how to get at people and grip their attention.
>
> Every human being likes to see himself in reading matter— just as he likes to see himself in a mirror. The ideal article for any publication (so far as "reader interest" is concerned) would be one in which every reader would find his own name.
>
> The ideal illustration would be a group photograph of all the readers, so that each reader could have the fun of finding himself in the picture.
>
> Once in a while the newspapers print a flashlight photograph of a thousand men having dinner together. When they do, each one of those thousand men takes a special interest in that photograph. He shows it to his family, and he invents ways and means to bring it to the attention of his neighbors.
>
> Newspapers are read widely because the individual reader sees himself constantly in the paper. I do not mean that he sees his own name. I mean that he reads about things happening to individuals which might happen to him, and he keeps comparing himself with what he reads.

Topics closely related to the reader, his family, his hobbies, and his affairs are the surest approaches to his interest.

THE UNUSUAL. The unusual is the basis of much which we call news. Changes, departures from the expected and routine, are usually productive either of thought or of amusement. Note the following item:

> HUNTSVILLE, Ala.—The claim of Joseph Jones of Merrimac to hospital attaches here that he had "some bean" was borne out today when his story that he had been kicked by a mule on the head and that as a result the animal was lying helpless with a broken leg was investigated and found to be true.
>
> Jones said his way was blocked by a stray mule and he made a threatening gesture to frighten it away. It refused to stampede, however, meeting the assault with a well-

directed kick to the brow. The mule's leg was broken in
two places. It was pronounced a helpless cripple and shot.
Jones will recover.

Neither Jones nor the unnamed mule is of interest or significance in
himself. Jones made the news columns only because the incident in which
he was involved reversed the usual results of such encounters. The story
fits well the timeworn formula, *"If a dog bites a man, that's not news;
if a man bites a dog, that's news."*

WELL-KNOWN NAMES. The reader readily gives attention to timely
items concerning prominent persons or places.[1] An unusual incident is
news but such an incident in which a well-known personality is involved
is choice copy.

STORIES OF COMBAT, OF STRUGGLE BETWEEN OPPOSING FORCES. Most
of the big news featured by newspapers involves a contest. Sports, business, and politics, three of the most productive news fields, are all of competitive character. Crime news presents the criminal and law enforcement
officials in conflict. Big aviation news is chiefly a report of man's struggle
against nature. Stories of adventure present their heroes in conflict with
varied dangers. The romantic appeal also involves conflict of emotions,
desires, and wills. Even the story of mystery finds man in a struggle to
reveal the unknown.

FAMILIAR SUBJECTS. Familiarity paves the way for interest. Timely
information concerning persons and places with which the reader is acquainted intimately often will produce more thought and comment than
far more significant facts will arouse. Gossipy personal items are particularly valuable, as has already been noted, in the small-city and rural newspaper.

MAGNITUDE AND SIGNIFICANCE OF EVENTS. Items which present vast
figures or deal with the activities of masses of persons have appeal because
of the sheer magnitude of the concepts with which they deal. The huge
banner headline gets the reader's attention because of the compelling
power of its great size. The mind reacts in similar fashion to magnitude
of concepts presented.

An item sometimes gives rise to thought not because of itself but because of its probable consequences, its significance. An account of the
passage of a new law is often of little interest *per se* but of great concern
because of consequences. Significance of the event is frequently a factor
contributing additional appeal to accounts having other strong interest
elements. A presidential election commands interest because of the newsworthy names involved and the element of struggle but produces even
greater reader-interest if the issues involved hold widespread significance.

HUMAN-INTEREST INCIDENTS. Intimate glimpses of the lives of others

---

[1] Discussed at length in Chapter X, *Names Make News.*

touch the reader's emotions. Stories lacking significance and newsworthy names often are highly desirable copy because of their so-called human-interest values.[1] Man possesses natural sympathy for other beings like himself. As he reads of the joys or sorrows of another, they tend to become his own. True, if the reader is to feel this emotional transfer, the original state of feeling must be reproduced skillfully by the writer. The human-interest incident will be page-one copy as treated by one reporter and material fit only for the wastebasket as it comes from the typewriter of a less skillful writer. If reader-interest is to be assured, both intimate emotional content and appropriate presentation are essentials.

ANIMAL STORIES. Accounts dealing with animals also have effective appeal. Reader-reaction to animal stories is similar to that accorded human-interest stories. The psychological basis for this attitude remains doubtful but the frequent presence of this reaction is certain. A zoo assignment is often the city editor's answer to the problem of a dull news day.

---

[1] This is taken up in detail in Chapter XXIII, *The Human Touch Makes the Feature.*

Chapter VII

BUILDING THE STORY

Perceiving the law that all news drama begins at the climax, American journalism established the rule which still prevails for "straight" news—tell your story in the first sentence, expand it a bit in the first paragraph, then go back like a novelist to the beginning of the affair and relate it all in detail.—Will Irwin.*

THE STORY CONSISTS OF TWO MAIN PARTS

The conventional news story has two parts: the lead, the body. This is true even though news stories may be organized in many patterns. (One pattern, however, is standard and most commonly employed.)

The Lead Summarizes The Story. It serves three functions.

1. It answers the questions: *who, what, when, where, why,* and *how.*

2. It emphasizes the news feature of the story by placing it in the initial position.

3. It provides such quick identification of persons, places, and events as is necessary to an understanding of the story.

How to make it do these three things will be considered in the following chapter, *The Technique of Leads.*

The Body Is An Elaboration Of The Lead. The lead may be regarded as an outline for the body of the story.

When the facts are clear and well organized, the body will expand each of the points included in the lead in the same order in which the lead has stated them. This plan of organization can be followed most definitely when the story deals principally with expository material. Minor details not included in the material outlined by the lead may be presented in the order of their interest, those of greatest value being reported first and those with least appeal being used last.

"Block" paragraphs, each a separate unit without transitions connecting it to that which precedes or follows, are employed as much as possible in the body of the story. Such paragraphs may be shifted about or eliminated in editing of the copy without rewriting of other portions of the story.

Note the application of these principles in the following example. The

---

* From *Propaganda and the News* by Will Irwin, p. 59. Copyright 1936. Used by permission of the publishers, McGraw-Hill Book Co.

lead paragraph features an interesting phase of one speaker's address and gives his name and identification, the occasion, place, and time. The second paragraph completes the lead summary by listing the other speakers. The first paragraph could stand alone as a brief. The first two paragraphs constitute a tightly condensed summary and could stand alone. The next three paragraphs elaborate the idea featured in the lead. Remaining paragraphs are devoted to remarks of the three speakers listed in the second paragraph, each being mentioned in the order in which his name appeared in the earlier summary. This story could be cut at the end of any paragraph except the eighth, which requires the next paragraph to make its meaning clear.

1. The texts of Shakespeare's plays are still "hopelessly or almost hopelessly corrupt" in many places, despite all the work of eighteenth, nineteenth, and twentieth century editors and scholars, Dr. Samuel A. Tannenbaum, physician and Shakespearean scholar, told yesterday afternoon's audience at The New York Times National Book Fair in the International Building, Rockefeller Center. "Corrupt" was used in the sense of "garbled."

2. The large audience heard old and rare books discussed also by Henry W. Kent, president of the American Institute of Graphic Arts and secretary of the Metropolitan Museum of Art, who presided, and by Dr. A. S. W. Rosenbach and John Winterich.

3. The reason for the uncertainties in Shakespeare's texts lies mainly in the fact that his transcribers and printers often erred in reading his manuscripts, "the sort of thing that happens, even today, when a compositor has to decipher an author's handwriting and the latter does not read proof," Dr. Tannenbaum explained. "Shakespeare never read proof on any of his plays."

4. Shakespeare's manuscripts were written in the "secretary Gothic script," a style of writing so different from our Roman script that persons unacquainted with it cannot read it or even think of it as being English, Dr. Tannenbaum said.

5. "That Shakespeare also wrote the new Roman script, which was then coming into fashion among scholars and aristocrats, is proved by his signatures, of which there are only seven in existence," he continued. "In Shakespeare's handwriting there are extant today only the seven signatures and the words 'by me' on the third page of his will."

6. Although many persons regard book collecting as a recent innovation, Mr. Kent said, it is really very old, and collectors of the past are responsible for many of the world's great libraries.

7 Dr. Rosenbach described his experiences in collecting outstanding rare volumes and warned facetiously that "it is sometimes dangerous for women to possess rare volumes—they might for that very reason receive offers of marriage."

"That sounds fantastic, but it is true," Dr. Rosenbach continued. "I can only quote the celebrated case of a great feminine amateur at the beginning of the nineteenth cen-
8 tury. Miss Richardson Currer owned a valuable library containing over 15,000 volumes including a beautiful copy printed on vellum of the 'Book of St. Albans,' 1496, written by the first woman sports writer, Dame Juliana Berners.

"Richard Heber, probably the most enthusiastic book-collector who ever lived, tried to wheedle it out of her by hook or crook. Not succeeding by nefarious ways, he took
9 the honorable method of proposing marriage. The lady, not caring to share the volume with a husband, indignantly refused. Good for her!"

10 It is possible to be a book collector "without being sued for non-support," Mr. Winterich said.

"Anybody who can afford to buy an occasional new book can afford an occasional old one," he explained. "I am afraid that as we look around at the glamorous rare books
11 and manuscripts in this Book Fair, we are likely to be at first delighted, then appalled, and then disheartened. What chance has any of us to possess such volumes?"

Mr. Winterich explained various types of collecting that may be enjoyed by persons without great means. One of the finest collections of Thomas Hardy material was assem-
12 bled by a mail clerk in the Middle West who recognized the genius of this author and began to collect his books before prices climbed.

Mr. Winterich told also of an orthopedic surgeon who collects books on the history of the crutch, an up-State
13 executive of a glass company who collects books on glass, and a New York barber who has built up a collection of books about his calling.

When the facts of the story include strong narrative elements, three methods of organizing the body of the account are available.

1. Narrative material presented in chronological order may precede presentation of nonnarrative facts.

Note in the following example that a summary lead is followed by a detailed chronological narrative with the last two paragraphs of the story devoted to unimportant nonnarrative material.

SUMMARY
LEAD

Matt Hoffmann, 33 years old, a small time beer peddler, was shot and killed late Thursday night after a struggle outside a roadhouse in Glenview. His body, with bullet wounds in the head, was found last eve-

ning in a cornfield near the village of Aptakisic, in Lake
county, about eight miles from the scene of the battle.

Hoffmann's wife, Anna, answered a telephone call at
about 10:30 p.m. Thursday. The caller was Jack Hackney, owner of a roadhouse on Harms road south of
Lake avenue in Glenview. He requested that two half
barrels of beer be delivered at once to his place.

The Hoffmann home is on Glenview road, just inside
the limits of Wilmette. Hoffmann arose from bed and,
clad only in his trousers, under-clothing and bedroom
slippers, left in his car with the beer.

According to Hackney, he had made the call on behalf of a man known to him only as Jake Schrieber.

"I met this Jake about two weeks ago," he said. "Matt
introduced him to me. He said that if Schrieber ever
wanted any beer delivered to him at my place I should
make the call. That's what I did, and Schrieber was
standing by me when I called.

"A few minutes after that Schrieber walked outside.
He said he'd be back inside an hour and to tell Matt
to wait. I think there was another man and maybe
two with Schrieber, but I don't know.

"Along about 11 o'clock, or maybe a little later, a
car came into my yard. Then, in about ten minutes
more, I heard somebody yelling 'Help, Jack!' I was
afraid to go out and there was some more noise. I
didn't hear any shots fired, but pretty soon two cars
drove away and I called the police to tell them I
thought Matt Hoffmann had been kidnapped."

Chief of Police Roy Miller of Glenview and Lieut.
James Meyering of the county highway force investigated. In the yard in front of Hackney's place they
found the two half barrels of beer, abandoned; two
shells from a .32 caliber pistol, and a pool of blood.
They were convinced then that Hoffmann had been
killed on this spot and his body carried away.

Efforts were made to find the missing man, but no
trace of him or his body was found until Roman Raupp
and Clarence Weidner, sons of farmers living near
Aptakisic, discovered the body in the cornfield.

Deputy Sheriff John De Smidt of Lake County rec-
ognized the victim as Hoffmann and Sheriff Lester
Tiffany of Lake county ordered the body taken to
Libertyville.

According to the police information, Hoffmann had
won the enmity of a rival gang of beer runners who
hoped to take over his territory. These men are believed
to have come down from Wisconsin.

Mrs. Hoffmann said she did not know from whom

CHRONOLOGICAL
NARRATIVE

NONNARRATIVE
FACTS

her husband bought wholesale, and she had never heard
of Schrieber. Hoffmann was the father of three small
children.

2. Nonnarrative facts may be presented first with the chronological
account following.

In the following example a two-paragraph summary is followed by a
paragraph of additional detail. Then follows the chronological account
which completes the story.

SUMMARY
LEAD

One man was in critical condition in St. Joseph hospital early today from burns after a rescue from a burning house in which firemen and a police officer braved fire and smoke to save him.

The man is Joseph Spade, 69, blind, who was found by firemen sitting on the edge of a bed in a smoke filled room of a house at 611 Carbon street after Patrolman Dan Simmons had been driven from the place by fire and smoke.

ADDITIONAL
DETAIL

Spade's condition was said to be critical early this morning and a priest was called to the hospital shortly after his arrival to administer last rites of the Roman Catholic church.

CHRONOLOGICAL
ACCOUNT

The fire was discovered by Patrolman Simmons as he was passing in a prowl car. He ran to the front veranda and broke open a screen door.

He was met by Mrs. Charles Gamerdinger, 60, who was overcome by smoke as the patrolman arrived. He carried her to the home of a neighbor next door.

The patrolman then learned that Spade was in the burning building and he returned there to get him. He made little progress inside the house as he was beaten back by dense smoke and fire.

When firemen arrived Patrolman Simmons directed them to save the man. Fireman Ray Worth of Engine company 2 crawled along the floor of the house to the bedroom where he found the man in a cloud of smoke and flames shooting all around him.

An ambulance was called from St. Joseph hospital.

3. More important nonnarrative material may be followed immediately by the chronological account and finally by less important nonnarrative material.

In the following story the first paragraph of summary lead is followed by six paragraphs of detail. The chronological narrative as told by an eyewitness is presented in the next three paragraphs and followed by several paragraphs of nonnarrative material.

Drunken abuse heaped upon his family over a period of five years ended last night for Benjamin Sanford, aged 54, when he was shot to death by his daughter-in-law, Mrs. Lorena Hayes of Kenosha, Wis., who was visiting in the home near Berlin Center.

Mrs. Hayes was lodged in the county jail here by Deputy Sheriff Benny.

"I hated to do it, but I just had to," the pretty black-eyed brunette sobbed.

Sanford was shot in the abdomen, chest and shoulder. He died at 1:30 a.m. today in Salem City Hospital.

Mrs. Sanford, aged 50, and her son Clyde, aged 19, born of a former marriage, witnessed the shooting. She did not know her husband had died until newspapermen called this morning.

"So he's dead, eh?" Mrs. Sanford asked. "Well, I won't miss him much—excepting his nagging and fighting."

Mrs. Sanford said she and Sanford were married seven years ago and that Sanford had worked but seven months since. "He was drunk all the time," she declared.

"Yesterday he came into the kitchen and abused Lorena and me because supper wasn't ready," Mrs. Sanford continued. "Finally he called Lorena a name.

" 'Don't you call me that name again or I'll shoot you,' Lorena said, but my husband just laughed.

"Lorena went into the living room and got a small revolver and as she entered the kitchen Sanford called her the name again. She fired once but it didn't seem to affect him. He walked to the porch and got a mattock, raised it above his head and started for Lorena. I heard two more shots and my husband walked out on the porch and sat down. Suddenly he collapsed and I ran across the street to the Engle home."

The son, Clyde, corroborated his mother's story.

Mrs. Hayes and her husband Lawrence Hayes have been married for four years. They came here three weeks ago for a visit. The husband, a truck driver, returned home last Friday and Mrs. Hayes had intended leaving on Monday.

Besides the sons, Clyde and Lawrence, Mrs. Sanford has another son, Emerson, who is serving a term in the Mansfield reformatory and a daughter, Mrs. Bertha Paxon, near Lisbon.

Mrs. Sanford said she has supported herself and family by making baskets which she sold along the highway. Clyde worked for farmers during threshing season.

Facts are not presented strictly in order of their importance, inasmuch as supporting details are often used to elaborate on important points. This is shown effectively in the following diagram.

DIAGRAM OF NEWS–STORY STRUCTURE

Width of lines indicates relative importance of material.
Capitals indicate news feature of story.

LEAD
(Feature)
General
summary
{ VIGOROUS OPPOSITION TO SECTIONS OF THE PROPOSED CHARTER OF INTERNATIONAL TRADE ORGANIZATION OF THE UNITED STATES WAS VOICED BY TWO SPEAKERS *Monday as public hearings on the charter opened at International House.*

Point 1
Point 2
{ The speakers were Ben J. Williams, representing the Association of Commerce and the New Orleans Cotton Exchange, who said adoption of the charter would bring about "world regimentation," and R. J. Urruela, city director of international relations, who attacked one section which he said "would put governments into business."

Other
summarizing
detail
{ A dozen others, representing various civic and business organizations, appeared before a four-man panel of federal government branches' representatives to give full support to the charter.

Elaboration
of *Point 1*
{ In his talk Mr. Williams declared "cartels, tariffs, as well as other barriers, must be eliminated or reduced to the extent that they will no longer hinder a large volume two-way flow of goods and services over international frontiers."

"But," he said referring to the proposed charter, "it seems to us inconceivable that a document intended to accomplish the removal of barriers to world trade would provide for the creation of intergovernmental commodity arrangements which would regulate production, trade and prices of agricultural commodities.

Further
expansion
of *Point 1*
{ "It is our opinion that the adoption of this charter in the form presented would accomplish exactly the opposite of the objectives sought, that the result would be world regimentation and the elimination of every vestige of freedom, both economic and social."

Elaboration
of *Point 2*
{ A middle-of-the-road stand on the charter was taken by Mr. Urruela, who lauded its purposes as "lofty," but at the same time attacked it because in his opinion it would "put governments into business."

Further
expansion
of *Point 2*
{ "The main trouble with the charter is that it will definitely place the governments in business," he said. "It will also mean that the government will have to determine, through action of ITO, of course, when a commodity becomes burdensome, when it becomes a surplus. Here free trade disappears. It is the government who will determine when a commodity is a burden and when it is not."

Minor detail
not covered
in summary lead
{ Clair Wilcox, chairman, director of the office of international trade policy, department of state, and the three other panel members, John Pierson, department of labor, Robert P. Terrill, department of state, and Nathan Ostroff, department of commerce, were welcomed to the city by Mayor deLesseps S. Morrison.

THE CONVENTIONAL PATTERN HAS EVOLVED
FROM USE

The form of the conventional news story has been shaped by reading habits and publishing methods.

Summary Leads Serve The Hurried Reader. In writing the conventional news story, the reporter is essentially preparing two stories, one being the highly condensed story in the lead summary and the other the more detailed account presented in the whole story. Lead summaries permit hurried readers to scan the entire news of the day in a few minutes. The complete stories serve more careful readers who desire full details.

Stories May Be Cut Easily. The conventional news story even after it has been set in type may be cut to any desired length by the simple process of throwing away its later paragraphs. If necessary, this process may be continued until only the lead is left standing alone as a highly condensed account. Arrangement of material in order of diminishing interest and use of block paragraphs make this possible.

Publishing methods, particularly of larger daily newspapers, require such hurried cutting of stories frequently. If a story is too long to fit the space which has been allotted to it in the page dummy, the make-up editor with the deadline hurrying his decisions merely drops off as many of the later paragraphs as necessary to fit the story to space available. A paper which publishes several editions must cut many stories after they are in type. A story which may be worth several paragraphs in a state edition, because it deals with a news event in the outer circulation territory of the paper, often deserves only two paragraphs in the city edition. Many stories which are allowed to run to some length in early editions must be cut to give place to later news in following editions. If the story has been cast in the conventional form, rewriting or resetting of the story is not necessary in this situation. The story is cut by merely discarding its later paragraphs.

Conventional organization of news matter facilitates the work of the copy desk also. If the reporter's story is longer than the editors believe it should be, its length may be reduced by the simple process of eliminating its last paragraphs. However, if the material has not been organized in the order of diminishing interest, a complete rewriting may be necessary. Use of block paragraphs in the reporter's copy enables the copy desk to reorganize the story if need be by cutting the copy and pasting it together again in the desired order.

SUSPENDED INTEREST CHANGES THE PATTERN

Suspended interest is the device most frequently employed in news stories which depart from the conventional pattern.

Weekly publications and dailies issuing but one edition are able to make more use of news stories which depart from the standard pattern than are metropolitan dailies. Community newspapers have not fully realized these possibilities and have imitated the stories of the metropolitan press. Such publications as *Time* and *Newsweek* have demonstrated the reader-interest which the weekly can develop in news presented in a fresh, unconventional way. Their example and increasing outside competition may serve to enliven tomorrow's community newspaper with more dramatic news presentation.

The Chronological Account Is Simple, Effective. The simplest way to maintain suspense is to record the events in the order in which they occurred. If the incident which forms the basis for the story possesses a true climax, this method of organization, which is applicable only to stories of definitely narrative content, may be highly effective.

The following story illustrates the application of this organization technique to an extremely brief wire story.

> UNIONTOWN, Pa.—Frank Pelone, a stable boss, today found a stick of dynamite and put it in his hip pocket. Later, while working in the stable, he was kicked by a mule. The dynamite exploded, blowing Pelone to pieces and destroying the stable.

The next story makes a more sustained use of chronological development but it also is an unusually brief example of this story type.

> For three weeks Mrs. Rose Zeherle of 9526 Avenue M, South Chicago, received letters signed "Black Hand," bearing the traditional skull and bones and demanding $3,000 from her, threatening her with death if she did not pay.
>
> She did not pay and yesterday received a more urgent one stating she would surely be killed if she did not wrap up $10,000 and place it under a certain tree near 95th street and Avenue M.
>
> Rose went to the station and told Sergt. Joe Hennessy and his bureau squad about it. The sergeant and his men went to the tree and stationed themselves at vantage points. Rose placed a bundle of newspaper where she had been instructed to put the money.
>
> After dark a figure slunk out of the dark to get the package. The detectives seized Frank Hockovar of Lemont, Ill. Rose told the police he used to patronize a restaurant she once operated.

Suspense May Be Created In Many Other Ways. Many devices, limited only by the ingenuity of the individual writer, may be employed to create and maintain suspense. The story may use a "teaser" lead which reveals just enough to indicate the character of the story, to promise the reader something, and to lead him on into the body of the tale. Follow-

ing this type of lead, the body of the story may be handled in a chronological arrangement. Another method reveals the story bit by bit, holding
back at least one important element until near the end of the story or
perhaps until its very conclusion.

The following example illustrates the use of the "teaser" lead and the
bit-by-bit method of revealing the facts.

> OMAHA (UP)—Lady Norfolk, world champion pullet,
> is hearbroken.
> Half a dozen times yesterday she started for her nest, ex-
> pecting to lay her usual daily egg. But each time she
> turned away and returned to the exercise pens. For the
> first time in 173 days Lady Norfolk, familiarly known as
> Babe Ruth, could not lay an egg.
> Finally it dawned upon her that something was wrong.
> "They changed your feed, dearie," whispered Carrie Na-
> tion, a trouble-making pullet from Kansas.
> "They double-crossed me," cackled the little white leg-
> horn. "They took away my proteins and fed me nothing
> but carbohydrates—just when I was beginning to get good.
> I could have gone 300 days easily."
> Change of diet for Lady Norfolk was ordered by her
> owner, A. R. Lander, Norfolk, Neb. Lander feared his
> prize pullet might meet the same fate as Lady Lindy, who
> died after establishing an American record by laying 149
> eggs.

Occasionally a reporter hits upon an unusual idea for organization and
presentation of his facts. Here is a strikingly unconventional example.

> New York, Feb. 23 (AP)
> THE following item is of
> NATIONAL interest—one of those
> PUZZLERS in fact. The writer is in
> LEAGUE with the group. When you've
> FINISHED reading this with
> ITS lack of journalistic
> CONVENTION you may say: "At
> LAST—Good
> NIGHT!"
> THE clue to the
> ORGANIZATION
> MEETS your eye by reading
> AGAIN, this time looking only
> AT first words of sentences.
> LIMA is a bean and also an
> OHIO town. Solution was no
> LABOR, was it? Good
> DAY.

CHAPTER VIII

THE TECHNIQUE OF LEADS

The lead, or introduction, is the most important part of a news article. It should be clear, provocative, and so simple that anyone can understand it. If it has a sharp adjective or adverb, so much the better. Usually it should start with a name, a noun, or an article, rarely with a participle, a preposition or a quotation. Some papers have a rule against starting a lead with "The," but there is little justification for such a " 'Hell!' said the Duchess" philosophy.

The lead should be a promise of great things to come, and the promise should be fulfilled. It should be as direct as, "President Roosevelt, speaking yesterday to 500 Gold Star Mothers in the Smithsonian Institution, accused Joseph Doakes, one-legged mestizo Montana prospector, of unlawfully hoarding farina." And go on from there.

—STANLEY WALKER.*

THE LEAD MUST ANSWER CERTAIN NATURAL QUERIES

Writing the lead for the conventional news story requires the exercise of great care. The lead serves to summarize the story by answering the questions *who, what, when, where,* and often *why* and *how;* and it serves to emphasize the newsworthy event.

It Must Summarize The Action Of The Story. This requires answering the six questions which the reader may be expected always to ask; and it requires stating the result or, in a continuing story where the final result is not known, the latest important development. In the case of a disastrous fire it is not sufficient to write as a lead, "Fire broke out at 7:30 P.M. in the Hartman block at 317 Main street," and then to report the details of the story. Much better would be, "Damage estimated at $16,000 resulted from fire which destroyed stock and fixtures of the Rand pharmacy in the Hartman block at 317 Main street last night."

It Must Emphasize The News Feature. The news feature of any story is the most interesting or significant aspect which it contains. It is the fact which should be the basis for the top deck of the article's headline. The feature is emphasized by placing it first in the lead. The first phrase of the lead, sometimes called the "show window" of the story, should direct the reader's attention to this feature.

ANSWER TO QUERY. The feature may be the answer to any one of the six natural questions.

* From *City Editor* by Stanley Walker, p. 156. Copyright 1934. Used by permission of the publishers, Frederick A. Stokes Co.

1. *The "Who" Lead.*

> John A. Wert, 71, former mayor of Ogdensburg, died at 4:10 o'clock Tuesday afternoon in Hepburn hospital here from injuries suffered in an automobile accident near Waddington last Saturday.

2. *The "What" Lead.*

> MILWAUKEE.—Derailment of a speeding Milwaukee Road passenger train, in which 11 persons—six passengers and five of the crew—suffered minor injuries, was attributed by railroad officials today to a defective rail, which plunged three cars into a ditch and sent two others off the tracks.

3. *The "When" Lead.* The time at which an event takes place is rarely the feature of a story. Inexperienced writers often have a tendency to open their stories with the time of the occurrence, perhaps because of the fact that "Once upon a time" has been the traditional beginning for folk and fairy tales, our most universally familiar form of narrative. Occasionally, however, the time at which an event has taken place has significance:

> On its first day's run after a close-down to remodel and install new machinery and equipment, the Utah Sulphur Corporation mill at Sulphurdale, 20 miles east of Beaver, was destroyed by fire Tuesday afternoon.

Time and occasion are often closely related, with the result that when the occasion has significance, a *when* lead which includes also an indication of the setting for the story may be used:

> VATICAN CITY.—On the eve of the eighth anniversary of his coronation, Pope Pius XII told the Associated Press in his Vatican conference Tuesday that nations must surrender some of their sovereign rights if a just and lasting peace is to be achieved.

4. *The "Where" Lead.* The scene or place of action, likewise, is rarely the news feature of the article. It most frequently becomes significant in connection with some special occasion which provides the setting for a story, as in the following lead for an article written in advance of a national sprint regatta at the University of Washington:

> SEATTLE.—Down at the University of Washington's weather-warped old shellhouse tonight as the last sleek galley was stored away the men who know their crew racing were high on Harvard and Cornell—but keeping their fingers crossed.

Sometimes a single word or phrase will supply the answer to the question *what* as well as *where*. In these cases, this word or phrase may well be first in the lead:

> Northern New York lay under a blanket of snow today after sinking temperatures brought a new reversal in a week of quick-change weather.

> PORTLAND, Me.—This city, where Henry Wadsworth Longfellow was born February 27, 1807, is planning to designate the week of February 25 as Longfellow Week in commemoration of his birth and is asking Governor Horace A. Hildreth to proclaim the celebration state-wide.

5. *The "Why" Lead.* Sometimes the news feature of a story will be the answer to the question *why* in terms of motives:

> In what police listed as a suicide pact, a World War veteran and a woman died of carbon monoxide poisoning yesterday morning in a closed automobile parked in a field in a deserted district of Bayside at 216th street near Seventy-third road, Queens.

More frequently the news feature is provided by an answer to the question *why* in terms of causes:

> An overheated furnace was blamed by firemen for a blaze that caused several thousand dollars damage Tuesday afternoon to a home owned by James Nolan and occupied by William Koenig at 84 Lewis street.

> Failing to get out of the path of an oncoming truck despite warning shouts from his companions, Robert Wortrecz, 48, of 619 East Washington street was crushed to death Saturday night between the machine and the stalled truck he was assisting in pushing on the Syracuse-Watertown highway at Hastings, a few miles north of Central Square.

6. *The "How" Lead.*

> Trapped in an overturned automobile, Hugh Buckler and his son, John Buckler, both actors of British birth, were drowned at midnight in Malibu lake, the sheriff's office was informed today.

LATEST DEVELOPMENT. Some newspapers, particularly metropolitan publications issuing frequent editions, often make the latest important development of the story, rather than an answer to one of the customary questions, the feature of the lead. This practice is followed primarily to furnish material for new and different headlines for the story as it progresses from edition to edition.

> CAIRO, July 8 (AP).—The Palestine war was on again tonight. The UN Mediator gave up hope of stopping it and tried instead to spare Jerusalem's holy places from destruction.

It Must Furnish Identifications Needed For Clarity. Persons, places, and events frequently must be given quick identification to make the lead clear to the reader. These bits of information may be considered as parts of the answer to the *who, where,* and *what.*

PERSONS. Persons are identified ordinarily, as may be noted from the examples of leads given earlier, by their names, addresses, occupations, current or former titles or distinctions, ages, or connections with the story in hand.

Where a person has various possible identifications, those not used with the first mention of his name may be used later as synonyms or appositives if subsequent references to the individual becomes necessary in writing the story. First mention of a name should be accompanied immediately by identification. In crime and accident stories, the identification includes the age. In most other types of news, the age is not used unless it happens to be definitely a part of the story.

Careful identification of persons figuring in an item not only helps the reader to a clearer understanding of who's who in the story but also is a protection against libel actions. Two persons of the same name are often discovered but each fact of identification which is added decreases the likelihood of confusing the individual involved in the story with another of like name.

PLACES. Places are identified with relation to better-known geographical names and as to their previous identification with important news. Thus, an example of the lead already given identifies the village of Hastings as being "a few miles north of Central Square," a larger town. The second method of identification of places is illustrated by such a phrase as "Madison Square Garden, long the scene of Gotham's major political and fistic battles."

EVENTS. Events are identified as to their purpose, their relation to other contemporary or previous events, and the auspices under which they occur.

LEADS VARY IN FORM

Leads for the conventional news story are varied in structure, organization, and length.

The Lead May Open With Any Of Three Grammatical Forms. It may begin with the subject, a phrase, or a clause.

The Subject Of The Sentence.

> A mother was killed yesterday in Brooklyn in a futile attempt to save her 5-year-old daughter from death under the wheels of an automobile.

A Phrase. The phrase may be participial, infinitive, or prepositional.

1. *Participial Phrase.*

> Injured in saving their baby from an oncoming automobile, a young man and his wife are in critical condition in City hospital today.

> Stretching their home court winning streak to nine straight games, the Chicago American Bears handed the front-running Indianapolis Kautskys a 55 to 47 National Basketball League setback before 5,200 fans today.

2. *Infinitive Phrase.*

> To assure prompt delivery of gift packages, post office patrons were urged today by Postmaster H. J. Hart to co-operate with the local postal force by doing their Christmas mailing early.

3. *Prepositional Phrase.*

> With the San Francisco County Branch as host, the Music Teachers' Association of California will hold its thirty-seventh annual convention here next week.

A Clause. This may be conditional, causal, substantive, concessive, or temporal.

1. *Conditional Clause.*

> If the new deal in Siwash University athletics is to accomplish the sweeping changes which seem to be desired, most alumni are of the opinion that the administration should use a new deck.

2. *Causal Clause.*

> Because he served the wrong-sized fish to the wrong persons a local restaurant manager faced arrest today.

3. *Substantive Clause.*

> What the OPA endeavored to do in keeping down food prices and preventing general inflation, San Francisco housewives are determined to carry out.

4. *Concessive Clause.*

> Although facilities for treating the mentally ill are con-
> centrated in metropolitan communities, mental illness is as
> great a threat in the country as in the city, a recent survey
> cited by the American Public Welfare Association reveals.

5. *Temporal Clause.*

> BUENOS AIRES.—After three weeks of civil war,
> neither the Paraguayan government nor rebel forces have
> been able to score decisive gains in the military or political
> field.

Of these three types, the subject beginning is most favored by contemporary news writers. Survey of news columns will reveal the fact that
the lead beginning with a common or proper noun is employed more
than all the other types combined.

Special Forms Of Leads Are Available For Complicated Stories.

THE 1–2–3–4 LEAD. This device for the lead is useful where a story
presents several features of like importance. It has the further advantage
of providing a clear-cut outline which the reporter may follow in the body
of the story. Although referred to as the 1–2–3–4 lead, it may be used for
stories involving fewer major features than four:

> San Franciscans are going to pay a lot more money to
> run their city beginning July 1. Yesterday they were of-
> fered this choice:
> 1—Either pay an increased tax—$7.05 to $7.55 on each
> $100 of property value;
> 2—Or, enact new taxes and borrow money through bond
> issues.

The 1–2–3–4 device may be used without numbering the major points
set forth, as in the following type of lead used by the Associated Press on
occasions when the Supreme Court hands down several decisions at once.

> The Supreme Court Monday:
> Upheld the sale of the Pullman Co.'s sleeping car busi-
> ness to 43 railroads.
> Approved the treason conviction of Hans Max Haupt,
> father of one of the German saboteurs executed during the
> war.
> Decided that a New York court could change a Florida
> decree which gave a mother custody of her young son.
> Ruled that truck company employees who spend a sub-
> stantial part of their time in work affecting the safety of
> interstate operations are outside the provisions of the wage
> and hour law.

> Overturned an ICC order which allowed railroads to
> charge more for hauling grain eastward when it is shipped
> into Chicago by river barge than when it comes from the
> west by rail or lake ship.

THE TABULATED LEAD. This form is more frequently used than the
1–2–3–4 type. It is useful when a news situation involves many angles.
Press associations slug it as an "undated" lead and use it to summarize
stories which originate at different points but concern the same news
situation. It may be used also with local stories having several distinctly
separate angles.

> INSURGENTS REPORT MADRID has offered to sur-
> render if concessions are made.
> REBELS CUT ELECTRIC LINE to Madrid, declare
> move has shut off four-fifths of capital's supply of current.
> FRENCH FOIL BOMBING plot on Spanish ship at
> Marseilles dock.
> SIX GOVERNMENT VICTORIES claimed by Madrid
> on several fronts; loyal planes bomb Fascists.

THE CAPSULE LEAD. This form employs a blunt, generalized summary.

> Syracuse celebrated Armistice day yesterday.

> James M. Mead may run for vice-president in the 1952
> elections.

Leads Vary In Length. The lead may require a single sentence or
several paragraphs. Its length is determined by the complexity of the
story. The greater the number of facts essential to the summary, the
longer the lead. Examples given here have ranged from a single brief
sentence to the several paragraphs of the lead for the story on Supreme
Court decisions. In many newspaper offices, however, the term "lead" is
used referring to the first paragraph of the story only.

FEATURE LEADS INVOLVE SUSPENDED INTEREST

Leads for unconventional or informally organized stories are known
as featurized leads and ordinarily involve at least a degree of suspended
interest. Variations in form of the lead for the story which departs from
the standard pattern are limited only by the writer's ingenuity.[1]

The "Once-Upon-A-Time" Beginning May Have Its Place Here.

CHRONOLOGICAL STORIES. The lead for chronological stories sets forth
the beginning of the action.

---

[1] Only a few of the more useful and common forms are listed and illustrated here.

Fire broke out in Al Holst's garage, which he valued at $1500. He called the fire department.

Policeman Donald F. Curran of the Aurora police force sauntered down one of that city's shadowed streets early yesterday morning. Policeman Curran was garbed in a woman's cloak. A saucy bonnet sat upon his head.

MODIFICATIONS OF CHRONOLOGICAL ORDER. Leads for stories which reveal one major fact or more before proceeding with a chronological account vary greatly in method and form. Each promises the reader interesting things to come.

The engineers who built the Holland Tunnel undoubtedly were fine men in their chosen profession, but in planning that great project they apparently never realized that some one might wish to bring a giraffe from Jersey City to New York.

The sultry looking brunette sat there on the diving board, dripping with water. She picked up a gadget, turned on the juice and she was dry.

The arrival of twins, a big moment in any family, hardly caused a ripple in the routine at the Walter Pearson home —Mrs. Pearson didn't even call a doctor.

"Teaser" Leads Follow Many Formulas.

LEAD USING WELL-KNOWN PHRASE OR QUOTATION.

Time marches on. But not for Jim Ten Eyck.

LEAD BEGINNING WITH A DIRECT QUOTATION.

"I am going to the electric chair but they are sending an innocent man," was the answer of Michael Figmann, Hanover Township miner, today to the verdict of a Criminal Court jury, which found him guilty of first degree murder with death as the penalty in the bomb slaying of Thomas Maloney, insurgent mine leader.

LEAD OPENING WITH A QUESTION.

When can you be arrested for driving without an operator's license and get away with it?

THE PARODY LEAD.

Where, oh where has little Prince gone?
       [Story concerns a lost dog.]

Lead Beginning With A Paragraph Of Direct Quotation.

"Extension of Christian ideals in every aspect of life and in all countries around the world is the best means of safeguarding humanity against another terrible World War which might easily blot out the human race."

This assertion was made today by the Rev. A. Stanley Trickett, associate secretary of the Methodist Board of Missions, guest speaker at the closing session of the Syracuse-east district of the Methodist church.

Lead Beginning With A Verse Or Jingle. The following example also illustrates the parody lead.

Waiters come and waiters go, George has flat-feet and Nick is slow. We've yearned to see a waiter able to more than shuffle toward our table.

Hail then one who's not so slow.

[*Story concerns a waiter's race.*]

Lead Employing Literary Allusion.

Like carrying coals to Newcastle, the steamship Derblay emerged from Bering Sea recently with more than 150 tons of Alaska tin ore consigned to Singapore, Straits Settlements.

The Descriptive Lead.

BAKER LAKE, N.W.T.—Huddled miserably in a wretched snowhouse, sick, weak, and half mad with pain, 24-year-old Dave Irwin of Sarcoxie, Mo., was found last week by native hunters from Baker Lake post.

Albert Callahan is 6 feet tall, husky and a subway guard. Ordinarily he spends his time opening and closing the doors of subway trains and seeing that they admit a proper number of passengers.

CHAPTER IX

WHEN THE STYLEBOOK IS THE MASTER

One of the many revelations that come to the new recruit in journalism is the amazing diversity of "style." One paper may capitalize a liberal percentage of all the nouns in the language, while another may capitalize scarcely anything but its own name, and perhaps that of the Deity.—E. L. Shuman.*

THE NEWSPAPER FORMULATES ITS OWN STYLE PATTERN

A newspaper's "style" is its manner of spelling, punctuating, capitalizing, and abbreviating; it commonly includes also its rules for writing and preparing copy.

Nearly Every Paper Follows A Style. Whatever a newspaper's regular practices may be constitutes its style. Only the paper that disregards consistency fails to have a style, and there are few papers of this type. Although a stylebook may not be used, a general pattern usually is clearly evident in the newspaper's columns.

Newspaper And Literary Styles Differ. Newspaper style is broader in scope than literary style. Style in the literary sense means "the arrangement of words in a manner which at once best expresses the individuality of the author and the idea and intent in his mind."[1] In the newspaper sense it means the way a paper's editors want writers to spell, punctuate, capitalize, and abbreviate, what forms writers are to follow in presenting tabular or other special material, and what typographical rules the writers are to observe.

THERE ARE VALID REASONS FOR NEWSPAPER STYLE

Newspapers follow a style in order to obtain uniformity of practice, to avoid confusing readers, and to achieve pleasing typographical effect.

Uniformity Avoids Errors. Errors are more readily avoided when practice is uniform. A paper that sometimes spells out a high number and other times puts it in figures, especially when dealing with sums of money, greatly increases the possibility of mistakes. Uniformity is especially important to the typesetters, whose composition work is done by

---

* From *Practical Journalism* by E. L. Shuman, p. 70. Copyright 1920. Used by permission of the publishers, D. Appleton-Century Co.

[1] From *A Handbook to Literature* by Thrall and Hibbard, p. 424. Copyright 1936. Used by permission of the publishers, Doubleday, Doran and Co.

an almost mechanical process of co-ordinating mind and muscle. It speeds the operations of typewriting and typesetting.

.Uniformity Facilitates Reading.   Consistency of style helps readers to enjoy the paper. Readers, often confused by the modern newspaper's efforts to present facts in attractive, startling, and unusual ways, are all the more puzzled if the newspaper cannot agree with itself on how to spell or abbreviate. Most readers peruse their papers rapidly; consistency of style helps them to do so. A fast reader who must stop often to untangle a style confusion soon changes to a paper that does nothing to impede his reading.

A Well-Chosen Style Improves Appearance.   Small as the individual style practices or rules may seem, collectively they affect the typographical appearance of the paper. A newspaper that capitalizes a great many words tends to look spotty. Its lines become so irregular and broken that the reader is influenced unconsciously to dislike the typographical effect. Inconsistent use of figures is similarly displeasing.

A STYLE IS LEARNED

Newspaper workers are guided by stylebooks, vocal instructions, and study of their paper.

Stylebooks Are Common.[1]   Many papers provide printed materials for the guidance of their employees in the matter of style. These are of two main types:

1. A booklet or sheet prepared by the editor and printed especially for his paper.
2. Similar material prepared for group use by a school of journalism or a press association.

There are variations. Sometimes the guide may be a mimeographed sheet, a printed leaflet, or a 100-page book. Some papers use the stylebook of another publication. There are differing views, also, on the use of printed sets of rules. For example:

1. Editors who favor such books of regulations say they make for uniformity, easy reference to usage, accuracy, and a high literary level.
2. Editors who discourage their use say that they slow up production, inhibit the writer, place the newspaperman's attention upon unimportant details that had best be reduced to a few general rules which copyreaders can remember without difficulty. They point out, too, that rules soon become obsolete.

---

[1] Please refer to *Appendix* for a model style guide of average length that might be followed by a newspaper or magazine which does not want to be either ultramodern or ultraconservative.

Verbal Instruction Is Needed At Most Times. Even with stylebooks, reporters will overlook details. It is at this point that verbal instructions become necessary. Whether or not a reporter has a printed guide, he usually is given a few general instructions about style from the city or managing editor.

The Newspaper Is Its Own Style Guide. Every copy of a carefully edited paper serves as a style guide worth following. When in doubt a reporter should be able to turn to any copy of his paper and find answers to questions of style and form. The alert reporter or copyreader, on taking a new job, always makes a detailed study of his paper's practices. The experienced reporter or deskman soon can grasp a paper's style in this way.

The Staff Must Know The Style. Style rules which are not practiced are meaningless. Rules cannot be enforced successfully unless the entire newspaper staff learns and follows them. Two groups in the editorial department are held mainly responsible for knowing and enforcing style: reporters and copyreaders. Reporters are expected to follow style when they write; copyreaders must assure consistency and unfailing use. In the mechanical department proofreaders are delegated to watch for style observance.

NEWSPAPER STYLES VARY

Except where a group style sheet is being followed, the styles of no two papers are alike; even if the major rules are the same, there are numerous variations in details.

Variations Have Many Causes. Differences can be traced mainly to the growth of style by accumulation. Newspapers change management and editorship; a new owner or editor builds upon, discards and substitutes portions, or otherwise alters style practice. Eccentricities and inconsistencies creep in during these changes. Other causes are typographical alterations that make style changes necessary; injection of new words into the language; new trends in spelling, punctuating, or other parts of style; copy coming from many different "foreign" sources; and failure to apply rules of style to the fullest extent.

Policies Differ Regarding Capitalization And Spelling. There is so little standardization in the style of newspapers that only a few groupings can be made among them.

THE "UP" STYLE VERSUS THE "DOWN" STYLE. A paper that capitalizes as commonly taught for correspondence or as do the editors of literary periodicals—many letters capitalized—is said to follow the "up" style. The converse is the "down" style. Thus the first would print it "John Street"; and the second would have it "John street."

MODERN OR SIMPLIFIED VERSUS STANDARD SPELLING. The school of editors who favor simplified spelling instructs reporters to shorten words as much as possible in accordance with a list of such words. Thus "staff" becomes "staf," "sheriff" is made "sherif," and "thorough" appears as "thoro." Those who follow the standard practice depend upon one of the better dictionaries for their authority.

MAGAZINE STYLES ALSO VARY

In a large measure, what has been said with specific reference to newspapers might also be said about magazines.

Quite apart from literary style, which is another matter altogether, magazines vary among themselves as much in "style" as do newspapers —perhaps more. Stylebooks may, and generally do, govern magazines as well as other journalistic media. They are a great boon to editor and reader alike.

CHAPTER X

NAMES MAKE NEWS

And what a mixed company inhabits the Temple of Universal Fame!
—generals, ministers, charlatans, jugglers, dancers, singers, million-
aires. . . .—ARTHUR SCHOPENHAUER.

WHAT'S IN A NAME?

The answer is:—Everything. As far as newspaper readers are concerned, Shakespeare was wrong when he said that a rose by any other
name would smell as sweet. The fact that, after himself, any human being
is most interested in other human beings is an important factor in determining news values.

Interest In Persons Is Universal. Newspaper readers are interested
in that which is familiar to them. They like to read about themselves,
persons they know, those with whom they are acquainted, those of whom
they have heard, and about the great world of persons who have become
conspicuous in the news.

Places And Things Have Interest. The interest readers have in what
is familiar to them extends beyond persons to places and things that they
may not know personally but that they recognize as important or prominent.

PROXIMITY HELPS DETERMINE NEWS VALUE OF NAMES

Since man is interested first in himself and then in his family and his
neighbors, local events interest readers because they know the places and
persons concerned. In part, persons, places, or things that go to make up
news excite a degree of news-interest in proportion to the closeness of
their relation to the reader's personal affairs, his home, and his business.
His immediate concerns come first in a scale of values. Beyond that he is
interested in his city, his county, his state, his nation; and finally he is
interested in foreign countries.

Curiosity Is The Psychological Basis For Interest. Human nature is
the same in a large city or a small town. The average person is more
interested in his neighbor than in the latest decision of the Supreme
Court. In one way or another, that curiosity must be satisfied.

If anything of news value occurs to him, his vanity is satisfied when he
sees the event chronicled in print even though it may be given as little
as an inch of space on an inside page. Most newspapers print items whose

only excuse, on the basis of news value, is the inclusion of one or several names.

Names Are Handled In Routine Departments. Since relatively few people participate in events of general significance, all newspapers give space to material that is more important for its name value than for any possible news value.

A heavy contribution to the news columns is made through routine lists—births, deaths, building permits, fire-department calls. Other lists are compiled occasionally, such as those of jury panels or of guests at an important social affair or a commencement; even a metropolitan newspaper may print a list of persons graduating with honors from the state university.

Society and club pages run heavily to names. That this is an important consideration in maintaining circulation is indicated by the fact that the *New York Herald Tribune* runs as much as ten columns a day on the activities of the most prominent summer resorts.

In the weekly or small daily newspaper considerable space is given to personals. The more columns of news of this sort, the better the paper fulfills its purpose, for in this field there is no competition between the weekly and the metropolitan daily. Metropolitan dailies use as a substitute for the personal-mention columns the news of groups and organizations with which individuals are associated. In an effort to present as many names as possible, some newspapers have established special sections where readers may find (*a*) brief news items about persons or minor events, (*b*) editorial-comment columns, (*c*) political gossip, or (*d*) out-and-out gossip columns about local people.[1]

Names Of Local People Have Special Appeal. Prominence of names influences the decision as to whether or not the news is of local interest. While names in themselves have a definite news value, at the same time some attempt must be made to choose facts and happenings which have informational and interest value to enough persons to give the stories some sort of news standard. If a man from New York were arrested in Chicago on the charge of forgery committed in the West, New York might use the information and Chicago not give it a line even though the arrest were made in Chicago. If the man were unknown and the forgery small, it is possible that even in New York the arrest would not be reported. If a Mrs. Jones of Cleveland dies in Florida, the Cleveland newspapers might not give it a line, since the item would interest only a few neighbors. However, if she had resided in Paducah, Kentucky, her death would be worthy of some mention in the local press—readers know about Mrs. Jones. On the same basis, if hers were an old Cleveland family, one of influence or wealth, or if she had been prominent in civic

---

[1] See William E. Hall, *Reporting the News,* pp. 237–40. Copyright 1936. D. C. Heath and Co.

affairs, many readers would be familiar with her name and her death would be given considerable space.

Some standard then must be used in determining news value of local names. When an event has passed such a test, it is an excellent practice to get into the news as many names as possible which have a direct bearing on the story.

PROMINENCE IS AN IMPORTANT FACTOR
IN NEWS VALUES

Prominence implies the widely known. Readers have a primary interest in names of persons with whom they are familiar. Certain persons come to be a part of the experience of most newspaper readers; they gain a hold on public imagination, and whatever they do, no matter where they are, is news. It may be name, position, or wealth alone that gives an item news value. The public is interested in the holiday plans of the President of the United States, the breakfast eaten by a champion football team, the advice of a prominent banker, the costume designed in Paris for a much-talked-about actress.

Bases For Reader-Interest Are Varied. The interest in the achievements or position of important people extends into their private lives, and the public is interested not only in their accomplishments but also in what they eat, in their recreation, in what they wear, and in their friends. The following are factors in the public preoccupation with the great or near-great.

Persons who have achieved great things, or have startling adventures, attract to themselves romantic interest. It makes little difference what these particular individuals accomplish. Charles Lindbergh made the first solo flight from West to East across the Atlantic; Madame Marie Curie spent years of grueling research that led to the discovery of radium; Edison accomplished the seemingly impossible in the field of applied science; Albert Einstein advanced the theory of relativity. Winston Churchill's leadership and unforgettable speeches became the living symbol of Allied resistance in World War II. All these people did things outstandingly well, and the idea of perfection is in itself romantic, since it is unreal so far as ordinary human performance is concerned.[1]

Historical position in itself contains romantic appeal. This makes former King Edward VIII, now the Duke of Windsor, a notable figure, and for that reason, his personal doings become of moment. The birth of a child to Princess Elizabeth of Britain and her consort, Prince Philip, has world-wide romantic appeal. Similarly, the goings and comings of Madame Chiang Kai-shek of China or of Mrs. Eleanor Roosevelt of America are good copy for newspapers everywhere. Other people travel,

---

[1] *Ibid.*, pp. 288–91.

have children, and marry divorcees; but their doings have little news value.

Apart from the romantic interest in the great or near-great, the personalities of certain such people gain more of a hold on the public imagination than those of others. Schumann-Heink and Greta Garbo were real news for many years. Other singers and movie stars came and went, but they did not capture the public imagination so completely. Both Charles Evans Hughes and Cordell Hull may be considered greater statesmen by future historians than George Catlett Marshall, but as Secretary of State he occupied more space in the newspapers than either of them.

A high position itself gives added importance to news concerning the person who occupies that position, even though the reader may never have heard of him before.

Authority is another factor. Officials of nations, leaders in the various professions, artists, musicians, or literary people can and do speak with authority, and what they say is significant. The expert is always good copy.

There are many cases of persons who have caught the public fancy by winning a prize fight, or producing the greatest number of children in a specified time, but for the most part their fame is short-lived. The public places little or no value on the opinions or activities of an ex-child actor.

The Real News Value Of Prominent People Should Be Recognized. Actors, travelers, authors, engineers, bankers, each has his particular sphere of accomplishment. The most important ones are copy at any time, but in presenting these people to the public the reporter must not indulge in the practice of quoting them on questions about which their opinions are of no value. These people have made great contributions to society and in fairness both to them and to the public they should be presented in such a way as to share their experience with the newspaper reader, whether it is the personality, the appearance, or the speech of Sir Lawrence Olivier or Dr. Vannevar Bush's description of atomic engineering.

News Values Are Relative. News values of persons vary from city to city, and from newspaper to newspaper. Editors attempt to give their readers news which conforms with their point of view. Opinions of people vary on politics, religion, social welfare, morals, international affairs, or on any other topic which influences the welfare of large groups of people. In a city where most of the population is of one religious faith, a public statement by the head of that church may be worth a column of page-one space, and, in another city where there are few members of that church, the same statement may be worth no more than a paragraph. Newspapers in any one city may also appeal to special groups of people, and, in such cases, persons who may interest readers of one newspaper might be unknown and lacking in interest to readers of another newspaper.

IMPORTANT PLACES ARE NEWS SOURCES

Size and prominence of places, like the importance and prominence of people, determine the news value in many cases and make news from them more important and interesting even though it may consist of no more than gossip or trivial happenings.

Newspaper readers come to associate in their minds certain kinds of news with certain localities. At the mention of such places as Reno, Tia Juana, or Gretna Green, the reader pricks up his ears with the expectation of a choice bit of spicy gossip. Broadway, Greenwich Village, or the Ghetto, as well as other names with like associations, add picturesqueness to a story. Readers are interested in the district in which wealthy and fashionable people live, and references to the Gold Coast or Park Avenue give added value to a story. ·

Readers come to attach more importance to news from certain cities than from others. London and Paris are easily the most popular. Newspapers print daily news from these cities which would not be news at all if the events happened in Pine Bluff, Arkansas, or Poplar Bluff, Missouri. Moscow is another favored city. If Russian women begin using cosmetics, it is news. The women of America would have to stop using cosmetics to make copy.

NEWS VALUE LIES IN SPECIFIC THINGS

News value is also attached to specific things known to newspaper readers, and the factors of size and prominence determine their value also. A great hotel excites more interest than a small one; a mansion has more news value than a cottage. Things which are a part of the experience of all are news.

Real estate landmarks are news at times. In a city without a skyscraper, the building of the first one is front-page copy. In New York it has to be a Radio City to excite attention.

Historic sites may also figure in the news. The *New York Times* gave a column to the celebration of the fiftieth anniversary of the Statue of Liberty, giving historical information as well as the details of the ceremony to take place. Such historic spots as Washington Monument, the White House, Buckingham Palace, or the tomb of the Unknown Soldier in Arlington Cemetery also excite interest. Everyone can identify Plymouth Rock. Other rocks might disappear without attracting attention, but not Plymouth Rock. It is a part of the experience of all, and because it is shared by all, the interest in it is obvious.

Large institutions, because they are generally known, attract attention to news involving them. The Library of Congress, Rockefeller Institute, the Y.M.C.A., the American Legion, these and many others, excite interest. Scientific research conducted in a large university attracts more attention than the same experiment conducted in a smaller school, not that one is more important than the other, but that the research is associated in the minds of the readers with the better-known school.

Important businesses—that is, familiar names of great ocean steamships, railroad companies, or manufacturers—increase the news value of stories in which they appear.

CHAPTER XI

POLICE–BLOTTER STORIES

Reporting at police headquarters was like a college education in this, that one had to take several courses all together. There was the police news, police policies and politics; the Ghetto, with its synagogues, theatres and moral struggles; the strikes. . . . It differed from college in this, that I was interested in each of these courses and could see that they belonged together. They all contributed to the learning of life as it is lived.*

PRACTICALLY ALL NEWSPAPERS PRINT CRIME NEWS

A large portion of the public has a tremendous interest in certain crimes, mysterious happenings, or unusual events that arouse its curiosity and awaken its sympathy.

A Reporter Must Deal With Crime News. The interest in police-blotter stories is not always a healthy one, but it is a factor with which the reporter and news editor must deal. The veteran reporter knows, and the cub reporter learns, what O. O. McIntyre meant when he wrote of the active reporter, "He deals with the stuff that is stranger than fiction."

Attempts have been made from time to time by certain newspapers to keep crime news out of their columns, but almost all of them have soon abandoned this policy. Today, among American newspapers, the *Christian Science Monitor* stands practically alone in its policy of consistently minimizing ordinary crime news.

The Printing Of Such News Is Regarded As A Duty. Most newspapers rightly regard the publishing of news of crimes as part of their duty to give their readers a true picture of happenings in the world. For millions of readers who have neither the time nor the inclination to visit courtrooms, the newspaper accounts of crime are the only definite information received about the dangers and evils of present-day life. The well-conducted newspaper's responsibility is to give the news of all phases of human activity fairly and impartially, so that the reader may get a reasonably true and complete picture of the world in which he lives.

---

* From *Autobiography of Lincoln Steffens*, p. 231. Copyright 1931. Used by permission of the publishers, Harcourt, Brace and Co.

THE CUB REPORTER OFTEN BEGINS HIS NEWS WORK ON THE POLICE BEAT

When a new man reports to the city editor, he is usually hustled off to the police station to begin work where most reporters have begun, namely on the police beat.

The Reporter Begins To Find His Place. If he has just been employed on a city daily, he may find his duties to be a part of a well-established routine of checking reports at the police and detective bureaus in the central station or in one or more of the suburban stations. In the small town he will visit the police station, the sheriff's office, the coroner's office, and probably a dozen or so public or semipublic places such as the city court, county jail, the railway and bus stations, local hospitals, the coast guard. Some of these places he can reach by telephone, and, as he becomes more experienced in his news gathering and slowly perfects his contacts with his news sources, he can keep in touch with most of them by simply calling the rounds.

He Gets Acquainted. The new man on the police beat will spend much of his time getting acquainted with various persons from police officials and detective officers down to telephone operators and record keepers, for he will need, as time goes on, a large number of personal contacts if he is to keep in close touch with the accidents, fires, emergencies, homicides, and other events which furnish much of the raw news material for the day's newspaper.

Records And News Bureaus Give Him Valuable Tips. The records at the police station will give him valuable tips or leads, for the police get information first regarding most of the unexpected events in a city. For follow-up stories he will get announcements from police officers, statements of their theories about certain unsolved crimes, confessions, letters, ransom notes in the case of kidnappings, reports on tests made by fingerprint bureaus and chemical or ballistic experts, and various and sundry bits of evidence that find their way into news columns.

While cubbing on the police beat, the reporter learns much from the reporters from other papers or news bureaus. He will be able to appraise their methods, to improve his chances of *not* overlooking important clues, to observe the actions of men with a well-developed sense of what is news and, equally important sometimes, of what is not. He will also pick up from them much information about the reliability of certain news sources.

He Masters Practical Details. The young reporter learns on this beat how to master certain practical details of his job. First of all he comes to realize the news value of the names of important persons either directly or indirectly related to a crime event. He learns that some places give to a news event a greater significance or greater interest than others. For example, a man caught trying to enter the White House with a concealed weapon or dropping a bomb in Wall Street, although no damage may be done in either case, makes front-page news.

He learns to check carefully entries in police records by consulting telephone and street directories, for he soon discovers that patrolmen not only frequently misspell names but also give incorrect addresses. The young reporter learns to recognize facts, to weigh statements, confessions, and the like, and is constantly alert for improper motives or other attempts to deceive. He soon discovers that some people court publicity and are ready with opinions or theories that may be entirely worthless, while others, for one reason or another, are inclined to be reticent, suppressing facts or information that if revealed would often prove helpful in unraveling crimes. In the midst of mystery, confusion, excitement, or the calm following a storm, the young reporter must learn to keep a cool head and an open, alert mind and in all his actions to keep constantly before him the first law of good reporting, namely, the cultivating of accuracy.

OBSERVANCE OF ETHICS IS IMPORTANT IN POLICE REPORTING

The reporter's whole duty in helping his paper mirror the world is to get his facts straight at all times, to report them promptly to his paper, and, if he writes the story himself, to play up only important or significant facts and to furnish such details as the interest of normal readers justifies and good sense and good taste dictate.

All Reporters Must Observe Codes And Ethics. The young reporter will find it necessary to get a thorough grounding in newspaper codes and ethics and to familiarize himself with the law of libel. A discussion of the latter may be found elsewhere in this book. It should be remembered that all libel laws are made by state legislatures and that they vary in different states. The reporter will find it necessary to have a working knowledge of the libel laws of the state in which his paper is located.

Good journalists observe a code of honor. Although newspapermen lay no claims to being gentlemen of honor, there are a number of things that no self-respecting reporter will do. He will not fake news. He will write a fair and impartial report of a political speech, for example, although he and his paper may both be of the opposite political faith. He will try to get both sides in controversial matters. He will not suppress news that should be printed. He honors those who tip him off to news. He invariably knows more than he writes.

If the policy of the paper he works for goes beyond this in its efforts at sensational treatment, the reporter's only recourse is to seek employment on a paper conducted more in keeping with his notion of ethics.

Ethical Methods Are Desirable In Handling Crime News. Knowing that many of their readers have an intense interest in crime news, certain papers indulge in sensational excesses in their treatment of news.

Such methods undoubtedly increase the sales of certain types of newspapers, but are contrary to sound public policy.

Much criticism of the press with reference to the handling of news of crime and court proceedings is heard, and a portion of the press should be censured for its unethical methods.

Newspaper practices that invite unfavorable criticism include the following:

1. Excessively large headlining of crime stories.

2. Too large a percentage of space given to news of this type.

3. Pressing the police into revealing details of their activities and publishing them, thus aiding criminals still at liberty to escape.

4. Glorifying criminals or making heroes of them by undue publicity.

5. Aiding other criminals by printing reports of crimes in such detail that the same methods may again be used.

6. Reporting details of sordid crimes in violation of decency and good taste.

Local police officers would do well in dealing with the press to adopt the custom followed by federal officers, commonly known as G-men, who refrain from showing their hand while pursuing criminals or working on a crime.

It is not necessary to discuss here the many ways in which the better class of newspapers co-operate with the legal forces in winning public support for the suppression of crime and the upholding of law and order.

While running down clues in crime cases, seeking motives of perpetrators, and the like, the police reporter will learn, especially if he is working in a large city, of that strange pattern of life known as the underworld, with its lawless characters and antisocial organizations. He may learn that this demimonde is not without ramifications that extend even into the official life of the city. No one knows more of the mysteries of modern life than the seasoned reporter, and much of the knowledge that he acquires in newspaper work can hardly be called reassuring. The cub will do well to learn to take such knowledge in his stride, for while it may not increase his wisdom it will add to his understanding.

NEWS VALUES ARE FEATURED IN REPORTS OF ACCIDENTS AND CRIMES

Generally speaking, the importance of the event from a news standpoint is determined by the extent of injuries to persons, damage to property, etc., and in almost all cases the collecting of this kind of information is more important than the writing of the stories.

Fires Are An Important Unexpected News Event. Care must be taken to get all the essential elements of the story of a fire. If lives were lost the names and addresses of the dead are the first thing to obtain. If a school building containing children was destroyed, names and ages of the children who were lost and names and addresses of the parents should be obtained, also the names of firemen or spectators killed. The names and disposition of injured and the names of persons who escaped injuries should also be noted. Other details include the time the fire started and the probable cause of it. For information of this kind, first-hand opinions of fire chief, police officials in charge, superintendent, or others in charge of the building destroyed should be obtained.

Next in importance to persons killed or injured is the property loss. This includes the building itself, records, equipment, furnishings, and the like. An effort should be made to determine the insurance coverage. Other details should be sought if time will permit, such as incidents of escaping from fire, experiences of relief workers and others giving aid, other buildings threatened, success or failure of fire fighting, heroism and rescue work, prominent persons participating, and so on.

In writing the story of a fire, the lead will usually suggest itself. If lives are lost, the opening paragraph usually begins with that fact, together with the *what, when,* and *where* of the event. This statement is immediately followed by a list of the names of the dead, giving as far as possible their last known addresses. A separate line is usually given to each person. Then follow the names and information about the disposition of the known injured and of the unknown dead and injured. The rest of the story will give the essential news facts in the usual manner of news-story writing. With a wealth of material at hand, the skillful reporter will give facts simply, so as to allow space in the early paragraphs for the news facts of outstanding importance.

Accidents And Wrecks Are A Type Of Police-Beat Story. Unexpected events resulting in loss of life or loss of property or both are handled by the reporter much as a fire story is handled. The reporter's first duty, after notifying the city desk of the accident, is to get to the scene of the event (unless otherwise directed by his superior) and get the news facts as quickly and as accurately as possible. In the case of large-scale accidents, the newspapers organize on a large scale for the complete and accurate gathering of the news. Here again names of persons killed, the names of the injured, the names of prominent persons who escaped injury, the cause of the accident, and all the related details must be quickly obtained. The reporter will observe the customary precautions in interviewing eyewitnesses to get a check on each statement he gets.

In writing the story care must be taken to avoid fixing responsibility because of the danger of libel until there is an inquest or other report from persons authorized to investigate the affair. When prominent persons are concerned, an accident that did not actually occur but was narrowly averted may make a front-page story.

Homicides Are A Source Of News. When the body of a dead person is found, the police are invariably notified at once, and the proper entry is made in the records. The reporter who gets the tip will hurry to the place where the body is and watch closely the early developments. If the person is prominent, or much interest is shown by the police in the crime, or if there is other evidence of unusual news value, he, of course, will immediately telephone the city desk. The story should be written in the same style as any other news story.

Chapter XII

WHEN OTHERS COME TO TOWN

> Reports of speeches are one of the commonest types of news stories.
> To the uninitiated the job of reporting a speech seems a simple assign-
> ment. But the apparent simplicity of the task is misleading. Reporting
> a speech so that persons who did not hear it will get the gist and sig-
> nificance undistorted demands skill of a high order.
>
> —William E. Hall*

PREPARING FOR THEIR ARRIVAL IS THE FIRST TASK

Visits paid to a city by distinguished speakers and by delegates to meetings and conventions not only must be covered by local newsmen, but also
must be preceded by advance stories which reporters have to prepare
long before those events occur.

Information May Be Gathered From Various Sources. Preliminary
announcements of speeches ordinarily are sent to the newspaper for publicity purposes. From this material the reporter can obtain the speaker's
name and subject, the local auspices under which he is to speak, the time
and place of the address, and sometimes brief biographical material in-
dicative of the speaker's importance or the authority with which he
approaches his subject. Additional biographical information can be obtained in the newspaper's reference room, particularly in such publications
as *Who's Who in America, American Men of Science,* and *Leaders in
Education.*

The reporter should contact the source of the publicity release to obtain
names of the local committee which is arranging for the address and any
other local news angles such as the fact that the speaker will be a guest
of an old friend while in the city. Questions concerning arrangements
made for local entertainment of the speaker may produce several such
angles.

Arrangements for meetings and conventions are always known to a
local committee or representative. Organizations sponsoring meetings and
conventions often have a publicity chairman who can be of much service
to reporters. The careful newsman will not be content, however, merely
to use the facts in the releases which the publicity representative furnishes.
He will contact the local committee on arrangements and in the case of

---

* From *Reporting the News* by William E. Hall, p. 328. Copyright 1936. Used by
permission of the publishers, D. C. Heath and Co.

important events may call upon the management of the hotel where the meeting is to be held and upon other sources such as the convention secretary of the local chamber of commerce. Hotel men frequently can give the most accurate information as to probable attendance.

From these sources the reporter will learn:

1. Time, place, and auspices of the meeting or convention.
2. Details of the program.
3. Important business, particularly that involving controversial issues, to come before the meeting.
4. Names of local persons making the arrangements.
5. Names of all local persons involved in the program.
6. In case of a convention, names of officers of the organization.
7. Probable attendance and names of well-known persons expected.

If the meeting or convention is an important one, not all of this material will be available for a single story. The reporter may follow the making of plans during several weeks after the first announcement. He will write a series of articles as information becomes available bit by bit until the day before the opening of the convention, when his final advance story will record early arrivals, probable attendance, details of the first day's program, and a recapitulation of outstanding facts included in earlier stories.

News Values Must Be Carefully Judged In Writing The Advance Story. Stories dealing with events of this sort have a tendency to become stereotyped. Opening paragraphs especially are subject to this fault. Leads beginning "A meeting will," "An address by," "The purpose of," "Plans are being made" should be taboo.

Announcements of speeches are simple stories. News of this kind can be told briefly. Interesting biographical details concerning the speaker are the only type of information which will require much space for the telling. Care must be taken to avoid editorial comment concerning the speaker. Statements such as "Dr. Hardy is well qualified to discuss all phases of psychological research" should be avoided. If such material is included, the source of the opinion must be stated. An even better practice is to include biographical facts from which the reader may draw his own conclusions concerning the speaker's qualifications. Leads of such stories may feature:

1. The name of the speaker. (This is a natural beginning, especially if the person is newsworthy.)
2. The subject of the address. (This beginning should be used only when the subject is timely and of special interest. If the subject is more interesting than the speaker it may well come first in the lead.)

3. Information indicating the speaker's significant connection with his topic. (If a foreign correspondent just returned from a battle front abroad is to lecture on a subject connected with that conflict, the fact of his firsthand relation to his material may be featured.)

4. Purpose for which proceeds from a lecture are to be used.

Advance accounts of meetings feature their programs. These stories run longer than do announcements of speeches and usually are organized to conform to the conventional pattern. Outstanding speakers, special events, and major business to come before the gathering will furnish material for the feature and lead summary. In selecting these materials the reporter must remember to evaluate them in terms of popular interest rather than in terms of their importance to the special group concerned in the meeting. In covering a meeting of astronomers, for example, he must remember that, although a paper on a new method for measuring the heat of stars may be the scientific cream of the program, the lay reader will be more interested in a discussion of possible relation between sunspots and weather on the earth.

COVERING THE EVENT IS THE MORE DIFFICULT ASSIGNMENT

The story written after the speech or meeting and containing an account of it requires greater skill in gathering facts and in writing them than does the advance story. The reporter must make adequate preparations for such assignments.

Content Of Addresses May Be Obtained In Two Ways. First, manuscripts of important addresses may be obtained in advance of their delivery or after delivery if necessary. The reporter should make arrangements well in advance of the date for the address to obtain an advance copy. Having obtained it, he should be present at the address [1] to be certain that the speaker follows his text and to catch sidelights which will add interest to his article. If an advance manuscript is not available, the reporter should contact the speaker before the address is delivered and ask for the manuscript so that he will know whether to take detailed notes. Manuscripts obtained in this way should be handled very carefully and they should be returned to the speaker, if he so desires, as soon as possible.

Second, the reporter may take notes as the speech is delivered. In taking notes, the reporter should endeavor to obtain material which will enable him to write an accurate summary of the speaker's thought. This is more important than concentrating on getting down extensive direct quota-

---

[1] Reporters who put too much faith in advance texts of speeches often find to their sorrow that the speaker has changed his mind and contradicted opinions included in his prepared material.

tions. If he is not certain of his ability to get the direct quotations verbatim, he should content himself with setting down the speaker's main ideas as a basis for a careful summary.

Writing The Speech Story Is Primarily A Problem Of Organization. Most speech reports conform to conventional news-story organization. An analyzed example is given in the diagram of news-story structure in an earlier chapter.[1] In these stories, especially, it is well to regard the lead as a separate story in itself for the hurried reader and to make the body of the story expand the outline of the lead summary. The problem is that of selecting proper materials for inclusion in the lead.

THE BEGINNING. Any of six beginnings may be used in the lead:

1. Indirect quotation of the speaker's most significant statement.
2. The keynote, a concise summary of the central thought of the address.
3. Direct quotation of a striking or significant statement. (This is the easiest beginning and, hence, has become so common that it is barred by many city editors.)
4. The occasion and circumstances.
5. The speaker's name.[2]
6. The title of the address.[2]

THE HANDLING OF QUOTATIONS. Handling of quotations is the chief problem in writing the body of the story. Special points should be watched.

1. Direct and indirect quotes should be alternated to avoid monotony.
2. Less than a complete sentence should not be used in direct quotes.
3. When direct quotes are begun again following use of indirect quotes or summary, a new paragraph should be started.
4. Phrases such as "said the speaker" should not precede quoted material but should be buried in it or used at its conclusion.
5. In indirect quotations the speaker should be referred to frequently enough to make the authority for the statements clear at all times. If this is not done, statements indirectly quoted may appear to be those of the reporter.

MISCELLANEOUS SUGGESTIONS. Here are some miscellaneous suggestions for the writer of speech reports.

1. If the speaker or his manner of delivery is interesting, give the reader a visual impression of him through narrative and descriptive touches. For example, note this effect in the following report:

---

[1] See Chapter VII, *Building the Story.*

[2] Least desirable. Its use frequently results in leads which do little more than confirm announcements made in advance stories and which are by no means newsy.

> More than 100 persons from the Host church and Temple street mission heard the slender flashing-eyed youth sing "On the Other Side" and other revival hymns in syncopated rhythm that kept feet tapping.
>
> They watched him strip off his coat to expose rolled-up sleeves, red tie, white belt, and green suspenders. Stamping across the platform, clapping his hands ecstatically and shouting hoarsely, he drew repeated "amens" from the congregation with an impassioned warning against "selling your soul to the devil for nothing."

2. If the lead plays up a single idea from the speech, the story should protect the speaker and the reporter by summarizing the whole speech in the paragraph following the lead. This will avoid distortion of the speaker's point of view.

3. Get variety in verbs of speaking, but avoid overly colorful extremes such as "barked," "growled," "snarled."

4. Get the spirit of the speaker as well as the substance of his speech, to make certain an accurate report.

Officers Provide Much Material For Convention Stories. Contacts with the officers in charge of a meeting can be of much value to the reporter. The president or chairman can tell him of changes and unexpected features in the program. The secretary can supply the spelling of names, copies of resolutions, and other detailed information. If the gathering is not an important one, the reporter will spend only enough time at the sessions to contact the proper officers and will depend upon them for his information. Manuscripts of addresses included in the program he will obtain in the manner already outlined.

Full coverage of such events includes not merely gathering material for the main article but also picking up feature angles for side stories. Items about the oldest delegate or the delegate who has attended every convention of the group are resorted to frequently when more novel features are not available.

Meeting Reports Usually Take The Inverted Pyramid Form. Accounts of meetings rarely can be presented in chronological order. The various items included in the program are reported in the order of their importance instead of in order of their occurrence. Thus, the opening address of welcome by the mayor may be crowded into the last paragraph of the story (where it is likely to belong).

Significant phases of the program are summarized in the lead and each is then presented in greater detail in the body of the story.[1]

This manner of organizing the meeting report is shown graphically in the diagram accompanying this chapter. It indicates the way the chrono-

---

[1] For an example of such organization please turn to story on pages 66 and 67.

Diagram Comparing Outline Of Program For A Meeting With Outline Of A News Story Reporting The Meeting

Program Of A Meeting	Organization Of The News Story Reporting The Meeting
1. Address of welcome	Feature **5A**
2. President's address	Lead summary **6A - 4 - 3**
3. Speech	Elaboration of **5A**
	Additional matter from **5**
4. Speech	Elaboration of **6A**
	Further detail on **6A**
5. Speech **5A.** "Newsiest" material presented in the program	Elaboration of **4**
	Further detail on **4**
	Elaboration of **3**
6. Debate and adoption of resolutions **A-B-C**	**6B** **6C**
	7
7. Election of officers	**2** **1**

logical outline of the program is altered to put important things first in the story.

Points to be covered in the meeting or convention story, any one of which may provide the feature for the lead depending upon individual circumstances, are:

1. Summaries of addresses of popular interest.
2. Resolutions and motions adopted.
3. Controversies developed concerning business of the meeting.
4. Officers elected, committees appointed.
5. Attendance: numbers, notables.
6. Selection of place for next meeting.

Chapter XIII

THE CIVIC PROJECT IS NEWS

It is impossible to measure the constructive and beneficent influence which a local paper can exert by the recognition and encouragement of ideas, aspirations, plans and movements which tend toward the well-being of the community.*

CIVIC PROJECTS HAVE MANY ORIGINS

Whether local changes or improvements are suggested by the newspaper or its readers, or whether they are necessitated by unforeseen happenings, the newspaper regards them as being newsworthy.

Some Projects Have Official Status. When changes are voted by the municipal government, they carry an official status, and the newspaper is essentially a chronicler rather than an instigator. The newspaper may or may not agree with the ordinance calling for the change, and may even wage battle in the editorial columns against it, but nevertheless it views the project as news and accords the story merited space. A press fight against the change may even be carried on in the news columns by printing interviews with those opposed to the project and by the publication of stories from other cities showing unfavorable experiences with similar plans. This may be continued until a referendum decides the issue.

Service Clubs And Societies May Initiate Projects. When civic-minded groups sponsor a movement which aims to further the city's development, their program loses its private character and becomes of quasi-public nature. The plans and activities relating to this project are recorded on the news pages in proportion to the amount of interest the plan creates and the relative importance it possesses in civic development. Its value as news is no longer related to its sponsors but to what it promises to the population of the area.

Philanthropists May Donate For Improvements. The activities of important men make news, but when these activities concern endowment by philanthropists or other individuals for civic improvements they make major news. The donation for a park, playground, social center, or museum transfers a private act into a public good and leads to many future news stories. If this donation is for a public building, it is news during the erection of the structure, at its dedication, and at the innumerable

* From *The Community Newspaper* by Harris and Hooke, p. 110. Copyright 1923. Used by permission of the publishers, D. Appleton-Century Co.

meetings and functions it houses during its lifetime. Such a civic project is news not only at its inception but also for many years thereafter.

Readers May Suggest Civic Changes. Individual readers imbued with community pride and eager for their city to progress may suggest through

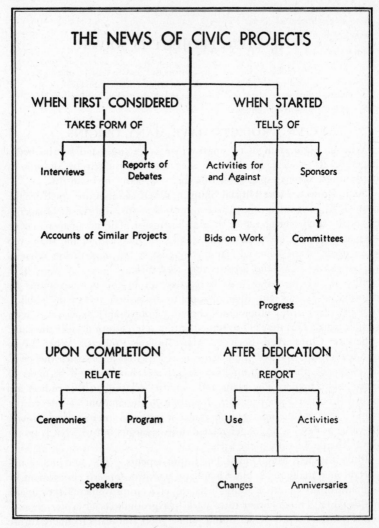

the forum column changes which the newspaper is glad to further. Many of the ideas suggested by readers present insurmountable difficulties and are hence not pushed by the press. But the newspaper acts as a clearing-house in publishing and backing constructive ideas for civic change.

What an individual could not carry out by himself he may be able to accomplish when his suggestion is adopted by the press and later by the public. It becomes news when meetings are held to discuss ways and means for carrying out the project. It continues as news until the project is carried out or abandoned.

The Press Initiates Civic Projects. Because of their extensive and detailed knowledge of the community and its needs, newspapermen are among the first to know what projects are most feasible. Some of these projects the newspaper advocates for a long-term program knowing that such plans can move but slowly. Others it advocates as immediate projects to be carried through at once and to the fulfillment of which it devotes its news and editorial columns and all the constructive driving force of the press. The projects which it wishes to support become planks in its platform. As one project is completed and becomes a living reality, it is replaced by another so that the press can be a continual force for civic improvement.

SOME CIVIC PROJECTS ENCOURAGE LOCAL TALENT

The urge for self-expression in the fine or applied arts finds release in local contests sponsored by community groups.

Community Drama Is Encouraged. Such great movements as the little theater in America have had their modest beginnings as local drama groups which earned a sponsorship by civic groups and the press. The original formation of such groups, their selection of plays to be produced, the appointment of casts, the announcement of the director, the dates for the performances, and the reviews of the productions are all occasions which are newsworthy and which the press regularly prints. Such accounts become even better news when the success of the dramatic functions leads to the establishment of a theater building, whether converted from old uses or newly built for the purpose.

Music Festivals Are Arranged. Youthful and adult lovers of music are encouraged by regular festivals, usually appearing annually, which are sponsored by local groups and which provide for competition among individuals and organizations. The final civic festival is usually preceded by smaller community festivals or contests where winners are selected for higher competition. Because of the great number of contestants and the intense interest aroused, the newspaper has opportunities to use many news reports. Particularly here is there a chance to use the press dictum that "names are news." The announcement of the project, names of sponsors and entrants and winners of the elimination contests all occasion news stories prior to the final festival.

Art Displays Create Interest. Displays of art, whether amateur or professional, have a cultural value at the same time that they stimulate and encourage local artists. Whether such displays are sponsored by the press or by civic organizations, they are given news space and frequent editorial support. Contests may be arranged at which judges select the best amateur efforts and accord them an exhibition with other artistic work of value. Or traveling exhibits may be brought into the city and displayed under the auspices of local groups as a means of entertainment and encouragement to those in the community who are artistically inclined. Although most of these exhibits are of paintings, similar displays may be arranged for other of the fine and applied arts such as sculpture, architecture, and tapestries.

Forensics Are Encouraged. Debate and oratory contests stimulate thought while providing an outlet for useful talent. Occasionally these contests are developed by forensic societies, but they are usually instigated by the newspapers. In the smaller cities similar contests such as spelling bees are arranged through the co-operation of the schools. The contests may be arranged on geographical or community lines, such as townships, and thus provoke a healthy intercity rivalry. The types of contests vary and may include such widely different ones as sewing, folk and ballet dancing, cooking, cornhusking, and the like.

THE COMMUNITY PLANS RECREATION

Faced with the problem of healthy entertainment for leisure time and for keeping their youths and adults away from harmful diversions, the city and quasi-public groups have arranged for playgrounds, parks, and social centers.

Parks Are Created. Rapid growth of cities coupled with inefficient planning in earlier days created the problem of space for parks. Newspapers and philanthropists as well as certain public-minded groups now see the need for more parks and hence purchase proper sites, raze the buildings, or otherwise prepare the area for the landscaping, planting of foliage, and building of roadways. Each step of the process makes news stories.

Playgrounds Are Constructed. To keep children off busy city streets and to provide healthful recreation, space for playgrounds becomes a necessity. As in the case of parks, sites for playgrounds are selected in various sections of the town and are developed and equipped over a period of years. Each step of this development makes newsworthy accounts. And as in the case of the parks, the playgrounds are the scenes of many events including games, speeches, and picnics, which in themselves are worthy of news mention.

Social Centers Are Inaugurated. For evening recreation, particularly for those seeking companionship as well as play, the press and other socializing agencies have created social centers scattered through the neighborhoods and within easy access to everyone. The establishment and location of these centers make news as do also many of the activities carried on in these centers. In some cities this work is so organized that reporters regularly cover the activities.

Civic Sports Are Encouraged. Friendly competition of neighborhood teams and leagues organized on a civic basis provides contests which throughout the year are worthy of news mention in the columns of the press. Sports vary with the seasons, but there is no time when the average city finds itself without a sport sponsored by community leaders and developed on a city-wide plan. Stories of the games with the box scores and summaries of the more important contests not only are good news stories but also encourage the continuation of the civic progress.

Community Buildings Are Purchased Or Erected. As a public meeting place where town and country meet or where different factions in the city mingle for public discussions on important questions, there are buildings variously called the community house, auditorium, or town hall. Whether these buildings have been erected by municipal funds or by private philanthropy or public donations, they acquire a public character, and their use is regulated by a civic body, official or semiofficial. The acquisition of such a building was a civic project which furnished news until its completion and which continues to be of importance because all functions held in such a building must, by their nature, have a public interest.

CIVIC EFFORT CREATES BETTER HEALTH FACILITIES

Without the constant reports in the press regarding the activities of such groups as the sanitary boards, the fire and health departments, and the traffic section of the police force, their work would be greatly hampered, for the regulations and requirements of these health and protection agencies make important news accounts.

The Press Exposes Laxity In Civic Boards. The press's acceptance of its duty to report carelessness or inefficiency in such civic institutions as the emergency hospital and the health department protects the public at the same time that it makes news. The vigilant press is here a public servant as well as news gatherer and by truthful news accounts provides assistance to the civic organization. It also exposes the cases of individual physicians and laymen who are practicing illegally and unethically. On the other hand, the press has an equal duty to report constructive changes in hospital regulations and facilities or orders of the medical board which make for better health.

It Helps Preserve Sanitation. When storms or other conditions interrupt the normal sanitary measures, the press reports the situation and the regulations or suggestions for improvement. Poor water or dangers of contamination, flies, mosquitoes, or other pests occasion news accounts that may lead to campaigns initiated or at least supported by the press which bring about better sanitary control.

Safety Measures Are Urged. The ceaseless struggle to prevent loss of life, carelessness in traffic, in construction of buildings, in large gatherings, and in fire prevention prompts the newspapers to consider as important news the announcement of added regulations or the enforcement of existing ordinances and safety decrees. As a part of this plan, the press throws into prominence the names of reckless violators of safety measures and gives accounts of such occurrences unusual display.

CHARITY RECEIVES CITY-WIDE SUPPORT

The care of the needy, whether in regularly planned community drives or in emergencies caused by fire, flood, or other disasters, is a community project enlisting the support of all agencies and necessitating the best efforts of the press.

The Annual Charity Fund Is A News Source. The yearly campaign for funds to be divided among various social agencies provides many news stories. These may be in the form of announcements of workers for the drive, amounts of donations, names of large donors, human-interest stories of the most needy cases, and interviews with those most concerned in promoting the success of the campaign.

The press initiates its own charity funds. To care for those not provided for by annual charity funds and to aid in times of minor, unexpected disturbances, the newspapers inform the community of the need and take charge of the fund. Such newspaper charities provide funds for coal, ice, milk, health camps, and similar aids.

The Press Takes Command In Times Of Stress. When flood or pestilence visits a community the newspapers report news of the calamity and recovery. They may, and often do, furnish the directing force and leadership while appraising the situation and reflecting the conditions in the news columns.

DEVELOPING THE CIVIC SPIRIT MAKES NEWS

There are occasions when the community expresses itself through feelings rather than material projects and where reports of manifestations of this spirit in themselves make news.

Historical Projects Are Examples. Even though through lack of funds or other causes a tradition is not embodied in visual substance, as a statue or a building, this spirit may manifest itself by gatherings of those interested. Programs may be arranged at which speakers extol the historical traditions of the vicinity. These traditions may refer to a man or an event, and they may ultimately result in some material symbol of that tradition. But the feeling of historical reverence makes news even while it remains in the emotional phase.

The Spirit May Be One Of Good Fellowship. It is newsworthy when leaders in a community arrange for meetings at which gather representatives of near-by communities or factions within the community itself. At such meetings there is evidenced a spirit of helpfulness of townspeople toward rural residents and a sympathetic understanding on the part of the farmers of the problems of those residing within the limits of the city. Such meetings are news, as they report the status of a spirit which makes for civic development.

A CIVIC PLAN DEVELOPS NEWS

Any local change of city-wide interest, such as a new civic building, a playground, or a park, is news at its inception and through all its stages and may continue as news even after the fulfillment of the original conception.

The Original Suggestion Is News. If the project is feasible, whatever its source and nature, it becomes news at the first announcement. At this stage the project may be an idea rather than a plan, but it arouses discussion and leads to action. The pros and cons are debated in the press in the form of interviews and statements.

When action by city officials, private citizens, or groups who are sponsoring the measure insures that the project is to be carried out, the news acquires a positive character. The stories now record the names and activities of those who are carrying the venture into its more definite stages. Its development is progressively sketched by accounts in the press.

Human-Interest Stories Support The News. Feature stories tell of the anxious expectancy of children for their playground or the dangers in building a bridge or the difficulties met by a contractor in digging a tunnel through quicksand. Through these stories the citizens become more aware that this project is their own.

When the building or playground or park is ready to fulfill its function, the newspaper records the plan for the dedication and opening. Names of speakers and committees and arrangements for the entertainment are announced by the press. The event itself may furnish the newspaper display in proportion to the city-wide interest it has aroused.

The Civic Project Is The Scene Of Future Stories. Many of the civic projects, such as buildings, parks, playgrounds, or services, continue to make news because they are the meeting point of large groups and because in them or through their aid public functions are performed. The project which was news at its inception continues to live as a news source because of the service it performs to the city and its people.

Chapter XIV

THE CALENDAR AS NEWS

Seasons do for time what tidiness does for space.—SAMUEL BUTLER*

THE CALENDAR IS A RECORD OF NEWSWORTHY EVENTS

Besides being a register of the days, weeks, and months of the year, the calendar is also a record of numerous events which recur at regular intervals but which have enough variety of detail to make them newsworthy.

It May Be Used As A "Future Book." Because of this regularity, the newspaper editor can use the calendar as a "future book" for planning in advance articles (news stories and news features) appropriate to these events. Such articles have both timeliness and immediacy. Therefore they aid the "spot news" stories—i.e., those of unpredictable and unexpected events—in giving the newspaper its character as a day-by-day chronicle of contemporary life.

There Are Three General Types Of Stories. Calendar news stories and news features come under three general classifications—seasonal, holiday, and anniversary.

The *seasonal* story deals with human activity as it is affected or modified by factors peculiar to the four seasons of the year.

The *holiday* story is concerned primarily with the news of the celebration itself—still it frequently is the story of some "by-product" of that day.

The *anniversary* story links the past with the present, interprets one in terms of the other, and shows the significance of their relationship.

THE SEASONAL STORY REFLECTS THE SPIRIT OF THE SEASON

Seasonal stories are alike in reflecting the spirit, or the characteristic activities, of the season in which they are written, and they change in detail as the seasons themselves change.

Weather Is A Primary Source. One of the primary sources of seasonal stories is the weather and its variations in: (1) spring, (2) summer,

---

* From *Further Extracts from the Note Books of Samuel Butler,* edited by A. T. Bartholomew, p. 62. Copyright 1934. Used by permission of the publishers, Jonathan Cape, Limited.

(3) autumn, and (4) winter. The weather itself is always a topic of interest to people, and naturally enough they are interested in stories based upon the variations of weather in the four seasons. Typical of certain of the stories reflecting these variations are:

SPRING—which brings news of melting snows, the breakup of ice jams in rivers, excessive rainfall—any of which may result in floods that threaten human life, property, or welfare.

SUMMER—which produces its news of droughts, of heat waves and the comparisons with record high temperatures of past years, of electrical storms, tornadoes, and the freakish behavior of lightning.

AUTUMN—which is the season of the "melancholy days," of "October's bright blue weather," of Indian summer, of "dry spells" which bring in their wake forest fires, of "frost upon the pumpkin," and of the various proverbial "signs" by which the amateur weather prophets foretell the kind of winter ahead.

WINTER—which is productive of news of the first snowfall, of long periods of extremely cold weather, of sudden freezes and sudden thaws, of interviews with "old timers" who reminisce of the deep snows and low temperatures of yesteryear.

Man's Activities In Each Season Make News. The great variety of news stories and news features relating to the activities of mankind, as they are affected or modified by the seasons, are indicated by the following suggested topics:

SPRING—Roller skating and marble games as harbingers of spring; "the first robin"; sales of farm machinery, garden tools, and seeds; planting gardens; plowing and sowing and planting of grain; house cleaning; new buildings; new automobiles on the highways; new clothes (the Easter Parade); moving day (March 1 in the country, May 1 in the city); "spring fever"; spring colds and other epidemics peculiar to the season; renewed activity on the tennis court and golf links; opening of the baseball season.

SUMMER—Schools close and graduates begin seeking jobs; June, the gift month for graduates and brides—its stimulation of business; organized playground activities; vacation time; travel at home and abroad; increase in motoring (and in accidents); circus parades; height of the baseball season; horse racing; cultivation of crops (prospects and prices); hints to housewives on summer menus; summer excursions; picnics; swimming (and deaths by drowning); heat prostrations (and how to avoid them); fishing; "dog days."

AUTUMN—School begins (enrollment, new courses, new teachers); off to college; football season; harvesting and marketing crops (big yields, prices); fall plowing; cornhusking and husking bees; gathering nuts; burning leaves; county fairs; hunting season; election time; harbingers of the approaching winter season.

Winter—Skating, skiing, tobogganing, and other winter sports; bob-sled parties; basketball season; taffy pulls; new indoor games originated; dances and parties; Christmas shopping and its stimulation of business; harvesting the ice crop; the jingle of sleigh bells; maple sugar time; wild geese flying north and other harbingers of spring.

RED–LETTER DAYS ARE NEWS PEGS

Holidays are shown on the calendar as "Red-Letter Days." Every one of these offers a news peg upon which to hang an appropriate news story or news feature.

Some of our red-letter days are legal holidays when all business activity ceases and man gives himself up to recreation, amusement, and good fellowship. Others are occasions which custom decrees shall be commemorated with special ceremonies by individuals or organized groups. Some are religious in origin, some are patriotic, some represent survivals of ancient superstitions, and others are products of more modern traditions and customs.[1]

Despite the fact that these holidays are celebrated regularly year after year, all of them can be used as the basis for stories if given a fresh appeal with a local or timely "tie-up." Every month in the year has one or more such days which suggest appropriate stories, as for example:

January. The first day of the first month leads off the holiday parade with New Year's Day to recall past celebrations of the day, as compared with the present, and to inspire some new variation on the ever-popular theme of "New Year's Resolutions." January 17 is Franklin's Birthday, which inaugurates Thrift Week and makes appropriate stories about savings banks, the amount of money in savings accounts, et cetera. Every four years January 20 is Inauguration Day—a time for recalling ceremonies in the past when other presidents took the oath of office. January 30 is both Franklin D. Roosevelt's Birthday and "March-of-Dimes Day," honoring his struggle against infantile paralysis and dedicated to aiding other sufferers from that disease.

February. February has ground-hog day (how many people believe, or toy with, the superstition about his seeing his shadow?) and Valentine's Day (changing styles in the tokens of love). Lincoln's Birthday and Washington's Birthday (celebrations in the schools and by patriotic organizations) are other days of note which are always productive of good copy.

March. March brings St. Patrick's Day ("wearing of the green") and the earliest possible date for Easter (eggs, rabbits, new clothes).

April. This month is ushered in by April Fools' Day (tricks to watch

---

[1] For a list of these days see *The World Almanac*.

SEASONAL CALENDAR FOR NEWS AND FEATURE WRITERS

	MAR.	2	Texas Independence Day	(Tex.)
		15	Income-Tax Day	
		17	St. Patrick's Day	
		22	Earliest Date for Easter Sunday	
S	APR.	1	April Fools' Day	
P		5	Booker T. Washington Day	
		13	Thomas Jefferson's Birthday	
R		19	Patriots' Day	(Me., Mass.)
I		21	San Jacinto Day	(Tex.)
		26	Confederate Memorial Day	(Ala., Fla., Ga., Miss.)
N			Arbor Day	(Varies in different states)
G			Easter Sunday	(Variable)
	MAY	1	May Day. Child Health Day	
		8	V–E Day	
		10	Confederate Memorial Day	(N.C., S.C.)
		20	Mecklenburg Independence Day	
		22	Maritime Day	
		30	Memorial (or Decoration) Day	
			Mother's Day	(Second Sunday)
			Easter Sunday	(Variable)

	JUNE	3	Jefferson Davis' Birthday	(Ala., Ark., Fla., Ga., La., S.C.,
				Tenn., Tex.)
S		6	D–Day	
U		14	Flag Day	
		15	Pioneer Day	(Ida.)
M		17	Bunker Hill Day	
M			Commencement Day	(Variable)
E	JULY	4	Independence Day	
R		13	General Bedford Forrest's Birthday	(Tenn.)
		14	Bastille Day	
		24	Pioneer Day	(Utah)
	AUG	1	Colorado Day	(Colo.)
		6	Atom-Bomb Day	
		14	V–J Day	
		16	Bennington Day	(Vt.)
			"Dog Days"	(Early July to early Sept.)

	SEPT.	6	Lafayette Day. Marne Day	
		9	Admission Day	(Calif.)
A		17	Constitution Day	
U			Labor Day	(First Monday)
T			American Indian Day	(Fourth Saturday)
	OCT.	9	Leif Eriksen Day	
U		12	Columbus (or Discovery) Day	
M		19	Yorktown Day	
N		27	Theodore Roosevelt's Birthday. Navy Day	
		30	Halloween	
	NOV.	1	All Saints' Day	(La.)
		11	Armistice Day	
			Election Day	(First Tuesday after the first Monday, every 4 years)
			Thanksgiving Day	(Last Thursday)

	DEC.	10	Wyoming Day	(Wyo.)
		25	Christmas Day	
W		28	Woodrow Wilson's Birthday	
I	JAN.	1	New Year's Day	
		8	New Orleans Day. Jackson Day	
N		17	Benjamin Franklin's Birthday	
T		19	Robert E. Lee's Birthday	
		20	Inauguration Day	(Every 4 years)
E		29	William McKinley's Birthday	
R		30	Franklin D. Roosevelt's Birthday. March-of-Dimes Day	
			Child Labor Day	(Last Sunday)
	FEB.	2	Ground-Hog Day	
		12	Abraham Lincoln's Birthday	
		14	St. Valentine's Day	
		22	George Washington's Birthday	
		29	Leap-Year Day	(Every 4 years)

out for), and it also contains Army Day, April 6 (national defense, new weapons, pacifism).

MAY.   May opens with May Day (Maypole dances, May queens, and other survivals of old English customs, Communist or other parades), which is also Child Health Day. May 8 brings V–E Day to recall the Allied victory over Germany in World War II. Mother's Day and Memorial, or Decoration, Day are rich in possibilities for a wide variety of human-interest stories.

JUNE.   June is marked by D–Day (the anniversary of the landing on the Normandy beachheads in 1944), Flag Day (historic associations, proper method of displaying the flag), Children's Day (special programs), as well as Father's Day (inspired by sentiment or commercial interests?).

JULY.   July has one of the most important of all holidays—Independence Day, with its variety of methods of celebration and customs, all suggesting interesting stories.

AUGUST.   For so many years lacking in a day for nation-wide observance, August gained two in 1945—August 6, when the first bomb was dropped on Hiroshima to usher in the Atomic Age, and August 14, the day of Japan's unconditional surrender.

SEPTEMBER.   September begins with Labor Day (picnics, parades, the laboring man's part in the political and economic history of the country), continues with Constitution Day (the problems of the present related to the ideas of the men who wrote the Constitution), and ends with American Indian Day (the varied contributions of the red man to our history, customs, and traditions).

OCTOBER.   This month recalls two rivals for the honor of being the discoverer of America—a Norseman on October 9, Leif Eriksen Day, and an Italian on October 12, Columbus Day (methods of celebrating these days by racial and other groups). Theodore Roosevelt's Birthday is also Navy Day (reminiscences of T. R. by local citizens, interviews with ex-sailors, discussions of America's place as a sea power), and, of course, Halloween is another red-letter day in this month with its rich background of superstition and ancient customs which make possible many timely articles.

NOVEMBER.   November brings Armistice Day (interviews with World War I veterans: "Where were you on November 11, 1918?") and that ever-important native American festival, Thanksgiving Day (difference between old-time and modern celebrations of the day, the turkey as the "national bird," etc.).

DECEMBER.   December needs no holiday other than Christmas, and the many festival events surrounding its celebration, to make it notable as a source for calendar news. From the first of the month until the twenty-fifth any type of story relating to the "Yuletide season" is appropriate.

In some respects it offers the greatest opportunity for newsworthy features of all kinds—for the old and the young, for all Christian nations and peoples.

PAST EVENTS MAY BE PRESENT NEWS

The anniversaries of notable events in the past make these occurrences news for the present if the connection between them is shown by the news writer.

Birthdays Of Notables May Serve As News Pegs. "Lives of great men oft remind us . . . ," said the poet Longfellow. There is inspiration for the present generation in the deeds and achievements of those who have gone before. For this reason, the birthdays of notable men and women are also red-letter days on the calendar and provide news pegs upon which to hang a story recalling who they were and what they did. Especially interesting are interviews with descendants of these notables or with people who knew them and participated in the events which made them notable. Typical of this kind of story is one headlined:

SON OF SITTING BULL RECALLS DAY WHEN "LONG HAIR" (GENERAL CUSTER) AND HIS TROOPERS RODE TO THEIR DEATH ON THE LITTLE BIG HORN

Rehearsing History Provides Many Other Days. Anniversaries of battles, beginnings and endings of wars and other events in military, political, economic, and social-culture history, as well as birthdays of important personages, are occasions for rehearsing those bits of history as news stories of present-day interest. This kind of story has special value if the significance of the event, in the light of later events, and its bearing upon present conditions are emphasized. Also, as in the case of the story swung on the birthday of a notable, it has increased human interest if it is based upon an interview with living persons who participated in the historic event the anniversary of which is being celebrated. An example is some such story as one headlined:

HE GUARDED F.D.R. AT CASABLANCA—FORMER GI HAS INTERESTING
REMINISCENCES OF HISTORIC MEETING IN NORTH AFRICA
WHEN ALLIED LEADERS MAPPED FUTURE COURSE OF
WAR AGAINST AXIS

CHAPTER XV

THE PRESS AND THE SPORTSMAN

Most of us who love adventure must live it vicariously . . . by watching stronger men struggle in the war of sports . . . by steeping ourselves in the printer's ink that writes strange tales across white paper. . . . In the process of getting away from ourselves . . . from the routine of office and factory and the common monotony of home . . . uncounted millions have found the supreme stimulant in sport. It holds the thrill of the battlefield . . . the romance of the stage . . . the ambition, joy and sorrow of life itself.—JACK KOFOED.*

THE SPORT PAGES REFLECT MAN'S COMPETITIVE URGE

From the time he's a boy in grade school until he enters the competitive world of business, man is engaged in pitting his own abilities and skills against those of others. Nowhere does this competition appear in keener form than in the world of sports. Uncounted millions of fans spend billions of dollars annually to see and participate personally in the adventure of competition.

Sports Stories Have Tremendous Reader-Interest. Sports are classified as amateur and professional depending upon whether the athlete receives money for his performance. Both branches of sports rivalry, however, command a large following of enthusiastic and even rabid fans.

According to a study of reader-interest on 100 newspapers, 95 per cent of the men absorb themselves in the sports page—only the comics and editorials surpass this showing and then only by 1 per cent. While the figure for women drops off to 82 per cent (fifth place), that's still surprisingly high.[1]

Sports Are Divided Into Two Main Kinds. Amateur and professional sports events contribute mutually to the promotion and stimulation of interest in each other. Sports may be classed as amateur even though the group sponsoring them, as in the case of universities, may receive profit from the efforts of the athletes. This is true only when the institutions themselves are not organized on a profit basis. Educational and char-

---

* Columnist and feature writer, the *Miami Herald;* formerly sports columnist for New York papers (*Post, Journal,* and *Telegram*). Used by express permission of Mr. Kofoed from his book *Thrills in Sport*, p. ix. Copyright 1932.

[1] From *The Continuing Study of Newspaper Reading*, 100-Study Summary, conducted by The Advertising Research Foundation in co-operation with the Bureau of Advertising of the American Newspaper Publishers Association.

itable groups are the two chief examples of organizations permitted to retain amateur standing for themselves and their athletes and yet charge admission for their sporting events.

Amateur Sports Command An Increasing Following. Coming into prominence in the 1920's and growing by leaps and bounds in the decades since, amateur sports, both of a team nature and those primarily emphasizing individual competition, have secured an enormous increase in popularity. As a result, many newspapers are devoting more and more space to chronicling these amateur events. However, there still has been too much tendency to cling to the traditional stress—for example, professional baseball—and ignore the millions of skiers, golfers, or tennis players.

This interest in amateur sports often has centered around college and high-school athletics, such as football and basketball. In their seasons, other school sports, including rowing, track, tennis, golf, swimming, hockey, and softball, receive attention and take their place in the news.

Over and beyond the enthusiasm of alumni for sports news involving their alma maters, there is a general clamor for information about amateur athletic activity. Amateur sport assumes national and international rank in contests sponsored by the Amateur Athletic Union and its subsidiary organizations and in the main Olympic games. Furthermore, personal participation in individual sports—such as hunting and fishing, golf, tennis, bowling, skiing—contributes directly to personal enthusiasm; and more millions of Americans each year are being added to the ranks of those who take part in such a sports program.

Many Fans Follow Professional Sports. The great interest of the sportsman in professional events has encouraged newspapers to give ever-increasing space to this kind of news. So great is the interest that sports, which were formerly confined to amateur performances, are now developed on a professional basis. Particularly is this true of football, basketball, golf, tennis, and hockey, which were first presented and popularized by colleges. The interest in baseball has become nation-wide, culminating yearly in the World Series but fostered throughout the season by professional leagues of various classifications in all sections of the country. Newspapers for years have published late editions to satisfy the craving of fans for the latest reports on their favorite teams. As long as a professional sport remains clean, newspapers legitimately meet the demands of the fans. Wrestling, boxing, and horse racing are examples of sports which have their chronic ups and downs. Editors have become suspicious of certain performers and promoters in these "fringe" territories.

Horse racing, once referred to as "the sport of Kings," is now of personal interest to millions who follow the sport avidly. Race-track reporting has become almost an art in itself.

The sports writer should constantly guard against any encouragement to the gamblers and win-at-any-price touts. While the will to win is laudable, the victory compulsion has been overplayed on the sports page and too many sports stories have, intentionally or unwittingly, stimulated the gambling fever.

PRECONTEST STORIES ARE NEEDED FOR ALL SPORTS

Whether the performers are amateurs or professionals, the public demands sports articles which predict the outcome of the contests by analyzing the athletes and other factors. This is true in all sports coverage but especially in football, baseball, and boxing because of their popularity.

A Major Football Game Requires Several Advance Stories. If the teams are old rivals or are evenly matched, the public wants searching analyses by football experts as to their chances. The writer makes such analyses after visiting the opposing camps or by scanning all available information as to the strength and weaknesses of the two teams. He will take into consideration such factors as the following: the relative weights and experience of the opposing players; the records of the coaches; number and ability of reserves; the comparative scores of the past season; injuries and ineligibilities; weather conditions as they may affect one team or the other; morale; handicaps such as lack of practice; the recent records of the teams. During the entire week or so before the contest the writer must revise his judgments as the above factors may change. For the public insists on knowing the latest news concerning its favorites and their chances of winning the game. The football expert writing a precontest account is an observer as well as a reporter and must express his opinion after weighing the various factors.

World Series Games Occasion Many Advances. When the American and National league races are close, pregame stories are given before each contest but the demand for "dope" stories is greatly heightened immediately preceding the World Series. The hitting and pitching records of the two teams are compared and major attention is given to the star performers. Because professional baseball is big business as well as an interesting sport, attention is paid to such items as probable attendance and money splits to the players and the clubs. But the chief interest to the public is what the baseball writer has to say about who is going to pitch and what are the probable lineups. Interviews and predictions are secured from rival managers, pitchers, and team owners. Each newspaper will run pregame accounts daily during the period immediately preceding the opening of the Series.

Newswriting Serves The Reader, Not The Promoter. The sports writer's first duty is to the reader. The sports writer's job is not to beat the publicity drum for the promoter.

REPORTS OF THE GAME ARE EAGERLY AWAITED

The manner of reporting athletic events varies with the sport and with the amount of space a newspaper can devote to it; articles may be detailed play-by-play accounts, or lead stories emphasizing the high lights or giving colorful reports of the crowd and side-line events.

Play-By-Play Account Is Detailed. One of the most difficult tasks of a sports writer is to handle a complete play-by-play report of a major contest such as football. In such a report he must give on every play the name of the person carrying the ball, the position through which he carried it, the number of yards gained or lost, and the opposing tackler who brought down the ball carrier. This play-by-play report, when run by the newspaper, is preceded by a brief lead which gives the score of the game, the deciding factors in the result, and the particular feature angle of that particular contest. At the end of the play-by-play account there is appended a summary including statistics. Play-by-play stories demand close observation together with ability to work at top speed. Naturally a knowledge of the sport is essential. This means that the reporter has to know the rules and the records of the past as well as a multitude of details regarding the players, the officials, and the plays.

Newspapers Play Up Lead Stories. In addition to complete play-by-play accounts, some newspapers also will present a story of the game which centers on the high lights and more important plays. Many newspapers, which do not have space to present the play-by-play story, will give space to such lead stories on local or regional athletic contests.

Such stories center around the scoring plays in football or the hitting rallies in baseball. They discuss the crises of the games, the star performers of both teams, those plays which are crucial and have an important effect upon the outcome. Play-by-play accounts are run chiefly by afternoon papers while morning papers tend to use the lead story on the high lights. There is great room in this type of sports reporting for individuality and style and colorful reporting.

Brief Sports Stories Are Also Used. Newspapers at some distance from a sports event often may carry briefer stories, generally supplied by the press associations. These may vary in length from one hundred to four hundred words, depending upon the judgment and decision of the individual sports editor, although the wire service generally carries an adequate story which may be cut to suit individual needs. Most of the stories center on straight news reporting of the sport event with, however, a sports flavor. They stress the score, the winner, outstanding incidents, and how the outcome of the game affects the season's standings of the teams or individual players.

Major Sports Events Call For Color Stories. Color and human-interest features, or "with" or "side" features as they are called, are presented in the sports pages in connection with contests which attract large crowds because of traditional or intersectional rivalry. These human-interest and feature reports describe the crowd, important or newsworthy personalities among the spectators, activities between the halves, and similar angles which develop from side-line activities. Such accounts are generally written as separate stories and, in the case of major contests, will often be covered by a feature specialist rather than by the sports writer who is reporting the game. Often the two men collaborate on the play-by-play, the color story, and the lead story on an important contest, each doing his share of the job but often assisting the other.

The Sports Reporter Needs Objectivity In The Press Box. In the press box, covering the game, the reporter's job is to see and record the action. To do so, he must be cool, never losing his objectivity as an observer even in the most heated moments of action. He cannot afford to take sides or dispute decisions. He must be constantly on the watch for unusual incidents or angles, which he may play up in the lead of his story. While the sports writer, under the legal privilege of fair comment and criticism, has considerable latitude as to criticism, prediction, and personal opinion, he should remember that his story may legitimately deal with the game or the athletic competition as such but not with the personal reputation or conduct of the participants. In other words, what is presented to the sports fan by the athlete or the team for public approval and exhibition is within the realm of the sports writer's justifiable criticism. When he goes outside the active field of the sports contest he forfeits his legal protection.

THE FANS WANT FOLLOW–UP STORIES

On the days immediately following major sports contests, fans scan the newspapers for additional explanation of the outcome of the games.

Follow-Up Stories Furnish Post-Mortem Analyses. Later reports discuss the condition of players injured in the contest, the psychological factors influencing the game, the statistics and what they indicate. These accounts should be invariably written by experts, as they require sound judgment and a thorough knowledge of the sport. Logic and analysis are called into play, and the emotional and colorful factors are subordinated. Although personal opinions may be injected into this type of follow-story, unreasonable local bias or prejudice should not be allowed to creep in.

Often accurate and careful pregame analysis will remove the necessity for lame excuses by sports writers who climbed too far out on a limb. A follow-up story should never attempt to single out goats and it is not the sports reporter's job to hire or fire players or coaches.

The Sports Column Should Offer Constructive Suggestions. The goal of many a sports writer is to have his own individual sports column in which he can write about athletics from the angle of his own opinion. While such columns make excellent reading when well written, they may serve as vehicles for personal favoritism or unreasonable critical attacks. Very few sports reporters are sufficiently expert to start running a team from the columns of their newspapers. They should confine themselves, therefore, to legitimate and constructive comment. Or they may call attention to the performance of certain athletes, which, because of lack of space, cannot receive sufficient attention in the stories of the game itself.

Many sports writers, when they become sports columnists, take on the aura of authority and circle their brows with a halo. Running a column does not make a sports writer omniscient. While one or two sports columnists have developed reputations on a basis of their inability to predict correctly, going out on a limb or master-minding with continuous inaccuracy is a certain way to win the contempt or disapproval of the fans. While prediction is a regular part of sports columning, it should be kept within the limits of probability. At no time should a sports columnist set himself up as infallible.

FANS ENJOY FEATURES ABOUT THE ATHLETES

Readers of the sports pages desire avidly human-interest stories and anecdotes about their favorite heroes. Individual stars have their own following; in addition, sportsmen want to know about new prospects on their way up.

The Personalities Of The Stars Attract Attention. Little incidents in the life or play of the athletes are stressed in the personality features written about them. Dressing-room anecdotes, superstitions of the players and coaches, their idiosyncracies, their biographies are related to the thousands of fans. Press associations and syndicates add to the material gathered by the writers on newspapers or magazines and assemble innumerable stories about the major athletes of all sports. More latitude is given to the writer of sports features than is permitted in most other sections of the newspaper, for the sportsman is an ardent fan and desires his stories to have zest and color. The sports writer must cater to the hero-worship of the sportsman, but he should stay within the limits of the truth and avoid gilding an idol with clay feet.

Interest In Some Stars Never Dies. While sports features are usually seasonal in that they discuss the leading athletes of the current sports season, some of the greater athletes make good stories the year 'round. Others, all-time favorites in the hearts of the fans, remain legend for years after they have ceased active participation. No matter what the season and no matter how the years go by, sports-page readers will continue to digest eagerly the feature epics of such great athletes as Babe Ruth, Jack Dempsey, Jim Thorpe, and Charley Paddock. These stars have so captured the imagination of young and old sportsmen that interest in them does not die.

SOME SPORTS EVENTS ARE NATIONAL SPECTACLES

Because of the great tradition and universal following of such sports events as the Rose Bowl, they have developed into climactic points of the season in which they occur. Such events are a sportsman's paradise.

When either amateur or professional spectacles have been held annually over a long period of years they develop a tradition and glamour which set them apart from the other sports contests. To handle such stories as those occasioned by the Kentucky Derby, the Rose Bowl game, and the World Series, newspapers send their star reporters, while the press associations also delegate their specialists to write innumerable stories based on the contest itself as well as on the crowd and spectacle.

NEWSPAPERS BUILD LOCAL AND MINOR SPORTS

In addition to handling the news of major amateur and professional sports, newspapers provide coverage for many local athletic activities and for minor sports fields. Such individual-participation sports have received a tremendous impetus in the last ten or fifteen years and a great reservoir of reader-interest has been created as a result.

Papers Cover Local Baseball, Basketball, And Bowling Leagues. Names are always news and many names occur constantly in the minor and individual sports programs which may be found in any town, no matter how small. Newspapers, realizing the extent of local sports enthusiasm, often capitalize on coverage of such events and give considerable space to its promotion. Often, the sports department and the promotion department of the newspaper work actively to organize such local leagues and individual sports events. They arrange for the contests and the tournament, provide prizes, and keep a constant running stream of stories and summaries of events. Local health and recreational conditions are often aided by such newspaper activity, while the sport itself gains a material advantage from reader-interest and the availability of local news on the sport. Thus a wholesome and effective backlog of local sports enthusiasm is built.

Newspapers And Athletic Organizations. Many amateur groups are assisted by the newspapers to carry on athletic programs culminating in contests and awards. Such groups as the Catholic Youth Organization and the Young Men's and Young Women's Christian Associations co-operate closely with the newspapers, furnishing news to the press and in return receiving helpful publicity. Interest in such athletic programs has increased so rapidly that newspapers have had to expand their sports sections. In some cases, however, they have chosen to reduce the amount of space given to professional sports. Newspapers have initiated such programs as the Golden Gloves contest which have brought forth national athletic figures and, at the same time, have stimulated athletic competition. They have incidentally promoted their own sports pages simultaneously, so their venture has been only partly altruistic.

Commercial And Industrial Firms Sponsor Sports. Business institutions as well as charity groups have, for various reasons, become interested in sponsoring sports programs among their employees and associates. News of these activities is furnished to the newspapers by the publicity men of these institutions or by a member of the newspaper staff. In recent years women have become active participants in sports as well as ardent spectators at major games.

THE SPORTS REPORTER MUST HAVE SPECIAL QUALIFICATIONS

The sports writer must be able to attract the general reader of sports. At the same time he must display his knowledge of the specialized techniques of individual sports, so as to gain and hold the confidence of the fan and expert in those particular lines of athletics.

The Sports Reporter Writes For The Average Reader. The sports page today is written for the average newspaper reader who enjoys athletic events but has no special knowledge or background in them. These stories are primarily for the enjoyment and information of the ordinary reader rather than the sports expert. Unusual and technical terms, which would not be understood by the average reader, should be avoided. With the growth of participation by women in athletics and the great extension of sports participation in recent years, the sports pages have more readers than ever before. Always, in the event of some especially outstanding and nationally prominent sports story, a new group of readers is created who are not used to the day-by-day coverage. For these reasons, the sports reporter and the sports editor must remember that they are writing first of all for Mr. and Mrs. America, fascinated by the appeal of sports, but without the skill or know-how of an active athlete.

The Sports Reporter Must Use Good English. There was a time in American newspaper practice when the sports writer took pleasure in conjuring up a weird and mysterious language of his own. In this occult tongue, he referred to the "keystone sack," the "coffin corner," the "casaba," and other inventions often of his own imagination. Some of these started out as an attempt to develop a picturesque patter for descriptive purposes. Others were closely related to the intricate technical playing of a game. In any case, they too often were incomprehensible to the average reader.

The better newspapers today keep the use of technical phrases and words down to a minimum and discourage the constant use of a specialized slang or jargon which discourages the ordinary reader. Good sports writing, as with any other type of expression, is writing in good English with clear and forceful diction. The vitality and virility of sports reporting demand vigorous expression and a terse, crisp style.

Where definite technical expression is part of legitimate reporting, such as the use of "par" in golf, "punt" in football, "strike" in bowling, certainly no one can object. This is part of the necessary vocabulary of the sports writer, just as references to "bulls and bears" are part of the atmosphere of the financial page.

The Sports Writer Has To Be Able To Turn Out His Story With Speed. Because of the great interest in sports results and because events of some sports, such as football and hockey, are played at a mile-a-minute clip, the sports reporter has to be able to work fast and to get his story out accurately. Inasmuch as many contests are played with alternate periods of fast action and "time out," the reporter has some time to catch his breath. But while play is on, the sports writer must be able to see and to note all that he sees, and to pound out a rapid running story on many occasions while play is in progress. Then at the end of the game he shoots in by telegraph or telephone the final score followed immediately by a bulletin giving the lead details on the game. This calls for the ability to produce under pressure.

The Sports Writer Must Be Fair. While the sports reporter for a sports page in a local paper is probably the most consistent and faithful follower of local teams and local athletes, he should not let local pride and prejudice interfere with fair and accurate reporting. As a definite and defensible practice, he will give the play and the emphasis to the doings of local men and the local team, but he should not distort or twist facts in order to justify local defeats. Thus, the reporter at all times should avoid a rabid partisanship which results in misrepresentation or inaccuracy. His job is a constructive reporting which will capitalize on local news in the spirit of fair play and good sportsmanship.

The Sports Writer Needs An Encyclopedic Memory. Legends of the past and rules of the particular sport being covered should be available, like a complete set of files, in the mind of every sports reporter. Many is the time when he is the ultimate authority in his town for all disputes concerning sports. In the course of covering an athletic event, he should be able to reach into the proper drawer of his memory and pull out the pertinent facts or decisions. Who won the World Series in 1910? What great punters also were superlative passers? How high should the basket be in basketball?

Immediate answers to these and a million other questions must be at his disposal without a second's hesitation. If he has cultivated and made a point of learning this background, he can truly write and be recognized as a sports authority. Without this background, he seldom will have the proper perspective or judgment to report current events in sports. Such a display of expert knowledge will do more to establish the reputation of a sports page than any other single quality.

The Young Sports Reporter Must Become A Minor Sports Specialist. If you're heart and soul determined to write for the sports page, become a minor sports specialist. Oh, yes, that also means that you should know about football and baseball and basketball. That'll be taken for granted. But the press boxes are full of men who can rattle off the football rules glibly but know nothing about a "split," a "christy," or a "tack." If you are an expert on a couple of minor sports as well as the big three of the sports world, then you've got two strikes on the other fellow already when it comes to getting a job or that all-important raise.

THE SPORTS PAGE FURNISHES SUMMARIES FOR THE STEADY FAN

The box score in baseball, the summaries in track, the lineup and summaries in football—these form a bible for avid sports followers which they read and pore over with persistent and devoted interest. In these summaries are many details and facts which reveal high points of the contest involved.

The form in which sports summaries are presented varies little from paper to paper throughout the United States. However, these summaries must be accurate, detailed, complete. A definite tradition or pattern for this detailed type of sports reporting has been generally adopted. It is considered the most important part of the sports coverage of an event by the regular and constant follower of that particular sport. If it is not accurate, if it is not complete, the fan soon rebels and registers his indignation. Every sports reporter must know how to handle summaries. For this reason, the following examples are presented in four major sports.

Football

Pos.	Collier Tech (13)	Bay State (6)
L.E.	Smiley	Jones
L.T.	Kelley	Dunstan
L.G.	Wallace	Bell
C.	Dexter	Jordan
R.G.	Waters	George
R.T.	Drury	Thorpe
R.E.	Keeler	Whalen
Q.B.	Lawson	Barton
L.H.	Tyler	Good
R.H.	Janes	Schram
F.B.	Nash	Nelson

Score by periods:

Collier Tech	0	0	13	0–13
Bay State	6	0	0	0– 6

Touchdowns—Collier Tech: Nash 2.
        Bay State: Nelson.
Points after touchdowns—Collier Tech: Lawson.

Substitutes—Collier Tech: Muster, Clay, Belton, ends; Mayland, Mathews, tackles; Ball, Burke, guards; Clay, center; Fisher, Reilley, Swartz, backs. Bay State: London, end; Connor, tackle; Hendricks, Devine, Bainter, guards; Gebhart, center; Fitzwarren, Rossman, Buck, backs.

Officials—A. Buckhouse, Boston; P. Miller, Philadelphia; E. Hunter, Boston; F. Benton, Boston.

Baseball

AMERICAN LEAGUE RESULTS YESTERDAY

New York, 6; Cleveland, 3 (night)
   Detroit, 2; Washington, 1 (night)
     Chicago, 8; Boston, 3 (night)
       Philadelphia, 9; St. Louis, 5 (night)

STANDING OF THE CLUBS	New York	Boston	Cleveland	Philadelphia	Detroit	Chicago	Wash'ton	St. Louis	WON	LOST	Percent	Games behind
New York	—	10	9	10	9	12	10	14	74	44	.627	—
Boston	5	—	6	10	11	13	14	13	72	48	.600	3
Cleveland	8	11	—	7	9	10	12	12	69	51	.575	6
Philadelphia ...	7	6	11	—	7	15	11	9	66	54	.550	9
Detroit	11	6	5	11	—	9	14	12	68	56	.548	9
Chicago	6	5	7	4	8	—	11	10	51	69	.425	24
Washington ...	4	3	8	4	4	6	—	11	40	78	.339	34
St. Louis	3	7	5	8	8	4	6	—	41	81	.336	35

American League Games and Pitchers Today

New York at Cleveland (night)—Raschi (15-7) vs. Benton (4-4).

Boston at Chicago (two)—Parnell (19-6) and Kinder (15-5) vs. Wight (11-9) and Kuzava (8-3).

Philadelphia at St. Louis (night)—Scheib (8-9) vs. Ostrowski (7-8).

Washington at Detroit—Calvert (6-14) vs. Gray (7-9) or Hutchinson (13-4).

PENNANT RACE AT A GLANCE

	W	L	Pct.	G.B.	To Play
Boston	95	56	.629	——	3
New York	95	56	.629	——	3

Remaining Schedules

New York—Home (3); Boston, 2; Philadelphia, 1.
Boston—Away (3); New York, 2; Washington, 1.

WASHINGTON (A. L.)	ab	r	h	po	a	NEW YORK (A. L.)	ab	r	h	po	a
Yost 3b.....	4	0	2	0	2	Rizzuto ss ..	4	1	1	2	4
Simmons lf.	1	0	0	2	0	Mapes rf....	5	0	1	4	0
Stewart lf...	1	0	0	1	0	Johnson 3b..	3	0	0	0	1
Mele 1b....	4	0	0	7	0	DiMaggio cf.	2	0	1	2	0
Vollmer cf...	5	1	1	7	0	Henrich 1b..	3	1	1	8	0
Lewis rf....	4	0	0	1	0	Lindell lf...	4	1	1	2	1
Dente ss....	4	1	1	0	3	Coleman 2b.	4	1	2	2	1
Kozar 2b...	2	1	0	3	0	Silvera c....	3	0	0	7	0
Robertson 2b.	1	0	0	0	0	Byrne p....	1	0	0	0	1
Evans c.....	2	1	0	3	0	Pillette p....	0	0	0	0	0
Early c.....	1	0	0	0	0	†Woodling .	0	1	0	0	0
Harris p....	3	0	1	0	1	Reynolds p..	2	0	0	0	2
*Coan	1	0	0	0	0						
Haynes p...	0	0	0	0	0						
Totals ...	33	4	5	24	6	Totals ...	31	5	7	27	10

*Fanned for Harris in eighth.
†Walked for Pillette in fourth.

Washington   000   400   000—4
New York   000   401   00x—5

E—DiMaggio, Mele, Kozar, Johnson, Coleman. RBI
—Vollmer, Harris 2, Yost, Henrich, Coleman, Mapes.
2B—Rizzuto. HR—Vollmer, Henrich. S—Rizzuto.
Left—Washington 9, New York 9. BB—Off Byrne 3,
Harris 6, Pillette 1, Reynolds 2. SO—By Harris 3,
Byrne 1, Reynolds 5. HO—Byrne, 5 in 3⅔ innings;
Pillette, 0 in ⅓; Reynolds, 0 in 5; Harris, 7 in 7;
Haynes, 0 in 1. HPB—Byrne (Kozar). WP—Harris.
Winner—Reynolds (12-3). Loser—Harris (2-10).U—
Rommel, Stevens, Boyer and Passarella. T—2:36. A—
6,638.

LEADING FIVE BATSMEN

American League

Player and club	G	AB	R	H	Pct
Williams, Boston	119	432	121	154	.357
Kell, Detroit	109	434	79	150	.346
Dillinger, St. Louis	103	404	56	136	.337
DiMaggio, Boston	109	456	102	151	.331
Mitchell, Cleveland	112	476	74	152	.319

Runs Batted In		Home Runs	
Stephens, Red Sox	136	Stephens, Red Sox	31
Williams, Red Sox	122	Williams, Red Sox	30
Wertz, Tigers	101	Henrich, Yankees	22
Chapman, Athletics	83	Joost, Athletics	21
Henrich, Yanks	76	Kokos, Browns	20

Basketball

St. James University (55)	FG	FT	PF	TP
Dalton, f	2	4	0	8
Edison, f	2	1	1	5
Clay, c	4	1	1	9
Tucker, g	1	1	0	3
Nelson, g	1	2	0	4
Degnan, f	3	1	0	7
Johnson, f	5	1	1	11
J. Burg, c	0	0	2	0
Hess, g	2	1	1	5
C. Burg, g	0	2	4	2
Scanlon, g	0	1	0	1
Totals	20	15	10	55

Eddy College (32)	FG	FT	PF	TP
Staples, f	0	1	1	1
Thule, f	4	1	3	9
Travis, c	1	0	0	2
Hopper, g	4	1	4	9
Crane, g	1	0	1	2
Rosen, f	0	0	1	0
Peters, c	2	0	0	4
Newburg, g	0	0	1	0
Benton, g	0	1	2	1
Fredericks, g	1	2	2	4
	13	6	15	32

Halftime score—St. James 30, Eddy, 14. Missed free throws—Dalton 2, Edison, Nelson, Johnson, Hess 2, Staples, Travis, Rosen, Benton, Fredericks, Herron. Officials—Henry Zeller, Joe Marion.

Track or Swimming

The summaries:

220-yard free style—Won by Smith, Georgia; Burke, Maine, second; Anders, Florida, third. Time—2:28 1-5.

Fancy dive—Won by Zimmerman, Georgia (88.5 points); Sumter, Florida (87.8), second; Patterson, Maine (85.4), third.

Chapter XVI

WOMEN "ARRIVE" IN JOURNALISM

By slow degrees she [the newspaper woman] has moved out of the false framework of legend and prejudice that has surrounded her for the last fifty years, although there is no denying that she is still a negligible factor in the newspaper office, and is there only because of her own insistence, not because anybody wanted her. She has her own compensations, however. Invariably she likes her work beyond all telling. Adventure, excitement, romance, danger, praise and blame, glamour and drudgery keep her spinning self-forgetfully day after day in the dizzy world inhabited by ladies of the press.—ISHBEL ROSS.*

WOMAN OFTEN HAS THE INSIDE TRACK

Department store and retail store advertising, specialized trade publications, publicity, and promotion positions—all these, as well as the women's pages of daily and weekly newspapers, are the women's world of journalism. In this area, woman is supreme and the poor male is distinctly second choice.

Woman's Reign In Store Advertising Is Assured. Whether it be the fabulous metropolitan department store or the smart specialty shop, if the store caters to feminine customers most of its retail advertising will be best handled by women. In fact, through such work women, like Dorothy Shaver of Lord and Taylor's, have risen to the top executive direction of the entire store operation. When it comes to merchandising for other women, it is only natural that women have the inside track.

Generally, the woman who reaches a top advertising position has served an apprenticeship behind the counter, learning how to sell and getting acquainted with customer wants and prejudices. She has worked into the advertising staff and then into writing copy and preparing layouts. From there, the step to the position of advertising director may have been a long one—but it's a natural line of promotion.

Woman Has A Domain In The Specialized Trade Publication. Trade publications there are of infinite variety, and a large number of these deal with products or subjects of special appeal to women, restricted primarily to their needs and interests. To cite a few: *Women's Wear Daily, Better Homes and Gardens, American Cookery, Modern Beauty Shop,*

---

* From *Ladies of the Press* by Ishbel Ross, p. 600. Copyright 1936. Used by permission of the publishers, Harper & Brothers.

American Childhood Education. It has made sense for women to write and edit such periodicals for they know how to write for women.

Specialization in this field of journalism often demands a specialized background, training in home economics or in the fine arts of horticulture. But it is a domain for the woman in which she has turned the tables on her masculine competitor—here, *he* has to prove he's as good as a woman.

Publicity Offers Opportunity For The Woman's Touch. When it comes to promoting a new book, publicizing a new lipstick, handling news and information services for an appropriate type of industry or for a women's college, the woman journalist has the edge on any man. That's why you find women monopolizing the publicity jobs in book-publishing companies, or handling women's cosmetics accounts in many advertising agencies. At an airline's cocktail party in connection with a new international route, they'll brightly serve you with canapes or flight data. For the exclusive girls' school, they'll be treating the better residential areas with teas for doting mothers and awkward daughters.

The Woman Runs The Women's Page. Practically every daily newspaper, whether large, small, or medium, has a woman's page or pages which feature fashions, recipes, lovelorn columns, advice on child training, society news, interior decoration hints, gardening tips, and a potpourri of assorted feminine furbelows. From time immemorial, this newspaper section has been the woman journalist's private preserve. Again, special training in home economics can help a lot in smoothing the way for the woman's-page worker, in making her copy more professional and authoritative.

There Are Other Feminine Strongholds. The teaching of journalism in high schools is one field in which women have been active for many years. Supervision of high-school publications and the first injection of printer's ink into the youngsters' veins, these have been and will continue to be the responsibility and privilege of many a woman journalist.

Radio journalism has opened a new territory: radio programs for the housewife, radio advertising and continuities which stress the home and the woman's angle, radio scripts ranging from the eternal soap opera to national comedy shows. In a few outstanding instances, journalism-trained girls going into radio have even advanced from script girls, on the production side, into full direction. This is equally true in television.

Free-lance writing also gives the woman journalist a career fortress of her own. For the general woman's magazine such as *Ladies' Home Journal,* fiction and articles offer the woman writer a better chance than the man—and the tables of contents bear loud testimony to the way the feminine free-lancer has responded. For trade and class publications which emphasize woman's interests, the woman writer again can out-write her masculine competitor. In fact, in every area which touches the feminine heart and mind and pocketbook, the free-lancer from the distaff side holds all the winning cards.

THE WOMAN COMPETES ON EVEN TERMS

While a few jobs, notably on press associations and in some areas of daily newspapering, are monopolized by men, World War II proved that women could handle any position in journalism. Many hard-boiled male executives revised long-standing prejudices and swung to wholehearted praise for the feminine performance.

The Woman Journalist Won Her Place The Hard Way. Although World War II gave new journalistic opportunities to women and proved that they could compete with men, all too seldom do the press associations give women a chance to show what they can do. Quite a number of editors still retain the city-room bias against having skirts around a city desk or sending a girl out on the police beat.

The war did win many editors over; they stated that the future would find competence succeeding, regardless of sex. There was no branch of journalism, from front-line battle action to press-association bureau managing, in which women did not distinguish themselves. On the home front, the shortage of men opened many doors hitherto closed. Some of these swung shut again, with "V" days, but many are still open to the woman who can compete.

Women Are In Newspaper Work To Stay. While the woman's page, society news, and sob-sistering (human-interest and feature writing) have long been women's own preserve in journalism employment, some women operate at the very top. In 1946, according to an *Editor and Publisher* compilation (April 20, p. 19), 121 women directed 131 American daily papers as publishers, presidents, general managers, or editors.

There is no area of newspaper work, whether daily or weekly, where the woman is not found. General reporting, Washington coverage, around the rim of the city desk, departmental editing of book reviews or dramatic criticism, even the sacrosanct sports staff—all have experienced the feminine invasion. On the weekly, many women run their own papers, managing or participating in all operations from sticking type and running the jobber to writing the editorials and keeping the books. Many others give their husband-owners strong support in a team work and partnership which know no favoritism for sex.

The local ad staff of the newspaper has found the woman a pretty handy member of its production system. Not all papers have an all-woman staff of eleven girls, as did the *Monroe* (Louisiana) *News-Star* and *Morning World* in 1945, but there's a place on every staff for some women, says Frank E. Fehlman, *Editor and Publisher* staff writer. He adds the following elaboration of his statement.

At this point we want to go on record as being very definitely in favor of women's handling certain classifications of retail accounts. During the past three years we have seen many women in many markets successfully sell and keep alive the local advertising of stores that have been short of merchandise.

When it comes to women's, young misses' and children's and babies' apparel, they can analyze and more quickly prepare newsy ads than men. Those who live with their parents or who are married can usually do a better job with food accounts. They do a swell job with stationery and office supply stores because so many of them have come up from the ranks of stenographers and office jobs. They do good work with florists, undertakers, beauty shops, drug stores and book stores.[1]

The Advertising Agency Has A Place For Women. From bottom to top, women may be found competing on even terms in advertising agency work. In fact, on certain accounts, they'll run the men ragged. General headquarters for American ad agencies is New York City; there, at least nine feminine vice-presidents operate in the leading companies. Every single one has risen to her executive job since 1940.

Writing copy and research studies on merchandising are green fields for women in the agency work. However, one may have to be willing to start at the bottom, as receptionist or stenographer perhaps. One of the woman executives, Jean Wade Rindlaub,[2] of Batten, Barton, Durstine, & Osborn, comments:

> Being a woman can be both a handicap and an asset in the advertising field. You can't trade on being a woman, for it won't work, but your knowledge gained from cooking dinners, running a household, taking care of children, etc., can come in very handy.
>
> There are and always will be some agency jobs for which men are better fitted but there are some too, for which women have shown they are especially qualified, as more and more agencies are realizing.

Another, Van Davis [3] of Ellington & Company, adds:

> The fact that you're a woman doesn't need to be a handicap in business, provided you don't ask for special favors. While the advertising agencies on the whole have been slow to recognize women, many more of the sex have been making headway in the last five years. And it's a trend that makes so much sense when you think about it!

---

[1] *Editor and Publisher,* December 9, 1945, p. 64.

[2] *Ibid.,* November 2, 1946, p. 10.

[3] *Ibid.,* November 2, 1946, p. 58.

Women Abound On Magazine Staffs. Not only do trade publications and women's periodicals offer special opportunities to the woman journalist, but general magazines employ her as an editorial assistant or departmental editor. She also may work on the art, advertising, or circulation staffs. Many a magazine of national circulation depends heavily on its women readers, who look over the manuscripts and sift out the chaff.

Women Also Succeed In Other Journalism Careers. Women often have followed successful careers in some of the other vocational fields of journalism. Syndicates and feature services offer jobs ranging from the routine staff chores to national columns, particularly in such specialized women's interests as the home, fashions, child training, beauty aids, interior decoration, recipes, advice to lovelorn. A few women produce cartoon panels or fiction, many deal with features on a broad variety of subjects.

Book publishers often have women employees. They may work in the business office on clerical duties, they may engage in advertising new best sellers. Closely allied with the latter activity, a number carry on promotion for the book house and still others, as readers and assistant editors, aid in the selection and preparation of manuscripts.

Many phases of journalism call for art work, either photographic or creative drawing. Women photographers such as Margaret Bourke-White have acquired world reputations. Women illustrators for books and magazines are numerous. In advertising, in cartooning, they have evidenced first-rank ability. Many a department store ad or sketch in the *New Yorker* carries a woman's initials or name.

Early Women Journalists Were Unique. Before women found acceptance in journalism, adventurous girls in skirts to their ankles made a solitary path. Often, in their day, they were regarded as unwomanly, uncommonly bold, unseemly. But the Margaret Fullers of the 1840's and the Nellie Blys of the 1890's paved the way for Dorothy Thompson and Ishbel Ross and Anne O'Hare McCormick of today. To these early women journalists, all girls aspiring to the company of ink-stained wretches owe a deep debt of gratitude today. Their road still is not easy. It is not filled with glamour, whatever Hollywood dreams up. A sound journalism education, in which specialized backgrounds in home economics or fine arts or economics must have a place, is the starting point. Talent and good fortune and hard routine work all play their part. But the door was opened by the sisterhood of Dorothy Dix and Jenny June.

To have a specialty, based on specialized training, is the consensus of informed advice to the would-be woman journalist. From the pioneering of a few brave feminists, women have advanced, through skill backgrounded on ability, to a respected place in journalism.

CHAPTER XVII

COVERING THE BUSINESS BEAT

The world of business is not simply made up of machines and merchandise, of counting houses and factories. It is the expression of, indeed the very means of existence for, civilization.—JULIUS KLEIN.*

WHAT IS THE BUSINESS BEAT?

Whether in big city or small town, the business beat means the coverage of stores, industrial and wholesale concerns, trading in commodities and other goods, the personalities and activities of all the millions of human beings who work for a living. The business beat covers everything from whether Charlie Brown, operator of the men's shoeshop, has a new clerk to the purchase by the Northern Pacific of twenty new giant Diesel locomotives.

Men and women are vitally absorbed in the job of making a living. Business news means coverage of the organized aspects of that job; it's the story of how people go about earning their bread and butter. Nevertheless, for all its practicality and materialistic aspects, it is packed with the thrill and emotion of the daily struggle for existence.

The Reporter Covers Local Business, Retail. All business is local, the advertising bureaus and agencies tell us; all business is local because sales and purchases are made in the home-town market. And the local nature of all business becomes particularly evident when one realizes that the largest manufacturer still depends upon ultimate retail sales to the individual consumer. While many a metropolitan newspaper has realized the importance of business news for many years, all too often smaller dailies and weeklies have passed up their best bet in this field. They have neglected the small local retail merchant, not realizing that his activities make news, and important news, for the community. While they have tried to dredge him for advertising dollars, they haven't realized that he also was a legitimate news source. The Depression helped to change some of this. It focused the eyes of newspaper editors for the first time on the important aspects of workaday living, getting and keeping a job. It made them realize that business in their own little community was vital front-page news. Unemployment and business failures forced them into giving headlines to business news.

---

* From *Whither Mankind,* edited by Charles A. Beard, p. 84. Copyright 1928. Used by permission of the publishers, Longmans, Green & Co.

The hardware store, the women's specialty shop, the small factory handling local commodities, these are important to the community in which they exist and also have a bearing upon the growth of the state or entire region.

The Reporter Covers Local Business, Wholesale. The possibilities of local business news are not exhausted with the retail shop or store. Moving into larger units of operation, the local wholesale organization is important. It may distribute drugs; it may be the center of a regional chain of independent grocers. In any case, its activities not only contribute in an important way to the success of the community in which it is located but also influence the entire county or trade area.

From the wholesale house, a reporter gets news not only of his own home town but also of surrounding communities which make up the circulation territory of his newspaper. He is able to watch the business temperature and health of his whole area. As wholesale activities go up or down, he can follow the growth or decline of local trading areas and can observe the maturing of infant industries. Through the wholesale house again, he can see the industrial affiliations of his own community with larger industrial centers throughout the nation. While all business is local, the local wholesale business is an important ganglion in the nerve network of business which stretches beyond the home town.

Relationships With Labor Must Not Be Overlooked. Careful and accurate coverage of labor news often will demand the complete attention of several reporters on a large metropolitan paper. However, in the small town, it is generally feasible and necessary for the same individual to cover both business and labor news. The activities of these two major aspects of our society are so closely interrelated that they naturally fall into the province of one reporter.

But however the actual news coverage may be handled, the business reporter must keep closely in touch with developments on the labor front. Inescapably, union activity affects the business in which the union operates. A wave of strikes means business loss and failure. A shortsighted employer may harm not only his own business but under some circumstances the lives and welfare of his workers and many others in the community. Therefore, the business reporter must follow news of the labor beat also, even if he does not have the actual responsibility of writing the stories. In order to cover his business beat properly, he must know economics, and political science, and sociology. Certainly, he cannot be ignorant of the fundamental history and principles of management-labor relationships.

Local Or Regional Industries Generate News. The reporter on the business beat always should be conscious of the fact that certain local or regional business activities often dominate or have tremendous influence upon the life of his community and the surrounding areas. It may be the raising of sugar beets, or it may be a lumbering or mining activity. Perhaps it's the making of men's hats or the growing of cotton, or the dairy industry. Whatever the local situation, this absorption in one or two or even three main industrial or agricultural activities means that all other life in the community or the area is closely connected with the dominant business activity. The reporter must be able to see and appreciate these ramifications; it is his job to tie them together to make meaning. An alert reporter will have no real difficulty.

Commodity And Stock Markets Create News. In many American cities and towns there are commodity markets which are closely connected with the life of the region. The commodity may be tobacco in Lexington or cotton in New Orleans or metals in Spokane.

The activities, the sales, the purchases, the daily transactions on these commodity markets are vital and fundamental business news. They demand daily coverage which is accurate and complete. In all of America's major cities, but especially in New York and Chicago, commodity and stock markets are a major part of the business picture.

Too often the markets have monopolized coverage of the business beat. What Wall Street does, what happens on the grain exchange in Chicago, these events may shape the destinies of an entire continent—and did, back in the Depression days of the 1930's. Actually, the Depression was probably more responsible than any other circumstance for the development of business news as vital front-page stories and a regular beat for coverage. For the first time, editors became conscious of the news possibilities inherent in this bread-and-butter activity of all men. They began to cover it thoroughly and have kept on doing so.

Although the market pages of metropolitan papers are filled with columns of information (quotations, figures) about the various commodities and stock markets, even smaller dailies will often carry quotations pertaining to their own communities. Press associations and private wires carry market quotations all over the country and they are a regular part of many newspapers.

THE SOURCES OF BUSINESS NEWS ARE MANIFOLD

The cub reporter, assigned to the business beat, may be completely bewildered. What kind of news is he expected to get and where? How does he go about finding out what has happened in this store or to that industrial leader? Where and what are the sources of the news that he is expected to get?

The Retail Store Has Many Potentialities. Every man and woman has occasion to visit retail stores almost daily in his life and yet the business activities on the retail level have been grossly neglected by too many papers. Although much of business news has not been intelligently handled and reporters have missed the human interest and drama, there is no need for this. It has taken *Fortune* magazine to show how vital and absorbing business coverage can be. Labor news was kicked around badly for years and still is, at the retail level.

Where, at the retail level, does the reporter look for his stories? The answer is simple—in the retail store, from its owner, the salesman behind the counter, its customers. What elements of story-interest may there be to the reporter and the reader? To name a few: changes in working hours, wages, conditions; expansion, changes, and alterations in the physical plant; expansions in service or lines of products carried by the store; changes in price, especially when they are part of an important local or national trend; personal items, emphasizing names, about the store clerks, the department managers, the owner; trips taken by store executives and their buying excursions; promotions and changes in personnel. All of these mark but a few of the possibilities for story coverage on the retail avenue.

The Wholesale Company Is An Important Source. While every news angle mentioned in regard to the retail store can also apply to the wholesale company, a number of other developments and news possibilities come into the picture. New processes, research, new machines and inventions—all of these may become part of the wholesale picture; as has been suggested, the relationships of retail units in the community, the region, with the wholesaler are all grist for the reporter's mill. The relationship of the wholesaler with the manufacturer or large distributor often should be followed. Through the wholesale establishment, the reporter is able to keep in touch with important local industries on the manufacturing level or with major commodity producers. The wholesaler can give him the over-all picture. In the wholesaling house, the reporter should be in contact not only with the president and top executives but also with department heads throughout the plant. To do this, he must familiarize himself with the operation and with the lines or products with which it is dealing.

The Chamber Of Commerce And Other Trade Associations Develop News. Business news often originates in the offices of business associations and trade organizations. These may include the chamber of commerce, the real-estate board, the better business bureau, the credit associations, and all the multitude of luncheon and service clubs, such as Rotary, Kiwanis, and Lions. At the meetings of these organizations, the reporter is brought into close association with business leaders in the community, programs which they are planning, and business trends and developments. In the luncheon get-togethers he has an opportunity to participate with them in more informal moments and to get to know them as individuals apart from their offices.

The Transactions Of Banks, Real-Estate Firms, And Transportation Lines Are News. Three main business activities in every community serve as sources of business news for many other lines of business activities. These are the real-estate agencies, the banks, and the transportation lines.

From the real-estate agent, the reporter has an opportunity to find out about sales of business property in the community and of residential property. He gets details on real estate involved, new uses to which it is being put. He finds out about new construction, new buildings, new residences, periodic reports on building and real-estate activities. Thus he often gets a hint of new businesses coming and of expansion in old ones. Much of this news may be legitimately worked up into a real-estate page, which may serve a merchandising co-operation function and offer the paper an opportunity to secure new advertising accounts. Merchandising pages of this kind may be utilized not only in connection with real estate but with almost any other business activity of the community. In construction, in transportation, in wholesaling, in food merchandising, the business reporter and his paper have a chance to capitalize in a perfectly legitimate way on the advertising and news interest of the business beat.

From the bank and the banker, the reporter not only has a full opportunity to cover banking news such as annual meetings and reports, monthly statements, the growth of assets, nature of investments, amount and character of loans, the ratio of loans and discounts to deposits, co-operation of banks with government agencies such as F.D.I.C., but also, as he gets to know the banker closely, he may obtain and investigate valuable tips on business developments within the community.

From the offices of transportation lines, such as the railroads and airlines, the reporter is kept in close touch with the comings and goings of businessmen and business products. From their reports on car loadings and freight movements, he has a chance to follow the business and industrial activity of his region. Often they can tip him off about the visits of important business leaders or industrial figures to his community. The transportation lines afford him an index to the business health of his town.

The City Hall, The County Courthouse, The State And Federal Agencies Must Be Covered. The city hall is the clearinghouse for a variety of business activities. From the registrar of deeds comes information on the sales or transfers of property. The city treasurer has the tax rolls, records of tax payment, sale of municipal bonds, the financial condition of the local government. Estates and wills are filed in probate court. Other important sources are the referee in bankruptcy, the building inspector, the public-utilities commission, the city engineer, and the board of public works.

From the county courthouse and the county building the business reporter will get other stories which are vital to his business needs. From the county treasurer and county assessor comes county-tax and property information. From the county treasurer he gets a great deal of licensing and permit news. In the county agricultural agent, the reporter finds a well of information regarding agricultural developments and their relationships to business and industrial activity. County courts often will be dealing with matters of concern to the business world. Activities of such law-enforcement officials as the sheriff, the prosecuting attorney, and the coroner, may have their relationships to business also.

In practically every town today, there are state and federal offices which again are related to the business of that community. State and federal employment offices, the post office, income-tax bureaus—these and many other governmental activities have a direct effect upon business life. The business reporter must keep on top of all these news sources and be prepared to check them regularly.

The Labor Unions Are Increasingly A Vital Source. As already indicated, the business reporter cannot neglect his labor news and labor sources. He may not have responsibility himself for that beat, but he must keep in touch with labor developments. Otherwise he cannot understand what is going on in the business scene. Local offices of the A.F. of L. and C.I.O., the local headquarters of various unions, the central trades and labor council, these are some of the sources of labor news and labor activity which inevitably affect the business picture also.

The Wire News Should Be Watched. From the teletype ticking off state, national, and international news, the business reporter often may get his cue for stories affecting local businesses or industries. Over the U.P. wire comes a Washington, D.C., account of how Congress has put a new tariff on wool imports. The reporter in Montana or some other wool-growing state knows that this calls for a local follow and local coverage. This is but one example of how wire news may stimulate local business coverage. The smart business reporter will have his telegraph editor primed to keep him informed of such business developments and wire stories.

The Trade Publications Should Be Followed. Practically every business and industry has its own publication or periodical devoted to news and personalities in its particular field. The publications cover changes of ownership, new inventions and developments, alterations, new plants, personal chit-chat about individuals in the business or industry, industry-wide surveys, and a great mass of similar material. From them, the business reporter may get a great many tips on what is to come, may follow the trend of what is happening in the business or industry, may keep in touch with what goes on in other industrial areas beyond his community. The trade publication, ranging from the house organ of a single business to the industry-wide publication covering the entire country, is one of his best sources of background and actual news.

Corporations Supply Copy. Much business news is contributed voluntarily by corporations and individual business firms. This copy is often prepared by a publicity man whose duty it is to place his employers and their point of view before the public. News of this kind, separated and sorted out from the chaff of raw publicity, can give the reporter useful assistance regarding dividends, bonuses, new construction plans, and new equipment.

In the last analysis, the reporter covering the business beat must remember that all of these sources are useful to him but most useful of all is regular and daily coverage of his beat, the business firms in his town, and the businessmen who run those firms.

WRITING BUSINESS NEWS REQUIRES SPECIAL QUALIFICATIONS AND TECHNIQUES

If public confidence in business news is to be maintained, the newspaper must be fair, accurate, and impartial at all times. A test of news value on a business story is whether it has actual news interest for many readers, aside from its purely commercial slant. Consider the rights of the *reader* first, not the interest of the individual business or businessman.

The Business Reporter Needs Background. Any reporter needs a wide knowledge of politics and economics, but the business news writer must be as much if not more of an expert than the political editor. He has to understand laws governing business activities, he must know something of sales management and advertising, the organization and standing of the important industries, and, in addition, must have the vocabulary of business. The commodity-exchange reporter must understand how economics affect that sphere of business. He should have enough commercial geography to know where various items are produced and the situations and conditions which affect their prices. In essence, this means that the business reporter must have an education founded primarily upon economics, history, political science, and sociology. For him to have some training in commerce and allied fields is likewise essential.

On this, as on almost every other beat, a reporter cannot get to know his news contacts too well. The people with whom he deals daily—bankers, clerks, wholesale operators, retail grocers, farmers, and all the other individuals who make up the great world of business—these he must know intimately as friends, and he must know their backgrounds. Names are news in any phase of newspaper work. Friendly relationships mean good news sources also, everywhere. In business news, the reporter's success will be largely based upon his friendly and cordial relationships with the businessmen and business firms with which he is dealing.

Finally, if there is a local commodity or local industry which is preeminent in his community, the business reporter should know the details of that commodity and its production. He needs to be able to talk the language, he should know his way around thoroughly, so that the producer, be he farmer or miner, will regard him as an intimate and also an expert.

Feature Copy Must Be Prepared. Men on the news staff may be recruited by the business reporter to contribute to special sections which may not appear daily, but perhaps once or twice a week when whole pages will be given over to real estate, automobiles, or construction work. The business reporter or editor of course should serve as the director of these pages and supervise the activities of the men writing for them. As has been suggested, such pages also may furnish helpful merchandising co-operation with local merchants. When handled as news, in such a fashion, they are always legitimate, but should avoid the suggestion of free publicity.

Also, under the surface or surrounding the regular news story breaking on the business beat will be a great number of features. These should not be overlooked. The life story of the owner of a dime store may be fascinating. Misadventures of a little boy lost in the department store may make your readers hold their sides with laughter. The very story of what happened to the tree cut down and sawed into house lumber in your own area may be as thrilling as a novel. This feature material is there always for the intelligent and imaginative business reporter.

The Business Column Has Its Place. Not the least valuable contribution which the business reporter can make to the business welfare of his community is his own personal column, in which he discusses the more informal activities and news events in the business community. For this column, he should save the little human-interest story, the careful ventures into legitimate speculation on business developments, the miscellaneous but absorbing by-products of his business beat. Here he may present them with his own individual personality. This business column should form the heart of his business page.

Accuracy Is All Important. The work of the business reporter is of a complicated nature. Most of the copy is segregated into special sections. This makes it easier for businessmen to locate information they seek daily. It also makes it easier for them to find mistakes and errors in business copy.

Furthermore, the reporter must play fairly with his sources and the public. In a labor-management dispute, he must deal equitably with both sides.

The newspaper itself represents a large investment of capital and it cannot afford the antagonism and mistrust of large sections of business over a long period of time. Therefore, the business reporter must be certain that he presents accurately and completely both the background information and the business news which he is covering.

While the newspaper itself is a business enterprise and must protect its own investment, the reporter cannot forget that the newspaper is also a quasi-public utility. It is essential that the newspaper make a strenuous effort to protect the interests of the public while reporting the news of business accurately in the light of the facts.

Check, recheck, verify. Then write cautiously, remembering that drastic revisions of the libel laws forbid the publication of comment which might subject a man or business firm to financial loss or injury.

Forecasts And Comments On Trends Are Danger Zones.   The role of the business prophet is fraught with danger. Be careful of interpretation. When you enter upon predictions and forecasts, you are entering danger zones. Consider the number of prophets who have gone wrong in the past, those who predicted no depression when a depression, indeed, was right around the corner. Forecast and interpretation are always accompanied by accusations of bias. Unless you are indeed an expert, leave prophecy to the expert.

This does not mean, however, that the efficient reporter should not analyze factors in business situations so that he may recognize important news as it develops. Out of the welter of bond quotations, he may detect a consistent public interest in government bonds, even though these are long-term bonds bearing a low interest rate. What effect has this upon the market? The stock exchange is relatively quiet but there is heavy trading in the bond market. Why? Certain clues emerge from tendencies in business activities, heavy industrials, public utilities, investment trusts, the grain and cotton exchanges. These things make the story.

In writing this copy, the reporter must consider the average reader and attempt to make his story comprehensive and understandable. He must give legitimate news of trends and developments.

The Reporter Should Write English, Avoid Routine.   Some business reporters seem to think that the hallmark of the expert is an incomprehensible jargon of mysterious terms. The mark of a good business reporter is his ability to write simple, good English, so that any reader may understand it. Many a businessman or stock buyer may read the business stories, but they are open and available also to any reader of the paper—or they should be. Simple, ordinary, and good English will provide a key for any reader.

While much of business news, particularly that dealing with quotations from various exchanges and markets, is of a regular and daily nature, it should never be allowed to fall into a routine pattern. When the reporter becomes a routine workman he forgets the news possibilities inherent in even the smallest change of the quotation board or ticker tape. He begins to write in routine ways, using the same hackneyed expressions every day. His leads fall into certain routine structures. His habits and ideas alike suffer from the commonplace. The routine has no place on the business page. While regular and daily items recur in much the same form, the business reporter should ever avoid the routine handling of this news.

INDUSTRIAL JOURNALISM SUPPLEMENTS THE BUSINESS BEAT

Industrial journalism is very close to the business beat.[1] This, in itself, is the business which produces periodicals devoted to single industries or trades, or to groups of people having common business or industrial interests. Its aim is to inform as well as to entertain.

In its effort to make a comprehensive coverage of its particular field, the services an individual magazine renders the industry it represents are multiple.

At the present time the industrial press occupies a position of commanding importance in all business activity. Editorial contents often include general information, feature material, technical information, educational material, news and general articles. In short, the industrial publication does more intensively for one industry what the newspaper attempts to do in a limited way for all industry. It has editorial and statistical departments, market reports, digests of current literature, legal opinions, and news items.

One of the services of the industrial press is to further better understanding between industry and the nation; that is, to guard the interests of both the industry and the public at large through legislation, elimination of objectionable advertising, and enlargement of markets. In this, most of these journals work with the daily press. Many of the industrial papers co-operate directly by sending proofs of important articles to the newspapers of more general circulation.

---

[1] For a complete presentation of industrial journalism, see Chapter XXXVII, *Publishing the Business Press.*

CHAPTER XVIII

COVERING THE LABOR RUN

Labor reporting may cross the police beat, the Supreme Court, and the political forum in a single day, so the labor reporter should be nimble-footed, resourceful. But the good labor writer will be more than that. Through fair dealing, he will have the confidence of both sides in the continuing labor-management relationships he chronicles. He will be able to screen facts from propaganda, without making it an issue. The job is tedious; it is often exciting; it is always important.
—HAROLD W. WARD.*

LABOR'S PUBLIC RELATIONS NEED A BETTER PROGRAM

Labor leaders themselves have bemoaned the lack of good public relations for labor. This has been due to many factors: labor's own lack of an informational program, adverse publicity from other interested sources, failure by the newspaper and reporter to comprehend properly the necessity for expert reporting of labor news, and a false concept that news is only the sensational and dramatic. Some American newspapers and some labor unions today are taking steps to meet these difficulties.

The Importance Of Labor Must Be Recognized. Approximately 60,000,000 Americans work for a living, according to figures of the Department of Labor. About 15,000,000 of these are organized in labor unions, the A.F. of L. or the C.I.O. or independent organizations. Our civilization is primarily industrial; it depends upon the joint and mutual co-operation of labor and management in serving the ultimate consumer. As workers ourselves, we are vitally concerned in the welfare and activities of other workers. As potential employers, we recognize the vital relationship between capital and labor. Labor is important. Front-page stories throughout the nation testify to its importance as news. Therefore, newspaper men and women are concerned with its program of public relations, the coverage of the labor run, and the extent and influence of the labor press.

How May Labor's Public Relations Be Improved? Many a union leader and many an experienced, responsible man would state vigorously his opinion that something is very wrong with labor's program of public relations. Professional publicists often agree. Different causes are assigned,

* Written expressly for this book by Harold W. Ward, Associated Press, Washington, D.C.

however, in these opinions. In some quarters it is charged that unfair reporting by the newspapers, radio, and general magazines is, to some extent, responsible. Others ask, with some degree of justice, whether management has done any better job in presenting its viewpoint. Sociologists may say that in any state of upheaval and always in areas of conflict or controversy, there will be disagreement rather than a totally favorable reaction to a public relations program. Some union men will blame themselves and their unions for faulty and inept public relations. Whatever the cause, there seems to be general agreement that something needs to be done.

From the standpoint of the journalist, a few things could be done to improve the program of public relations for labor. The most important would be the establishment of a daily information service by every union organization—local, state, or national. Through the following steps progress could be made:

1. By educating the worker regarding the labor movement and the values of proper relations with the general public.
2. By appointing union members to specialize in and handle publicity and news.
3. By establishing men in regular bureaus on a state and national scale, both for individual unions and major associations.
4. By making use of the services of large advertising and public relations firms.

LABOR IS NEWS

News of labor commands front-page headlines, but often overlooks the daily commonplaces of the worker's life such as his picnics and his family activities. A few first-class dailies are recognizing that a labor reporter is an asset to a news organization—especially a labor reporter who has the background of authority and can write as an expert.

Front-Page Labor Stories Require Expert Handling. The reader is accustomed today to the sensational front-page story about labor which plays up strikes and industrial disputes which have reached the stage of violence. Congressional action regarding labor's activities, relations of labor to victory during war, or to prosperity during peace, have been prominently reported. When labor-management relations reach their crucial stage and affect great industrial organizations or the economic life of an entire region, the newspaperman has to play this news on the front page. It is front-page news and belongs there. As such, there is one important caution for the reporter and the make-up editor to keep always in mind—be fair. Present both sides—it means that you have to have statements or news from both sides. Be sure that your head and the lead upon which it is based present the news accurately and without taking sides.

Labor news is front-page, often; when it attains front-page prominence, its presentation needs to be in the hands of experts.

Labor Stories Should Get Regular Daily Coverage. A few years ago, a reporter who devoted his entire time to covering news of labor was an oddity on the staff of even the largest daily papers. One of the pioneers in this field, the *New York Times,* put Louis Stark to work as a labor reporter, covering labor news and industrial events on the labor run. This precedent, one of many moves by farsighted newspaper editors toward expert, specialized reporting, has been followed by a number of other papers, although chiefly in metropolitan areas. The *Editor and Publisher Yearbook* for 1947 listed a hundred and forty-six labor editors on different papers in the United States, although many of these are not on a full-time basis. That still means, however, that practically eight out of every nine American papers are without a labor editor or specialized labor reporter. Partly because of this fact, partly because of unthinking tradition on the city desk, labor news to many papers means the front-page, sensational variety which breaks after trouble has arisen in our society.

The important kind of labor news, many editors believe today, is the news which treats of labor as the business page might handle the activities of business. When John Luigi gets promoted to assistant foreman, a little note about that gets into the labor page or the labor section of the paper. When the United Boilerworkers Union goes on its annual picnic, that gets coverage by the labor reporter. When the union co-operates with management of the company in setting up a program of mutual co-operation and progress in promoting more profits for both management and labor, that gets into the paper.

When more newspapers are doing this kind of job of covering the labor run, the readers will be better pleased and better informed, labor itself will respond, and all elements in our society will benefit. It's just doing a better professional job of newspapering.

THE LABOR REPORTER SHOULD OBSERVE FUNDAMENTAL PRINCIPLES

Impartiality is the golden rule for the labor reporter. Impartiality depends very largely upon reporting which is accurate. To be accurate, the reporter has to know what he is writing about; that is, he must have a background in sociology and economics. Finally, the reporter needs to be well acquainted, on a personal and human basis, with the labor leaders and labor men with whom he is dealing.

Impartiality Is Vital. This standard has always been of utmost importance.

> Perhaps in no field is the charge of news distortion so often made as in that of industrial controversy. Responsible journalists do not contemptuously dismiss such charges without considera-

tion. They recognize that journalism has no greater task than to give the public all the truth that can be found about conflicting interests underlying class antagonisms. The main hope of better social and economic conditions lies in a well-informed public opinion.[1]

This is a fair and reasonable statement of the labor reporter's problem in covering his field today.

The labor reporter must deal fairly with both sides. Although it is easier, perhaps, to obtain a statement from management, the reporter should never overlook the worker's point of view. Readers are equally interested in the ideas of labor, and it is essential to present the views of this group. It is even more essential to present them impartially and with complete fair play. That is simply good reporting on the American newspaper.

Inasmuch as the activities of unorganized labor are not available readily for news coverage, news about labor is usually news about labor unions. Except during an industrial crisis, labor news receives less publicity than may be justified by the facts. When this is true, it is unfortunate. If there is news value in the disputes between labor and capital, there is also news value in the internal affairs of labor unions, the resolutions passed, officers elected, meetings held, negotiations undertaken, the conferences and conventions.

A Labor Reporter Must Be Accurate. His quotations should be checked and double-checked. His statements in regard to a labor dispute, for example, have to present the points at issue clearly and correctly. Not every "strike" is a strike. Not all "lockouts" are lockouts. To find the kernel of truth in this shell game demands unerring skill and untiring persistence. The labor reporter has to do it. This often means that he must know price changes and wage formulas. It means that he has to see and get both sides. It means a devotion to accuracy and a constant search for the facts which may reveal the truth.

What Does The Reporter Need To Know? In school, the embryonic reporter had better get acquainted with economics and sociology, especially those phases of the subjects dealing with labor. Certainly, he ought to know something about history and political science. If he takes some courses in the department of commerce or school of business administration, all to the good. He ought to know something about distribution and its methods, marketing, industrial production, problems of management, the sources of commodities and the operation of exchanges which deal in those commodities, transportation lines and rates. While he can't get all this in college, packed in with the other things he needs in his journalism

---

[1] From *The Conscience of the Newspaper* by L. N. Flint, p. 61. Copyright 1925. Used by permission of the publishers, D. Appleton-Century Co.

training and general education, he should build himself into an encyclopedia on these and allied subjects before he is ready to tackle labor reporting. Certainly he should know all he can about the history of labor, the development of labor organizations, unionism, the labor picture in other countries, and state and federal legislation on the subject. This knowledge of his will extend to such matters as the very definite and technical differences between mediation and arbitration. It will cover the labor universe in all its aspects. The labor reporter must know the answers.

The Reporter Ought To Know Labor Leaders And The Rank And File. In some towns, covering the labor run can be a pleasant as well as a paying job. Cordially welcome, the reporter is a regular visitor at meetings at the union hall or labor temple. Union leaders are counted as his personal friends as well as business acquaintances. In other places, the reporter too often may feel that he is working ever among suspicious and sometimes hostile news sources. That, it's easy to realize, complicates the job of getting the news and further complicates the job of presenting it impartially. It's an old story that cultivation of news sources pays off in news stories. This is just as true on the labor run where knowing Joe, the union business agent, as a fellow fisherman may well help out on the daily run of visiting his office. Friendly visits, with time out for a little human touch, make life pleasanter and turn a chore into a daily adventure.

It's not enough to confine one's acquaintance on the labor run to the labor leaders. Don't forget that the rank and file exist and that much of your daily coverage should concern their activities and their lives. It's as important to find out how Harry feels as he operates on that power lathe as it is to spend time with George, the union secretary. The rank and file may not be running the union at the top but they and their views eventually get attention. They deserve their full share of daily coverage and the wise reporter knows the worker as well as his story.

LABOR NEWS IS OF VARIOUS TYPES

There are at least six main types of labor news which the labor reporter should figure on covering regularly or occasionally. These are: daily and regular stories, a weekly labor column, local follows on press association stories, articles, labor features, coverage on labor-management controversies.

It's The Daily Coverage On The Labor Run Which Counts Most. Far from concentrating only on the sporadic outbreaks of industrial warfare or disputes which crop up in labor-management relations, the labor reporter should concentrate on such events as meetings of labor unions, meetings of central trades councils, social activities such as picnics and benefits, activities of the women's auxiliaries of labor organizations, news about individual rank-and-file members as well as the officers of the union, trips made by union members on their vacations or on business, births of babies, marriages, deaths. In other words, handle the labor run as a regular news run.

Most important of all, remember that news that is worth while for the community, beneficial to the progress and development of labor-management relations and industrial and economic peace, is of prime importance to the labor reporter. It is this type of constructive coverage on the labor beat which will pay off in the long run, not only for the paper but for the whole community.

The Labor Reporter May Develop A Regular Column.   Once a week, or more often, the labor reporter will do well to supply his paper with a column of labor news which will emphasize the human side of the labor run or its more informal aspects. This column should contain such materials as will not be suited to news stories or news items. The labor reporter may exercise some opportunities for injecting his own personality, even his own ideas and opinions, to a limited extent, in the paragraphs of such a column. In it, he may draw his conclusions as to labor developments and relate them to other aspects of the city's life.

Local Follows On Press-Association Stories Should Not Be Overlooked.   The wide-awake labor reporter who is on his toes often will see in press-association stories, dealing with the state, regional, or national scene, an opportunity to write local follows emphasizing the local angle, or developments from such news-service accounts. Such follow-stories, which may deal with a local shoe factory and its labor market in relation to rising prices of leather or with similar local situations relating to the broader national picture, afford a fine opportunity to capitalize on the reader's interest in his town.

Press association stories often will be roundups dealing with employment conditions, changing prices, manufacturing developments, commodity production, or industrial disputes. They should be accompanied by local stories calling attention to local conditions. The labor reporter will get comments from local labor leaders, rank-and-file workers, business officials, chamber of commerce officers, and ordinary citizens who may be affected. This ability to stress local follows often will depend upon careful co-operation between the telegraph editor of his paper and the labor reporter himself. They localize the wire copy and bring it down to earth in his town.

Interpretative Articles May Be Produced.   In interpretative articles, his regular column, or special feature stories, the reporter who has background and knowledge of labor activities often can do a service by analyzing trends as they develop. In the complicated industrial and economic world of today, the labor reporter has the duty of careful, accurate, and unbiased interpretation to make the news intelligible for his readers. In analyzing trends, he is not playing the part of a prophet but rather that of a research expert who takes the known facts and draws certain logical conclusions from them. When a labor story deals with complicated problems of contract adjustments, prices, and formulas of wage increases, the reporter can perform a real service in such interpretation and analysis. Always remembering his duty to all readers, no matter what their economic position or occupational status, he attempts to follow the daily scene and interpret it in the light of the past and to draw certain valid conclusions as to the future.

Labor Features Offer Opportunity To The Reporter.　Features dealing with labor activities in his city offer a more lively and even more informative picture of the community. The labor reporter will do his part to furnish such feature coverage for his paper. It may be a story dealing with the father-and-son combination who have worked fifty years in the same plant. The feature may concern the long-standing and amiable relations between employees and employers in a factory. Or the labor reporter may write about the manufacturing process, in terms of the human element engaged in it. In any case, a feature story from the labor run will offer both information and entertainment for the casual reader. To be effective, it often should be accompanied by good photographs taken in local plants or businesses. Such feature coverage, if skillfully handled, can gain the good-will of news sources among labor and management both.

Labor-Management Controversies Call For Skillful Reporting.　While there has been criticism of newspapers on the charge of biased coverage of labor disputes with management, such criticism may be avoided by the labor reporter if he keeps industrial conflict in its proper setting. It should not be played up in the vocabulary and terminology of military war. While the newspaper itself is a capitalistic enterprise, with decided interests of its own in labor activities, many newspapers have dealt equitably and amiably for years with their own employees who are union members. Reporters should examine the facts carefully in labor disputes and avoid sensationalism. While strikes may be called by unions, lockouts also may be declared by employers. Before the term "strike" or "lockout" is used the reporter must be certain of his facts.

Violence is not always union-induced; unwise police officials or quick-tempered business executives may produce unfortunate results also. While news of this type has to be covered and often gets front-page play, the labor reporter will be certain to see that there is a fair presentation of both sides, that the issues are presented from both the union and the management points of view, and that he does not stir up more trouble himself by inept handling which pours oil on already present fires. The editor of the newspaper does well to express his interest in the welfare of the entire community rather than in the personal desires of any single minority group. If the labor reporter, when confronted with labor-

management controversy, keeps his head and remembers his whole duty
as a reporter, he will be doing his job.

THE LABOR PRESS OFFERS JOURNALISTIC OPPORTUNITY

Weekly, monthly, and even daily union publications and newspapers
are found in every section of the United States. A growing and important
phase of journalism is manifest in the labor press. The problems and
policies of the labor press, its professional activities in journalism, and its
extent are matters with which every labor reporter should be familiar.

In a survey by *Fortune* magazine,[1] it was stated that the United States
labor press comprised 928 publications. These ranged from official national organs, "charged with promoting the policies set by the unions'
national conventions and top executive boards," to small weeklies which
sometimes are published by local unions only for local circulation. The
national labor papers, such as the *C.I.O. News,* the *American Federation-
ist,* the *U.M.W. Journal, Labor,* and others often are circulated to the
entire national membership of the union. Others may have state circulation of several thousand, or may drop down to comparatively small circulation ranges of a few hundred.

Today, it is clear that labor as well as business has its own important
papers and offers its own editorial interpretation of events for the workingman. The labor press, therefore, may not be ignored in any chapter
dealing with the reporting of labor news.

Labor leaders themselves have deplored the fact that many people working on the labor press have not had journalistic training and therefore are
handicapped. Without such training in reporting or editing, the worker
on the labor press often has failed to present labor's point of view effectively. There are a real field and a real opportunity for service to not only
labor but our entire economic life, in better-trained professional journalists who assume positions on labor papers.

What the future holds for the labor press in America depends of course
on the future of labor itself. As unions grow and expand in strength and
wisdom, the labor press also may expand and develop. If labor experiences
declining fortunes, its ability to support a press of its own will suffer accordingly. With better-trained staff members, wider and less partisan out-
look upon its functions, and more complete coverage of its own labor
area, the labor press can give a service to labor and the whole community.

---

[1] September, 1944.

CHAPTER XIX

THE MARCH OF SCIENCE AS NEWS

*Science owes its effective ministry as much to the interpretative mind as to the creative mind.—GLENN FRANK.**

SCIENCE KNOWS NO BOUNDARIES

The interest in science is so universal that scientific news, whatever its origin, is used by the press of all countries and is relayed throughout the world provided it be so written that the layman can appreciate and understand it. For example, nuclear fission, with its unlimited uses, has focused unprecedented attention upon all natural and physical sciences.

The World's Wires Carry Science Stories. While pure science can be understood by but a few, applied science telling of discoveries, inventions, or applications that may change man's life and work is of as much interest in Australia as in New York. Such spot news is put on the wires of the great press associations or individual newspapers and carried to all corners of the earth. From lone and hitherto unknown research workers, from the floors of convention halls where scientists meet, from the laboratories of big industrial concerns, from the fields, the chemical plants, and the factories come announcements that surprise and interest the world because of their general application to all men. These spot news stories necessarily are brief and carry only the main facts as written by general reporters who leave the more detailed and interpretative accounts to general and technical magazines and professional journals.

Prior to World War I, the seriously-treated science story in the daily press was a rarity. Just as that conflict gave impetus to research and development, it also accelerated the development of science writing. People heard about poison gas, long-range guns, and dirigibles; they wanted to know more about them—their effectiveness, limitations, and how they came into being. The "Sunday-supplement" type of exposition, straining for the spectacular and sensational, based upon science—real and fancied—became popular. It was not until the middle 1930's that sound, accurate science stories in the press, without sacrifice of popular-interest values, became general.[1]

---

* Formerly president of the University of Wisconsin.

[1] Concurrently, there was a wave of progress in medicine and biochemistry— examples: sulfa drugs, photofluorography for speedy and economical X-raying of the

World War II found many of the nation's leading dailies, as well as the wire services, staffed with men and women fitted by training and experience to meet the demand of a more discriminating public for good science stories. This trend has continued in both the general and the specialized press.

Various Media Carry The News. Magazines, trade journals, house organs, the radio, and the newsreels, as well as the metropolitan and non-metropolitan press, have been alert in recognizing the reader-, listener-, and audience-interest in this type of material. Peacetime as well as wartime applications of scientific research are presented in all of these journalistic media.[1]

What the busy wires cannot carry is printed in the magazines as follow-up accounts which give the background, color, and significance of the news already published in the daily press. Here trained writers who are specialists in the handling of science news report accurately and interestingly to the laymen, industrialists, businessmen, housewives, and others who know the value of science.

Demand Continues To Increase. More science stories, photos, and articles are appearing in the public press than at any other time in history. The demand for qualified science writers exceeds the supply. No longer is their product generally regarded as "filler." Even so, the feeling persists in some conservative papers that the buyer of a five-cent daily simply is incapable of comprehending a description, say, of a solar eclipse. Furthermore, it is true that some newspapers still consider science writing a sideline, assignable to some reporter who has some spare time and a flair for writing the rare and unusual. In general, however, a notable advance has been made in recognition by the American press of the public's interest in dependable and accurate, yet simply written, accounts of happenings in the world of science.

SCIENCE NEWS SATISFIES MANY INTERESTS

Science news is of many kinds and is of interest to all classes of readers as it ranges from the romantic to the extremely technical and philosophical.

Tales Of Adventure Make News. The daring of such adventurers as Roy Chapman Andrews, who explored the Gobi desert, and William Beebe, who studied the flora and fauna at the bottom of the seas, has brought the elements of personality and romance into science accounts

---

chest, immunization against tetanus, and, later, penicillin and streptomycin. The result was to expand the size of the reading public for explanatory stories that were simple yet possessed the unmistakable ring of dependability.

[1] All media of education and information today are aware of the public interest in cooking by radar and in vaccines that give protection against influenza and plague, as well as in the sonic airplane and the guided missile.

and has thus dramatized in narrative form what otherwise might have been dull reading.

Prophecies Of Progress Make News. What the scientist finds in his laboratory is appraised on the editorial page where a reflective writer prophesies as to its worth to the human race. The editorial appraises by (1) measuring, (2) weighing, and (3) predicting on the basis of somewhat similar past scientific findings and the present industrial and commercial civilization.

When news breaks of such scientific discoveries as atomic energy, safety glass, and television progress, it occasions further news. Alert reporters interview other scientists, business and financial leaders, and heads of allied industries to see what the discoveries may mean in the progress of industry and finance. The stories are based on opinions and guesses but are scarcely appraisals, for they follow too closely after the original event.

Lure Of The Unknown And Mysterious Makes News. Universal wonder concerning life on the planets and inaccessible parts of the earth causes avid reading of anything outside the commonplace. Semipopular stories tell of Byrd's experiences in Antarctica, the flight into the stratosphere, life on Mars and the moon, the eclipse of the sun, Halley's comet. What astronomers and explorers found and what they believe about the unknown is related in the newspapers and magazines.

The Urge For Riches Makes News. Revolutions in industry and finance are almost daily recorded in science stories telling of new discoveries and inventions. When scientists working individually or in the employ of big commercial laboratories discovered the formula for rayon and invented the zipper, million-dollar industries arose while others went into eclipse.

The Wish For Change Makes News. Because of man's eternal restlessness he reads with pleasure any news telling that science has found another way to change man's way of living. Through news stories science has taught the readers unique ways to spend idle time, novel methods of entertaining, and easier ways to work. Science cures man's dread of monotony.

The Appeal Of Philosophies And Isms Makes News. To each decade come its philosophies or its favorite isms, which are recorded in the daily press and in special and esoteric publications. In such accounts there are explained the theories of such cults as Theosophism, nudism, and spiritualism. As no cult is without its leader, these stories are usually built around personalities such as Father Divine, the modern exponent of a "primitive" cult.

The Wish To Live Makes News. Man's natural wish to prolong his life results in avid reading of stories predicting a longer expectancy in the life span and explaining the methods and discoveries which make

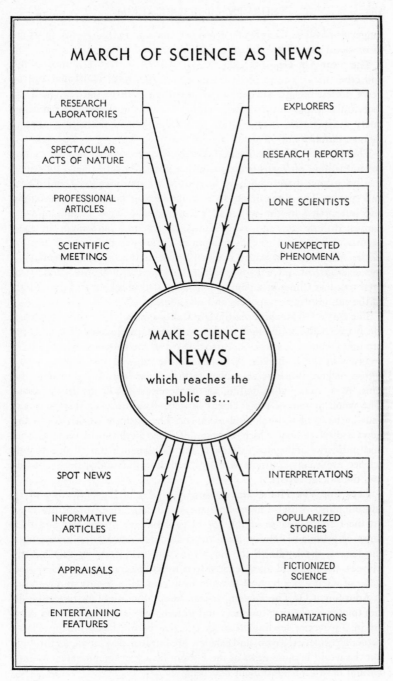

MARCH OF SCIENCE AS NEWS

RESEARCH LABORATORIES

SPECTACULAR ACTS OF NATURE

PROFESSIONAL ARTICLES

SCIENTIFIC MEETINGS

EXPLORERS

RESEARCH REPORTS

LONE SCIENTISTS

UNEXPECTED PHENOMENA

MAKE SCIENCE
NEWS
which reaches the
public as...

SPOT NEWS

INFORMATIVE ARTICLES

APPRAISALS

ENTERTAINING FEATURES

INTERPRETATIONS

POPULARIZED STORIES

FICTIONIZED SCIENCE

DRAMATIZATIONS

longevity possible. Each reader has a personal and selfish interest in stories of oxygen tents, ultraviolet ray, sun-bathing, and food preservation.

The Fear Of Death Makes News. Cures for cancer, tuberculosis, and other major causes of death are among the most widely read of all news stories, because such news is important both to the mass and the individual. Important also are scientific accounts of preventive medicine, safety measures in transportation and industry, and decreasing rates of infant mortality and of death in childbirth.

The Mystery Of The Past Makes News. Excavations of ruins and the unearthing of fossils make news that is eagerly read today, for it tells the living how those who have been dead for centuries lived and played and fought. The signs of an ancient age as dug up by the archeologist and interpreted by the writer of science paint a word picture of what happened those eons ago. King Tut-Ankh-Amen, Montezuma, the ruins of ancient Rome, and the civilization of the mound-builders are familiar to the American newspaper reader because of the dramatic accounts of the exploits of adventurous archeologists, Egyptologists, and their brethren. Faint lines of a papyrus are translated into bold and living lines in the columns of newspapers and magazines.

The Strife Of Machine And Man Makes News. Eternal is the struggle between the individual worker and mass production that has been brought about by scientific discoveries and inventions. Thousands of Negroes in the South are disturbed by the news of the invention of a cotton picker. Workers in rubber factories fear loss of employment because of a science story telling of the development of synthetic rubber. The whole system of employment in several industries is thrown out of gear by news of technological advances. The business world sees in this news a displacement which must result in severe losses in some sections and industries and gains in others. The news which started out as pure science eventually finds its way to the business columns, the want ads, and the suicide reports.

Love For The Home Makes News. Stories of the perfecting of air conditioning, of useful home appliances and decorative furnishings interest the readers because of the appeal to their love of comfort and their sense of pride and beauty. Such news accounts interest the homeowner, the tenant, the landlord, the housewife, the manufacturer and his employees, the financial agencies involved in all the transactions. Here, too, news of science has become news of business and of beauty and comfort.

Adornment Of The Person Makes News. Since earliest times the desire to appear pleasing to others and to feel well dressed has caused interest in discoveries leading to more effective personal adornment. Plastic surgery, cosmetics, rayon, and celanese are familiar developments throughout the world because news of these scientific achievements caters to one's natural desire for adornment and beauty.

Preparation For War Makes News.   When nations prepare for war they hold as secret the discoveries of new ways to deal death, but when war comes, and sometimes earlier, the secrets of the chemists and the physicists leak out. When the armistice comes, the lessons that science bequeathed to war are converted into peacetime industrial undertakings.

SCIENCE NEWS HAS DIVERSIFIED APPEAL

As science news satisfies many interests, it appeals to young and old. Everyone who reads is almost certain to be a ready consumer of some kind of science news.

It Appeals To School Children.   From the primary grades upward, youngsters constitute a reading public. What child does not wonder what causes thunder, why grass is green, where the sun goes when it "sets," or why wood petrifies? Science stories go far toward supplementing formal learning processes.

It Attracts "Escapists."   The speculative story, whether it be on evidence that Mars is inhabited or the prospect of 90-minute flights from New York to San Francisco, or whatever, always finds an eager reader in the individual who would get away from the commonplace. Such persons made the books of Jules Verne best sellers—and their number is legion.

It Interests The Housewife, Appreciative Of Labor-Aids.   Cooking with the sun's rays, the perfection of "tarnish-proof" silver, the invention of virtually any sort of gadget for which labor-saving claims are made—write a story about any of these and a sizeable reader-market among the country's millions of housekeepers is assured.

It Provides Solace To The Chronically Ill And Their Kin.   Although tremendous gains have been achieved in prevention, diagnosis, treatment, and control of disease, there still remain scores of infections and pathological conditions whose solutions continue to elude researchers. Sufferers from cancer, epilepsy, heart disease, diabetes, certain nervous disorders, high blood pressure, and arteriosclerosis—the list could go on almost interminably—are insatiable "fans" of the medical science writer. So are the relatives and close friends of these chronically afflicted. Consequently, when a physician reports on his tests of a promising drug or a surgeon discloses that a radical operation has brought improvement in some cases, these people want to know all about it—in language they can comprehend. The competent science reporter is soberly aware of his responsibility to the reader.[1]

It Reaches Scientists Themselves.   Geologists, physicists, and their colleagues are people—they are not strange folk. As people they are interested in news of all types; as scientists they are interested in all stories

---

[1] He will not "pipe up" his story in a manner that will generate false hopes, only to be followed ultimately by a cruel letdown.

that purport to interpret science and its developments to the lay reader. A rich find of dinosaur tracks in Colorado interests not only the paleontologist but the botanist and astronomer. All men of science have a common passion—the search for truth. They possess inquisitiveness. Science stories, in proportion to their substance and presentation appeal, exercise influence and serve to inform the scientist upon occasion even in his own field. During World War II, military and naval surgeons kept up with the less technical aspects of professional advances in their distant outposts through articles in popular magazines to a large extent.[1]

It Stimulates The Motiveless Reader. Finally, the science story, again depending upon a happy combination of interesting subject matter and skill of exposition, will attract the casual reader exactly as any good news story or feature will claim his attention. News stories sell themselves on their intrinsic merits—police stories, political stories, humorous features, and science stories all alike. Give any of them a good lead, sustained by an interest-retaining follow-through, and they will not want for readers.

SCIENCE WRITING TAKES MANY FORMS

The forward march of science is so complex that it takes many kinds of writing to introduce and explain it to its many kinds of readers. Science stories may be a stick in length or three columns, heavy or light of vein, of limited or universal appeal, strictly factual or generously interpretative.

It Breaks Forth As News. When any scientific happening is first announced, it usually appears in the form of a straight news story giving the *who, how, what, where, when,* and *why.* As authority is particularly important in a science story, and what that authority invented, said, or discovered has high value, the *what* and *who* are usually given the most emphasis in the first news story. Such first announcements may come from a chance talk with scientists, statements from heads of industrial and commercial laboratories, meetings of scientific associations, dramatic incidents (such as a stratosphere flight or the falling of a meteor), the adventures of explorers, the discoveries of excavators and archeologists, the results of inventor's labors. These first announcements must compete for space with all other spot news of the day and may be found on any news page in the paper. Usually they follow straight news style and are written by reporters not specially trained in the handling of science accounts.

It Informs. What the spot news story has been unable to do, because of lack of space and time, is performed by the follow-up account

---

[1] In some instances, this may have been from necessity rather than choice, since magazines were dispatched from the States by air as a recreational measure for the men, while scientific journals received a low priority for delivery. Yet this does not alter the fact that magazine accounts of the Stader splint, streptomycin treatment of tuberculosis, the Rh factor, etc., carried no little influence.

that is designed to give more adequate information. Here can be given the details concerning the discovery or invention which could not be given in the news story.

It Explains Or Interprets. The trained writer in science performs his finest task when he translates the acts and statements of the scientists to the readers of his journal. He makes his readers aware of the real meaning of vitamin, ohm, and watt. He makes known by interpretation what the scientific mind has done for the human race.

It Appraises. What may be the results of the discovery by scientists or inventors are measured by able newspaper and magazine men. They weigh what has been found and gauge its potentialities in its particular industry or competing ones. They determine as well as possible how the latest progress in science may affect matter and men. Theirs is the work of analysts who are at once scientific and practical. Contrary to the spot news story on science, the articles of appraisal are found on the editorial pages or in the financial and industrial sections, for their immediate interest is not so much for the public as for industrialists and financiers.

It Entertains. If a story is adaptable to light treatment, it may be presented that way. A science story need not be sober and "dignified." The fact that it elicits a few smiles does not mean that its quality is any the less. To the contrary, the knack of amusing while informing is much to be desired. The humorously slanted science article may have value in increasing the vocabulary of its readers and giving sugar-coated knowledge or practical guidance in how to use the lessons bequeathed by the workers in pure and applied science.

One Subject Type Is The Zoological Story. In almost any general circulation publication, two subjects are "sure fire": children and animals. The person who does not care to read about them is the exception. In any city that has a zoo or a park collection of animals, the alert city editor sees to it that this newsbeat is regularly and adequately covered.[1]

Another Is The Natural Phenomenon Story. This may be an event whose coming is known beforehand, such as an eclipse or a meteor shower, or it may be an unpredictable act of nature—a tornado, a serious epidemic, a volcanic eruption, an earthquake or a mysterious blight which deals disaster to marine life in certain areas of the ocean. A dual responsibility to the reader is presented: first, straight coverage of the event itself; second, ample background and interpretative information which will make for a clear, full appreciation of the precipitating incident.[2]

---

[1] When new animals arrive, the reporter will find out their native habitat, any peculiarities of the species and their zoological identification. Of course, he will not call a tiger *Felis tigris* but he may give the subject its scientific label once, for its scientific "color effect" and for the benefit of amateur zoologists.

[2] Let us say that, of a sudden, radio broadcasting and reception become gremlin-infested. The weakened signals and spotty transmission are traced to a sunspot

The Technical Story Is Yet Another Type. The "most important" newspaper stories are not necessarily the most widely read. They may possess real significance but they frequently run second, in number of readers, to the feature about a cat caught in a drainpipe or a child lost in the woods. A parallel exists with respect to science stories. Not infrequently there develops, on the floor of a scientific conference or in a professional journal, or in an interview with a researcher, a story so technical, albeit important, in nature that it cannot be reduced readily to laymen's language without distortion—for example, the discovery of intracellular chemical substances which may hold the key to anomalies in genetics. While this type of story may be popularized to a limited degree, the science writer knows that such a technical piece will not have universal appeal. In such cases, the science writer will do well to write the story as simply and clearly as possible, defining unfamiliar terms, of course, but avoiding carefully any overtone of "writing down" to the reader. The commission of that error will alienate scientists and succeed with few others.

THERE ARE VARIOUS WAYS OF GETTING AND WRITING THE STORY

While the science reporter follows substantially the same journalistic rules as the general-assignment or "beat" men, he carries a number of distinctive responsibilities. In addition to keeping abreast of the current scientific and professional literature, he must develop a talent for assessing —in advance—scientific meetings so that he will know which are worth covering and he must expect to do a large amount of legwork.

Scientific Literature Is Valuable Source. Almost invariably, the news break on a good science story comes with its publication in a technical journal or its delivery at a professional meeting. Exceptions include special announcements by governmental or industrial agencies, testimony of scientists before Congressional committees, and the spot news event, as an atomic bomb test or a demonstration of telemetering from a robot-manned airplane to ground instruments. The science writer will see to it that he receives certain journals regularly and has quick access to others. With the proper initiative and approach, he may arrange to get page proofs or advance clipsheets, permitting him to write his story with more deliberation and less haste. Proper credit to the journal concerned is always given.

flare-up. That story is told: what happened, the immediate results, economic losses, the ascribed cause, etc. Then, either as part of the same story, as a side-bar feature or as a follow-story, the sunspot angle should be explored from a scientific point of view. The reader will be told what sunspots are, something about their known periodicity, how large spots may be seen with the naked eye (through a smoked glass), and so on.

Attendance At Meetings Is Helpful. Ordinarily it is not possible for a science reporter to attend all scientific meetings. Further, not infrequently the smaller meetings are more productive as a source of newsworthy stories than the large ones. Some scientific gatherings have efficiently operated pressrooms, making easier the reporter's task.

Making The Rounds Is Part Of The Job. By establishing contacts with researchers and administrators of scientific enterprises in his city or town, then visiting or telephoning them with regularity, the reporter will not only pick up an occasional good story but also gather background information and keep himself informed of forthcoming meetings. The practice will also increase his chances of scoring beats on such auxiliary topics as laboratory construction, personnel changes, and administrative reforms.

The Writer Has Wide Choice Of Leads. When the science writer sits down to write his story, he is a newspaper reporter. That is to say, this specialist has no magical exemptions, no ready-made clientele which will be tolerant of license taken with good journalistic technique. Conversely, he is bound by no special restrictions. He has a story to tell and to sell, just like the colleague near-by writing about a murder or the one down the hall pounding out a piece on the sales tax. Whether his lead shall be a quotation, an eye-arresting statement, or a conventional *who-when-where* paragraph is for him to decide, just as his judgment largely decides how much space the story deserves. The end product must satisfy his editorial chief and finally the newspaper's reader-groups. However, it is well for the reporter doing "a piece" as a science writer to remember that he must bring the subject matter and the class of reader to whom he is appealing into harmony through his approach or lead.[1]

Checking For Accuracy Is Essential. All reporting should be presented clearly and accurately but science reporting is somewhat more exacting. Therefore the science writer who, for the sake of accuracy, would be relieved if his story were reviewed by the person whom it concerns yet who hesitates to request such aid because it might be construed as solicited censorship can resolve his problem easily. Let him simply explain to the expert that he wishes to make certain that a point or a set of facts has been expressed clearly and accurately. This is not censorship but merely a validation of fact procedure. Most professional persons are glad to co-operate fully and without censorship implications.

SCIENCE WRITERS MUST EVIDENCE UNUSUAL TRAITS

In addition to meeting the qualifications of the general news reporter, the science writer must have a passionate respect for accuracy; possess a

---

[1] Some of the more useful of the news and feature approaches are: The person lead, striking-statement lead, known-to-unknown lead, order-of-importance lead, and chronological lead.

talent for appreciating—and being able to describe understandably—the practical significance of a given set of facts; be ever mindful of the influence for good or for bad which his stories may exert, and be the owner of a healthy curiosity and a high index of suspicion, even in the manner of scientists themselves. Only those who are gifted with such unusual qualities, inherent and acquired, can expect to find pleasure and profit in reporting the march of science.

Accuracy Is Essential. Because science deals so much with living things and because its terms and measurements are exact to fractions and decimal points, the reporter of science must also be specific and accurate. He must know that lives and reputations, successes and failures, are to some extent dependent upon the accuracy with which science is reported to the world. The constant striving is for accuracy, clarity, and interest. And the greatest of these is accuracy.

Enthusiasm Is Important.   Science writing cannot be undertaken halfheartedly. A love and an enthusiasm for the sciences, and the stories they have to tell, are essential. A working knowledge of the various sciences' fundamentals is necessary, and must be gained by education and practical experience. Without this the value of scientific news could hardly be appraised. But one does not have to be a scholar. Possessing the verve and initiative that are needed, the writer soon learns that knowing where to go to obtain technical information is the important thing—not cramming his head with data for possible future use.

Curiosity Is A Vital Factor.   The journalist who continually wants to know the why of things has one of the first essentials of a reporter of science. He does not take things for granted. He is not ashamed to ask questions, questions which on the surface may seem to be naive, even silly. Facts and their meanings are not served upon burnished platters. They have to be dug out.

The Reader's Interests And Limitations Must Be Considered. The writer who knows his readers can effectively translate the developments of science into terms and parallels which a reader of limited technical knowledge can understand and appreciate.

Personality And Character Count. The gatherer of science news must be a respecter of confidences and a patient listener. He is courteous without being obsequious. Gradually he learns the idiosyncracies of leading scientists, how an approach that is successful in drawing out one—as in an interview or press conference—has to be modified when some other scientist is the subject. By the quality of his stories he demonstrates that he knows how to report and interpret facts reliably and without violating the spirit in which they are passed on to him.

CHAPTER XX

POLITICAL AFFAIRS CREATE NEWS

The present-day demand of the masses of our people for a real participation in the affairs of government, the increased size and heterogeneity of today's electorate, the geographic expanse to be covered, the importance of winning the Presidency and even local and state offices have brought about a high degree of organization of political news. The newspaper is the one indispensable medium for gathering and distributing this important type of information.—RALPH D. CASEY.*

LOCAL, NATIONAL, AND INTERNATIONAL POLITICS ARE NEWS

Events at home and abroad and the activities of political leaders and public servants demand skillful reporting by corps of well-trained news writers.

The Public Wants The Facts Behind The News. Economic and political crises have focused the attention of readers on local, national, and international news. Newspaper readers do not want merely to be amused. To be sure, they are not primarily interested in government, economics, politics, and foreign affairs as such; but when hard facts strike their homes, their families, or their pocketbooks, they want to know the bases of newly aroused fears—they want to know what the government should do, can do, and proposes to do.

News Of Public Affairs Allows Readers To Watch Officials. Readers whose lives have been touched by the economic and political currents of their time use the newspaper to keep in touch with what government officials are doing. The newspaper offers the reader the best day-by-day check on his representatives and on foreign leaders whose activities may affect him as closely as those of his local public servants.

Reporting Public Affairs Requires Special Skills. Important news of public affairs is often extremely complex in its make-up. The recent increase in the number of technical agencies of government makes it essential for the press to focus the attention of readers on government units which can no longer be observed and controlled directly by the people. Technical problems of government cannot all be solved by votes. The people can determine only what men should manage the public's house-

* From an address by Professor Ralph D. Casey, chairman of the Department of Journalism, University of Minnesota.

167

keeping. The press, on the other hand, must describe and explain what these agencies are doing and how well they are accomplishing the job. To meet these demands reporters and correspondents are required to know the background of the public's business and to write skillfully—to crystallize clear-cut facts and meanings out of the intricate details of the news.

TRAINED MEN REPORT THE PUBLIC'S BUSINESS

The American press is organized to report systematically the news developed in the various governmental units in this country and in foreign states—that is, newspapers tap the main fountainheads of public affairs in county seats and in state, national, and foreign capitals.

Aside from the reporting of civic projects [1] and of news of municipal government, the press stations experienced reporters at the springs of news in counties, and in the state, the national, and foreign capitals. In each of these fields, the reporter-correspondent is charged with the task of sifting newsworthy stories out of a mass of facts and opinions. To assure the readers a proper understanding of the scene in which he is operating, the reporter also endeavors to look beyond the daily happenings or unexpected occurrences. He reveals the background and meaning of the news by showing a relationship and a continuity in events.

THE COUNTY'S BUSINESS IS NEWS

Readers are aware of public affairs centered in the county because the county, as the traditional administrative division of the state, conducts much of its business directly with the residents.

The County Seat Is A Source For Local And State Business. Counties serve as administrative branches for the state. Together with the cities, the counties serve as centers for supervising elections, enforcing the laws, collecting taxes, keeping records, and administering justice. The reporter stationed in the county courthouse gathers official news close to the immediate lives of the readers. Because of the relations of the state and county with the towns, villages, and school districts, the reporter at the county seat may also keep the public informed of important news concerning these local governmental units.

The Reporter Gathers County News Systematically. Each day he visits the various administrative offices seeking timely news. Although the precise organization of offices for conducting the public's business within the county differs in various states, the departments may be grouped under eight main headings.

FINANCE. The assessment and collection of taxes and the bookkeeping for the county are functions which the press reports regularly.

---

[1] Discussed in Chapter XIII, *The Civic Project Is News.*

PUBLIC WORKS. The building and maintenance of roads, parks, bridges, and public buildings are an important source of news.

ADMINISTRATION OF JUSTICE. Court trials, whether civil or criminal, yield significant and interesting stories.

LAW ENFORCEMENT. The sheriff's office, charged with law enforcement as well as many civil duties, must be watched carefully by the courthouse reporter. The county jail, the offices of the coroner, prosecuting attorney, and various special county investigators provide much news.

PUBLIC RECORDS. Departments for issuing licenses, registering deeds, keeping statistics, recording mortgages, wills, affidavits, and papers in court cases are mines of good news stories.

HEALTH AND WELFARE. Supervision of health, county hospitals, county nurses, and poor relief is a function of county government which is the subject of reports by the press to its readers.

SCHOOLS AND LIBRARIES. Progress and supervision of public education are watched closely.

GENERAL ADMINISTRATION OR GOVERNING BOARD. Rules and policies respecting the public's business are usually developed by a special board, sometimes called the board of commissioners or the board of supervisors. News is sought from it. However, in some states the county manager has taken the place of such a board as the chief administrative or policy-forming official. Where this is true the manager's office is covered with care by the courthouse reporter.

In addition to these primary departments other divisions such as election commissions, county agricultural agents, and veterans' relief bureaus are sources of news in many county courthouses.

The Reporter Scratches Below The Surface. Adequate reports of the public's business and common interests supplement the personal and neighborhood news.

A conscientious study by the press of governmental organization and public welfare has turned up important examples of community service. Competent reporters of the county's business go beyond the obvious task of gathering the news. They examine pay rolls and vouchers, assessment rolls, the methods used by the county for purchasing supplies, the disposition of cases reported to the county attorney's office, and numerous other sources of information. Readers are thereby acquainted with the manner in which the public's business is conducted over a period of time. The newspapers also consider the need for reform. For example, in recent years the press in various parts of the country has served the community by supporting such developments as:

1. Consolidation of county offices.
2. City and county consolidation.
3. County zoning.

The press provides an important community service by giving space to these suggestions and by supporting them if it believes that they will serve the public interest. The leadership of the press in county zoning is a good illustration.[1]

Nonofficial Public Organizations Yield News. Associations or private agencies which have no direct connection with government exert an influence on public affairs which the press must also report intelligently.

POLITICS. Political issues in the county reflect a clash of issues and personalities which the press reports for its readers. Individual politicians, party organizations, and assemblies such as party conventions are important sources of political news.

LABOR, AGRICULTURE, BUSINESS. Whatever affects the workingman, the farmer, and the businessman of the city or county affects the public welfare in general. Whatever is interesting or important to any of these groups is important to the community and to the press. Reporters familiarize themselves with the organizations of these social and economic groups and strive to report their activities objectively.

MISCELLANEOUS ORGANIZATIONS. Recreation and sports, social activities, study and adult education, promotion of patriotism, the interests of war veterans, public morals, and other special interests are assisted by organizations which influence the public and its business and so provide news.

EACH STATE HAS ITS INDIVIDUAL NEWS INTERESTS

The federal organization of the nation sets each state apart as a distinctive news area. Although some news within the state transcends boundary lines, a common news interest confined within state boundaries also exists.

Special Coverage Provides State News. Crises and developments national in scope sometimes alter the extent of power and influence of the state over its citizens, but in normal times the public business of the state is especially close to the average newspaper reader. The great news-gathering agencies recognize this and provide special reports for their clients within each state. However, only the metropolitan papers report the news directly from the state capital; others rely on their press agencies.

---

[1] Promotion of public welfare and prosperity is a desirable aim for counties as well as cities. Consequently, a movement has gained force in recent years, reported and discussed in the press, for zoning the land outside of the cities for agriculture, forestry, and recreation. Some lands are suitable for forests but not for farming; some are adapted to sport and recreation but not to crop cultivation. By restricting the use of lands to purposes for which they are particularly fitted, the county, as well as states, can save settlers many heartaches, can economize by avoiding useless improvements and facilities, can protect land values, and can correct past mistakes made in the utilization of lands.

Regular News Sources Are In The State Capital. The statehouse reporter, like the courthouse man, visits the various offices regularly in his quest for news. Experience teaches him which offices to watch constantly and which need be visited only occasionally. Among the main sources are:

GOVERNOR. The governor's office is a fountainhead for news concerning policies, politics, and items involving the leading personality in state government.

SECRETARY OF STATE. Important records are available in this office such as lists of political candidates filing for office and automobile registration.

ATTORNEY GENERAL. Opinions affecting the state, counties, cities, and towns, and stories regarding court cases involving the state are among the news items sought in this office.

OTHER STATE OFFICERS. Although the organization of government differs somewhat among the states, such officials as the state auditor, comptroller, adjutant general, and state commissioner of education are on the "must" list of the statehouse reporter.

COMMISSIONS AND BOARDS. Most states have important agencies such as the conservation commission, tax commission, banking commission, insurance commission, industrial commission, highway commission, liquor-control commission, pardon board, prison board, and department of agriculture. None of these sources is overlooked.

APPELLATE COURT. Decisions of cases appealed to the highest state court often yield important news articles.

Recognition of the important relations which exist between divisions of the state government and the press is shown by the increasing number of press or information bureaus set up by state officials to act as links between state departments and the press.[1]

The Press Observes The Legislature Closely. When the people's representatives meet in the capitol, the legislative reporter informs the readers of political trends, maneuvers in the legislature, and progress of important legislation. Before the session begins the reporter lays the foundation for the strenuous work which lies before him. By observing party platforms, studying the governor's message, writing letters to legislators, compiling data on new legislators, turning back to newspaper files of other years to observe the usual cycles of news during the session, and discussing prospective legislative activities with state officials, he prepares himself for the rush of activities. When the session has begun, he keeps up his daily personal contacts with session leaders, follows the day-by-day

---

[1] Although the capital correspondent can receive assistance from the state publicity men, he must equip himself to evaluate such news. Official state directories and manuals help. He must, however, be acquainted with political alignments in the state, and with the procedure in the courts, commissions, and legislature, as well as with his paper's policies.

legislative calendar, watches the important committee hearings, collects a file of bills and resolutions, covers party caucuses, keeps in close contact with the governor's office, and watches the progress of proposed legislation.

While the statehouse man is following the people's business in the capital, part-time correspondents scattered over the state contribute political news from their local communities.

The press keeps in touch with special sources of information which it can tap for state news. These sources are analogous to those discussed heretofore in connection with county news.

THE PRESS WATCHES THE PEOPLE'S BUSINESS IN WASHINGTON

Newspapers in democratic countries play an important role in national government. The people must be supplied with adequate information regarding the backgrounds of national policies and activities.

Newspapers Stimulate Interest In Government. Critics assert that one of the greatest difficulties in national politics is to get the thoughtful attention, criticism, and consideration of the citizens. In recent years, however, Americans have learned that actions of the federal government may affect them vitally and directly. Moreover, the accretion of power in Washington and the commanding position of the United States in world affairs has made the capital a prime source of international as well as national news. To meet this demand for news of the federal government and to carry out its responsibility as a mirror of political, social, and economic affairs and a commentator on the national scene, the American press has organized a corps of trained men to report the news from the nation's capital. These are called Washington correspondents.

A Maze Of News Sources Challenges The Correspondent's Skill. Press associations and individual newspapers post correspondents in Washington in an endeavor to cover countless "warehouses of information" which exist in the capital. The total number of Washington correspondents reaches into the hundreds. Only a few examples of the principal news sources can be given here. They include:

THE PRESIDENT. The chief executive stands in the forefront of the administration as a symbol of national government and as an originator of policies and laws. Unlike the heads of many foreign states, the President confers directly at stated meetings with the corps of correspondents in Washington.

CABINET MEMBERS. The executive departments yield news, often in detail, of policies and administrative acts which are of vital interest to newspaper readers. The State Department, for example, maintains a unit which supplies official news through its outposts abroad to the world's press. This activity is an attempt to tell the world the facts about our country. It recognizes also the close relationship today between statecraft and information channels.

CONGRESS. Despite the importance of the President, Congress is still a great force standing between the people of the country and the numerous groups seeking special privileges. It continues to be the seat as well as the symbol of representative government. It is, in fact, the bulwark of democratic government.

The national legislative sessions are attended and reported by trained newspapermen who have facilities for transmitting quickly to their bureaus in Washington, or to their newspapers elsewhere, the news which develops from one minute to another. Little would be known about the people's representatives and their activities if it were not for the systematic manner in which the press reports the news of Washington.

The correspondents do not stop with reports of the Congress in session. They establish close contacts with individuals [1] in both Houses and endeavor to investigate the background of legislative affairs.

OFFICIAL PRESS BUREAUS. The complexity of national government has led to an increase in the number of official publicity officers and bureaus in Washington. The departments of government as well as scores of commissions, boards, and special divisions have established contacts with the press through persons, usually former newspapermen, who furnish correspondents with news of their units. This is sometimes called the "handout system." The extent of governmental activities today makes it almost impossible for the correspondents to gather independently all of the news which is available in government circles. On the other hand, the correspondents need use only that news from the official press bureaus which meets their needs and interests. The correspondents can select, discard, rewrite, use for tips, or sample only occasionally the material contributed by government publicity men.

MISCELLANEOUS OFFICIAL SOURCES. The Supreme Court, the foreign embassies, and the national headquarters of political parties are other important sources of news.

The *Supreme Court,* in which important decisions and interpretations of the nation's laws are made, is a difficult assignment for the reporter. The Court represents, nevertheless, the third or judicial branch of national government, and its activities have always been vastly important to the nation.

The *foreign embassies* are a source of news pertaining to foreign affairs, and in a sense the Washington correspondents who report news of the embassies supplement the work of the foreign correspondents.

The principal *political parties* maintaining headquarters and press bu-

---

[1] Congressmen, who usually do not have the personal responsibility which rests on the chief executive and his departments, generally discuss public affairs freely with the correspondents.

reaus in Washington are news centers immediately preceding and during national elections.

SEMIOFFICIAL AND PRIVATE ORGANIZATIONS. Private and group organizations of every description maintain headquarters in Washington in an effort to guard their interests and to influence government policy. Many of these organizations are heavily endowed with funds to carry on their work. Because of the great influence which many of these agencies exercise, and because of the pressure which they exert on government policies and Congressional legislation, the correspondents attempt to maintain a watchful, ever critical, eye on their activities.

The Press Seeks To Meet Demand For Fair Interpretation. A deluge of facts alone concerning government operations is confusing and often meaningless. Dispatches from Washington, particularly signed articles, attempt to give the readers a pattern of news which they can understand by showing the background and meaning of events. Comments on the editorial page also attempt to interpret important news from the capital.

These methods have failed, in recent years, to supply the demand for clear and concise explanations or the "lowdown" of the events unfolding in Washington. Press associations and correspondents for individual newspapers are attempting to meet this demand by contributing political columns or commentaries on the news. A number of correspondents are now specializing in writing and distributing these "dope" columns to scores of newspapers. Obviously, the reader must follow these columns with a discriminating eye and must evaluate them on the basis of the news dispatches and other sources of facts. The political columnists have, nevertheless, successfully provided clear, brief, crystallized, and intimate word pictures of backstage scenes in Washington.

THE PRESS DIGS DEEPLY INTO FOREIGN NEWS SOURCES

Both World Wars I and II and the postwar periods of each taught the American people and the press that nations are interdependent and that foreign news is important because events in world politics have repercussions which spread into all corners of the world.

Newspapers Supply Most Of The Information On Foreign Affairs. Because the press is one of the few regular sources of information concerning foreign affairs, it carries a heavy load of responsibility as a factor in maintaining understanding among peoples of the world. This responsibility has been increased in recent years because of the unprecedented interest in foreign news arising from a succession of crises which are likely at any time to affect any nation in the world. Readers are aware that a political explosion in Berlin, Moscow, Rome, Tokyo, Athens, or some other foreign capital may affect them as gravely as an important event in their own state or city.

POLITICAL AFFAIRS BECOME
HISTORIC MOMENTS—

From the *Washington Post*, August 15, 1941; the *Washington Evening Star*, December 8, 1941; the *Washington News*, December 8, 1941; and the *Baltimore Sun*, July 9, 1949. Reproduced by courtesy of the publishers.

While it is true that foreign news still is concerned largely with crises, the press has made notable advances in the presentation of week-by-week reports describing and explaining the social, economic, and cultural trends abroad.

The Writer's Style Affects Public Acceptance. The amount of foreign news which appears in the newspapers is determined largely by the editor's estimate of reader-interest. That interest depends on the importance to the reader of the particular event and the style and manner in which it is presented to him. It is generally recognized that the mere significance of a news item does not necessarily cause people to read it. The news must be presented interestingly, understandably, and accurately.

The foreign correspondent is, therefore, confronted with the broad problem of presentation. Ideally, he should be an effective writer, because his style contributes to the force of the appeal made by his dispatches. The attention which the reader gives to foreign reports, the extent to which his interest is stimulated by them, the degree to which he retains an impression of the stories, and the reaction which he, as a citizen, manifests after reading dispatches from abroad are factors which are shaped in part by the writing technique of the correspondent.

Foreign News Services Face Numerous Obstacles.[1] Much of the selection of foreign news for the reader is done at the source. Foreign correspondents are constantly trying to overcome the obstructions which are placed in their way by interested parties. Even the best-equipped and the ablest correspondents carry on a perennial fight with agencies which seek to prevent the dispatch of objective reports. They are also confronted with practical limitations imposed by their employers and by the readers.

Among factors which operate to obstruct and to limit foreign correspondents are:

PROPAGANDA AND CENSORSHIP BUREAUS. Two-thirds of the world is ruled by governments which impose rigid censorships on news. Correspondents in these countries suffer from restrictions and constant attempts to poison their dispatches with propaganda.[1]

SPEED. Despite the complexity of developments in foreign affairs, speed is demanded of the correspondent. The news must be timely and fresh. The reporter often has little time to balance the evidence carefully and to develop continuity in the day-by-day dispatches. Moreover, the center of foreign news shifts constantly from one country and continent to another, thereby breaking the running story of one news event and demanding hastily developed impressions of another.

COST. The cost of transmitting foreign news is very high, and only important dispatches, which are independently gathered, can usually be sent. Press associations and a few of the larger metropolitan newspapers

---

[1] See Chapter XXXIII, *The World's Press Systems.*

WORLD EVENTS CREATE NEWS
EARLY IN WORLD WAR II

From the *Washington Post*, February 13, 1942; March 18, 1942; July 10, 1943; and July 26, 1943. Reproduced by courtesy of the publishers.

which can afford a large budget for gathering foreign news spend hundreds of thousands of dollars annually to meet the demand for news from abroad. The reader, on the other hand, pays only a pittance for the service.

READING HABITS.   After the foreign correspondent's reports have run the gauntlet of editorial policies in the home office and the competition from news of local, state, and national importance, the dispatches must arouse the interest of the reader. The reports must be interestingly written, clearly presented, and tersely developed. This is especially necessary because foreign news is often hastily read.

Foreign News Sources Are Varied.   Foreign correspondents search all avenues open to them for news facts and background information. Among the sources commonly used are:

LOCAL NEWSPAPERS.   The correspondent keeps in touch with fertile sources of information by reading carefully the national press.

LOCAL PRESS SERVICES.   In addition to news supplied by major press associations operating in the countries in which they are stationed, special news services conducted by native reporters are usually available to correspondents in foreign capitals.

OFFICIAL PRESS BUREAUS.   Governments throughout the world maintain bureaus which distribute official statements, arrange for interviews with important officials, and sometimes prepare news articles for distribution to newspapermen. The degree to which these bureaus are helpful to the correspondent differs widely in different countries. Usually, regular conferences for correspondents are also held in government departments and foreign embassies.

POLITICAL ORGANIZATIONS.   Unless factions opposed to the government in power have been completely suppressed, the opposition leaders are sources of information which the correspondent taps in an effort to balance the evidence submitted by officials.

PERSONAL ACQUAINTANCES.   The correspondent builds up connection with officials, foreign diplomats, local residents of his own nationality, and other "tipsters" who are invaluable to him in his efforts to get the news.

PART-TIME CORRESPONDENTS.   Natives, often newspapermen, residing in cities throughout the country, supply the correspondent with tips and news items from their news areas.

Chapter XXI

COLUMNS AND COLUMNISTS

> Ah, ye knights of the pen! May honor be your shield and truth tip
> your lances! Be gentle to all people. Be modest to women. Be tender
> to children. And as for the Ogre Humbug, out sword and at him.
> —William Makepeace Thackeray.

COLUMNS PROVIDE TODAY'S PERSONAL JOURNALISM

Personal journalism of today finds its most extensive expression
through the medium of the column. The production of a column is at
one and the same time both an art and a technique of the writing profession. It is personal journalism at its best for it is responsible journalism in the sense that a columnist always writes as an individual. His by-
line is his trade name and this name is fully as important as the title
which happens to be given to the column he produces. No journalism
has a more personal appeal, a more authoritative influence, or a more
useful contribution to make in disseminating news and views whether
it be to inform, to influence, or to entertain.

There Are A Great Variety Of Columns Today. The words "column"
and "columnist" may be interpreted by different people to mean quite
different things today despite the general categorical classifications which
have been adopted for convenience of description. Some columns do not
really fall into any single class. For example, Dorothy Thompson is often
a news commentator and a political analyst at the same time. Similarly,
though primarily an essayist, Westbrook Pegler also purveys behind-the-
scenes information which amounts to well-documented "gossip." Any
reader is apt to become confused if he tries to "type" today's columnists.

Even so, there is some value in categorical distinctions and those generally recognized are three in number. They are: (1) the personal editorial or essay column; (2) the round-about-town or gossip department;
and (3) the humor column or "colyum." Although the last two are of
significance, it is the first classification which includes the most generally recognized names. This does not mean that they are necessarily
better columnists—though most of them are—but it does indicate the
current taste in personal journalism. Characteristics and examples are:

Personal Editorial Column. The personal editorial or essay column is an opinion column bulwarked by facts the author believes to be

true dealing with topics of the moment or of current interest. Most columnists in this category may be classified as:

1. *News commentators,* such as Leland Stowe, William L. Shirer, Dorothy Thompson, Robert C. Ruark, and Constantine Brown.

2. *Political analysts,* such as Walter Lippmann, Frank R. Kent, Marquis Childs, Thomas L. Stokes, David Lawrence, and Carroll Binder.

3. *Discursive essayists,* such as Samuel Grafton, Frederick C. Othman, Herb Graffis, Westbrook Pegler, Eleanor Roosevelt, Cedric Adams, Billy Rose, E. B. White, Henry McLemore, and Charles E. Tracewell.

4. *Sports writers,* such as Grantland Rice, Joe Williams, Jimmy Cannon, and Lawrence Perry.

5. *Advice commentators,* such as Dorothy Dix, Emily Post, Elizabeth Woodward, Antoinette Donnelly, Angelo Patri, Morris Fishbein, and Herman N. Bundesen.

ROUND-ABOUT-TOWN DEPARTMENT. The round-about-town or gossip department consists of a budget of gossipy items collected by the columnist for their human-interest value and to satisfy the desire of newspaper readers for "behind-the-scenes" glimpses of celebrities. Examples of such columns are those of:

1. Walter Winchell and Alice Hughes, written from New York.

2. Drew Pearson and Hope Ridings Miller, written from Washington.

3. Louella Parsons and Hedda Hopper, written from Hollywood.

HUMOR COLUMN. The humor column or "colyum" is most frequently a melange of editorial paragraphs, epigrams, gags, wisecracks, humorous and sentimental verse, puns, verbal and typographical oddities, vestpocket essays, etc., the product of the "colyum conductor" (columnist) and his "contribs" (contributors). A leading exponent of this type of column is Charles L. Collins, with his "A Line o' Type or Two" in the *Chicago Tribune.*

"Columning" Is Not A New Development. Although all of these types of columns and columnists are looked upon as comparatively recent developments, some variations of them have been found from the earliest days of American journalism. Perhaps the first bid of a columnist for contributions was James Franklin's announcement in the second issue of the *New-England Courant* (1721) that he "earnestly desires his friends may favour him from time to time with some short Piece, Serious, Sarcastick, Ludicrous, or other ways Amusing." When his younger brother Benjamin began writing his "Silence Dogood" letters in the *Courant* and later in his own *Pennsylvania Gazette,* he used many of the methods in vogue among columnists today to get contributions.

John Dickinson's "Letters from a Farmer in Pennsylvania to the Inhabitants of the British Colonies" which appeared in the *Pennsylvania*

Chronicle (1767–68) was in effect a personal editorial column, as were "The Federalist" letters, written by Alexander Hamilton, James Madison, and John Jay under the name of "Publius" in support of the ratification of the Constitution and first printed in the *New York Independent Journal: or General Advertiser* (1787–88).

The first trend toward the humor column was shown in 1795–99 by the department "The Dessert—From the Shop of Messrs. Colon & Spondee, wholesale Dealers in Verse, Prose and Music" in the *Farmer's Weekly Museum,* published at Walpole, N.H., by Joseph Dennie. It consisted of a variety of reading matter in prose and verse by Dennie and a number of voluntary contributors from various parts of New England.

The "colyum" as an institution in the modern newspaper, however, did not make its appearance until the eighties with Ambrose Bierce's "Prattle" column in the *San Francisco Examiner,* Henry Ten Eyck White's "Lakeside Musings" in the *Chicago Tribune,* and Eugene Field's "Sharps and Flats" in the *Chicago Daily News.*

COLUMNS SERVE A SIGNIFICANT PURPOSE

The importance of the column as an integral part of modern American journalism is shown by the prominent position it is given on the front page, the editorial page, or the sports page and the devoted followings which the various columnists have gained.

Intimacy With The Reader Is Promoted. The column answers the need for a closer personal contact between the publication—newspaper or magazine—and the reader. "Today's industrial world is a landslide toward the impersonal. Men have fewer friends—but we crave them, and the 'colyum' is one of the newspaper's most effective methods of meeting this cry for personal contact. Don Marquis, who served many years as a newspaper columnist, confirmed this point of view thus: 'The colyum's success, of course, indicates a public preference for direct contact with an individual rather than with the anonymous editorial output of a corporation.'" [1]

Reader-Interest Must Be Maintained. While the chief purpose of the humor column or "colyum" is to entertain, this is also true, to a lesser degree, of the other types—the personal editorial or essay column and the round-about-town department. Whenever any columnist ceases to entertain, when he loses his audience, his usefulness to the newspaper or magazine ends.

Jay E. House, for many years columnist for the *Philadelphia Public Ledger,* once declared:

---

[1] From *Pathways to Print* by Harrington and Martin, p. 194. Copyright 1931. Used by permission of the publishers, D. Van Nostrand Co.

Writing a column is a fine job. It is composed of about equal parts of labor, work and worry. A column hound toils and slaves to get out his column and then worries his head off for fear he'll go stale and lose his job. All that is expected of a column hound is that he be amusing or clever in twenty-five or thirty different ways every day. A vaudeville performer can go out with one act and get it booked weeks solid. The next year he can go over the same circuit with the same act. . . . A column hound must have a new act every day.[1]

Most Columns Have A Serious Purpose Today. This is indicated by Don Marquis's declaration that "Its persistent suggestions are frequently more influential, casually and entertainingly presented, than the direct propaganda of the formal editorials in the newspaper." To that may be added the admonition of C. H. Thompson, columnist for the *Kansas City Star*, "Tell something the reader already knows, but has forgotten, or come to regard as an experience peculiar to himself. This tends to show him that his lot isn't much different from that of others. If a columnist can succeed in making his readers realize that we are all about the same kind of folk, it ought to make them more tolerant and less selfish, and therefore happier." [2]

The fact is, columnists today—particularly news commentators and political analysts—have not only a serious function to perform by stimulating public discussion of affairs of the day but also a continuing obligation to measure their facts and comments by commonly accepted ethical standards geared to reality and their consciences.

THE COLUMNIST NEEDS SPECIAL QUALIFICATIONS

The outstanding characteristic of all columnists, whether essayists, writers of gossip columns, or conductors of "colyums," is individuality. Beyond that, however, columnists must have a keen sense of discernment, an aptitude for analysis and synthesis, and experience which has both breadth and depth. All of this must be pointed up with writing skill.

Originality, Creative Ability, And Rich Background Are Essential. Rather than to try to imitate the style and methods of established columnists, the would-be columnist should seek to blaze new trails, try new methods, and establish precedents. The latter, however, requires consummate skill born of natural aptitude, varied experiences, and imagination. Ordinary industry is usually necessary but is never enough to make a good columnist. It has been well said with special emphasis on the conductor of the humor column:

---

[1] From *The Editorial* by L. N. Flint, p. 243. Copyright 1928. Used by permission of the publishers, D. Appleton-Century Co.

[2] *Ibid.*, p. 247. Used by permission of the publishers, D. Appleton-Century Co.

To be successful as a column conductor demands of the writer maturity, richness of background and experience, an aggressive philosophy of life, and a style forceful and flexible beyond that which passes as adequate for the ordinary levels of editorial production. The writer must be essayist as well as critic and while holding to his main attitude must be able to vary his tone from satire to occasional flippancy and from humor to homily. . . . The columnist of today is not so much the man of wit and sophistication who knocked about town and wrote of the oddities which only a grotesque soul can coax from the daily scene, as a writer with facile pen who, conducting a well-planned humorous campaign or ringing the changes on established humorous devices, draws to himself the contributions of articulate stenographers, college wits and business men.[1]

Resourcefulness In Securing Subject Matter Is Needed. So far as is known there is no way of "getting contributions." One columnist put it well years ago when he said: "Go everywhere for material. There are fields, of course, that the columnist learns to avoid from being bruised on previous invasions. He should learn the value of chronic good nature, stern fairness, a sense of kindly humor rather than of the ridiculous, a terse style, and uncompromising loyalty to the newspaper."[2]

Resourcefulness in getting material means simply using all possible means of ferreting out facts suitable for inclusion in the kind of column which is being written. It takes different techniques for different people upon different occasions. There are no formulae which may be counted upon to substitute for ingenuity.

Today's Senior Columnists Have Rich Backgrounds. Although there appears to be no single essential "ingredient" for a successful columnist, there are some general characteristics common to most senior columnists. These may be presented best as lettered case studies:

Case A. Born Plattsburg, Missouri. Educated private academy and business college, Cincinnati. Worked as reporter, feature writer, political commentator, telegraph editor, city editor, and managing editor of newspapers in Ohio for nine years; associate editor of a magazine for one year; news editor of the *New York Evening Mail* for one year. Wrote widely syndicated column for more than twenty years.

Case B. Born New York city. Educated at Harvard University with graduate work in philosophy. Phi Beta Kappa. Varied career for seven years, then officer, United States

[1] From *Pathways to Print* by Harrington and Martin, p. 196. Copyright 1931. Used by permission of the publishers, D. Van Nostrand Co.
[2] From *The Editorial* by L. N. Flint, p. 248. Copyright 1928. Used by permission of the publishers, D. Appleton-Century Co.

Army assigned to Military Intelligence. Magazine writer and author of books on political affairs; associate editor of the *New Republic;* later editor of the *New York World.* Newspaper columnist for more than twenty years.

Case C. Born Lancaster, New York. Educated Lewis Institute in Chicago, Syracuse University, and the University of Vienna. Worked as Publicity Director, upstate New York Women's Suffrage campaign for two years; social work for three years; foreign correspondent for *Philadelphia Public Ledger* and *New York Evening Post* for eight years (at Vienna four years, at Berlin four years). For more than twenty years a free-lance writer, best known for widely syndicated newspaper column.

Case D. Born Tipton, Iowa. Educated through high school. Since twenty years of age worked for the *Los Angeles Times* as reporter, war correspondent, editorial writer, Washington correspondent, and editor. For some time writer and supervisor of movie stories for D. W. Griffith, Cecil B. DeMille, Mack Sennett, Jesse Lasky, Eric Von Stroheim. Wrote a daily column for more than twenty years.

Case E. Born Murfreesboro, Tennessee. Educated Nashville Military Academy and Washington University School, and Vanderbilt University. Phi Beta Kappa. Worked successively with *Nashville News, Forester Magazine, Atlanta Journal, Cleveland News, Nashville Tennessean,* all within a period of ten years; with *New York Mail* for three years, and then *Herald Tribune* for more than twenty years. Served as officer in World War I. Writes widely syndicated sport column which has been his specialty for more than thirty years.

Case F. Born Evanston, Illinois. Educated Phillips Exeter Academy and Swarthmore College. Phi Beta Kappa. Worked during World War I with American Friends Service Commission in Serbia, Montenegro, and Albania; instructor in industrial geography, University of Pennsylvania, one year; lectured on American, Australian and New Zealand chautauquas; foreign correspondent in Far East for newspaper syndicate, one year; foreign correspondent for newspaper syndicate, one year; lecturer in commercial geography, Columbia University, one year; foreign reporter for three years, working for Japanese newspapers; editorial staff the *United States Daily* and *Baltimore Sun* for many years. Conducted widely read and universally discussed column syndicated throughout the United States for many years.

Case G. Born Chicago, Illinois. Educated Northwestern University and the University of North Dakota. Worked in college as football quarterback and publicity man; later became a professional football player with the Philadelphia Eagles; but soon turned to sports reporting; became a reporter for the Chicago *Sun-Times*. Has conducted round-about-town gossip column for more than five years.

Chapter XXII

THE INTERVIEW AND THE INTERVIEWER

Of all forms of journalism, the interview is perhaps the most polished and most entertaining. The average newspaper reader might think that it is nothing more than a record of a conversation, but in reality the interview demands a great deal of skill and certain definite qualities on the part of the interviewer.—EMIL LUDWIG.*

READERS MEET NOTABLES BY PROXY

Through the medium of the printed interview newspaper readers meet by proxy and learn the views and personal characteristics of notables in the news.

The Interviewer Is An Emissary. The interviewer acts as an emissary for the newspaper readers who cannot hope to meet and talk with all the important and interesting people they would like to know. He seeks out the notable, asks the questions, records the answers, and gives his readers also a word picture of the celebrity's appearance and characteristics.

The Value Of The Interview Is Established. Interview stories are especially interesting to newspaper readers for a variety of reasons:

First, the spoken word, quoted verbatim, gives life to the story. The person interviewed seems to be talking to each reader individually. The description of him in his surroundings helps the reader to see him as he talks. Second, events, explanations and opinions given in the words of one who speaks with authority have greater weight than do the assertions of an unknown writer. Third, the interview is equally effective whether the writer's purpose is to inform, to entertain, or to furnish practical guidance. . . . Discoveries, inventions, new processes, unusual methods, new projects and marked success of any kind may be explained to advantage in the words of those responsible for these undertakings.[1]

Interviews Are Of Three Principal Types. Interviews fall into three generally recognized classifications.

FACTUAL NEWS INTERVIEW. In the factual news interview, the opinions of an authority on some subject of current news interest are sought

---

* From "Emil Ludwig, Famed for His Reporting, Tells the Art of the Interview," in *Editor and Publisher*, July 18, 1936.

[1] From *How to Write Special Feature Articles* by W. G. Bleyer, p. 56. Copyright 1920. Used by permission of the publishers, Houghton Mifflin Co.

and recorded for their news value. Such an interview might be head-lined:

> MONEY EXPENDED UNDER GI BILL FOR EDUCATION
> OF VETS IS "AMERICA'S BEST INVESTMENT
> IN DEMOCRACY," SAYS EISENHOWER

FEATURE OR PERSONALITY INTERVIEW. In the feature or personality in-terview, the emphasis is laid upon the personal traits and point of view of a celebrity. Example:

> THE UMPIRE OF THE TOWN MEETING—GEORGE
> DENNY TELLS WHY HE THINKS THE NATION
> NEEDS "UNFETTERED EXCHANGE OF
> OPPOSING VIEWS"

BIOGRAPHICAL INTERVIEW. In the biographical interview are told the achievements, personal characteristics, and philosophy of a celebrity. Example:

> CHAMP OF CHAMPS—THE GREATEST ATHLETE OF ALL
> TIME, HIS ACHIEVEMENTS STAND UNMATCHED IN
> SPORTS HISTORY, BUT THE ROAR OF THE
> CROWD HAS DIED AWAY: MEET THE
> JIM THORPE OF TODAY

Group Interviews Sample Public Opinion. Closely akin to the fac-tual news interview is the group interview. This consists of getting the opinions of a number of persons instead of just one person on some sub-ject of current interest. "Quite undistinguished individuals, if they are typical of a class or representative of a large body of opinion, frequently have extremely valuable conversation to offer. For authoritative stuff on labor problems among the stevedores, for instance, the writer may regard an interview with an ordinary longshoreman as of equal value to and perhaps more interesting than an interview with the president of a docking corporation or with a noted labor leader." [1] Group interviews appear in either of two forms:

INQUIRING REPORTER TYPE. In the inquiring reporter type, the an-swers to a certain question by a number of persons selected at random at some certain place are set down just as given.

SYMPOSIUM TYPE. In the symposium type, the statement of the topic is followed by comments on the subject from various individuals. These statements are then compared, contrasted, analyzed, and interpreted with the idea of arriving at a consensus on the topic by a representative group of citizens or by representative members of a trade or industry.

---

[1] From *Magazine Article Writing* by Brennecke and Clark, p. 247. Copyright 1930. Used by permission of the publishers, The Macmillan Co.

"FIRST CATCH YOUR RABBIT"

"Before you can have rabbit stew, first catch your rabbit." Similarly, before the interview story can be printed certain preliminaries are necessary.

Formulate An Intelligent Plan. Sometimes interesting and valuable interview stories result from a chance meeting or a "lucky break," but the majority of them are planned in advance. Most interviewers arrange in advance, by telephone or by letter, for an interview, but some believe that the best results can be obtained as the result of an informal call. "I believe it is poor policy to notify a business man in advance that I am coming to interview him. Even an American wouldn't be quite natural under such conditions. He would do one of two things, according to temperament. Either he would be so embarrassed at the idea of being interviewed that he would shut up like a clam, or he would rise to the occasion and give an imitation of a speech he heard someone make at the last state convention." [1]

But whatever the difference of opinion on making preliminary arrangements, most interviewers agree on the following procedure:

1. Inform yourself as thoroughly as possible about the career, interests, hobbies, etc., of the person to be interviewed.

2. If possible, study pictures of him. "Photographs are the most valuable aid since nothing reveals a man's personality more clearly than his physiognomy," says Emil Ludwig.

3. For the factual news interview, make sure you are familiar with the subject on which he is to be interviewed. Make out a list of specific questions to be asked and arrange these in as logical an order as possible to aid you in guiding the interview.

4. Keep in the field of his interests. "It is a mistake to assume that because a man has distinguished himself in one field, he will be an authority on any other. Interview a distinguished physician on the endocrine glands, but do not expect him to talk intelligently and originally on labor problems; and do not try to get expert musical criticisms and appreciations from a person whose sole interest in life is politics. This mistake is frequently made." [2]

Conducting The Interview. Methods of conducting interviews will vary somewhat according to the person, place, and time. But the following hints have the indorsement of many well-known interviewers:

1. The indirect approach to the subject is often the best. Get a man to

---

[1] From "Interviewing Business Men" by Jesse Rainsford Sprague in the *Saturday Evening Post*, January 27, 1934. Used by permission of the publishers, The Curtis Publishing Co.

[2] From *Magazine Article Writing* by Brennecke and Clark, p. 246. Copyright 1930. Used by permission of the publishers, The Macmillan Co.

talk about his hobbies or other subjects in which he is especially interested and which can be related to the main topic on which you are interviewing him.

2. Remember you are the questioner. Volunteer information on the subject only when it is necessary to stimulate the conversation.

3. Keep the atmosphere of the interview as informal as possible. Avoid unnecessary mention of the word "interview."

4. Unless the interviewee wishes to be quoted verbatim, avoid the use of a notebook or the too-apparent note-taking since this often makes him aware that he is going to be quoted and causes him to speak less freely. If note-taking is necessary, do it unobtrusively. Better still, listen attentively and as soon as the interview is over make notes on the essential information.

5. Keep your attitude and the interview plan flexible. If the interview which started out to be a factual news interview does not develop satisfactorily for an expression of opinions, change its purpose to a feature or personality interview and make mental and written notes accordingly.

6. In concluding the interview ask him if you may communicate with him again for additional details which may be necessary when writing the article. Also suggest that he look over the final draft of the article before publication to insure accuracy of quotation and interpretation.

THE STYLE OF WRITING SHOULD SUIT THE SUBJECT

Since the interview is largely written in direct discourse, the writer needs to avoid the danger of falling into a stereotyped form of "question-and-answer" diction. There is no one way in which this type of article should be written. In brief, the style should be adapted to the subject.

The Lead Strikes The Keynote. Adapting the style to the subject is especially important in the lead in which the writer strikes the keynote of the whole article. One thing the lead should do is to establish the importance of the person who has been interviewed and the value of his opinions (if a factual news interview) or the human-interest values in the story about him (if a personality or biographical interview). The lead may be a summary of the whole story; it may be the most striking statement made by the interviewee; it may emphasize the character portrait idea; or it may be concerned with the setting of the interview or the unusual circumstances under which the interview was obtained.

The Body Of The Article Requires Variety And Proper Emphasis. In writing the main text of the interview story, the following general principles may well be observed:

1. To avoid monotony of tone and typographical appearance of the interview when it appears in print, direct quotation should be varied with indirect quotation which gives accurately the sense of what the

interviewee said, with descriptive passages giving glimpses of his personality and with bits of description to suggest the atmosphere of the interview.

2. Your personality as interviewer should be kept out of the story unless it will add life to the story by heightening dramatic interest.

3. Since readers are interested in answers rather than in questions asked, the questions should be subordinated as much as possible. Sometimes they may be embodied in the replies and again they may be merely implied or entirely omitted.

Chapter XXIII

THE HUMAN TOUCH MAKES THE FEATURE

*Write about what you know and write truly. Write about people
you know that you love and hate, not about people you study about.*
*—Ernest Hemingway.**

THE FEATURE ARTICLE PLAYS UP THE HUMAN–INTEREST PHASE

The feature article has been called the news writer's masterpiece because a minor news event is created a major news item by accentuating
the human-interest element, and, as such, it shares importance with the
more newsworthy story or editorial review, comment, or opinion.

It Centers Around Some Emotion. In some respects the feature article
is little more than the most human side of the news "played up" so as
to attract interest, center attention, and fascinate the emotional senses of
the average reader. In order to do this, the feature usually centers around
some single basic emotion or takes its point of departure from some item
of current interest. The reader is not moved by the importance of the
tidings, but rather his attention is impelled by the human touch which
builds the feature around one of the emotions which may be love,
hate, curiosity, fear, humor—or what-not. By exercising literary ingenuity
the feature writer makes the simple thing a vital one, the commonplace
item an important happening. And when completed, the feature article
usually satisfies one of three purposes: (1) it entertains; (2) it informs;
or, (3) it teaches.

It Resembles The News Story. To a certain extent, depending upon
its purpose and point of departure, the feature article resembles both
the news story and the editorial article. It resembles the news story insofar as it deals with facts, and whenever it has the element of timeliness—that is, when it is "hung on the news peg." It differs from the
news story in that it is frequently longer than its news value justifies, is
more detailed, and does not follow the more standardized form of journalistic presentation. Further, many features do not have to give serious
attention to timeliness, for they are "evergreen" or "good any time."
From another point of view, the feature resembles the editorial article

---

* From "Old News Man Writes" in *Esquire,* December, 1934, p. 25. Used by permission of the publishers, Esquire, Inc.

whenever it seeks to interpret, accentuate, or conceal news facts, or any part thereof, to the benefit or detriment of another part. However, it differs from the editorial as it surveys the facts impartially, and does not present the opinions of the writer.

FEATURE ARTICLES MAY BE DIVIDED INTO TYPES

Feature articles may be divided into certain types, although sometimes clear-cut division is difficult because many of them overlap—still, the more usually recognized classification is helpful.

Human-Interest Sketches. Some human-interest sketches emphasize humorous or pathetic incidents in the day's news, as a feature headlined:

> CANADIAN GUIDE FIXUM: HE PACKUM
> CAMERA IN ICE LIKE FISH!

Others reveal the romance of the routine job by a "glorification of the commonplace," as is done in one headlined:

> INTRODUCING: THE MAN WHO FIXES YOUR
> TELEPHONE; "TROUBLE SHOOTER" IS A
> POPULAR FELLOW WHEN THINGS GO
> WRONG

Interesting-Persons Narratives. Feature articles are written about men and women whose stories are worth telling because they are historical characters in whom interest survives long after they are dead, thereby justifying a biographical feature such as:

> ETHAN ALLEN, THE HERO OF TICONDEROGA,
> WAS THE ROB ROY OF A WILDERNESS
> COMMONWEALTH

Or the story may be about "headliners of today" who are interesting because of (1) their vivid personalities or important position in contemporary affairs; (2) their achievements; or (3) their uniqueness, as illustrated by these typical headlines:

1
> THE LADY WHO SCARES POLITICIANS—A FROWN
> FROM ANNA STRAUSS IS BAD NEWS FOR
> CONGRESSMEN BECAUSE SHE'S PRESIDENT
> OF LEAGUE OF WOMEN VOTERS

2
> THE MAN WHO SAVED A THOUSAND LIVES—HERE
> IS THE INSPIRING STORY OF DR. CHEVALIER
> JACKSON, INVENTOR OF THE BRONCHOSCOPE

3
> HE IS THE LAST SURVIVOR OF THE "LOST BATTALION,"
> U.S. INFANTRY UNIT WHICH WROTE GLORIOUS
> PAGE IN HISTORY OF WORLD WAR I

Autobiographical Human Documents. "Human documents" which relate a personal experience, viewed objectively, are illustrated by an article headlined:

> I TEACH THE "THREE R'S" IN MOUNTAIN SCHOOL
> —AND SOME OF MY "PUPILS" ARE OLD ENOUGH
> TO BE MY FATHER OR MOTHER

The article may deal with more intimate personal matters, viewed subjectively and presenting some phase of life not usually exposed. Typical of the "confession story" is one headlined:

> I WON A BATHING BEAUTY CONTEST AND A TRIP
> TO HOLLYWOOD BUT I LOST THE LOVE AND
> FRIENDSHIP OF THE PEOPLE WHO MEAN
> MOST TO ME

Historical Features. Historical features, although dealing with events or personalities of the past, have interest for present-day readers because the facts they give (1) are timely; (2) are unique; (3) throw new light on a familiar story; (4) debunk popular beliefs; (5) promote a better appreciation of "minor prophets"; (6) offer interesting speculation revolving around the word "if." Typical of the variety in features of this kind are those headlined:

> 1   WEST VIRGINIA PREPARES TO CELEBRATE CENTENNIAL
> OF ITS JOINING THE SISTERHOOD OF STATES

> 2   SAMUEL P. CARTER WAS ONLY AMERICAN WHO EVER
> HELD RANK OF GENERAL IN ARMY AND
> ADMIRAL IN NAVY

> 3   NORTH CAROLINA EXCAVATORS FIND CLUES TO "LOST
> COLONY"—EVIDENCE OF ANCIENT FORT LINKED TO
> DISAPPEARANCE OF SETTLERS IN 1591

> 4   PAUL REVERE WASN'T ONLY "MIDNIGHT RIDER" IN
> '75; TWO OTHERS HAD EQUALLY IMPORTANT
> ROLES IN AROUSING PATRIOTS TO FIGHT

> 5   A PIONEER OF THE WEST WHOM HISTORY FOR-
> GOT—THOMAS FITZPATRICK, MOUNTAIN MAN,
> DESERVES RANK WITH KIT CARSON
> AND JIM BRIDGER

> 6   IF PICKETT HAD CHARGED AN HOUR EARLIER AT
> GETTYSBURG, WHOLE COURSE OF AMERICAN
> HISTORY MIGHT HAVE BEEN CHANGED

Travel Sketches. Travel sketches satisfy a human desire for more knowledge about things outside our immediate experience by telling of

(1) unusual or interesting people or (2) unusual or interesting places, as illustrated by articles headlined:

> 1   THE JACKSON WHITES ARE ON THE MARCH AGAIN—ANOTHER
>   BLOW FALLS ON STRANGE, TRAGIC RACE OF HILL-BILLIES
>   THAT LIVES WITHIN 32 MILES OF NEW YORK CITY

> 2   A MODERN GULLIVER'S TRAVELS IN NOVA SCOTIA—MEDLEY OF
>   TONGUES GREETS TRAVELER AND CURIOUS WILD LIFE
>   SCURRIES TO COVER AS ROAD UNRAVELS

Interpretative Features. Interpretative features inform, instruct and make clear to the reader the background and below-the-surface phases of (1) social problems; (2) economic problems; (3) political problems; and (4) problems of everyday life, as revealed in these typical headlines:

> 1   "OPERATION TEXTBOOKS"—INFLUX OF VETERANS HAS CHANGED
>   WHOLE PATTERN OF COLLEGE EDUCATION IN U.S. TODAY

> 2   THE FARMER TAKES A REST—RURAL LIFE ASSUMES NEW ASPECTS
>   DUE TO INCREASED MECHANIZATION OF AGRICULTURE

> 3   IS HE YOUR PRESIDENT OR THE POLITICIANS'?—AMERICANS
>   BEGIN TO TAKE STOCK OF THEIR METHOD OF CHOOSING
>   CHIEF EXECUTIVE

> 4   A NEW DESIGN FOR LIVING—SCIENCE IS AFFECTING MORE THAN
>   YOU REALIZE WHAT YOU DO EVERY MINUTE IN THE
>   24 HOURS OF YOUR DAY

Popularized Science Articles. Popularized articles, bridging the gap which for so long separated the scientist and the journalist, present scientifically accurate facts in nontechnical, easily-understood language, as is suggested in this headline:

> JUST HOW VITAL ARE VITAMINS TO THE HEALTH AND HAPPINESS
> OF THE HUMAN RACE?

Practical Guidance Articles. Practical guidance articles appeal to the reader because they tell him (1) how to do or make things; (2) how to learn or collect things; or, (3) how to improve himself. Illustrative of these three types are articles headlined:

> 1   HERE IS AN EASY WAY TO ILLUSTRATE YOUR WRITINGS WITH
>   HOME-MADE LINOLEUM BLOCKS

> 2   COLLECTING STREET CAR TRANSFERS NOT AS SILLY AS IT SOUNDS
>   —THEY TELL HISTORY OF URBAN TRANSPORTATION
>   THROUGH THE YEARS

> 3   OUT THERE BOTH HEALTH AND WEALTH AWAIT YOU—GET ON
>   YOUR HIKING BOOTS—AND GO!

IN TECHNIQUE FEATURE WRITING IS SIMILAR TO OTHER WRITING

The technique of feature writing is similar to the technique of any expository or narrative writing since it makes use of (1) an introduction or a lead, (2) the body of the article, and (3) the conclusion.

The Feature Allows Latitude And Variety In Lead. Including, as it does, such a variety of expository and narrative types, feature writing allows considerable latitude in striking the keynote of the article. Hence the lead may be any one or a combination of two or more of the following types:

THE NEWS SUMMARY LEAD. Similar to that used in straight news writing, this lead is a condensed version of the whole story and embodies the "five W's"—*Who, What, When, Where,* and *Why.* For example:

> When the Democratic national convention in Baltimore in 1844 resulted in a deadlock between the two leading contenders for the nomination, Martin Van Buren and Lewis Cass, the weary delegates at last turned to a political "unknown" and chose him for their standard-bearer. Thus James K. Polk of Tennessee became the first "dark horse" candidate for President in our history.

THE DISTINCTIVE-INCIDENT LEAD. This lead snaps a word picture of the story in its most characteristic moment and at a point when it has reached its summit of dramatic interest. Thus:

> The eight black-robed judges of the Court of Appeals in Washington sat watching a lovely auburn-haired girl. With deft movements she daubed cold cream over the left side of her face, and wiping it off with a towel revealed a hideous flaming birthmark from chin to forehead. No longer did the judges see her beautiful hair, her blue eyes or her trim figure. All they noticed was that terrible disfigurement.

THE QUOTATION LEAD. A familiar quotation that is apropos to the theme of the story may be used to indicate to the reader what the story is going to be about. For example:

> "O, East is East and West is West
> And never the twain shall meet!"
> If Rudyard Kipling had visited an International House on the campus of one of our American universities, he might have revised those lines in his famous poem. For there East and West not only meet but they also live and work side by side in friendly fashion, *etc.*

THE SHORT SENTENCE LEAD. This consists of a single striking assertion which may be either a summary of the whole story or a statement of
the most significant fact in it, as shown by this:

> I am lucky.
> Remembering the serious things I used to read about
> making good in business, I guess I am lucky to be able to
> come right out and admit I am lucky instead of telling
> about long hard hours of practicing golf shots.

THE QUESTION LEAD. The question lead is similar to the short sentence lead but it is phrased as an interrogation, instead of an assertion, to
challenge the knowledge or interest of the reader, as is done in this opening paragraph:

> How much would a baby be worth to you?
> If you already have one, of course, there isn't enough
> money in the world to buy him—or her. But for a baby as
> a new investment, could you afford to pay from $30,000 to
> $40,000?

THE CONTRAST LEAD. This is a statement of two obviously different
facts with the purpose of emphasizing the fact that will be the theme of
the article. For example:

> On that June day it was an inferno of chattering machine
> guns, HE shells and bursting bombs. Here men died—in
> boats, in the surf, on the sand.
> Today little French children play happily on this spot.
> Their laughter rises above the soft splash-splash of the
> waves.
> This is the coast of Normandy—"Omaha Beach."

THE ANALOGY LEAD. This is similar to the contrast lead but it gains its
effect by showing the similarity between some well-known fact and the
fact that will be the theme of the story. Typical of such a lead is this one:

> Ironically, the animal whose name is a synonym for
> everything contemptible in the human vocabulary is, in
> many essential respects, the most similar of all animals
> to man. The basis of this similarity is the fact that men
> and rats are the only completely omnivorous animals.

THE PICTURE LEAD. A graphic description of the setting of the story
told in the article serves as an introduction to its action or the characters
in it. An example:

> The huge cell block was quiet—not the ominous calm
> preceding a riot, but a poignant stillness, as if a thousand
> ears were intently listening. Suddenly from the upper end

> of the block, a youth's full rich voice came ringing down the gallery, singing: "May I sleep in your barn tonight, Mister, etc., etc."

THE JANUS-FACED LEAD. A lead may look backward into the past or forward into the future for purposes of comparison with the situation in the present which is the theme of the story. Typical of this kind of opening paragraph is this:

> If the next 25 years bring about as much change in bathing suit styles as the last 25 years, heaven only knows what conditions will be like in 1975. The big break in beach fashions really began with "that saucy harem bathing suit, the newest and wickedest Parisian importation," as the stylewriters termed it. From then on suits became scantier and scantier until we have what we have today. So it seems only reasonable to ask the question: "What will they be, if at all, in another quarter century?"

The Main Body Is Developed As In Other Good Writing. In so far as feature writing is similar to any other expository or narrative writing, the main body of the feature article is developed in the same way as any other good writing. It should exemplify the three cardinal principles of (1) unity, (2) coherence, and (3) emphasis in its separate paragraphs and in itself as a whole.[1] This may be accomplished by (1) having a central theme or main idea carried throughout the article; (2) eliminating extraneous material and closely relating all the material in the article to the central theme; and (3) bridging the transition from each paragraph to the next one easily and smoothly and avoiding abrupt changes of thought.

The Conclusion Is Not Unlike That In Narrative Writing. The conclusion of the feature article, also, resembles the conclusion of other forms of expository and narrative writing. (1) It may be a condensed summary of the whole article, reviewing briefly the salient facts brought out in the article; (2) it may be the climax or highest point of interest in the article as it frequently is in a short story; or, (3) it may be a "cut-back" or "flash-back" to the introduction, i.e., a restatement of the "lead" phrased in somewhat different language but serving to emphasize the important statements made at the beginning and to "round out" the whole article.

---

[1] These cardinal principles are treated fully in all rhetoric and composition texts. A work which shows their practical application in a manner especially valuable for the feature writer is *Better Writing* by Henry Seidel Canby.

Chapter XXIV

NEWS FROM NEAR AND FAR

As the world shrinks and nations jostle one another, far neighbors become important. Correct and rapid information about them is at a premium.—Stephen Vincent Benét.*

MUCH OF TODAY'S NEWS IS NOT LOCAL

More than half of the news in most metropolitan newspapers is received from sources outside the city in which the newspaper is published and comes to the newspaper by mail, telephone, telegraph, cable, and radio.

The County Furnishes Neighborhood News. Because proximity, or nearness to the point of publication, is an important characteristic of news, news of the locality immediately surrounding the city of publication is carried in many city newspapers even though it may be of little significance otherwise.

State Lines Bound A Natural News Area. The unanimity of interests of the citizens of a state in their common government and in mutual problems results in the printing of much news which is of little or no interest outside the borders of that state. News of a new sales tax in Ohio would be of paramount importance in the Buckeye state but would be given little, if any, space in New York newspapers. Proximity again is a contributing factor in this interest as are state pride and loyalty.

National News Is Given Much Space. National news falls naturally into two classes: first, news from or concerning the national government, and second, news originating in states and cities within the country's borders. Both types occupy a great deal of space in the news columns with the governmental news getting a much larger proportion than it did ten, twenty, or thirty years ago.

Citizens and other residents have an intense interest in news of the country of their birth or adoption and especially in recent years in news about laws and other governmental activities. This interest in news originating within the boundaries of the reader's country is a natural one as long as patriotism and nationalism exist.

---

* From "The United Press" by Stephen Vincent Benét in *Fortune*, May, 1933. Used by permission of the publishers, Time, Inc.

Washington, New York, Los Angeles (including Hollywood), Chicago, and Detroit, in the order named, are probably the best regular sources of news of nation-wide interest today, although an event of sufficient interest or importance may turn the news spotlight of the nation on Aspen, Colorado, or Flemington, New Jersey, for days or weeks.

Treatment Of World News Varies. The amount of space assigned to world or foreign news varies from many columns in the eastern metropolitan newspapers to much less space in the small-city dailies in the middle west.

World War II brought about much wider interest in world affairs on the part of all Americans whether on the seaboard or in the interior areas, once thought of as the stronghold of isolationism. As was the case after World War I, more space in all publications was given over to international affairs and it is unlikely that there will ever be a return to the days when a few sticks of type were thought sufficient coverage of foreign news in many small newspapers. Naturally, newspapers in the larger cities will continue to carry a higher proportion of foreign news because of the interest of their readers, many of whom are only a generation removed from foreign countries, and because the cost of obtaining and printing a large volume of world news is such that only the larger and more prosperous newspapers can carry it.

PRESS ASSOCIATIONS TRANSMIT MUCH NEWS

A great deal of the news from other cities, states, and countries is furnished to newspapers by press associations.

There are three major press associations, and one or more of these news services furnishes national and foreign news to practically every daily newspaper in the United States. These organizations are the Associated Press, the United Press, and the International News Service, commonly referred to by newspapermen and laymen as the A.P., the U.P., and the I.N.S.

Each of these three news-gathering and news-distributing agencies gathers news from the hundreds of cities and thousands of villages in the United States and distributes it to newspapers whose readers will be most interested in it. Foreign news is obtained by their own correspondents abroad and in some cases through arrangements with news agencies of other countries.

The news is gathered by a vast corps of reporters and is rewritten and edited in bureaus where it is put on leased wires which carry it direct to the offices of member or client newspapers. There are trunk wires connecting the larger cities from coast to coast and state or district systems or circuits which carry much of the trunk-wire news in addition to a considerable amount of news of interest only to their particular areas.

These major news organizations are similar in many respects but differ fundamentally on such important matters as determination of members or clients, financial setup, and rules governing the handling of their copy by newspapers.

The Associated Press Is The Largest. The Associated Press is the oldest and largest of the three agencies. It is a mutual, nonprofit organization of 2700 newspapers and radio stations in the United States. The number of newspapers and radio stations served in the world totaled 4000 in 1949. Members do not buy the service but pay assessments levied in advance on the basis of a budget.

Over its 318,400 miles of leased wires in the United States news is carried to morning and afternoon newspapers in every state. The A.P. operates a 24-hour leased cable from New York to London and leased teleprinter circuits from London to several European capitals. The A.P. output is approximately 1,000,000 words a day. Radio is also used by the A.P. in the distribution of news.

The A.P. also operates a national Wirephoto wire and a number of state Wirephoto networks. Photos transmitted by wire are mailed to members not having the wire service and more than 1000 newspapers receive this service in one way or another.

The chart on page 202 shows the main wire system of the A.P. bureaus, but does not include wires to many individual member newspapers.

The United Press Ranks Second. The United Press is a privately owned corporation which gathers news and sells it to 1036 newspapers and 1095 radio stations in the United States and to 920 newspapers and 154 radio stations in foreign countries. Founded in 1907 by E. W. Scripps, founder of the Scripps-Howard chain, and his associates, it is the number two press association in this country. The U.P. will sell news to anyone, anywhere, and supplies not only 3205 newspapers and radio stations, but special clients such as magazines, radio commentators, steamships, and business executives.

The U.P. early developed a strong coverage of South America and today also has many correspondents in the Far East and in Europe. It uses radio in gathering and distributing foreign news to a great extent, but continues to depend upon leased wires from London to a number of European news centers.

The U.P. was a pioneer in using feature stories and featurized news stories and it continues to emphasize the aspects of interest and readability in its news and radio reports.

International News Service Is Smallest. Third in size is International News Service, established by William Randolph Hearst. The I.N.S. serves 426 newspapers, 158 radio stations, and 62 special service clients in the United States and 302 newspapers, 19 radio stations, and 26 special service clients abroad. It also serves 29 television stations.

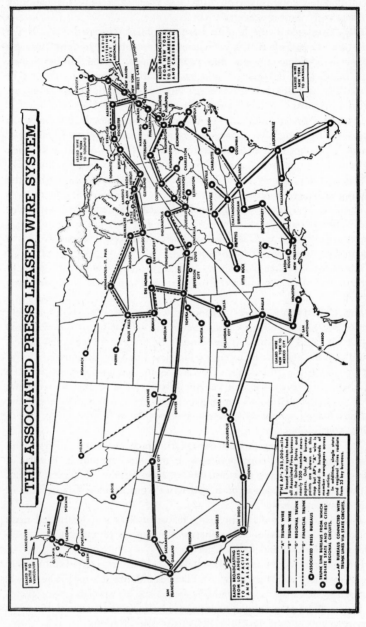

Printed, with modifications, by express permission of the Associated Press.

It operates 170,000 miles of leased wire in the United States and leases short-wave radio transmitters to distribute its news throughout the world.

Somewhat more sensational than the other two services, I.N.S. does not, however, go to the lengths that the Hearst newspapers do in the various ways characteristic of this chain. If it did, it could not have the large clientele that it has among newspapers of opposing political, economic, and social beliefs.

MOST NEWS COMES BY TELEGRAPH

Telegraph news may be sent to a newspaper by any one or all of three methods of transmission. These are by automatic printer-telegraph machines, by manually-operated Morse telegraph instruments, or by messages over the wires of the telegraph companies.

Printer-Telegraph Machines Are Generally Used. By far the largest amount of telegraph copy comes into today's newspaper offices over what are commonly called printer-telegraph machines. Operating by means of a complicated mechanism based on electrical impulses, these machines reproduce on a roll of paper a seemingly never-ending stream of news at the speed of sixty words a minute. This news is typed in capital letters as shown in this actual Associated Press story:

> CD 20
>
> BULLETIN
>
> CLEVELAND, NOV 26—(AP)—EDWARD M. MC CARTY, U.S. CUSTOMS COLLECTOR AT AKRON, PLEADED GUILTY TO EMBEZZLEMENT BEFORE FEDERAL JUDGE PAUL JONES TODAY AND WAS SENTENCED TO NINE YEARS IN THE FEDERAL PENITENTIARY.
>
> H1039AES

The operation in receiving offices is entirely automatic, and a copy boy or the telegraph editor needs merely to snap the switch at the time the wire opens and tear off the typewritten copy as it is received. Offices usually have two machines for each wire so that if mechanical trouble makes one inoperative the other may be turned on and the flow of news goes on uninterrupted. Mechanics who keep the machines in repair are furnished either by the press association or the American Telephone and Telegraph Company, according to the ownership of the machines, which are not sold to the newspapers.

An operator in a bureau may send to one or a hundred or even more receiving machines simultaneously, depending on the wire hookup.

Morse Wire Has Special Functions. Not so many years ago all telegraph news was sent and received in the Morse code over clicking telegraph instruments by telegraph operators, a picturesque lot, many of whom developed into excellent newspaper reporters and executives. But today, except in isolated offices and for special events and services, the Morse telegrapher is a figure of the past. The printer-telegraph machines are faster; they do not need rest periods; and they are much cheaper for the press associations and therefore for the newspapers, because no operator is needed except at the sending point.

Financial wires, which are open for a few hours daily, and sports coverage for football and baseball games, where the material is sent direct to the newspaper from the press box in the stadium, provide the chief types of news that is still handled by the Morse operator with his key or "bug."

Some Types Of Story Are "Sent Overhead."   "File 500-word lead and summary overhead" may be the message received by a college sports reporter the day before a big game. Or the news editor, sending a reporter downstate on an important story, may say, "File a thousand words overhead by eight o'clock and keep us protected by phone until the final goes in."

"Filing a story overhead" means to send it by Western Union. A message is sent either day press rate (DPR), or night press rate (NPR), and in most cases is sent collect. Because newspapers have a rate much cheaper than that for private or commercial messages, it is important that the reporter filing the story remember to put DPR or NPR on his message. Night press rate is cheaper than day but the reporter uses whichever service is available at the time his paper wants the story.

Stories from Washington correspondents or from correspondents in the statehouse are usually sent overhead unless edition time is very close when the telephone is used.

THE TELEPHONE IS USED FOR SPOT NEWS

Because of its speed and its two-way communication the telephone is often used to get stories from near-by points.

Minutes Often Count.   The telephone today offers almost instantaneous communication with nearly every city, village, and hamlet in the country, and thus is an invaluable instrument in getting news quickly. Stories which break near edition time often can be tracked down and cleaned up after a few well-placed and judiciously handled long-distance calls. Questions can be asked and answered and all necessary information obtained in a fraction of the time needed in using any other means of communication.

Many newspapers have standing rules that county and near-by correspondents use the telephone to report important deaths, accidents in which there are fatalities, and other significant spot news. As will be pointed out later, the bulk of the news from these correspondents is sent by mail, but no newspaper wants to be scooped on a good story for the sake of saving a small telephone bill. Prompt communication is a big factor in cities having several competing newspapers.

Accuracy Must Be Checked. When the telephone is used a careful check is made in most offices in order to be sure that names and other facts in the message are correct. The name or word is spelled so that no mistake can be made, as for example, "Tompkins. . . . T as in Thomas, O as in Oliver, M as in Mary, P as in Peter, K as in Kate, I as in Ida, N as in Nellie, S as in Samuel. . . . Tompkins."

Transoceanic Telephoning Is Now Common. Newspapers in the largest cities do not hesitate to use the transoceanic telephone to get the latest developments on stories of vital importance or great interest. London newspapers frequently get into contact with American editors by telephone to obtain up-to-the-minute information on stories which are of interest in England.

Naturally, the vast majority of the more than two thousand daily newspapers in this country do not use the transoceanic telephone at all or the long-distance service to any great extent. Their operating budgets will not bear the expense and they get their near-by news by mail and their other outside news from a press association.

SOME NEWS IS SENT BY MAIL

Much news and feature material, including county correspondence, political columns from state and national capitals, columns of general and special interest, comics, and departmental offerings, is received by the newspapers by mail.

County Correspondence Is Generally Mailed. The bulk of the news from towns surrounding the city of publication comes to the newspaper in the mail. The small-town correspondent knows when the mails close at his post office and it is his job to see that his daily letter is mailed in time to make a certain train or bus and yet not be so early that he will miss last-minute, good news items. As has been said before, he has definite instructions as to what stories he is expected to telephone but probably 95 per cent of his stuff is mailed.

State And National Political Columns Are Posted Regularly. Many of the daily and weekly political columns from the state capital or from Washington are mailed to the newspapers. They contain no spot news and the cost to the syndicate furnishing them and, of course, to the newspaper printing them is much less when they are mailed than if costly telegraph tolls were paid on the thousands of words. Some few of the columns are sent by telegraph, but they are the exception. If a newspaper has a statehouse correspondent who supplies considerable copy for the Sunday paper, almost invariably it is mailed Thursday or Friday so that it may be set into type on Saturday.

Feature Columns, Departments, And Comics Are Mailed. Feature columns, departmental features, and comics are sent by mail. Newspapers get most of their feature and departmental material from syndicates which distribute most of their wares by mail. New York and Hollywood columns are most commonly mailed once a week in printed form, and one of the copyreaders or editors clips out each day's release, pastes it on a piece of copy paper, and sends it to the composing room to be set.

Departmental features, which include such varied reading fare as advice to the lovelorn, Sunday-school lessons, how-to-be-beautiful columns, advice to parents, recipes and patterns for women, the daily short story and the never-ending serial, and daily poems are sent in printed or mimeographed form in daily or weekly doses, according to the policy of the syndicate furnishing them.

Comics are sent in mat form usually weekly. The syndicate usually tries to be from ten days to two weeks ahead of publication, and the deskman who handles the mats files them carefully in the order of their publication. The month and day of publication are usually noted in a corner of the cartoon and newspapers are expected to observe these release dates.

Foreign News And Features Are Forwarded From New York. Features and interpretative and color stories from Europe and the Far East, and, in fact, from all parts of the world, are frequently mailed to newspapers from New York. Foreign correspondents also mail many of their stories to the press associations or newspapers for which they work, which in turn mail them to those newspapers buying that type of service. Much of the coverage of foreign countries is such that the cable and telegraph need not be used for many stories which will be as good two weeks or a month after they are written as they are on that day. The use of the mails thus saves sizable sums for press associations and newspapers employing correspondents abroad.

FEW NEWSPAPERS GET DIRECT CABLE NEWS

New York, Chicago, Philadelphia, Baltimore, San Francisco, and Los Angeles newspapers are about the only ones which get cable news direct from their own correspondents abroad.

The Cost Is Prohibitive. Because of the cost of maintaining a correspondent abroad and of paying cable tolls on his stories, few newspapers get their cable news direct. This does not mean, however, that the average newspaper does not get as good and as rapid coverage on foreign news as do the newspapers with their own foreign correspondents. The press associations have developed excellent foreign staffs, and the competitive spirit is so strong among them that a newspaper relying on the press associations' foreign correspondents may get even faster coverage on spot news than a newspaper with its own correspondents in the various foreign capitals. Because of the fact that the press associations supply domestic and foreign news to newspapers of varying policies and shades of political opinion, their coverage is much more likely to be impartial and more nearly accurate than that of a paper whose correspondent, consciously or not, may write stories which he knows will please his publisher or editor. Foreign news is cabled to New York and put on the press-association wires almost instantaneously so that individual newspapers the country over receive it with little time lag.

The Cable Desk Exists On Some Papers. Newspapers which get direct cable news from other countries have a special cable desk where the cable editor and his assistants take the messages which come in "cablese" and rewrite them into intelligible English. Often a cable of no great length may be expanded into a story more than a column long by the judicious insertion and addition of facts which the cable editor has filed away, either in his desk or in his mind, from previous cables, from the correspondent's mailed stories, or from his own general background of knowledge.

The foreign correspondent, knowing that an event is scheduled to take place at a certain time, may have sent a lengthy descriptive and historical story by mail some weeks before the date. On the date a brief cable message releases this story and adds a few necessary last-minute changes or details. These will be skillfully woven into the story by the cable editor so that the finished product will look as if the entire story had been cabled direct from the foreign country.

NEWS IS TRANSMITTED BY RADIO

Radio is used to gather news by few United States newspapers, but its use in distributing news has become common with the press associations. Besides world-wide radio news gathering and distribution, there are local uses.

The three press associations and other agencies, including Press Wireless, supplement their news-gathering and news-distributing facilities by using radio to broadcast news from a central point to multiple destinations. News from out-of-the-way places is also sent to central distribution points by radio. Transmission of news by radio is still not generally efficient enough for entire dependence to be placed upon it.

Occasionally newspapers are enabled to obtain almost instantaneous reports from scenes of floods, tornadoes, or extensive fires and explosions which temporarily have interrupted telephone and telegraph communication. Amateur radio operators get in touch with fellow amateurs who in turn relay the reports to newspaper and press-association offices.

Newspaper offices in many cities today are equipped with radio receiving sets over which they obtain the city and state police broadcasts and in some instances broadcasts to firemen. Utilization of radio thus speeds up the handling of crime and disaster news although most of the messages received are of such minor importance that they do not figure in the news.

Radio transmission of news will become more general within the next decade.

Chapter XXV

THE REWRITE MAN REVAMPS THE COPY

A good rewrite man? Give him five facts and five minutes and he can hammer out a story that sings. He's the news room's word artist—a doctor for ailing copy, a teacher for cub reporters. For the harassed city editor, he's something like an extra arm.

—I. William Hill.*

THE REWRITE MAN'S RELATIONSHIP TO THE NEWSPAPER IS A SPECIAL ONE

As a worker inside the editorial department he performs many duties the public and even his fellow writers know little about. He is a writing craftsman with special understanding of the news and valuable reportorial experience.

He Is A Graduate Reporter. Some reporters do better work in an office than on the street. The reverse also is true. A man or woman adept at understanding other persons can gain entrance to important sources of news. He or she might not be able to assemble notes and prepare a brilliant story. When given the facts the other type of reporter can equal with his writing the brilliance of the news gathering. From this second type comes the rewrite man. Usually, however, he is a competent street man who is more valuable in the office than outside.

He Has A Place In Every Large Office. The small newspaper cannot afford expert news writers assigned only to the rewrite desk. Therefore the rewrite man is found most often in the editorial department of the metropolitan paper and the big bureaus of the press associations. There may be four or five in those offices, one in the office of a moderate size daily, none on a country weekly or small-city daily staff.

THE REWRITE MAN'S JOBS ARE MANY

He has numerous distinct functions to perform, ranging from telephone reporting to getting stories from office callers.

He Takes News Over The Telephone. This is the rewrite man's primary work. Let us say that a street or "leg" man covers a story in an outlying section of the city. He does not have time to return to the office and write the story himself or, even if he did, the story might be of such a nature that the rewrite, possessed of the facts, would do a better job.

---

* Written expressly for this book by I. William Hill, City Editor, the *Evening Star*, Washington, D.C.

Therefore the reporter telephones the editorial office, asks for the city desk, tells what he has, and is connected with a rewrite man. The street man has assembled his notes so he can give the details in good form, beginning with a lead, and progressing through the normal structure for a story. The rewrite may change that form if he wishes but at least he has the story in the shape most useful to him. He either takes notes or writes the story directly upon his typewriter, using headphones so his hands are free for typing. After he has checked the story where necessary and added any data the reporter was unable to obtain at the scene, he turns the copy into the city desk for treatment just as if the street reporter himself had submitted it.

Improving Copy Is His Job. If a regular reporter writes copy which displeases the city editor, or for some other reason must be rewritten, that executive turns to the rewrite man for assistance in recasting the story properly. If the original author is there and not crowded with other writing he may be asked to do the rewriting, but very often a story for a current edition or issue goes to the rewrite man because the reporter is not available. Here, the rewrite man's mastery of the elements of news writing comes into play. He is an expert at improving leads, bettering story structure, and polishing language. He is familiar with the various types of leads and their effect upon the reader and has good judgment about where to place the climax of a feature yarn. He can see the high points of a dull story and almost instantly make a suggestion for brightening the tale.

He Also Is A Fact-Finder. The rewrite man serves his paper as a reporter in two ways. In one he may, by use of the telephone, clipping file, and reference books, gather facts and write a story on assignment from the city desk. In the other, he may supplement the work of a street reporter who either cannot or should not be expected to get certain types of information. An example would be a fire story. A prominent citizen is burned to death in a fire which also causes much property damage. The leg man covering the fire tells the rewrite man that the local resident was killed, but leaves it to the rewrite to consult books and persons—in brief, to obtain details on the leading citizen's biography.

He Rewrites Stories From Other Papers. All newspaper editors assign persons on their staffs to examine other newspapers. Where a paper is large enough to employ someone to do this exclusively, that person is known as the exchange editor. But even when there is no exchange editor some staff member examines carefully the news columns of newspapers competing with his own or published in near-by territory. Often this is the city or news editor.

Clippings deemed of local interest are assembled and handed to the rewrite man for his attention. He is expected to check the major stories and provide new leads, either by reorganizing the stories or obtaining additional information, to combine certain yarns according to advance instructions, or to prepare without more than superficial verification the minor items to be used as filler material.

Localizing Stories Is One Of His Tasks. When a press-association story of a general nature but capable of local application reaches the city desk from the telegraph or news editor, who has seen the possibilities, it is given to the rewrite man. He is expected to inject the local material. This he obtains from files or over the telephone from outside sources. It may appear as an add, insert, precede, box insert, new lead, or entirely new story. A common example is a story from a state health officer about the prevalence of some disease. The local health commissioner is asked for facts and comment. This copy is not necessarily only off the wire. It may be a story from any outside source—newspaper, publicity release, book, or magazine.

Checking And Rewriting Publicity Falls To Him. Publicity copy has such a wide range of quality the city desk rarely can be sure that what the mail has brought is to be trusted. Therefore the deskman tosses to the rewrite man a publicity release which can be checked locally and indicates that it is to be rewritten to a certain length. The checking is for accuracy's sake; the revamping is to avoid having stories similar to those in other papers, since there always are editors who choose to print a publicity piece verbatim.

He Prepares Miscellaneous Documents. Between more important jobs the rewrite man may be asked to take a letter that has come in the mail and rewrite it into a news story. This may require search for additional facts. Letters to the editor, when illegibly handwritten, must be typed before the composing room will accept them. Poems, certificates, affidavits, and other miscellaneous matter must be transformed into newspaper copy. All this is the rewrite man's job any time of the day.

He Interviews Office Visitors. Many persons come to newspaper offices with stories to tell. Someone must be ready to serve them. Since he is right at hand the city desk turns such visitors over to the rewrite man, who interviews them in no different fashion than if he had gone to their homes. He writes the story just as if he had returned from an assignment. This work calls for versatility. The rewrite man must know how to handle a wide variety of news, often pinch-hitting for departmental editors. He must know what facts to seek in speaking to persons bearing stories about rummage sales, church services, deaths, political corruption, personal activities, and solutions for an economic crisis, to mention some typical instances.

WHY IS REWRITING NECESSARY?

Rewriting improves stories, permits the newspaper to take advantage of news breaks, and keeps the paper up to the minute.

First Stories Are Not Always Best. Because production is hurried, the story a reporter writes is not necessarily the best that can be written. A second writing, whether of the work of a competitor or of a writer in the "home" office, may find new possibilities in the story, give emphasis to something neglected, take advantage of coincidences, or bring new background facts to bear. The structure, the diction, the lead, or some other specific part of a story therefore may be, and often is, definitely improved by rewriting.

The News May Change. Between editions the news, which never is static, may force a change in a story. So as to convey some information to the public a paper may carry one or two paragraphs on some important story in an edition. Within an hour its rewrite men and regular street reporters can add columns of information. As the day or night goes on the story gains in length and strength from frequent rewriting (which means adding, recasting, inserting, and rearranging material). An afternoon paper which rewrites from a morning sheet is likely to find new facts, corrections to be made in the original yarn, and other material calculated to alter the original.

The Paper Is Kept Timely. As a result of the changes in stories called for by the alterations in news, the paper is kept up to date. This is important because readers expect and should receive the very latest information. A rival journal may provide that information first if the paper is not working constantly to get the newest facts available.

STORIES ARE REWRITTEN IN VARIOUS WAYS

The rewrite man has the whole range of reportorial writing forms available in treating stories that come to him, and he uses them as best serves the news-hungry public and the news slant of his news organ.

The Lead May Be Changed. The rewrite man may alter the lead merely for the sake of a new one, or, perhaps, because the lead best suited to the story has not been employed. He can use the straight-news, shocker, situation, capsule, suspended-interest, sequence, descriptive, punch, interrogative, quotation, substantive-clause, summary, comprehensive, epigrammatic, metaphorical, or interpretative lead as explained elsewhere in this book.[1]

The Story Structure May Be Altered. When rebuilding the body of the story the rewrite man has the choice of three main forms and their variations. These are the main-point-first, the chronological, and the main-point-last forms. Popular ways to illustrate these are to select a triangle standing on one of its points to represent the first; a rectangle standing on one of its narrow ends for the second; and a triangle standing on its base for the third.

---

[1] See especially Chapter VIII, *The Technique of Leads.*

The Story May Be Given New Treatment. The rewrite man is at liberty to change not only the lead and the architecture of the story but also the type of story. The material may come to him to be rewritten, but of his own accord, or on suggestion from the city editor, he may deem it wise to rewrite a straight *news* story into a news *feature* or to reverse the process. The rewrite man is a writing craftsman in the most complete sense. He must exercise judgment, skill, and understanding along with an ability to retain the original flavor of the news item in question.

CHAPTER XXVI

THE COPY GOES UNDER THE PENCIL

> The unsung copyreader . . . is now the principal conservator of the proper standards of language in America. It is he who is safeguarding the soundness, purity, cleanness, and power of written expression from the degeneration which threatens it on all sides. He stands as a vigilant guardian over the words, phrases, and sentences which form the bulk of the reading of the people, and which, there, tend to shape unconsciously the standards of everybody's speech and writing.
>
> —ALLEN SINCLAIR WILL.*

COPYREADING IS NECESSARY

Accuracy of all journalistic copy is of major importance in six principal respects: as to factual material, as to grammar and diction, as to presentation, as to form, as to news slant and judicious statement, as to its "dress."

Copy Must Be Made Factually Correct. The newspaper cannot afford knowingly to permit errors and incorrect statements to be published. Inaccuracies break down confidence in the paper and are misleading to readers. Although reporters are held responsible for the veracity of their copy, a number of errors may be expected from them because journalists are as fallible as all other humans. Copyreading constitutes a check on reporting.

Copy Must Be Correct As To Grammar And Diction. It is of the greatest importance that copy be correct as to spelling and grammar and attractive as to diction. The editors of the best newspapers seek to be as careful about the language used in their papers as are the editors of the best magazines and the publishers of the best books. Faulty expressions, like other blunders, creep into newspapers because of the haste of production and the still low educational level of many newspaper workers. The copyreader is a primary guard against just such weaknesses.

The Newspaper's Individual Style Should Be Followed. A newspaper's style includes such matters as its rules for abbreviation, punctuation, capitalization, spelling, and the use of words. The copyreader more than anyone else is held responsible for conformity of all copy to these rules.

---

* From an address before a journalism convention by Professor Allen Sinclair Will, late head of the Department of Journalism, Rutgers University.

Approved Newspaper Form Ought To Be Met. Newspaper practice has selected distinctive ways of presenting facts and ideas, but reporters do not always use the most concise, simple, and effective means to offer their material. Especially do those who submit unsolicited material to the newspaper fail in this. The copyreader must use his pencil swiftly in reorganizing the manuscript so that it is free of awkward construction and is arranged logically. He must shorten or lengthen it as required.

Copy Must Be Free From Dangerous Or Harmful Statements. Libelous, unfair, irresponsible, absurd, or otherwise injurious and injudicious words, phrases, and sentences must be deleted by the copyreader, although he must guard against overdoing the blue-pencilling and robbing the paper of its punch and its power in attacking antisocial elements.

Copy Needs Effective "Styling" And Headlining. Copy must be marked so the printer will know how it is to be set. The parts of a story must be kept in order. Headlines must be written. A chart or schedule of the copy must be maintained.

COPYREADING STAFFS VARY

Large papers have elaborate copyreading staffs; small papers concentrate the responsibility in a few persons.

The Large Daily Uses Many Persons. Not only is there a slotman (chief copyreader) but also there are a half-dozen persons, usually men, who handle only the general news copy, although they may spend part of their time in performing other duties.

The general news copyreaders are grouped around the chief copyreader, quite often at what is known as a "universal copy desk." This is semicircular, with six or eight partitioned spaces before which sit the copyreaders. The slotman then "deals out" the stories as they arrive from the reporters (via the city desk and the copy boys) to the copyreaders. Some of the copyreaders may have special background knowledge or be adept at reading certain types of copy or facile at writing some sorts of heads. The slotman considers this.

In the departments—such as society, telegraph, sports, and those devoted to the arts—the one or two readers work under the direction of the department heads.

Small Papers Combine Duties. Small papers include copyreading as part of the work of most editorial department employees. Each departmental editor does his own reading. On a medium sized daily there may be one or two copyreaders and the city editor acts as the chief. On small dailies the city editor is the copyreader and a rewrite man or some other assistant may write the headlines. On a country weekly the editor fulfills all these functions.

Smaller papers do not require much of a copyreading force because the copy is low in quantity and there are no changes to be made for new editions.

A COPYREADER MUST HAVE A SET OF TOOLS

Certain definite copyreader's "tools" and basic equipment are essential as guarantors of accuracy, as well as for the promotion of efficiency and the meeting of copy schedules.

Writing Materials Are Basic. The copyreader must, first of all, be equipped with sharp-pointed, soft-leaded pencils. He must have available, also, such objects as erasers, shears, paste, paper clips, copy paper, spindles, copy hooks, a typewriter, and copy baskets. These will make his work highly efficient and orderly to those whose tasks depend upon him.

A Vital Part Of His Equipment Is Reference Material. Within easy reach should be directories, dictionaries, clipping files, almanacs, style guides, and similar guarantors of accuracy. On a large newspaper each department has its own set of directories. A well-stocked library and carefully maintained morgue are ready to give immediate service.

The absolute minimum requirements for a paper are a dictionary, almanac, telephone directories, city directories, encyclopedia, *Who's Who in America,* a Bible with a concordance, state blue book, synonym book, guide to grammar, atlas, a clipping file, and back copies of the newspaper.

Schedules Are Necessary. Schedules are needed for orderly handling of the copy. Large papers particularly find record sheets essential. The chief copyreader maintains one indicating when he received a piece of copy (which may be a story, insert, new lead, or other portion of a yarn), what size headline it was to receive, the reporter's name, the copyreader's name, and how long the story was and what length it was to be after it had passed under the copyreader's pencil.

The copyreader keeps a schedule of the copy he receives, recording on it his experiences with the manuscript, including a record of the head (two or three words as a guide line).

As a small paper consolidates copyreading activities, one schedule usually is sufficient for a country weekly or single-edition daily. This is kept by the editor in charge or his immediate assistant.

RECOGNIZED SYMBOLS ARE USED

The copyreader uses a set of symbols in handling copy which are generally recognized among editors and printers.

Copyreading Marks Are Not Proofreading Marks. There are about twenty-five symbols or short phrases known as copyreading marks. These should not be confused with proofreading marks, although there is some duplication. The copyreader uses his symbols on the copy. His work is done before the copy is set. The proofreader does his work with his set of symbols on proofs taken from type after the copy is set. Copyreaders indi-

COPYREADING SYMBOLS AND TERMS

The Symbol or Term	How Used	Its Meaning
⌐ ⌐	"Deadlines"	Note the quotation marks
══	John Smith	Set in small capitals
∿∿∿	city editor	Set bold face
───	reporter	Set in italics
⸲	John⸲ James	Note comma
⊙ ✗	the end⊙ the end ✗	Note period
more (or) ↓		Story is not completed
30 (or) ⌗		Story is completed
no ¶	no ¶ The city room	Do not paragraph
¶ ⌐ ⌐	¶ The ⌐The ⌐The	Paragraph
⌐⌐	The room ⌐city	Transpose words
∿	fliy	Transpose characters
stet	book *is* not	Restore the text
⌐ ⌐	Stoker⸲ ⌐street	Join separated matter
≡	Not ~~soon~~ here	Delete matter crossed out
≡	r̲	Make it a capital letter
/	✗	Make it a small letter
⊂	Re⊃porter	Close up
		city⏐desk	Separate
⌄	the⸝beat	Insert letter or word
◯	ave.	Spell out
◯	avenue	Abbreviate
◯	nine	Make it a digit
◯	9	Spell it out
⌐ ⌐	⌐The city room⌐ is ⌐in the rear of the ⌐building, he learned.	Indent on both margins

cate changes with symbols and alter copy with pencil around and between the lines of a manuscript. They are not expected—except on small papers —to rewrite copy entirely.

Symbols Avoid Detailed Instructions. The symbols are used as a form of sign language to avoid writing out instructions. The copy, when it reaches the printer, must be neat and exactly as it is to appear, in type, in the newspaper. The editors cannot turn over to the printers the responsibility of making the copy uniform and accurate.

To shorten the task of communication copyreaders make marks upon the copy which are understood by the printers. For example, a reporter writing in haste may typewrite the word "avenue" thus in his copy: "ave." Yet the style of his paper is to write this word out in full: "avenue." To save himself the work of writing the instruction: "Write this out in full," the copyreader merely circles the word "ave.," which is a signal to the compositor to set the type to read "avenue."

THE COPYREADER SETS TO WORK

The copyreader studies the manuscript carefully, using his symbols as he reads. He looks up names, verifies doubtful spelling, adds the components of a total, and is ever watchful for style variations and violations.

Because of the drastic changes he sometimes is forced to make in copy, a copyreader often is called a "copy butcher" by annoyed reporters. He really is a surgeon. Sometimes surgeons make mistakes in their operations; so sometimes a copyreader is overly severe. But ordinarily his work improves the story, just as a surgeon's generally aids a patient. In brief, the able copyreader is a careful, thoughtful, skillful technician.

ALL COPY PRESENTS PROBLEMS OF ONE KIND OR ANOTHER

Different types of copy bring up different problems for the copyreader. These include: general news, telegraph and cable, sectional stories, departmental copy, et cetera.

General News Copy Is Main Job. General news copy is the main fare of the copyreader. This consists of stories written by staff writers, reporters on local assignment, or authors of unsolicited material. It generally requires more careful reading than telegraph matter. Wire copy already has gone through several copyreadings; the local material may have been scanned by an executive editor but not inspected carefully for misspelled names or minor misstatements of fact.

Accuracy Is Vital. The copyreader of this general matter must bring all his keenness to bear upon it. He soon acquires a familiarity with names of persons and places that makes his work lighter, but he dares not trust memory too much, for an error about a local situation, about which many persons know, is far more detrimental to the paper than failing to note something incorrect in copy dealing with a distant point.

Included in this general copy will be straight or spot news stories, features, and the copy that does not fall readily into a formula. The copyreader must watch the news-story leads to see that they present the high point of the story first, unless a special order has exempted the story from orthodox treatment. He must see that all the essentials—the *who, what, when, where, why, how*—are in the lead and that the story is otherwise complete in structure. If the tale is written as a feature he must seek to inject the best elements of a feature into it at any points where the reporter has failed. For example, if the yarn is written in dialogue form, the copyreader can remove awkward and unnatural speeches or at least make them smoother. He can make sure the story-interest begins gradually, as it should in good features, and that it develops evenly, so the climax comes normally. The copyreader can insert whimsical and fanciful words and phrases that improve a feature so subtly that the reporter who wrote the pieces believes he injected them. When the copyreader also is the headline writer, he can do great service to a story by writing a distinctive headline.

Telegraph And Cable Copy Requires Special Handling. Telegraph and cable copy has a special problem for the copyreader. Although wire copy comes to the desk in good shape, that sent over printer machines is written in capital letters and therefore must be read as if all letters were "down." The copyreader underscores capitals. If the paper receives Morse copy, it is little different from locally written matter, since the telegraph operator knows the newspaper's style and types his material just as if he were a reporter back from assignment. Wire stories much more than local stories come in sections and each section is numbered and keyed in with preceding parts.

Cable stories reach most newspapers through their press association equipment and no longer require deciphering. Decoding is done at the central receiving offices. Where a paper receives direct cable matter it is sent in condensed form.

Stories Received In Sections Often Are Troublesome. Spot news stories frequently will reach the copyreader in small parts, so as to expedite the typesetting. Handling of copy of this nature requires concentration and accurate scheduling. Sectional stories may come from the paper's own reporters or, more usually, from the wire service. For example, a paper may receive a two-line flash that a boat has sunk. In a few moments a lead comes through, which, depending upon edition time, may be the first piece of copy dealing with this incident to go to the composing room. The lead may be two paragraphs long; six or more paragraphs may come in two sections of three paragraphs each. An insert to follow the first paragraph then may break in at this point or a correction may mean the alteration of the whole story as received thus far.

THE COPY GOES UNDER THE PENCIL

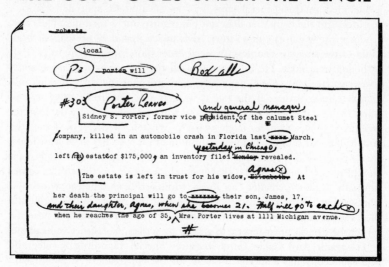

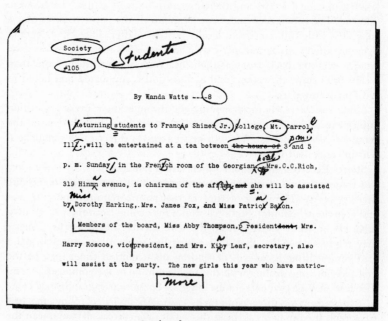

Continued on next page

N9251

PICTOU, NOVA SCOTIA, JULY 14 (CANADIAN PRESS) - THE ENTIRE
DOCK AREA OF THIS TOWN OF 3,000 WAS THREATENED TONIGHT BY A
ROARING WATERFRONT FIRE RACING OUT OF CONTROL. TWO DOMINION
GOVERNMENT FREIGHT SHEDS, A STRING OF FREIGHT CARS AND THEIR
CONTENTS, A REPAIR JETTY AND TWO SMALL SHOPS WERE BELIEVED LOST.

THERE WAS NO IMMEDIATE REPORT OF LOSS OF LIFE OR INJURIES,
BUT IT WAS BELIEVED THE LOSS WOULD AMOUNT TO MORE THAN $1,000,000
BEFORE THE FIRE COULD BE BROUGHT UNDER CONTROL.

AS CLOUDS OF SMOKE ROLLED OVER THE COMMUNITY, FIRE-FIGHTING
APPARATUS FROM NEIGHBORING PICTOU COUNTY TOWNS WAS CALLED IN TO
HELP.

THE CANADIAN GOVERNMENT STEAMSHIP ACADIA AND THE BEGONIA
MOVED OUT INTO THE HARBOR UNDER THEIR OWN STEAM AND DROPPED
ANCHOR IN A SAFE AREA.

—P236P—

The sectional story exists because news does not remain at a standstill. Fresh information creates new leads, adds, inserts, substitute paragraphs, corrections, accompanying or tangent stories, "lead alls," and precedes.

Departmental Copy Creates Special Problems. Terminology differs for each department of a newspaper. Copyreaders thus not only must have specialized knowledge but also must work within the bounds of their own departments. Copy may call for less rigid treatment in the sports department than in the financial division.

CRITICISMS AND REVIEWS. Most of the copy comes under a standing head and requires reading only. It will consist of music, art, literary, and dramatic criticism. Therefore the copyreader must have strong familiarity with the technical language and the outstanding names used in connection with the subject. The reader must help the critic or reviewer impart literary smoothness to his writing, for here some of the most finished writing may be done. Publicity must be deleted firmly and only honest appraisal permitted to go to the printer.

HUMOR AND OTHER COLUMNS. Editing the column is an exacting duty and calls for some knowledge of type by both the writer of the column and the person responsible for copyreading it (on most papers they are one and the same). Between them, they must make the column attractive in appearance by using various styles of type judiciously. The humor column usually must be made up by pasting small pieces together —a poem, a paragraph anecdote, another poem, a long quotation, still another poem, etc.—and calls for judicious selection of material. The use of asterisks, dashes, or type ornaments between items is a device which the copyreader should understand. He also should be prepared to write one or two line subheads for longer items.

Columns devoted to politics and other general subjects, written regularly by one or two persons, offer little worry to the copyreader. Usually he need read them only to watch for errors of typing or mimeographing, to detect any local tie-ups to be played up prominently, to mark such things as the column measure, if the article runs in a width not common to all columns of the paper, and to see that the copy conforms stylistically.

SPORTS COPY. It is expected that sports copy be far more informal than almost any other type of manuscript prepared for the newspaper. Personalized writing and the use of opinion are permitted extensively on the sports pages. This has made for more forceful and colorful writing than appears in other sections but also for more careless and inaccurate and unfair writing. Copyreading sports copy follows the lines of reading general news matter in all other respects. Slanginess, breeziness, and free interpretation are permitted under the wide latitude given sports writers.

EDITORIALS. Copyreaders rarely if ever have much to do with editorial column copy. Whoever edits it must guard against inaccuracy even more, if possible, than do the other readers. If he notes any dangerous statements it is his duty to call them to the attention of the editorial writer. At most he performs the routine duty of writing a brief headline and doing standard copyreading.

SOCIETY COPY. As does the sports editor, the society editor has a measure of freedom from the conventional practices of news writing. The sports editor may give evidence of this by breaking rules of grammar or peppering his copy with slangy yet effective phrases. The society editor does it by great use of adjectives and giving minute attention to details that would have no place in general newspaper copy. Copyreaders must protect themselves against falling into a rut in editing copy by challenging stereotyped formulas for stories when overused. Society-page material must be blue-pencilled heavily when it becomes gushy.

FINANCIAL COPY. Dealing as they do with vast quantities of copy made up of tabulations and other collections of figures, copyreaders of financial copy have a task that requires precision. Except in the major news stories, there is little need for or opportunity to attain journalistic heights in the writing. Accuracy is a far more important objective.

SYNDICATE MATERIAL. Syndicate and sometimes other copy comes to a newspaper office in a variety of forms—as a matrix, typewritten, mimeographed, multigraphed, as a metal cast, and printed. The copyreader identifies a mat or cast and turns it over to the mechanical department. A clipping or a printed story to be reset by his own composing room he mounts on a piece of copy paper, with wide margins to permit alterations, much as in proofreading. He proofreads, rather than copyreads, this sort of matter, which may consist of cartoon captions, illustrated features, straight news stories, departments, shorts, and that miscellaneous type of copy known as "grape" for filler.

MANY COPYREADERS HAVE OTHER DUTIES

Under some circumstances the copyreader may perform as many as eight duties in addition to reading copy.

Proofreading Is A Common One. On small papers he acts as the proofreader. Even though the composing room has one or two proofreaders, the copyreader on a small daily must give some time to scanning galley proofs and examining page proofs carefully for errors that may have occurred during make-up. Even on a large paper all who receive proofs from the composing room have learned the value of looking them over, for the perfect proofreader, like the perfect copyreader, is still unborn. On a weekly paper proofreading is regular fare for the editorial department.

Building Headlines Is Usually A Duty. Usually one-half the copyreader's work is the building of headlines for the stories he copyreads. He will be told to write heads ranging in size from eight-column streamer or banner lines to a head one line by one column. This is true especially on the smaller papers.

Knowledge Of Type Is Required. The copyreader must have a limited knowledge of the ways to attain variety in displaying body type. Not all copy for the paper is set in the same size body type or basic type face. The copyreader must know when to set the leads in slightly larger type, when to start a story or set an entire article in two-column measure, when to put certain portions in bold face or italics, and otherwise know how to give emphasis to the copy for reasons of policy or news interest. He acquires this knowledge by following the instructions of the editors, who usually make the major decisions about changes in type.

Make-Up Work May Be Another Duty. Making up the pages also falls to the copyreader on a small paper. He will be expected to plan the minor pages. The first and a few other important pages ordinarily are left to an executive editor. In addition the copyreader may have to do more than draw up a dummy. He may have to be on hand when the composing room make-up man puts the type into the forms.

Rewriting Is Often Required. The copyreading job frequently is combined with the rewriting job. On a large paper the rewrite man is an advanced reporter who receives news over the telephone and writes the stories as they come thus. He is a sort of complement to the "leg" man, who ferrets out the news but does not write it. The copyreader, being inside all day, is in a good position to fulfill this function and on the small paper it is a duty frequently performed between editing and heading up stories.

Preparing And Editing Cutlines Is Another Special Job. Reporters and copyreaders share this, at least at the writing stage. But the copyreader must know the paper's style of underline and overline to assure uniformity. Commonly these cutlines (the top part is called a caption and the bottom an underline) are prepared in two parts. One carries the caption or overline, with indication of size. In order to save writing out type sizes and styles each time, short cuts are used in indicating what is desired. The other sheet carries the underline and a partial repetition of the caption to make their union certain at make-up time. The copyreader, whether he writes or only edits these, must see that they are marked properly and that they are brisk, eye-catching, and comprehensive enough to give the picture meaning by itself.

Treatment Of Picture Copy Sometimes Devolves Upon Him. Photographic copy also appears on his desk. Not all copy set before the copyreader for his attention is manuscript. It also may be picture copy and therefore require special understanding of the news value and treatment of such copy. Among the duties connected with handling pictures are those of selecting the best copy—journalistically and photographically, marking the pictures so that the engraver will know how much to reproduce, and indicating photo combinations (layouts) or places for improvement at the hands of an artist.

Library Duties Are Often Necessary. Custodian of the library, or morgue, may be another title. If he puts some of his time in library work, as he may very well do on a small paper, the copyreader must know how to clip exchanges, his own paper, and other types of publications; be familiar with some system of filing this material; work similarly with mats, photographs, and cuts; assemble everything contributing to a complete and quickly attainable collection of information on the greatest possible number of subjects.

CHAPTER XXVII

HEADLINING THE NEWS

But the headline, whatever apologies may be made for its bad manners and its offences against good taste, remains one of the clearest illustrations of the temper of a newspaper,—of its sensational character or of a restrained desire to indicate the nature of the news beneath it without exploiting it.—LUCY MAYNARD SALMON.*

HEADLINES SERVE THREE FUNCTIONS

A good headline should advertise and summarize its story and beautify the page on which it appears.

The Headline Advertises The Story. That is to say, it should interest the casual reader to such an extent that he will read the story. A headline which does not arouse interest at first glance fails of its purpose. In the United States, thousands of persons "read" several newspapers a day. That does not mean that they read every word of every story; in fact, they do not read many stories at all. The determining factor as to whether a certain story will be read or passed by is usually the headline. The reader's eye sweeps rapidly over a page, stopping momentarily at each headline. Almost instantaneously the reader decides, from this briefest of glances, whether or not he will read a story. Therefore a good copyreader gives considerable thought to the headline which he prepares for any story, long or short, trivial or significant, dull or interesting. A poor advertisement (a perfunctory, careless, or sloppily-written headline) means no sale to the reader; a good advertisement (an attention-compelling, curiosity-arousing headline) means dividends in reader-interest.

What reader could resist reading the story under the following headline from the *Columbus Citizen*'s first page?

| Here's the Man Who Has the Jack
| To Buy the House the Cards Built |

Or this one from the same newspaper?

| 'Stars Fell on Alabama' and Ohio's
| Due to Get Her Share Monday Night |

---

* From *The Newspaper and the Historian* by Lucy Maynard Salmon, p. 52. Copyright 1923. Used by permission of the publishers, Oxford University Press.

These heads are excellent advertisements for the stories. They are striking; they compel attention; they arouse interest; they lead the reader into the story, without the slightest effort on his part, which is what every good headline should do.

The Headline Summarizes The Story. This summary may of necessity be one of four or five words in a one-line headline over a one-paragraph item, or it may run into as many as fifty or sixty words in a six-deck headline on a *New York Times* story. It is possible for a person to gain a fairly complete and not inaccurate picture of the day's news by reading only the headlines of a newspaper which has competent copyreaders who pride themselves on the quality of the headlines which they produce.

The headline "JOHN D. JONES, 67, DIES AT HOME" summarizes the story, and if the reader is not an acquaintance of the late Mr. Jones he probably will read no further. And yet, if a friend stops him on the street and says, "John Jones died yesterday," he can truthfully reply, "Yes, I saw it in the *Press.*"

The reader of the following headline in the *New York Times* had a good picture of the story which ran almost to two columns on pages 1 and 25:

GILBERT INSTALLED AS DIOCESAN BISHOP IN ANCIENT RITUAL

Bishop Manning Gives Oath to His Successor—6,000 See Solemn Cathedral Service

MILITANT CHURCH URGED

Lay and Clerical Dignitaries Hear New Episcopal Leader Challenge the Complacent

Americans have been criticized for being a nation of headline readers. This may be just criticism of the readers but it is high praise for the copyreaders who write the headlines. If a newspaper's desk force can write headlines so summarizing that the reader needs only to scan the headlines to get a picture of the day's news, it is doing its job well.

This habit of newspaper readers, however, puts a serious responsibility on the copyreader to be accurate and to mirror in the headline the exact meaning of the story. Exaggerated and misleading headlines have no place in the more carefully edited newspapers.

Headlines Beautify The Newspaper Page. Headlines, with their variety in size and type, do much to make the modern newspaper page attractive. A page of eight columns of solid body type looks uninteresting, gray, and colorless, as one can easily see if he turns to American newspapers of a century ago. There are no high spots, no foci of interest, no attention-arresting elements.

Today headlines introduce contrast, bringing black type and white space as a relief to the dull gray of the body type. Headlines properly placed bring balance, symmetry, and typographical beauty to a well-arranged page.[1]

HEADLINES VARY IN FORM

The headline varies from a one-column line of body-size type to an eight-column line of type several inches high.

Display Headlines Have Different Forms. These range from the one-column head in 8-point type to two-, three-, four-, five-, six-, seven-, and eight-column headlines in type from less than an inch to several inches in height.

On page one, heads of almost any width may be found, the size depending upon the importance of the stories, the policy of the newspaper, and the rigid mechanical limitations of eight columns.

ONE-COLUMN HEADLINES. Headlines one column in width make up by far the largest number written and, while limited to approximately two inches in width, they offer a wide variety in appearance, number of letters or words used, type faces used, and effects gained.

The *crossline* or *barline* is the simplest form of the display headline. It is merely one line a column wide in a type size often little larger than that in which the body of the story is set. The headlines over one- and two-paragraph stories are often simple crosslines. Typical examples are:

| Albion Officials to Run |

| MERIT AMENDMENT URGED |

| Gannett Group Names Keefe |

The *drop* or *step form* of headline is probably the most frequently used headline on longer stories in United States newspapers. It consists of two or three, and infrequently four, lines of type of the same length, somewhat less than a column in width, so that the first line is flush to the left, the second line centered, and the third line flush to the right. Though the most commonly used, it is a hard headline to write because each of the lines must be of exactly the same length as the other two.

---

[1] This function of headlines is discussed in detail in Chapter XXVIII, *Page-One Make-up.*

Following are examples of the drop or step type of headline:

LORAIN CRAWLS
OUT OF RUINS; —
FIND MORE DEAD
—*Chicago Tribune*

FOUR FLYERS FOUND
DEAD IN WRECKAGE
—*Baltimore Sun*

EXEMPTION OF TAX
ON DEBT PAYMENTS
ASKED BY BUSINESS
—*New York Times*

3 Beat and Rob Man, 73,
Of His Hearing Device
—*New York Herald Tribune*

The *inverted pyramid form* of headline is used less often than it was, but still is to be found in the top headlines of some newspapers.[1] Each of the three or four lines in this head is successively shorter than the line above it. An example of a top headline of this form is:

RAIN SEEN
FOR GAME
TODAY
—*Ohio State Journal*

The most recent development in the evolution of the headline in American newspapers is the "flush-left" headline which has no exact count for the units in each line, although there is a maximum which must not be exceeded. A section at the end of this chapter discusses this modern headline in slightly more detail. Examples are:

Church Towed
To Another Port
—*Ohio State Journal*

Educators Call
For Reform
Of Schools
—*Chicago Sun*

---

[1] However, the *inverted pyramid form* is used rather extensively by many newspapers as second and fourth decks or banks.

| Giants Spank Dodgers
| After Shaky Start
| In 9-5 Tussle

—Washington Sunday Star

MULTICOLUMN HEADLINES. Headlines two and three columns wide are used over feature stories and over news stories of importance in many newspapers. Generally speaking, the wider a headline is, the easier it is to write. There are more units in the multicolumn headlines and there is not the necessity of trying to crowd two or three words of eight to twelve letters each into a line which will take only eleven or twelve letters.

Some few newspapers use one-column headlines almost entirely, but most editors feel that the use of headlines of greater width gives the page a more attractive and varied appearance. Thus, both emphasis of the news and beauty of the printed page, which is discussed at some length in the chapter entitled *Page-One Make-Up,* enter into the practice of using headlines of more than a column in width.

STREAMERS OR BANNERS. The headline which extends across the entire width of the newspaper (usually eight columns), or across six or seven columns, is called a streamer, banner, or ribbon, the nomenclature varying in different sections. This headline is usually in large type—72-point (one-inch) or more—and is carried on the most important story of the day. Some newspapers use a streamer every day whether or not the news justifies its use. Others resort to the display only in instances of extremely important news. The streamer usually consists of one line of type but at times it may contain two or more. Sometimes a few words in extremely large, extended type are used, as in the following streamer:

BRUNO EXECUTED

—Chicago Herald and Examiner

The use of smaller type, however, permits the giving of more details, as in this two-line streamer which covered the same crime story in another paper:

STOICAL HAUPTMANN DIES IN CHAIR
MAINTAINING HIS SILENCE UNTIL END

—Baltimore Sun

Another example of how either one- or two-line streamers may be used to cover the same event with varying effects by different newspapers can be seen from the following:

STEEL WALKOUT IS AVERTED

—The Flint Journal

| STEEL STRIKE CALLED OFF;
| ALL MILLS ACCEPT TRUCE
—Chicago Daily News

STEEL FIRMS AGREE TO TRUCE

Big 4 Will Meet Board But Reserve Right To Reject Findings
—Youngstown Vindicator

The Headline May Be Made Up Variously. The headline consists of from one to eight, or even more parts, commonly called decks or banks. In the simple crossline form there is, of course, only one deck:

| Dies Unlocking Library Doors |
—New York Herald Tribune

In a somewhat longer story a second deck or bank, in slightly smaller type, may be added:

Odd-Jobs Man Arrested
In Murder of Widow

Had Burlap Like That Wrapped
Around Woman's Legs
—New York Herald Tribune

The third deck in a headline of four or more decks is usually a simple crossline. The fourth deck usually is similar in form to the second deck— as are the sixth and eighth decks, if the headline has that many:

BOSTON SYMPHONY
AROUSES AUDIENCE

Cheers Follow Performance of
Sibelius, Second Given at
Carnegie Hall

Women Toss Programs

Haydn Symphony in E Flat and
Finale of the Ninth by
Mahler Are Offered
—New York Times

In a two-deck headline the second deck either elaborates statements made in the first or gives further details of the story. In four-deck headlines, the fourth deck gives still further details. As in stories using summary leads, the most important facts are told first and these facts explained, if necessary, or less important ones added in succeeding decks.

Most of the modern headlines contain one, two, or four decks, although three and five decks occasionally are used.

The Kinds Of Type Used In Headlines Are Limitless. Even a cursory examination of several newspaper pages will convince the reader that the kinds of types used in headlines in the United States are virtually limitless. Gothic, Caslon, Cheltenham, Century, Goudy, Bodoni, and variants of the sans-serif modern type faces are much seen.[1] The type face of a newspaper is chosen because of the preference of the publisher, editor, or person who has the responsibility of deciding that question.

The use of capital letters in the top decks of the display headlines is still common and undoubtedly is approved in practice by the majority of the nation's newspapers. The capital- and lower-case-letter headline is becoming more popular rapidly, however, under the leadership of that typographically excellent newspaper, the *New York Herald Tribune*. There is much to be said for this headline. It is easier to read because the reader is habituated to reading body type set in lower case. Some newspapers are using a judicious mixture of capital-letter and lower-case headlines, not a bad compromise because it offers variety.

HEADLINING INVOLVES SPECIAL WRITING TECHNIQUES

The good headline contains brief, colorful nouns and vigorous, active verbs which vividly tell the story in a few words.

Language Of The Headline Emphasizes Brevity. The language of the headline is, of necessity, a brief clipped language written almost entirely in the present, historical present, or future tense in the shortest words possible because of the mechanical limitations of fitting metal type into newspaper columns of exact width.[2]

This does not mean, however, that slang and "headlinese" need run riot in display headlines. In spite of their brevity, headlines can be dignified, as any reader of the *New York Times* knows. On the other hand, they can utilize slang to the utmost and are a factor in creating it, as sport-page and tabloid readers can testify. The tabloid copyreader who

---

[1] See Chapter XLIV, *Mechanics of Publication*.

[2] The method of keeping a headline within the space of a column or more is referred to as "counting in." This means simply counting the spaces that go to make up each line of any given headline. In effect, there are so many units of space; each letter of the alphabet is counted as one unit except M and W (which are both counted as $1\frac{1}{2}$ units in width), I (which is counted as $\frac{1}{2}$ unit), and the spaces between words (which are counted each as $\frac{1}{2}$ unit). It is a purely mechanical process, but there is skill in using it well.

wrote "KING'S CANARY REFUSES TO CHIRP" over a story of an interview (or an attempted interview) with England's poet laureate worried not at all about dignity; whether his slang was justifiable or understandable is a matter of opinion.

Rules For Writing Headlines Are Not Complicated. There are a few universally recognized rules for writing newspaper headlines to which each editor adds his own variations. A headline should:

1. Tell the story accurately.
2. Contain a verb, but preferably not start with one.
3. Be in the active voice.
4. Be in the present, the historical present, or the future tense.
5. Never repeat words.
6. Avoid the use of articles.
7. Use few abbreviations except widely known ones.
8. Be typographically and mechanically perfect.
9. Not split a phrase between the first and second lines.
10. Reflect the tone of the story.

Almost all of these rules, except the first one, and probably the second, may be set aside in certain cases. Sometimes a headline in the passive voice is much better than if the active voice had been used. Now and then words are repeated. Articles are used freely in the newspaper which probably has the most carefully and accurately written headlines in the country—the *New York Times*. And so on. The function of the headline is to tell the story and if it does that it meets its first and most important requirement.

Feature headlines, like feature stories, are a law unto themselves. Their primary function is to attract attention to the story so that it will be read. They may violate any or all of the foregoing rules for news headlines but they should not be misleading. If they summarize the story as well as advertise it, so much the better.[1] The following headline is a good feature head:

Mr. Murnan Takes Wagers
On Speed and Endurance

Some Call It Bookmaking, But There Are Higher
Sounding Terms, Testimony Reveals
—*Columbus Citizen*

Problems Of Headline Writing Are Many. The headline writer faces many problems, chief among which are the speed at which he works, and the difficulty of getting words and phrases to fit in the narrow confines of the newspaper column.

[1] Several examples of typical feature headlines are given in Chapter XXIII, *The Human Touch Makes the Feature.*

TYPICAL NEWSPAPER HEADLINES

Flush-left headlines with decks and without decks; cap and lower case headlines; a four-deck and a two-deck cap headline illustrate the types of headlines most commonly seen today.

Four Die In Midair Explosion

TWA Craft Falls
In Bay After
Training Flight

Slightly Warmer To Follow Freeze

Snow Falls Here;
Low of 30 Seen

Fugitive Negro In FBI Custody

Ohio State Journal

Turkish Trip Starts Monday

Akron Beacon-Journal

HIGH COURT ORDERS CLASS FREIGHT CUT OF 10% FOR SOUTH

ICC Is Upheld, 7 to 2, in 1945
Finding of Discrimination
in Favor of Northeast

LATTER'S RATES GO UP

Majority Asserts the Present
Set-Up Retards the Advance
of the Southern Economy

New York Times

G.O.P. WAR ON BUDGET COLLAPSES

House Members Admit Cam-
paign for Cuts Will
Fall Short 50%

*Grade B Potato
Dumping Canceled*

Cleveland Plain Dealer

Bevin Places Peace Hope in Big 4 in Fall

Reviews World Situation,
Sees Parley at London
'Most Vital in History'

Points to Lessons Of Moscow Talks

His Speech to Commons
Avoids Giving Russians
All Blame for Deadlock

Long Distance Operators Here Return Today

Union Tells 5,000 Still Out
to Pass Western Electric
Pickets to Prevent Split

New York Herald Tribune

CITY DWELLERS FIND REST, FUN IN MANY PARKS

All Can See Trees and Flowers Daily

Chicago Tribune

---

*London 'Spivs' Wear 'Titfers'
On 'Loafs' And Drink 'Pig's Ear'*

Baltimore Sun

233

The speed difficulty never will be overcome so long as newspapers publish several editions daily. The good copyreader becomes geared to the
speed necessary and often does his best work under the greatest pressure.

The greatest obstacle in headline writing, however, is getting exactly
the same number of letters and spaces into each of the two, three, or
four lines of the headline's top deck. The maximum letter count of each
line in the average display head ranges from ten to fifteen letters, which
usually restricts the writer to two words or at the most three. In the step
form of headline each line of the top deck must count almost exactly the
same. In the pyramid form each line is successively shorter, making it
virtually impossible to get more than two words in the second line and
one in the third.

THERE ARE TRENDS IN HEADLINES

Headline styles change. The past century has seen the caption give way
to the many-decked one-column headline, followed in turn by the multicolumn horizontal display. The modern trend is definitely towards brief
one- and two-deck headlines, many of them with no rules except as to
maximum count.

Headlines Evolved From Simple Captions.

A CENTURY AGO. One hundred years ago newspapers used a label
head or a caption over news stories. These captions told little, if any, of
the news in the story, and were usually set in type not much larger than
that in the body of the story. The following examples from the *National
Intelligencer* are typical:

| SECOND TRIAL OF R. H. WHITE |

| For Burning the Treasury Building |
—*January 14, 1837*

| DEFENCE OF MAJOR GEN. SCOTT |
—*January 27, 1837*

| PROCEEDINGS IN CONGRESS |
—*February 10, 1837*

THE CIVIL WAR PERIOD. The Civil War brought larger headlines into
use, as did the Spanish-American War and World War I. Because of the
interest in the news, Civil War editors tried to attract readers' attention
to their stories by using headlines which hinted at, if they did not always
tell, interesting details contained in the stories. These heads were kept
within the bounds of a single column, although some of them ran to such
length that they almost filled the column. Verbs were used somewhat
sparingly and apparently there were no rules regarding their use. The

following headline from the *New York Herald* of June 30, 1864, is a typical headline of that period:

GRANT!

The Left Wing in Possession of the Waldon Railroad

PETERSBURG STEADILY SHELLED

Sharp Engagement Between the Rebel and Union Batteries

Hancock Again in Command of the Second Corps

Engagement of Rebel Troops in Petersburg

Narrow Escape of the Rebel Generals Bragg and Ewell

The Rebel Attack on the Second Corps

Interesting Account of the Whole Affair

HOW WE LOST THE GUNS AND PRISONERS

The Brilliant Achievements of Hancock and His Corps

&c.,   &c.,   &c.

THE HERALD'S DESPATCHES

The Second Corps

THE LATE NINETIES. The Spanish-American War found Pulitzer and Hearst battling in New York, each trying to outdo the other in typographical display. The eight-column streamer came into being and its use spread rapidly although some of the more conservative newspapers clung to the one-column heads.

The *Chicago Tribune* on May 2, 1898, carried the following three-line, seven-column streamer on Dewey's famous sea victory:

| GREAT SEA VICTORY FOR AMERICA!
| VENGEANCE FOR THE MAINE BEGUN!
| SPAIN'S ASIATIC FLEET BURNED AND SUNK! |

Six two-column decks on the left side of the page and six three-column decks on the right side gave details of the battle.

THE TWENTIETH CENTURY. The use of multicolumn heads has become general in recent years. Most newspapers use headlines several columns wide rather than one-column headlines with the resultant use of many decks. In the past decade there has been a swing back to the use of one-column headlines, except for streamers and on feature stories, but in most cases the maximum number of decks used is four, although the *New York Times* until recently used six and occasionally eight decks in its top heads.

The Trend Is Toward Shorter Headlines. This definite trend towards shorter headlines, which no one will deny, seems likely to continue according to many competent to judge. In fact, the use of one- and two-deck headlines, except for the day's most important story, is spreading, and this type of headline bids fair to be universally accepted.

Earle Martin, late editor of the *Cleveland News,* on becoming convinced that only one reader in ten reads "anything below the display bank of the headline," threw out everything but the display bank for headlines in the *News.* By doing so, he simplified the appearance of the paper, added to its attractiveness, saved two and one-half columns of space daily, and got an immediate favorable reaction from the reading public.

Dozens of newspapers, which for years used four-deck headlines on all top stories, now use but two decks.

No-Letter-Count Headlines Are The Newest Form. The flush-left, no-letter-count headline represents a new departure in headline trends. Using this headline, the copyreader has no worries about getting an exact count in the lines of his top deck, and can therefore concentrate on telling the story. Headline language becomes more natural. This new headline has much to recommend it and its widespread adoption in the past decade is an indication that readers like its appearance and readability.

Each of the two or three lines in the flush-left, no-count headline can be written without thought of unit count and no thought of length, except the maximum width. Most of the newspapers using this new headline have dropped second decks except on their largest stories. The reader thus gets into the story immediately after reading the comparatively few words in the one-deck, easily read headline.

Examples of this new development in headlines follow:

**North Siders
Laud New Bus
At Hearing**

—Columbus Citizen

Editor Fights
Ad Boycott

—Akron Beacon-Journal

Lewis Starts
Negotiations
With Coalmen

—Washington Times-Herald

Flier Killed in Crash
While Relatives Watch

—Philadelphia Inquirer

51 in Skokie
Subpoenaed
By Tuohy

—Chicago Sun

**Boy Bitten by Dog
Dies of Rabies**

—Cleveland News

**Frank Buck Hurt
Not by Tiger or
Lion But by Horse**

—Los Angeles Times

CHAPTER XXVIII

PAGE–ONE MAKE–UP

To make a favorable first impression, a newspaper must be attractive physically. For the dress of a paper—its physical make-up—is seen, and liked or disliked, before its contents can be appreciated.

—JOHN E. ALLEN.*

MAKE–UP REQUIRES CAREFUL PLANNING

The first impression made by a newspaper depends largely upon the appearance of its front page. If the headline advertises the story, page one advertises the newspaper as a whole, and its typographical appearance may be the deciding point in turning a potential reader into an actual one.

A Good Type Dress Makes A Good Impression. The importance of the general impression made upon readers by make-up, i.e., the arrangement of the type, the size of the headlines, the number of stories, the size and number of the pictures, should not be underemphasized. Sensationalism, restraint, blatancy, staidness, boisterousness, vulgarity, or moderation may be the impression the reader gets from a quick glance at page one.

Any one of these effects may be carefully planned. In fact, every good-looking page one is the result of planning. Two page ones with identical stories could produce entirely different effects on casual readers by the size and kind of headlines used. The hodge-podge effect resulting from a front page made up without careful planning presents a picture so obviously careless and slipshod that the reader may raise questions about the accuracy of the news stories and the dependability of the editorials.

A good front is not everything, but it is as distinct an asset to a newspaper as it is to an individual.

Each Paper Has A Make-Up Policy. Page-one make-up is handled by the managing editor or news editor in most offices although on small dailies this may be part of the telegraph editor's job. Some newspapers have a standardized make-up from which they depart only in cases of extraordinary news. Others change their make-up from day to day for the sake of variety. In the former case the task of the man in charge of make-up is easy; he has only to decide after conferences with the city and telegraph editors what stories go in what columns and the job is done.

---

* From *Newspaper Makeup* by John E. Allen, p. 1. Copyright 1936. Used by permission of the publishers, Harper & Brothers.

PAGE-ONE MAKE-UP
in TOWN and CITY

Typical examples of page-one make-up of twentieth-century newspapers. Used by express permission of the publishers of each of the newspapers.

But on newspapers where variety is sought, it is up to the man planning the page to evolve attractive typographical patterns for the eight columns and then order headlines to fit. He may use an eight-column streamer one day; a three-column, three-line head the next, and a one-column top on the big story the third day.

A dummy—a diagram of a page made out by the managing editor— is sent or taken to the composing room for the guidance of the printer who puts the type in the forms. The chart accompanying this chapter shows two page-one dummies. Frequently the managing editor goes to the stone in the composing room to superintend this process. Changes may be necessary and most managing editors think enough of the importance of make-up to be on the job to see that there is no slip-up in the last-minute rush before edition time.

Make-Up Is Secondary To News. Newspapers are NEWSpapers above all else, and if a big news story breaks at or near edition time, no managing editor will let the destruction of his carefully-laid plans for a good-looking page stand in the way of giving the story the space and display it deserves.

Beautiful examples of typography can be found in books and magazines, in posters, and other products of the job-printing shop where time is not an important factor. Typographical excellence is greatly to be desired in a newspaper, but in seeking this the wise managing editor never loses sight of the fact that his first and foremost duty is to present the news.

STYLES OF MAKE-UP VARY

Columns On Page One Have Different Values. Custom or reading habit has set values on the eight columns which make up a page of the average newspaper. As with other customs, this varies from time to time and in different localities.

Column eight, i.e., the right-hand column on page one, is generally regarded as the most important spot on the page, and therefore the day's most important story usually starts in that column.

In most sections of the country, column one is regarded as the second in importance. The day's next most important story will be found there.

Columns six, three, four, five, seven, and two follow in order of decreasing importance. Six and three are given third and fourth positions because in a paper made up with one-column heads these are the columns (besides eight and one) carrying top headlines. Columns two and seven rank much lower because headlines of the same size and type are seldom put next each other, and so the top of these two columns is generally filled with a photograph, a box, or a short feature article of little significance.

The middle columns—three and four—rank fifth and sixth in importance, and are used most frequently for important feature stories or for pictures.

In New York City and in other cities where newspapers are sold on news stands, they are likely to be folded twice instead of once and a different evaluation of the columns is made. Column eight remains the most important but column six becomes the second in importance, followed by five, seven, one, four, three, and two. With the paper folded twice, only the tops of columns five, six, seven, and eight are visible to the buyer, thus completely eliminating the pulling power of column one.

Five General Types Of Make-Up Are Common. Several different styles of make-up, each with its variations, are most generally used by newspapers in the United States. They may be classified as: balanced, contrast and balance, brace, broken or mixed, and circus types of make-up.[1]

BALANCED MAKE-UP. Balanced make-up, the chief exponent of which is probably the *New York Times,* strives for symmetry through balance. Headlines, art, boxes, and indented stories are arranged with this in mind. The reader gains the impression of restraint when he looks at the page. Absolute balance in make-up is possible and some few newspapers strive for it, but the danger of monotony is ever present. Most of the newspapers with balanced make-up use variations often enough to escape the deadening effect of sameness.

CONTRAST AND BALANCE. The contrast and balance make-up preserves balance, but attempts to get away from the perfect balance and symmetry reached when heads of the same size are put in the same places in corresponding columns. The make-up editor using this type of make-up can balance a three-column news headline at the top of columns six, seven, and eight with a three-column feature headline near the bottom of columns one, two, and three. He uses a two-column cut at the top of columns two and three to balance the two-column indented article at the bottom of columns six and seven. The entire page presents a pleasing picture—and a balanced one—without formality, exact balance, and the danger of monotony. He can change his effects daily and get a much more varied page than can the person who uses only balanced make-up.

BRACE MAKE-UP. The brace make-up, often referred to as the focused style, is used a great deal in New York City, where attention is directed to the upper right-hand corner of the page because of the way newspapers are likely to be displayed on the news stands.

A three-column head—although a two-column or four-column may be used—is usually put on the day's best story. This head spreads over col-

---

[1] Kenneth E. Olson, director of the Medill School of Journalism at Northwestern University, in his book *Typography and Mechanics of the Newspaper,* from which this classification was taken, discusses the problems of newspaper headlines and make-up much more completely than can be done in a volume of this kind.

umns six, seven, and eight with the story running down the eighth column. The rest of the page is so made up that this corner is thrown into
the limelight. Minor headlines are usually arranged in diagonal lines
across the page so that the eye naturally goes to the right-hand corner.
This diagonal line forms the hypotenuse of a right triangle—or the brace
of a wall bracket; hence the name. The *New York Herald Tribune* uses
this system of make-up almost exclusively. It is effective when one story
transcends all others in importance.

BROKEN OR MIXED MAKE-UP. Broken or mixed make-up is self-
explanatory. The make-up editor using this style of make-up tries to
avoid balance or any suggestion of it. Almost invariably the newspapers
using mixed make-up carry many stories on the page and strive for
variety in headline sizes and widths and often few, if any, of the column
rules are unbroken. The Scripps-Howard newspapers use this style. The
make-up editor is allowed complete freedom to obtain the effects he
desires, and many interesting and excellently made up pages result from
this lack of a definite pattern.

CIRCUS MAKE-UP. Circus make-up is broken make-up carried to the
extreme with headlines in glaring black type and with a dozen different
parts of the page fairly clamoring for attention. There is no focus of
interest, and because of this many feel that this style defeats its purpose.
Some evening newspapers which are conservative enough in their home-
delivered editions go in for circus make-up in early and late editions to
increase street sales. Other newspapers—the *Denver Post* being the outstanding example—use this sensational make-up in all editions; their
readers have become conditioned or inured to the daily fare of big black
headlines and accept as commonplace what is startling to the outsider.

Make-Up Has Special Terminology. Newspapermen, especially when
talking or writing about the problems and technicalities of make-up, use
many terms peculiar to the craft. This is sometimes referred to as press
jargon.

The special terms used by journalists and frequently referred to as
press terminology and jargon are defined in detail elsewhere in this
volume.[1] Certain of these technical terms are used extensively by all members of the craft, but a few are used most frequently by those concerned
with page-one make-up. Some of those most commonly used by the
make-up editor and his assistants are: art, bank, bold face, box, caption,
column rules, cut, cutlines, dashes, date line, deadline, ears, jump or
breakover, jump head, jump line, line over the top, name plate, make
over, pix, stone, tombstone, and underlines.

For example, "How many jumps have you?" is a daily question that
a make-up man in charge of inside pages asks the man in charge of

---

[1] See Chapter XLV, *Terminology and Press Jargon,* for definitions of craft terms
mentioned here and elsewhere.

PAGE–ONE MAKE-UP

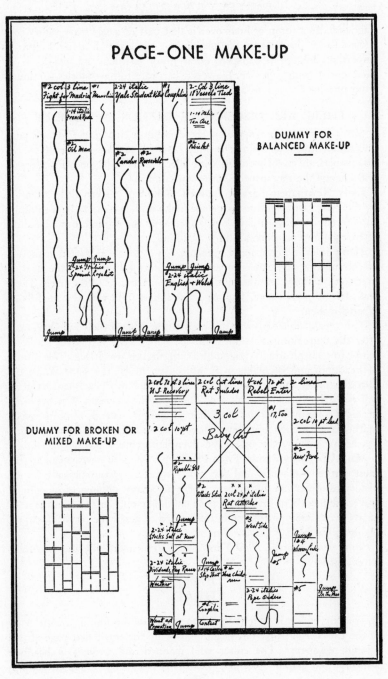

DUMMY FOR
BALANCED MAKE-UP

DUMMY FOR BROKEN OR
MIXED MAKE-UP

243

page one. As a jump or breakover is that part of a newspaper story continued to an inside page the meaning is perfectly clear. This term is important because newspapers often jump as many as two-thirds of their stories from page one. However, it is rare to have stories continued from one inside page to another.

THERE ARE DISCERNIBLE TRENDS IN MAKE-UP

Styles in newspaper make-up are constantly changing. Today's page ones have little resemblance to those of a century ago. Some of today's newspapers are experimenting with effects, which, if generally adopted, will change the newspaper's entire appearance.

Early Newspapers Largely Ignored Make-Up. Given little attention by the early printer-editors, page-one make-up has come to be a carefully considered part of each day's newspaper with one of the executive editors often spending considerable time planning it.

Many times in newspapers a century ago a story was started at the top of column one and carried over into the next column, and the next, if necessary, without any thought as to the appearance of the page. There was little, if any, display. The page was almost solid with the small body type used then.

This type of make-up was still used at the time of the Civil War, even after the one-column headline with its many decks was used. Little attempt to gain pleasing typographical appearance was made. The history of headlines and of make-up is, of course, much the same. With the introduction of the horizontal style of multicolumn headlines, attention was naturally turned to make-up. The Spanish-American War, reported in eight-column headlines and line drawings several columns wide, marked a great change in newspaper make-up. More and more attention has been paid to make-up as the twentieth century has advanced.

Make-Up Today Results From Planning. Modern newspapers are the most carefully planned and the most attractive typographically in the history of American journalism. There are many differences of opinion and consequently of practice in page-one make-up, but the front page of nearly every daily newspaper in the United States is the result of careful planning on the part of an editor.

Some years ago the *New York Daily News* used only the two four-letter words

BABY
DEAD

in type six inches in height to tell the story of the finding of the body of the Lindbergh baby. The headline took up the entire first page of this tabloid newspaper. The editor who planned and wrote that headline aimed at and got an effect just as carefully considered as the effects produced by the restrained, dignified, many-worded 42-point or 48-point eight-column streamers of several lines used in the *New York Times*.

The same effect could have been achieved in connection with the closely followed Judith Coplon spy trial in 1949 by the use of the following, on successive days:

JUDY
GLUM

COPLON
GUILTY

As stated in the chapter on headlines, the modern tendency is towards simpler headlines with fewer decks. And some of the experimenting editors have dropped all but the top deck in all headlines. This makes for a simpler and more easily read page one.

Generally speaking, the main trend in make-up today is towards greater legibility. To produce this, most newspapers have changed to a larger, more easily read body type. Many of them set this type on a deeper slug so that there is more white space between the lines. The attractive new-type faces, both in body type and headlines, have contributed to this legibility.

The flush-left headlines, which have rapidly come into use since the early thirties, bring much more white space to page one and add to the legibility of the type and to the attractiveness of the page by affording greater contrast between the black type and the white space created as a result of the irregular lines.

The *Cleveland News* and the *Los Angeles Times* are two of the newspapers whose front pages have irregular splotches of white space brought about by the use of flush-left heads. Differing in such details as type families for their heads, and the use of second decks, the make-up of these two papers presents the striking similarity of added white space not found in the average newspaper.

The Future Page One Will Be An Improvement. Tomorrow's page one will be more attractive, simpler, easier to read, less crowded, more distinctive, and will carry fewer complicated headlines than that of today.

The definite trend towards fewer decks in headlines, towards simpler, more legible type, towards the introduction of white space between the lines of body type and into spaces formerly crowded with black headline type, points towards further developments along this modern motif.

More beautiful type faces in the modern manner, more attention paid to proportion, and more study being given to physical appearance guarantee that, whatever its form, the future page one will be an improvement over the page of the present and that of the past.

Chapter XXIX

SYNDICATED FEATURES AND ILLUSTRATIONS

*The syndicate has enabled newspapers of every class to give their readers that "balanced ration" of mental food, and, through the cheap medium of the newspaper, has brought to the masses the stimulation of reading the words of outstanding leaders of thought in the world today. That fact, perhaps, has been the syndicate's greatest contribution to American journalism.—*ELMO SCOTT WATSON.*

SPECIAL FEATURES COMPLETE THE NEWSPAPER PATTERN

Interesting newspapers, appealing to readers representing a wide range of ages and social backgrounds, supplement the news and editorial columns with a great variety of special features. Interpretations of the news, pictures, cartoons, comics, serial stories, fashions and beauty hints, and a host of materials other than those supplied by the city and telegraph departments find their way into newspaper columns as a part of publishers' efforts to produce a well-rounded publication.

Special Features Stimulate Circulation. The tremendous growth in newspaper circulations in recent decades was accompanied by a significant expansion of space devoted to special features. Much of the rise in circulation is attributed to features which supply practical information, entertainment, and amusement. Editors and publishers discovered, at any rate, that special features developed and met demands of new readers, retained thousands of subscribers, and served to give a note of distinctiveness to their papers.

Publishers try to keep abreast of the trends in interest manifested by the readers of special features, and to uncover new types of reading matter and illustrations which will appeal to the public. In recent years, for example, pictures and comics, features dealing with science and health, and articles which discuss significant developments in public affairs have grown greatly in popularity. A phenomenon of the Depression years is said to have been the growth of the news-behind-the-news columns, which have developed into a business involving a gross income of hundreds of thousands of dollars annually.

Low Cost Encourages Expansion Of Features. Demands for special features resulted in a rapid growth of agencies which make a business of supplying the press with this material. By selling local rights for

---

* From *A History of Newspaper Syndicates in the United States, 1865-1935* by Elmo Scott Watson, p. 85. Copyright 1936. Used by permission of the author.

specific features to newspapers in hundreds of communities throughout the country these agencies need to charge each client only a fraction of the original cost of production. By assigning perhaps 15 per cent of the budget for the editorial department to the purchase of special features, the publisher can buy a wide assortment of reading matter to enliven the pages of his paper.

The temptation to fill news columns with nonlocal or "canned" features bought at low cost from feature services is regarded, however, as a serious threat to the individuality and effectiveness of the press.[1] Nevertheless, used with care and discrimination, nonnews features help to brighten and to balance the contents of newspapers. Used merely to fill the columns at small cost, they deaden the initiative of the local staff, standardize the contents of newspapers throughout the country, restrict the publication of fresh news, and deprive the press of its independence. Moreover, local features written by competent staff reporters rank first in appeal and reader-interest.

FEATURE SYNDICATES SUPPLY SERVICES TO 90 PER CENT OF THE PRESS [2]

Nearly 200 agencies supply the American market with nonlocal feature material by offering a great variety of separate items for sale to newspapers. Most of the weeklies and dailies supplement local news with features purchased from outside sources.

Syndicates Satisfy A Wide Range Of Reader-Interest. The feature syndicates keep a close watch on the rise and decline of news interests among readers. Directories show, for example, that features are available under the following classifications: [3] astrology, automotive, aviation, beauty, books, bridge, business, cartoons, children, columns, comics, cooking schools, editorial, fashions, finance, food, gardens, general health, household, motion pictures, news services, patterns, puzzles, photographs, religion, research, science, serials, short stories, sporting-page features, stamps. These titles represent main divisions of features which are available.[4]

---

[1] It is likewise a serious question whether the time spent by readers on columns filled with fiction, comics, sports features, and entertaining articles allows the reader to get more than a hazy impression of the significant news of the day. Daily publication of identical features in hundreds of newspapers also opens an inviting channel for the advocates of special interests to spread their colored viewpoints. Editors, therefore, attempt to achieve a compromise between the obvious appeal of special features and significant and objective news.

[2] See Elmo Scott Watson, *A History of Newspaper Syndicates in the United States, 1865–1935,* Chicago, 1936.

[3] Annual *Editor and Publisher* Syndicate Directory.

[4] The extensiveness of the business enterprises which sell features to newspapers is indicated by the list of 700 clients, controlling a circulation of about 15,000,000, served by one company which deals largely with the daily press. A syndicate which sells mainly to publishers of weekly papers has about 6,000 customers.

Among other classifications are agriculture, bedtime stories, dogs, foreign news, labor, manners, politics, questions and answers, radio, schools, Sunday magazine articles, theatrical news, verse, woman's page.

Most of the feature syndicates are private enterprises which concentrate exclusively on the business of selling and distributing their products to the press. Many of the metropolitan newspapers, however, sell the products of their staff writers, cartoonists, and comic-strip artists to other newspapers. In recent years the great press associations, particularly the Associated Press, have supplied their members or clients with an extensive feature service.

During the period of depression beginning in 1929, restricted markets and unusual competition resulted in numerous mergers and consolidations of feature syndicates. The emergence of the Associated Press as a source of supply to its membership for news pictures, comics, cartoons, and many other features increased the competitive nature of the business.[1]

Syndicates Supply Features In Many Forms. Some newspapers have limited facilities for setting up pages of feature materials and for reproducing illustrations. The feature syndicates are equipped to meet the needs of nonmetropolitan shops as well as the large daily newspapers. Among the forms in which features may be purchased are:

READY PRINT. Some of the small community papers buy features which are completely made up in page forms. That is to say, the newspaper purchases from a syndicate a stock of newsprint paper, half of which is already filled with features and advertising. Pages 2 and 3 of a four-page sheet are, for example, in printed form, and pages 1 and 4 are blank, reserved for community news printed in the local shop.

Sunday magazine sections of daily papers are also sold, completely printed.

PLATE SERVICE. Community papers are also a market for features which they receive in the form of flat metal castings, each a column wide, which are placed in the page forms in the local shop before the paper goes to press.[2] Complete articles, headlines, and illustrations are included on the plates.

MAT SERVICE. Newspaper shops which contain facilities for producing castings from stereotype matrices are supplied with a picture service or advertising service in the form of paper matrices. Small papers may receive illustrated articles in this form.

CLIPSHEET SERVICE. Most of the services distribute their features in the forms of printed clipsheets. Pages of features, printed on one side of the sheet, are received by clients, together with mats for the illustrations. The editor clips from the sheets whatever features he proposes to publish and sends the copy out to the composing room to be set up in

[1] See Chapter XXIV, *News from Near and Far.*
[2] See Chapter XLIV, *Mechanics of Publication.*

type. This service is kept close in the wake of the news. Airmail and special delivery are used to speed the packages daily from the distributing points to the newspapers.

The Individual Newspaper Arranges For Its Syndicated Features. Editors and publishers try to get as much as possible for the money which they spend on nonlocal features. They may select from one or more syndicates whatever special features they desire, a comic here, serial fiction there, and sporting-page features offered by a third agency. An alternative is to contract with one syndicate for a "blanket service" which offers a wide variety of features and pictures wherefrom the editor may select each day whatever meets his needs or desires. Many newspapers purchase such a service but supplement it with selected features from other syndicates.

Prices for specific features and "blanket services" vary greatly. The popularity of the feature, the circulation and importance of the newspaper which proposes to make the purchase, and many other factors enter into the terms of the contract. Wide distribution of a given feature results, however, in comparatively low prices for the right to publish locally the product of a noted writer or illustrator.

PHOTOGRAPHIC ILLUSTRATION IS A MODERN MEANS OF REPORTING NEWS

Illustrated tabloid newspapers, rotogravure sections in the Sunday papers, pages of news pictures in the daily press, news-picture magazines, the extensive use of sketches and photographic illustrations in news columns and magazine pages, and the coming of telephoto services are manifestations of a new era of pictorial journalism. The public likes picture stories, and publishers are meeting the demand for them as fast as technical developments and an expansion of sources for photographs permit.

Illustration Is Designed To Tell A Story. Illustration of any kind fails of its purpose if it does not tell or contribute to a story. Pictures used by the press generally deal with incidents, and even an illustration which is reproduced because of its artistic worth should have story value as well.

The nature of the modern press, particularly the newspapers, emphasizes certain requisites of illustrative art. Ideally the incidents involved in pictures should be caught at the high point of the story. This means that speed is important: speed in obtaining the picture at the right moment after a quick appraisal has been made of its story values, and speed in reproducing the picture in the newspaper.

Like timeliness, the other requirements for illustrations in the newspaper press are similar to those demanded of the news story. Action, life, prominence, romance, adventure, novelty, amusement, beauty, children, and other basic appeals to the public are used to gauge the value of illustrations in the press.

Editors Search The World For Good Pictures. Pictures submitted to the editor must pass a series of tests, and photographers and artists must have these in mind before they produce the illustrations. Pictures must not only tell the story adequately and fall within the limits imposed by cameras and the tools of the artists, but they must also be sufficiently clear and defined to meet the requirements of engraving processes.

Six important sources of pictures for the press are:

1. The feature and photograph syndicates.
2. Staff photographers.
3. The press associations.
4. Commercial photographers and amateurs.
5. Press agents.
6. Reference libraries.

Pictures For The Newspapers Are Carefully Edited. The news department selects from the syndicated material which it receives whatever pictures or mats contribute to the appeal and make-up of the news and special feature sections of the paper. Large newspapers and many small dailies also maintain an art department, which includes photographers who receive assignments for reporting events and personalities in pictorial form, and artists who prepare photographs, sketches, and layouts for publication. The city editor appraises the local pictures which staff photographers submit to him, picks the prints which best tell the story, determines whether all or part of the photograph shall be published, decides the size and form which the picture shall take, and marks the necessary instructions to the engraver on the print. Copyreaders [1] write the overlines and underlines, seeking to compress in a few clear and well-chosen words the essence of the picture story.

In addition to illustrations appearing in the news and feature columns, many newspapers publish picture pages and rotogravure sections. The staff member who selects, edits, and lays out these pages tries to achieve as wide and varied an appeal as is presented in the printed matter of the publication. News and feature pictures, covering the whole range of human events and interests, are assigned and placed in the layout in a neat and orderly arrangement of units. Variety among the specific pictures brightens the page and expands its appeal. Coherence, harmony, and unity in the appearance of the page as a whole contribute to a pleasing effect on the reader.

CARTOONS PUBLICIZE IDEAS

Cartoons and caricatures have long been popular forms of pictorial journalism in America, designed to simplify or to crystallize ideas regard-

---

[1] For further details refer to Chapter XXVI, *The Copy Goes under the Pencil.*

ing current affairs so that the reader can catch the meaning of the drawing at a glance. They are vehicles for humor and for ridicule, and they aim to entertain and to exert an influence on the public.

The Cartoon Is Effective As A Social Force. For generations the cartoon has had an important place in newspapers and magazines, particularly as an effective means of influencing public opinion. Its force lies in the ease with which the reader can catch the point of the drawing. Effective cartoons deal with a single idea, and any line or word which detracts from the simple unity of the subject is superfluous. While the subject matter covers a wide range of ideas and purposes, the typical cartoon deals with ideas and problems which have a political and social significance. Some cartoonists achieve their purposes by treating all subjects good-naturedly or humorously. Others exert an influence on the public by using a serious, stark, or sophisticated approach.

Artists Often Use Symbols. The necessity for presenting an unqualified picture, without details or explanations, has fostered the development by cartoonists of convenient symbols to represent countries, concepts, political parties and special interests. The Republican elephant and the Democratic donkey are familiar examples of symbols which were first made public in cartoons. While this powerful technique lends itself readily to exaggeration and perversion of fact, and while it is more effective as a weapon for ridicule than as a medium for expressing commendation and praise, it is nevertheless a forceful means of political and social education.

Metropolitan Papers Have Own Cartoonists. Large papers employ their own cartoonists. Thousands of others publish the products of artists who are under contract to feature syndicates. Whether the cartoons are printed on the front or editorial pages, they supplement the editorial comments and interpretations by using the effective and universal language of pictures to reach and to influence the public.

COMICS SERVE TO RECRUIT AND TO RETAIN A STEADY CIRCULATION

The "funny papers" attract readers who desire to follow daily the activities of their favorite comic characters. They also develop new readers and new subscribers among the boys and girls who are first drawn to the newspapers by comic strips.

"Funnies" Must Be Chosen Carefully. Proof of the popularity of comics is indicated by the constant growth in the number of daily strips and the number of pages in the Sunday comic sections. The comics, like pictures, have never failed to appeal to a large part of the American reading public. Today, hundreds of different comic strips are on the market, and a score or more of the most successful comic artists receive very high salaries.

A good comic strip develops a large and faithful following of readers. Consequently, editors and publishers try to select from the offerings on the market a representative list which will assure a steady circulation.[1] They follow announcements of new strips, knowing that the addition of a "bell ringer" is likely to result in a rise in circulation. They attempt to provide variety in the comic pages by selecting comics which will appeal to various age groups, to boys and girls and to men and women.

Formerly the comics were popularly called "funny pictures." The word "comics" implies that humor traditionally has been the essence of the strips. In recent years, a new form, filled with excitement, tragedy, adventure, sex and romance, has come into vogue. Humor is no longer an essential characteristic of the strips, although representatives of the two types are usually employed to give variety to the pages.

The comics are also classified into "gag" and "continuity" strips and "panels." The "gag" strips introduce a funny situation or idea each day. The "continuity" strips present a narrative or a continued story of incidents which, like chapters in a serial story, must be followed day by day. The "panels," increasingly popular, offer a single drawing containing a single thought or joke.

Critics See Good And Evil In The Comics. Comics brighten the newspaper pages and offer an escape to the public from the humdrum routine of everyday life. Readers get wholesome amusement from scenes which treat humorously many intimate and familiar details of family, business, and social life. Followers of the comics also project themselves into the roles of the characters which they follow in the comic strips and live vicariously the adventures, thrills, and other experiences of the heroes.

As long as good triumphs over evil, and as long as the comics emphasize clean humor, good deeds, decent manners, and good taste, parents express no fear over the influence which the "funny pages" have on their youngsters.[2]

---

[1] Some comics improve with age; others deteriorate and must be replaced in time. Some make a far better showing in the form of Sunday colored comics than in the black-and-white daily strips, and vice versa. Drawings which present the conversation in "balloons" are usually more successful than those which depend on underlines. These and many other considerations must be kept in mind by the editors who choose the comics.

[2] The coming of the strips which deal seriously with exciting adventures and crime thrillers has been accompanied by growing criticisms of some of the picture stories. Melodrama, filled with crimes of violence, tragedy, ugly and bestial situations, and suggestive attitudes toward sexual questions, has replaced, in some of the new strips, the fun which was formerly the essential characteristic of the comics. The question has been raised whether newspapers which present picture strips of this sort have a proper regard for their responsibility to society or for their power as socializing forces.

CHAPTER XXX

THE NEWSPAPER SETS ITS POLICY

An institution that should always fight for progress and reform, never tolerate injustice or corruption, always fight demagogues of all parties, never belong to any party, always oppose privileged classes and public plunderers, never lack sympathy with the poor, always remain devoted to the public welfare, never be satisfied with merely printing news, always be drastically independent, never be afraid to attack wrong, whether by predatory plutocracy or predatory poverty.
—NEW YORK WORLD.*

NEWSPAPERS ARE EITHER PARTISAN, INDEPENDENT, OR NEUTRAL [1]

Three policy alternatives face every newspaper: partisan, independent, or neutral—but to be either of the latter two does not mean the newspaper has neither principles nor policies.

A *partisan* newspaper is one that supports a political party or a factional group in any controversy in public affairs. Such a newspaper generally has deep-seated convictions concerning the broad issues of party or group values. Its partisanship may be the kind that supports a party or group year after year, whatever the issues; or it may be a partisanship applied to individual issues.

An *independent* newspaper owes no continuous fealty to a party or faction. It is independent in the sense that it may support a Republican program in one campaign and a Democratic program in another. The Scripps-Howard chain of newspapers is independent in this sense. An independent newspaper has convictions, which may cause it to become partisan in a campaign. But it makes up its mind independently of previous party or group allegiance. In fact, a newspaper without convictions on public issues is not regarded with great favor by the American public. Newspapers in small cities which have no competition, while calling themselves "independent" often assume a neutral policy in politics and upon community issues, serving all sides by printing all sides of those issues.

---

* From the *New York World*, May 10, 1883.

[1] The same may be said for other forms of journalistic media including magazines. In fact, much that is said in this chapter applies in some measure to all classes of journalism.

The newspaper may be neutral. *Neutrality* in journalism means a refusal to take sides. Many newspapers are neutral with regard to certain issues. Hardly a newspaper exists which is completely neutral upon all issues. Such a newspaper would be regarded as spineless. Just as the individual cannot escape taking sides against evils in life, so the newspaper necessarily has convictions against crime, corruption, and other evils in public affairs. However, a newspaper may adopt conscientiously a policy of neutrality on certain issues, e.g., in a labor war.

NEWSPAPERS REVEAL THEIR POLICIES

Principles are expressed in one or more of six ways: editorials, platforms, slogans, cartoons, news slant, sample ballots.

Editorials Enunciate Policies. The prime function of the editorial page is to declare the newspaper's principles and policies. It may argue, attack, criticize, and try to persuade the reader to accept its principles. Editorials often attempt merely to explain, but readers expect newspapers "to take a stand" upon important issues. Frequently unusually important, sensational, or special major policy editorials are removed from the editorial page and printed on page one, which by custom has been reserved for news.

"Platforms" Are Published. Many newspapers codify their policies into "platforms." These platforms are usually published at the beginning of the editorial page often under the "flag," or "masthead." They usually enumerate a number of projects or principles for which the paper stands.

Newspapers Adopt Slogans. Slogans frequently· are statements of policy regarding public issues. They may be published in the "masthead" or heading beginning the editorial page or at the top of page one.

Cartoons Reveal Editorial Attitudes. Editorial cartoons are editorials in pictorial form. They contain an argument, often suggested on the basis of an emotional appeal, which may be more readily grasped by the reader than the point in an editorial. Cartoons are published almost anywhere in the newspaper, although they are employed more generally on the first page and the editorial page.

News Stories May Express Editorial Policy. Policy may be revealed in the news in two ways. By a concentration of space and attention upon gambling or vice, for example, and the publication of an unusual amount of information about vice conditions, a newspaper expresses its attitude directly in this regard. Another and more subtle method is the selection of facts favorable to a cause and the suppression of facts unfavorable to it. This method is employed most frequently in heated political campaigns, particularly when the publisher is an active participant in the campaign. News columns which present biased information do not enlighten public opinion. Most newspapers feel their responsibility in this respect and strive to report all points of view.

Sample Ballots And Other Devices Are Used. Before elections newspapers frequently publish marked sample ballots to express their preferences for candidates and to influence voting. Other devices may include the raising of funds to fight evils, the issuance of free literature upon controversial subjects, and the setting up of bureaus to aid a cause.

SOME PRINCIPLES OF POLICY ARE GENERAL

Much success in journalism has been based on policies of public service. A newspaper whose policies do not conform with the public welfare does not succeed. This statement is a generalization applicable in a majority of instances. A newspaper's policy cannot conflict with the public welfare. It may conflict on one or more issues, but to continue to do so inevitably means that the public which has supported that paper will fall away. It may conflict with the welfare of one group and receive support from another group. Still, it must serve the interests of a very large public, if not always the entire public.

Certain abstract principles are espoused by all American newspapers. Among them are justice, liberty, patriotism, the sanctity of the Constitution, equable taxes, honest government, sympathy for the weak and distressed, and community improvement. Newspapers tend to adhere to those broad general principles which the people accept. However, they may champion concepts which may not be generally popular or understood, such as an international attitude in either trade or world politics.

OUTSTANDING PROGRAMS HAVE MADE HISTORY

While every newspaper has a program of public service, certain programs have won special fame as well as helped make newspaper history.[1]

The "Sun" Brought News To The Masses. The success of the *New York Sun* was founded upon the principle that public affairs should be brought to the level of understanding of the "mechanic" or common worker. To do so, human interest was mixed with fact. The *Sun*, begun in 1833, broke from the aristocratic and intellectual tradition of the older papers and wrote news for the common people.

Bennett And The "Herald" Developed Crusading and Sensationalism. James Gordon Bennett was a pioneer in independent journalism, in sensationalism, and in public-service crusades and "stunts." He reported politics and finance impartially, in contrast to the partisanship customary among older newspapers in 1835. He indulged in "stunts" by financing exploring expeditions, balloon races, the Stanley expedition to rescue Livingstone in Africa, and other exploits. These policies made the *New York Herald* successful.

---

[1] The historical aspect, as such, is given in Chapter III, *The Evolution of Journalism.*

Garrison Championed Abolition. Among editors with a zeal for the abolition of slavery, William Lloyd Garrison, stands pre-eminent. His great passion did not bring him wealth, but it gave him and his *Liberator* an enduring name.

Greeley Was A "Fighting Editor." Horace Greeley stood militantly for the principle of honest government in the interests of the masses of the people. He was a "fighting" type of editor who crusaded for causes by the score in his *New York Tribune*. A few of them were unfortunate. Most of them were dedicated to democracy, and he wielded tremendous power over public opinion and the course of government.

Watterson And The "Courier" Assisted Reconstruction. Col. Henry Watterson stood for the principle of friendship and unity between North and South. His newspaper was an influence for moderating the bitterness that prevailed in the decades following the close of the Civil War.

Nelson And The "Star" Stood For Community Service. Col. William Rockhill Nelson and the *Kansas City Star* vigorously pursued a program of civic reconstruction. Nelson was the aggressive fighter for reform and beautification who transformed Kansas City from a city with mud streets into a modern metropolis.

Pulitzer And The "World" Campaigned For Liberalism. Joseph Pulitzer fought for reform of everything in New York City that needed reforming from the milk supply to municipal administration. Later the *World* became the great exponent of liberalism among New York dailies. Its record of campaigns for the public welfare is imposing.

The "Times" Advocates Completeness and Accuracy. "All the News That's Fit to Print," accurately, completely, and impartially presented, has made the *New York Times* one of the world's great newspapers. Its zeal for completeness and accuracy is demonstrated in its publication of its *Index,* used by scholars in libraries throughout the world.

The "Christian Science Monitor" Meticulously Adheres To Objectivity. A policy of excluding news of crime and disasters and devoting its space to news of educational and constructive significance characterizes the policy of the *Christian Science Monitor*. Triviality finds no haven on its pages. The *Monitor* is worth-while reading. This policy makes it revered.

CRITICAL EVALUATION JUSTIFIES NEWSPAPER POLICIES

The press serves as a leader in a democracy—partisan, independent, and neutral policies are needed.

Newspaper Platforms Codify Opinion. The newspaper, by enunciating its creed in a "platform," gives public opinion, political parties, and public officials rallying points for action. In this way the press leads public opinion and brings pressures upon leaders in government.

Partisan Papers Serve. The newspaper which crusades for a party year in and year out aids in preserving that party as a force in American government. The two-party system has lived because it has had a press which maintained it. Partisan papers contribute, moreover, a crusading zeal in that discussion of issues which is needed in a democracy.

Independence Is A Valuable Policy. Independent newspapers are valuable because they weigh the issues and the merits of candidates before becoming partisan. Their programs have merit because they are not the product of continuous fealty to a party or cause. Frequently they serve as a corrective of the blindly partisan press. The trend has been markedly away from definite allegiance to a party and in favor of independence in politics. The weakening of party lines in America and the increase in the so-called "independent" vote may be associated with this trend in journalism. The consolidation of newspapers in many small cities, leaving but a single newspaper to serve the public, has impressed many publishers with their responsibility to be independent in politics.

Neutrality Preserves Impartiality. Impartiality in politics induces presentation of all sides of issues. Neutrality as a dominant policy is rare among newspapers, yet it is pursued frequently by all news organs upon numerous issues. The growth in the number of one-newspaper cities has been a factor in preventing newspapers from being partisan. When two newspapers served a community, each usually represented one faction or party and each could afford to take sides. The newspaper with a monopoly in its community must serve Republican, Democrat, capital, and labor alike, and neutrality often is the best policy. The merit in a neutral paper is the compulsion it is under to print all sides of public issues. Generally, the news columns are open to all the facts, whereas in partisan papers, they tend to reflect those facts which favor the cause espoused by the paper.

Chapter XXXI

THE EDITOR SPEAKS

Editorial expression shapes public opinion only if it adheres to the right, if it serves the public interest, if it is fearless, vigorous, unprejudiced and persistent; if it adheres to a reasonable policy well-grounded in experience and unassailable in purpose. Such editorial expression is effective if it comes from an independent, free, solvent newspaper which has won the confidence of its field and is beyond the reach of selfish interests.—ARTHUR C. JOHNSON.*

THE EDITORIAL PAGE IS A FORUM FOR THE EXPRESSION OF OPINION

Newspapers generally reserve one page as the mouthpiece of the editor and his readers where the news and tendencies of the day are discussed and analyzed and where debate clarifies issues and shapes convictions.

The Editorial Columns Expose The Policy Of The Paper. In comments and appraisals the editorial writers interpret the news of the day in accordance with policies of the newspapers which they serve. Fortified by knowledge and experience not available to readers of the news columns, the editor is able to analyze the news happenings and measure their worth. In the editorial columns the editor speaks boldly or gently as issues and policies demand. He may state with calm conviction, urge with force, or suggest with subtlety, but in all cases he hopes to influence or inform on news and issues of the times.

The Reader Has His Say. In letters to the editor the readers can express their personal opinions about anything and everything provided their statements are in good taste and are endorsed with the signature and address. This public forum serves a two-fold purpose: (1) It furnishes a safety valve for the release of emotional and intellectual promptings; (2) it keeps the editor in touch with his readers by throwing into emphasis those policies in which the readers are most interested or about which they are most articulate. Even letters from cranks or personal publicity seekers may disclose to the editor the temper of the people about certain events or unearth a situation which may be corrected by editorial crusading.

---

* Arthur C. Johnson, for many years editor-in-chief, *Columbus Dispatch,* in a symposium of opinions on the editorial page in *Editor and Publisher,* June 29, 1935.

Humor Columns Furnish Comedy Relief. The lighter touch is displayed in columns [1] which are the joint effort of the column conductor and his wide circle of readers. In limericks, pithy paragraphs, pungent poetry or prose, humorists such as Cedric Malcolm Adams of the *Minneapolis Star* and *Tribune* offer a potpourri which entertains as it informs. By a wisecrack or a quip the humor column may clarify a situation which news and editorial columns have made but more obscure. Through such characters as Archie the Cockroach, The Old Soak, and Senator Sorghum, humorists were able to expound sage philosophies and homely beliefs as they could have done with no other medium.

The Professional Offers Advice. Variety on an editorial page is enhanced by the syndicated columns of physicians and specialists on etiquette and moral and social conduct. Such columns range from advice to the lovelorn to remedies for the common cold. They present material which is personal in nature and which finds its best setting on a page of opinion and prediction.

Commentators Explain The News. The editorial page provides a place for a column of news behind the news written by special reporters who have unusual facilities for explaining behind-the-scene events. Because of the by-line or signature the columnists are permitted a freedom of style and expression which provides more background information than could an objectively written news story. They act as observers rather than reporters, and because their accounts are signed the newspaper does not accept responsibility for their views and need not agree with them. These special commentators can indicate their views as well as the facts on which these views are based. Their interpretations may be colored by individual preferences and prejudices.

Literary Works May Find Welcome Here. The best poetry of contemporary authors and of the old masters finds a place on the editorial page although it is denied reception in other sections of the newspaper. The publishing of work of literary merit encourages new authors at the same time that it increases the newspaper's opportunity to influence the cultural tastes of its readers.

What Other Editors Say Is Reported. By reprints from other newspapers on the "exchange" list, the readers are given the best thoughts of other editors in the state and nation. In this manner the page provides an escape from provincialism through presenting the viewpoints of many minds. It permits as well the opportunity to judge what are the problems in other communities and how those problems are being solved.

---

[1] For a more nearly complete discussion reference should be made to Chapter XXI, *Columns and Columnists.*

THE MAGAZINE EDITOR ALSO SPEAKS

The magazine editor exercises editorial leadership to at least the same extent as the newspaper editor. He does this in all the ways open to him, but especially in his editorial section and through his selection of articles, features, short stories, serials, or whatever is "grist for the mill" for the magazine concerned.

Since magazines are less standardized than newspapers as to their recognized functional purpose and as to their reader-class appeal, the magazine editor may not only utilize his editorial section for expression of opinion but may also, and frequently does, impregnate the entire magazine with an easily discernible editorial slant.

On the one hand, publications like the *Saturday Evening Post* follow an editorial policy not unlike that of most newspapers and limit editorial views to a specific section—often a single page; on the other hand, publications like the *Christian Herald* quite frankly promote their views by selection of material almost invariably in accord with their editorial opinions.

In a general way, magazines, reviews, and trade journals of all types may be classified for convenience into editorial categories based upon their social, political, or economic philosophy, or lack thereof.

EDITORIALS HAVE MANY FORMS AND PURPOSES

The form of an editorial depends upon its specific function, which in turn is modified by the importance of the subject, the aggressiveness of the editor, its relationship to other editorials in a series or campaign, and what particular response it is expected to elicit.

Some Editorials Inform. When editorials restate the facts of news stories or add other facts without explanation, their function is informative only. Such editorials are most frequently used when the editor has not had time to consider the stand his newspaper will take, when the issue is not yet clarified, or when the question is one of fact-finding rather than of interpretation. An editor who is lazy or indifferent may use this form in place of one of the others. Such editorials have their value, but they frequently indicate lack of courage or interest on the part of the editor.

Editorials May Explain. When an editor wishes to go into more detail than is possible in a news story because of its brevity and rigid structure, he may write editorials which explain the news facts but which do not add pertinent interpretation. In this form also the editor finds it possible to avoid stating his conviction or the policies of his newspaper. He adds an explanation which is not readily indicated in the facts available to the readers, but he comes to no conclusion and advocates no decision or action.

Richmond Times-Dispatch

JOHN STEWART BRYAN, 1871-1944
DAVID TENNANT BRYAN, President and Publisher
VIRGINIUS DABNEY, Editor

ESTABLISHED 1850: Published every day in the year at 110 North Fourth St., by Richmond Newspapers, Incorporated. Entered at the Post Office at Richmond, Virginia, as Second Class Mail Matter.

MEMBERS OF THE ASSOCIATED PRESS which is exclusively entitled to the use for publication of all news dispatches credited to it or not otherwise credited in this paper and also the local news published herein. All rights of publication of special dispatches are also reserved.

Telephone 7-1851
Adv. Representative: Sawyer-Ferguson-Walker Co.

SUBSCRIPTION RATES
By carrier, in Richmond, Petersburg, Hopewell, Daily and Sunday, 38c wk.; Daily only, 25c wk.; Sunday only, 10c wk. Elsewhere by carrier: Daily and Sunday, 30c wk.; Daily only, 25c wk.; Sunday only, 15c wk.
RATES BY MAIL—PAYABLE IN ADVANCE
	1 Yr.	6 Mo.	3 Mo.	1 Mo.
Daily and Sunday	$14.00	$7.50	$3.90	$1.50
Daily Only	9.00	5.00	3.00	1.00
Sunday Only	6.00	3.25	1.70	.60
Rates to Foreign Countries will be furnished upon request. Subscriptions by mail not accepted in localities in which carrier service is available.

Sunday, August 17, 1947

The Struggle Between Nature and Civilization

UNDERGRADUATE critics of THOMAS LOMAX HUNTER's frank analyses of world events have in the past made fun of his repetitious use of the words "tribes" and "tribal." To young or shallow thinkers it seemed as though he indulged in an anachronism. Yet MR. HUNTER, when speaking of "tribal warfare," probes close to the bedrock of the basic causes which stir up the recurring seismic disturbances of the international scene.

A recently published book by SIR ARTHUR KEITH, entitled *Evolution and Ethics*, sustains MR. HUNTER in principle. KEITH, too, believes, after more than 60 years of research in the field of international evolution, that the struggle of man to escape from the scourge of war is a struggle between "nature and civilization." He cites ample evidence to prove that wars must be attributed to "tribal expansion" and the resistance of "tribes" who seek to maintain their identity.

The tribal instinct, he says, has been the most important instrument of evolution; its urge toward growth and its resistance to the growth of neighboring tribes stems from the inherited instincts within the "genes," the determining factor transmitted by the parental germ plasm.

Tribes, he says, will fight to the death to preserve their racial, cultural and religious characteristics. He cites the Jews as an example of a race which has preserved its identity by rigid tribal rules for more than 6,000 years, and he perceives the same instinct in attempts of the white race to preserve its identity.

We need only scan the newspaper headlines of the last few days to realize how much mischief can be attributed to the expression of these tribal instincts. In Palestine the Jews are fighting the British who would deny them the right to strengthen the population of the area which they look upon as their tribal and religious homeland. At the same time murder stalks between Jaffa and Tel Aviv, as the Arabs and Jews dispute the right to that ancient strip of land.

In India, national self-determination, made possible by the withdrawal of British rule after three centuries, has resulted in a bloody tribal feud between Hindu and Moslem, because the independent mountain tribes of Northwestern India refuse to join their southern compatriots.

The formation of the Pan-Slavic bloc by Soviet Russia through the assimilation of the Balkan states behind their iron curtain indicates that the Soviet strategists are well aware of the power of ancient tribal instincts as an international cement. By the same token their envoys and agitators in the non-Slavic countries of Europe appear doomed to failure because of the resistance of nationalism.

SIR ARTHUR KEITH points out that the yearning of mankind for a reign of peace brought about by "universalism" has been frustrated because the separate nations or cultures comprised within established geographical regions will always hesitate to yield sovereignty, that is to say, to merge the identity of their tribe with alien tribes.

The late WILLIAM GRAHAM SUMNER, of Yale many years ago cited this same obstacle in the path to universal peace. He attributed wars to the dual standard of morality within the tribe: one set, highly ethical, enforced peace in the relations of people within the tribe itself; the other, highly uncivilized, code justified invasion, murder and looting, in its belligerent relations with neighboring tribes.

If we subscribe to this view, the present struggle "between nature and civilization" has arisen from the attempts of the "universalists," the ethical leaders of mankind, to establish the same high standard of morality prevailing in the "in-group" in its relations with "out-groups" with whom it competes in the international and interracial struggle for existence.

KEITH believes that that happy consummation can come about through two means: force and fear.

HITLER attempted to use brute force. He tried to impose "peace and unity" upon Europe—but with the German nation as "the ruling race." He failed because the tribal resistance he encountered proved too great when supported by those nations who have become converted to a higher and more civilized standard of international ethics.

Now that the peace efforts of the United Nations are approaching the defunct League of Nations in impotence, it is becoming more and more apparent that idealistic postwar dreams of permanent peace were wishful dreams, indeed, that peace and order can be imposed and maintained only by force, and that international laws without a unified international police force to enforce them are mere scraps of paper.

The only ray of hope on the international horizon is strangely enough, a hope derived from universal fear of atomic war—the fear that the next war will destroy friend and foe alike, and thereby civilization itself. This instinct of self-preservation may, in time, neutralize the potent tribal instincts which have twice involved the world in senseless orgies of fratricide.

A fine example of a lead editorial from the *Richmond Times-Dispatch*. Used by permission of the publishers.

Better Editorials Interpret. When an editor indicates the real significance of an event he is performing for the readers the valuable service of interpretation. Through his special knowledge acquired from research and advice of experts it is possible for the editor to point out the vital and perhaps hidden significance of what has been reported in the day's news. He views the events with his particular readers in mind and interprets the affairs of the world as to how they would affect the people in his own area. To many isolated items bearing on the same subject he may bring the thread of interpretation which correlates and binds them and thus discloses their real meaning. Although news items on the same subject may appear on different pages, the wise editorial writer notes their real relationship, explains that relationship and the possible reactions upon each other. He may bring into the same spotlight separate dispatches from Moscow, London, Paris, Athens, Shanghai, and Tokyo telling of developments in those areas. He then interprets the sum of these dispatches and what they indicate of the intentions of the powers as to matters of world concern.

Editorials May Argue. The cold, substantial logic of the best editorial minds finds expression in editorials which argue from cause to effect, clearly indicating the reasons why certain developments are expected. These are offerings that appeal to the intellect and which satisfy by their substance and clarity. They may not always convince because based on false assumptions, but if the original premise be true and the logic sound, the editor is performing one of his highest functions. They may concern public issues or public men, but they are almost invariably written about the more important situations of the time. Minor causes do not occasion argumentative editorials employing this form, for it provokes response from press and public.

Occasionally Editorials Urge Action. A public that is exhorted too often soon becomes deaf to pleas for decisive action, so editorials that incite responsive attitudes and deeds must be used rarely and at the right time. Editorials of this form are most frequently preceded by those of persuasion and argumentation and information so that their timing is consistent with the action desired on the part of the public. They may also be used in times of sudden crisis when imperative needs require that the editor exert unusually forceful leadership, but overuse of this editorial destroys its effectiveness. When an editor employs this form he hopes for a definite and prompt reaction.

Editorials May Crusade. When editors feel that a cause is particularly important they may run a series of editorials based on that cause and culminating in editorials of action. These are part of a newspaper's crusade and have made notable certain journals and certain men. They most clearly indicate the policy of the editor and his courage or lack of it. They expose corrupt local politics that need correction, advocate major improvements or champion a now forlorn cause that, if successful, would bring community betterment or individual progress. These editorials are closely related to the newspaper's policies and constitute a considered program.

Editorials May Lead By Persuasion. Many causes are easiest won by editorials which suavely and subtly convince rather than by the sterner type that demands or exhorts. When issues need no immediate settlement or are not paramount to the public's good, editorials may softly and adroitly secure consideration which more urgent methods would prevent. In such cases an editor demonstrates his knowledge of human nature and his balance on the relative importance of the various causes. Using wise psychology he convinces by inference and suggestion. Thus he expertly leads instead of drives.

Some Editorials Appraise. On occasion, editorials must offer an analytical judgment on some of the day's affairs. They must measure and weigh for the benefit of the readers who have not a comparable opportunity to judge the worth of statements, inventions, discoveries, or successes.

Sometimes They Announce Policies. The editorial page is usually reserved as the logical place for the newspaper to establish its stand and to affirm and defend that stand on current problems. Here the paper champions the plans in its program and here is its masthead flying its colors.

They Offer Entertainment. The pathos and comedy in the news are reflected in human-interest editorials of essay nature which entertain as they inform. In this category also are editorials on holidays, anniversaries, and similar occasions.

THE EDITORIAL PAGE REFLECTS LOCAL INTERESTS AND PRESSURES

The political, economic, and social philosophies and attitudes of the readers, the editor, and the owner are indicated on the editorial page by the very nature of the editorials.

Readers' Interests Are Evidenced. Whether the readers are mainly local or whether the paper extends to sectional or national areas is shown by the amount of provincialism on the editorial page. Local interests are shown by the attention devoted to near-by industries, local racial and social groups, and community problems.

Frequently the existence of one or more competing newspapers will influence the direction of editorial policies. It may cause a defensive attitude on some matters, a virile aggressive attitude on others.

The editorials show the interests of the readers by the nature of the discussion of social, economic, political, and religious questions. The incomes and living standards of readers are here shown as boldly as are their philosophies, and here is indicated the pressure of the men and groups to which the newspaper particularly appeals.

The Business Office May Direct And Influence. The editorial page may be influenced directly or indirectly, consciously or unconsciously, by the owner and the advertiser. The publisher necessarily has capital and secures other capital in the form of revenue from advertisers. He may then wish his editorial page to reflect the views of the business interests and employers rather than of other reader classes.

SKILLED ANALYSTS SHOULD WRITE THE EDITORIALS

What is said in an editorial is as important as the manner of saying it. Writers must have logical thought processes and a fund of knowledge upon which to draw. The editorial writer ought to combine common sense with erudition.

To understand the complex problems of today, the editorial writer must have studied both widely and deeply. He must be such a constant student that he can immediately appraise contemporary problems, estimate their worth, and interpret their meaning. He may need to be an expert in one or two fields or a near expert in many. In any event, he needs to be a qualified analyst.

If he is to translate the complexities of today's affairs into terms which the everyday man can understand, he must know how his readers live, act, and think. He observes them with sympathy and understanding. The successful editor knows and loves his people, and it is to them he speaks on the editorial page.

Even though the editorial page is usually anonymous, it should be an example of good writing. Clear, simple diction and vigorous but homely phrasing help the logical editorial thinker convey his interpretations to the readers. Clear thinking leads to clear and effective style. Poorly written editorials reflect upon the entire competence of the newspaper.

Since it is not usually possible for a newspaper to employ regularly qualified analysts in all fields, many newspapers supplement their staffs with free-lance experts in certain fields. These may be scholars, travellers, scientists, or other specialists of repute who are sometimes requested to contribute on an individually signed article basis. Such editorials are used most often in Sunday or other special editions.

THERE IS NO SET EDITORIAL STYLE OR STRUCTURE

There is no conventional form of the editorial as there is of the news story, nor is there a recognized style except that evidenced by the impersonal, anonymous approach and the expression of opinion.

Although there is no established structure that can be recognized, many editorials have two rather definite sections. These are an opening statement of the question and an interpretation or explanation of that state-

Speaking of Straws in the Wind

The Omaha World-Herald conducted a poll last month which adds a jot to the accumulating evidence that the buyer's market is here, not only for merchants, shopkeepers and the servicing trades, but for the Federal government. People are giving price tags a hard, unfriendly look, whether they are on washing machines or health programs, print dresses or farm subsidies, automobiles or government housing projects.

Brannan Spurned

Its price tag feature is what gives the World-Herald poll a special significance. The basic question is not "What will you have?" but "What will you pay for it?" The newspaper urged its readers to express themselves for or against several Federal spending measures before Congress and to mail their marked ballots to their Representative or their Senators. Sen. Wherry received 6003 of these ballots and inserted the tabulation in the Congressional Record.

Nebraska is one of the great agricultural States. Nevertheless, Nebraskans apparently take a dim view of Secretary of Agriculture Brannan's farm subsidy proposal, which would commit the Federal government to maintaining farm prices at the Himalayan heights of the last few years. Sen. Wherry's sampling shows 102 for the Brannan plan and 5384 against it. (Not every one of the 6003 ballot markers recorded a vote on every proposition.)

The reason for this astonishing 50-to-1 vote against the farm subsidy probably lies in the language of the question. This is the way the World-Herald put it:

"How do you feel about Secretary of Agriculture Brannan's farm plan, the cost of which Secretary Brannan himself is unable to estimate? (Sen. Byrd did not estimate the cost but others have suggested figures up to $10,000,000,000 a year.)"

A reasonable explanation is that the Nebraskans did not vote against subsidies but against their cost. Some

Appalling Price Tags

of the other questions asked by the World-Herald touched on spending not so close to the Nebraskan interest, but the propositions all carried price tags and the votes for and against were in almost the same proportion. A few samples:

The national health plan ($10,000,000,000 a year)—for, 99; against, 5828. The Federal housing program ($20,000,000,000 over 40 years)—for, 214; against, 5704. Federal aid to education ($300,000,000 for one year)—for, 514; against, 5320.

It would be wrong to conclude that Nebraskans are against all these things on principle, in ratios from 10 to 50. It is safer to say that they are against the cost of these things. Their balloting is an intimation of the rediscovery of an old, forgotten truth: that you can't have anything without paying for it. This truth had been entombed in the 1930s when a majority of the people was persuaded that you didn't have to pay for things; you merely voted for them, and owed the prices to yourself.

Nebraskans aren't a tribe apart. The magazine U.S. News conducted a survey by reading the mail of members of Congress, and last week it reported on the thinking of the home folks: "Congress finds a mood of caution taking hold all over the country. Letter writers say: Cut the cost of government. Avoid tax boosts. Do nothing to unsettle business, which already is having troubles. Pressure mail is discounted. But Congressmen heed letters from friends. These letters, on the conservative side now, are slowing the Truman program."

Members of Congress long ago penetrated the letter and telegram devices of the pressure groups. Some Representatives suspect their mail so deeply on the pressure ground that they keep branch offices in their home districts to keep them informed of how the voters really feel. And all members of Congress have friends whom they trust and from whom they get a stream of information. "These persons—more than the volume of the mail—are now cautioning Congress to go slowly with any new experimentation."

Liberals' New Line

Even the liberals, as the advocates of big government and free spending are called in this age of name transposition, have become sensitive of the middle class temper. Some of these liberals, who have been President Truman's pillar of cloud and pillar of fire, are even counseling lower taxes! The Public Affairs Institute, which is a liberal front organization, recommends that plans be made for public employment to combat the impending depression, but it concedes that higher tax exemptions and lower tax rates are required, "if consumer demand is to be promptly and effectively stimulated."

To cap the case, former Senator, former Supreme Court Justice and former Secretary of State James Byrnes, one of the most sensitive politicians of the age, has raised an alarm against the welfare state and demanded a reduction in Federal spending and Federal powers.

There seems to be a trend, a happy trend. Perhaps this will turn out to be one of those years of decision for which the historians are perpetually hunting.

A good example of an editorial reflecting opinion which is partisan, yet at the same time, responsible and informed. Selected from the *Los Angeles Times.* Used by permission of the Times-Mirror Company, publishers.

ment. The first part is usually very brief and may consist only of the news on which the editorial is based. It is the second section which is the important contribution of the editorial writer and which interprets, explains, appraises or performs the other specific functions.

Where a third section is added, its purpose is to drive home a last important thought or direction. This conclusion may be in the form of exhortation, plea, advice, or command. Or it may be a simple summary. Or it may be a separate important point towards which the other parts have been leading. Its appearance and form depend upon the nature of the subject treated.

No matter how difficult the subject, the editorial writer succeeds best whose style is clear, vigorous, direct, and simple. He does not alienate his readers by devious phrasings or by inaccurate statements or unfair reasoning. He writes as logically as he thinks. The editorial writer chooses words which accurately and fairly explain the situation with which he is dealing. And he strives to avoid ambiguous terms and those not easily understood. The accuracy and purity of his style are a reflection of his thinking.

THE EDITORIAL PAGE EXPRESSES THE PERSONALITY OF THE PUBLICATION

There is no other place in the newspaper for the editor to speak now softly, now with vigor to readers he thinks of as "his people."

It Is The Voice Of The Editor. Even though the editorial page carries a note of authority in impersonal language, the readers recognize that here the editor speaks. It is a more human and vital page than are those which carry the objective news stories which are stripped of interpretation and reasoning. On only the larger papers is there a successful masking of the editor's personality on the editorial page. On the smaller daily journals and in the weekly press the editorial page discloses the editor in the guise of a friendly critic, a sage philosopher, and a kindly friend.

It Helps Mold Public Opinion. The editorials appeal particularly to the leaders in the various social, economic, and political groups and through these leaders find their way to all levels of the population. By the high lights and emphasis which the editorial page throws on certain aspects of the day's news, it directs the reader's attention to the more significant and portentous occurrences. In this way it helps to direct the thinking on particular subjects and with emphasized viewpoints.

Editorials Keep Opinion Out Of The News Columns. Perhaps the greatest single advantage of the editorial page is that it provides a legitimate place for the expression of opinion and for the exposure of bias. Were it not for the editorial page, fact and opinion might be so mixed in the news columns that the reader could not distinguish between them. With the proper separation of opinion and fact each is accorded its true worth and is clearly discernible in its own light. Even partisan papers can keep fancy and bias on a page reserved for their expression.

Editorials Reflect Local Opinion On Vital Questions. Through the editorials newspapers are able to indicate to other editors how their own communities are thinking and acting in important situations. In this sense the newspaper is crystallizing public opinion and extending its influence rather than shaping public opinion. Through this reflection of public opinion statesmen and other leaders become informed as to the wishes of the public they represent and are better able to follow the dictates of their constituents.

Editorials Help Develop The Newspaper's Own Sense of Responsibility. When editors find it necessary to choose among subjects those that will best serve and develop the interests of their communities, they become aware of their leadership in its truest sense. The editor like the wise father realizes that his task is to advise sagely remembering that he is often held responsible for measures he advocates or warns against.

Editorials Provide A Chance For Community Development. On the editorial page the newspaper assumes its role of community leader. Here civic projects may be promoted far in advance of any developments that would warrant attention on the news pages. The editorial page makes possible a look ahead and the forecasting of plans and possibilities.

The Editorial Page Is A Potpourri. On the ideal editorial page is presented such a variety of material that there is something for all manner of men. Here happenings are explained in their true perspective, leadership is exerted, the busy are informed and the weary entertained. Here the editor converses with his people, reflects, or molds public opinion on important local and national issues. The voices of others are added to that of the editor, so that on this page are represented the viewpoints of expert commentators, column conductors, and the newspaper itself.

Articulate readers occasionally contribute very appreciably to the editorial page by submitting letters or extended comments on some issue of the day. Usually, these contributions are addressed to the Editor and express either righteous indignation or alarm and find their place, when printed, in a section titled "Voice of the People," "The Forum," or "Letters to the Editor." Occasionally, when a letter seems either very timely or very impelling, or both, it may be given a position separate from the section reserved for such communications.

An excellent example of this appeared on the editorial page of the *New York Herald Tribune,* June 12, 1949. Subsequently, it was republished in the magazine *Coronet.* Its length would normally preclude inclusion in a book of this character but as it is also a good example of literary journalism, it is reproduced as an illustration of this kind of journalism as well. Originally signed "Coriolanus," as shown, the writer, John Green Burr, has given express permission for its reproduction here.

TO AN ATOM SCIENTIST

Some Parental Reflections on Patriotism, Freedom and Responsibility in Field of Fission

To the New York Herald Tribune:

Among the problems stirred up by the investigation of the Atomic Energy Commission and David Lilienthal is a personal one. My son, now thirty-one, a Ph.D in chemistry and working for the commission in the non-secretive zone, wrote me the other day questioning the investigative action and upholding the rights of free speech and action on the part of young scientists. I cannot send you his letter, but your readers may be interested in my reply, which is appended:

"Dear Son:

"Your letter and opinions on the Lilienthal matter are, as you say young scientists are, so 'intellectually proud and socially naive.' I would emphasize the 'naive' if I were you, for a while, I think. You talk grandly about 'democracy,' you are 'proud' that young scientists do not like to be told what to do; you are quite sure that if these 'proud' scientists are so told only 'second raters' will take their place. But, nowhere, my son, do you mention the one word which this country needs to hear and which is as much a part of democracy as 'freedom,' and that is 'duty' or, if you choose: 'responsibility.'

"You talk about democracy. Did you ever stop to think who created our democracy? It wasn't the scientist. It was the layman, the statesman, the politician, the military man and the ordinary everyday business man and laborer. But now the scientist wants to take advantage of that democracy to do as he pleases irrespective of the rest of the country. I am quite sure that when he talks of 'freedom of speech,' of 'freedom to do as he chooses,' of 'individual liberty,' he doesn't know what he is talking about.

"Democracy is a society, son; a conglomeration of individuals gathered together in an attempt to live peacefully, happily and in prosperity. An individual living in a society has only such 'liberty' as will allow all others to have the same 'liberty'—he is free only to do such things as will not prevent the others from doing as much. In addition to considering the other individuals, he must consider the community as a whole. There is no such thing as absolute liberty of the individual—not in society! If you want it outside of society, go out into the wilds by yourself—and find out how much liberty nature allows you.

"Of course, it is true that the purpose of a democracy is to provide the maximum of 'liberty' for the individual—that is the basic idea back of that form of government. But—that does not include 'liberty' to the individual to destroy democracy, itself, does it? Especially by violence? Must democracy provide for its own destruction? Or is it democracy when the society provides for changes in accordance with the true will of the greater part of the society? Isn't it an absurdity to say that a society must acquiesce in its own suicide? Of course it is. Then, democracies, in providing for the welfare of the greater part of their members are justified—nay, required—to limit the freedom of those of the society who would destroy it.

"When the 'proud' young scientist refuses to do anything he is told—irrespective of whether it is for the good of others or the good of the community; when in his demand for personal freedom he does not stop to consider whether his acts are going to damage the country which has given him that freedom or his neighbors who have helped preserve it; in other words when the 'proud' young scientist forgets his duties as well as his responsibilities, he should be reminded of them—forcibly if necessary. And, if he resents that, then he had better get out and try it somewhere else.

"I would love to see him try it in Russia!

"We want freedom—all of us—just as much as we can have while giving the other guy the same thing and having a society which will work along those lines. We know that the Communist idea is entirely different. And we know that the Communist is determined to destroy our way of life by violence and through the use of trained minorities; Communism is not a political creed. It is a fanatical faith—a religion for its followers, an irrationality of belief that transcends reason. To talk about it as if it were a philosophy of the mind, another kind of political party, an idea to be discussed in the drawing room—that way lies suicide, for that is just what the Commie hopes we will do and it is just as dangerous as appeasing Hitler was.

"In dealing with communism we had better treat it as we would a forest fire: the only way to win is to put it out; you can't compromise with it.

"To train Communists, then, in nuclear research is just the same as setting up schools for murderers—murderers of democracy. I don't care whether the boy is just playing with it or not. You can't take a chance. Suppose he happens to have not been playing with it? What do we do, then, take his knowledge away from him?

"The atom bomb is not just the plaything of the scientists any more—to use, develop and handle according to his ideas of what should be done or how it should be done. When you boys invented that thing you entered the great, big world, outside of your laboratories, and became an integral and most important part of your society—all of your society: politics, business, government and all the rest of it. The lives of all of us may depend on the thing and what is done with it. And that means that our ideas of what is liberty of speech and what is security take precedence over yours—except as you are part of us—even if we're wrong!

"After almost sixty years of life, I have come to the conclusion that Plato was pretty nearly right: the only 'whole' men I have ever met have been the practical philosopher type: those men, who, having lived a practical life among the material facts of life, such as running a business, arguing cases in court, curing the sick, building bridges, have, in addition to that, acquired a 'classic' education—if subconsciously—a knowledge of history, of the philosophies (not deeply but casually), of literature and, to some extent, the arts. All the rest of humanity see out of one window only, that window through which they have been gazing so intently at their own particular interest: chemistry, physics, the counting house, Wall Street, the bank, the railroad, the art of painting, the joy

of words and so on. (I'm one of them!) None of us is to be trusted: we are not well rounded enough to be able to find the answers for humanity in this weird monster of a world that you scientists are creating.

"We are all valuable—immediately so—but we—all of us—ought to have keepers over us to see that we don't run berserk after our special interest. And the only ones competent enough to be such keepers are the practical philosophers.

"And that, I believe, is going to be the eventual end of democracy: a society intelligent enough to see that such are the men who ought to run government and, of its own volition, sensible enough to put them in that position.

"Of course that will happen about 100,-000 A.D. if you scientists don't disintegrate us first!"

CORIOLANUS.

Washington, D.C., June 5, 1949.

CHAPTER XXXII

THE PRESS AS A POLITICAL AND SOCIAL FORCE

It is the newspaper press that has made democracy possible. . . .
[The] development of the press has enabled news to be diffused and
public discussion to be conducted over wide areas. . . .—JAMES BRYCE.*
    A people without reliable news is, sooner or later, a people without
a basis of freedom.—HAROLD LASKI.**

THE NEWSPAPER IS A MOST POWERFUL AGENCY OF COMMUNICATION [1]

Among the instrumentalities of communication, the newspaper generally excels because of its technical facilities, its trained personnel, and its
immense public.

Equipment And Personnel Are Highly Developed. Compared with
other techniques for the communication of facts, ideas, and arguments,
the press possesses a mechanism which makes it the most powerful force
in public affairs. Its technical equipment includes news and opinion-
gathering stations manned by thousands of trained men throughout the
world; telegraph and wireless equipment that encircles every continent;
devices for instantaneous transmission of news pictures; and high-speed
machinery for manufacturing newspapers (in Chicago alone more than
a million copies daily, each containing 100,000 words or more). In
personnel the press is today employing the best minds obtainable. Its
writers are chosen among men educated in government and trained in
journalism. This huge mechanism operates to influence public opinion,
politics, and government.

The Newspaper Reaches An Immense Public. In America, the newspaper's public embraces all who can read. The circulation of the approximately 1800 American daily newspapers is approximately 50,000,000
copies among the 150,000,000 men, women, and children who constitute
the population. Day after day the press impinges itself upon the conscious-

---

* From *Modern Democracies* by James Bryce, vol. 1, p. 92. Copyright 1921. Used
by permission of the publishers, The Macmillan Co.

** From *A Grammar of Politics*, by Harold Laski, pp. 146–7. Copyright 1925.
Used by permission of the publishers, Yale University Press.

[1] Chapter I, *The Press as an Institution,* deals, among other things, with the broad
aspects of journalism as an agency of communication whereas this chapter concerns
itself principally with the newspaper as one of the instrumentalities of communication.

ness, the emotions, the fund of information, and the reasoning processes of the American public, particularly in the fields of politics and public affairs. No other force in public life unless it be government itself operates so persistently and so extensively in the size of its public and the scope of its subject matter as does the American press.

THE PRESS OPERATES AS A POLITICAL FORCE

The press acts in nine ways upon government and public opinion.[1]

The Newspaper Reports The News. Reporters and correspondents are stationed wherever government operates. They report the facts which the people in a democracy must have. American newsmen are located in every large city on the globe. More than 500 correspondents are stationed in Washington, around 450 at the seat of the United Nations at Lake Success, and a score or more in every state capital. In a political campaign, the newspaper publishes as news the candidates' records and speeches. What every public official does and says that is of public concern is sought eagerly by newspaper reporters day after day. A form of news presentation that has grown enormously in recent years is the news picture, which has brought government at home and in foreign lands closer to the people.

The Newspaper Interprets Public Affairs. Interpretive writing about government and politics is today an important part of the newspaper. The news needs interpretation because of the growing complexity of problems and issues in government. Interpretive writers for the newspaper write either special articles, which may be run in the news columns or on the editorial page under the writer's name, or "columns" under a standing headline like the "Washington Merry-Go-Round" by Drew Pearson, "On the Record" by Dorothy Thompson, and "Today and Tomorrow" by Walter Lippmann.

The Newspaper Criticizes, Attacks, Proposes. The critical function of the newspaper is employed on the editorial page to influence political and governmental affairs. Editorial writers study developments in government and politics and are prepared quickly to attack undesirable trends and movements and to propose reforms. Probably the most famous editorial of the last century was that entitled "The Prayer of Twenty Millions," written by Horace Greeley in his *New York Tribune* and addressed to President Lincoln during the Civil War in which he beseeched him to free the slaves at once.

The Political Cartoon Plays A Part. Newspapers exert influence in politics and government through cartoons. Political cartoonists are in reality editorial writers who employ the pictorial form rather than words.

---

[1] Most of the items discussed in this section are dealt with from the point of view of journalistic presentation in Chapters XIII, XXI, and XXXI: *The Civic Project Is News, Columns and Columnists,* and *The Editor Speaks.*

Their work should, of course, be distinguished from that of the comic-strip artist, who draws purely for the amusement of readers. John T. McCutcheon of the *Chicago Tribune* was a veteran in the use of ridicule, exaggeration, and imagery in cartoons to attack or praise events in government and politics. Such cartoons are frequently more effective than editorials. Another one of the great editorial cartoonists of this century, Clifford Kennedy Berryman of the *Evening Star* of Washington has played a continuingly effective role for many years.

Newspapers Conduct Campaigns. Movements are inaugurated by newspapers in the realm of public affairs. These movements take the form of crusades, campaigns, the raising of funds, and the conduct of special investigations by reporters relating to municipal or national government. Their purpose is usually to bring about reform, or to alleviate an evil in public life, or to provide funds and machinery for constructive improvement. Such campaigns are carried on in the editorial and news columns of the newspaper.

Newspapers Propagandize. Campaigns may assume the proportions of propagandizing movements. A continuous propaganda may be conducted for a political party, against weakened national defense, or in favor of private ownership of public utilities. The propaganda of patriotism, sacrifice, and military aggressiveness carried on by newspapers during World Wars I and II was on an enormous scale, aided by the government. Propaganda may be employed both in the news columns and in editorials. However, those qualified to judge feel that partisanship should be reserved for the editorial page where opinion, argument, and bias have their proper place.

Extramural "Promotional" Activities Are Organized. Newspapers affect political life by setting up mechanisms of public service outside their news columns. A taxpayers' service bureau may be promoted. A staff of experts may be employed to study a city's finances. Free voters' handbooks may be distributed. Polls of public opinion may be undertaken in advance of elections. Such polls not only reflect opinion, but they also influence voting. Even so, the validity of all polls came into serious question in the Dewey-Truman campaign in 1948 and their influence suffered appreciably. However, it is to be expected that polling techniques, in improved form, will continue to be used and, despite the possibility of error of a few percentages, they will provide an index to what large groups think and feel about public questions.

Newspapers Adopt "Platforms." A newspaper may codify its program of reform in government into a "platform." This program is repeated every day on the editorial page.

Advertisements Affect Voters. The advertising columns contribute to the power the press exerts in public affairs. These columns are open to all parties and candidates. Paid announcements inserted in them bring social issues and political candidates and their platforms vividly before the public.

THE NEWSPAPER'S TECHNIQUE IS PURPOSEFULLY DEVISED

The influence of the press in the sphere of politics and government has many different aspects.

Factual Reporting Enlightens Public Opinion. A people's knowledge of the facts about government is the very foundation of a democracy. Without the facts in public affairs, democracy falls prey to illusion and corruption. The most enlightened peoples have been those whose news columns have been kept free. Their enlightenment has preserved democratic and humanitarian government. Where governments or the newspapers suppress the news or distort it and fill it with propaganda, the product is ignorance, class hatred, international ill-will, and dictatorship. Moreover, the news in factual form permits the citizen to vote intelligently, pay his taxes on time, participate in political discussion and political organizations, and, in general, to play the role of a free man in a democratic form of government. Democracy, according to Joseph Barthélemy, the French political scholar, carries with it the idea or principle of publicity for all the acts, deliberations, decisions, and procedure performed in the name of the state.[1] The newspaper provides such publicity more effectively than any other agency.

Publicity Purifies Politics And Government. The news of government banishes secrecy and enforces among officials a sense of public responsibility. Secrecy, whether in local government or international diplomacy, permits chicanery and corruption. Joseph Pulitzer once wrote that crookedness can live only in secret places. Throw the white light of publicity upon it, he said, and sooner or later the people will laugh it out of existence or find ways of curing it. The *New York Times* published facts about the Tweed Ring, and the latter's tentacles upon New York political life withered and disappeared. Pulitzer exposed evils in prisons, the milk supply, and other public services, and cured them. Newspapers are engaged frequently in printing facts about crime, vice, spoils, and traffic hazards. Moreover, the publication as news of the acts and public statements of officials serves to keep them alert to their public responsibility. Police departments, governors, congressmen, all are cognizant daily of the reactions of public opinion to what they do and say. Without newspaper publicity, their allegiance could more easily fall to political machines and other selfish interests.

The Press Focuses Upon Issues. Newspapers bring public problems quickly before the public. They supply the arena of debate with issues.

---

[1] *Democratic et politique étrangere*, 1918, pp. 178 ff.

Newspapers do so in two ways: by reporting as news issues raised by men in public life; and by raising issues themselves in their news and editorial columns.

Interpretation Clarifies Public Affairs. Complex problems are simplified for the public by the newspaper. Interpretive writers, in the news columns, in special articles and columns, and in editorials both enlighten public opinion and rouse public interest concerning governmental problems by the very process of clarification. The touch of human interest, with which journalists are frequently expert, helps in making complex issues understandable and interesting.

"News" Propaganda Warps Public Opinion. The public may accept as fact one-sided information in the news columns. It cannot form intelligent opinion regarding national issues from a newspaper which fills its news columns exclusively with facts favorable to one party and unfavorable to another party. The full truth was not told about World War I until many years afterward, although, on the other hand, much of the "debunking" of America's idealism in that war was wide of the truth.

Press Criticism Aids Reform. Editorials which criticize, attack, or persuade are spurs to reformation in political affairs. Newspaper criticism has forced undesirable politicians into retirement. The *New York World* prevented the sale of government bonds at a discount through Wall Street. Nearly every newspaper has a long record of having brought about change, usually for the better, in public life.

Campaigns Effect Reforms. Newspaper crusades frequently bring about improvements in public life. Campaigns carried on in news columns by a concentration of facts and on editorial pages by a marshalling of arguments day after day effect reforms. The Pulitzer awards for public service have usually been given to newspapers which have crusaded over a period of weeks or months against evils, among them the Ku-Klux Klan, municipal corruption, and racketeering.

"Service" Activities Aid Government. Newspaper services related to public affairs facilitate good government. Bureaus of advice, handbooks for voters, studies of government finances, funds for the distressed supplement government services. Col. William Rockhill Nelson and his *Kansas City Star* engaged in activities which played an important role in "purifying" and beautifying Kansas City.[1]

"Platforms" Provide Rallying Points. A newspaper's "platform" published every day on the editorial page provides a code for discussion and action. Frequently the points in a "platform" are translated into law.

The Press Affects International Amity. International relations are

---

[1] Cf. Kansas City Star Staff, *William Rockhill Nelson*, 1915, and Johnson, Icie F., *William Rockhill Nelson and the Kansas City Star*, 1935.

influenced by great bodies of opinion played upon by the newspaper press. By lashing the public into a state of mind, newspapers have determined the course of international politics. The Hearst press is held responsible for helping create a war psychosis in the United States which brought about the war with Spain in 1898. Professor Fay of Harvard places part of the blame for World War I upon the state of mind of the peoples of Europe induced by the nationalistic press in each of the great nations of Europe.[1] Professor R. L. Buell exclaimed, "Try to picture Congress voting a declaration of war without the support of the Newspapers!"[2] In nations having a free press, the state of public opinion created by the press often thwarts the acts of diplomats, either for good or evil. Occasionally this effect is produced by exposing secret diplomacy. A notable historical example of the influence of a free press occurred when French and British newspapers revealed prematurely the Hoare-Laval proposals to be submitted to Mussolini in 1935 concerning the settlement of the Italian war on Ethiopia. Public opinion in England forced Hoare to resign; the compromise proposals failed and the League of Nations faced a major crisis. The supreme function of the press, according to Dr. Chao-Chu Wu, "is to foster among peoples and nations mutual knowledge which should modify national bigotry and prejudice, and to create in the people an international mind which will think not in terms of strife but of peace, not of suspicion and condescension, but of goodwill and sympathetic understanding."[3]

In nations where the press is controlled by the government, public opinion as an independent influence does not exist.

Advertising Columns Produce Results. Candidates and special-interest groups impress public opinion with their message through advertising. Railways and utilities have utilized advertising space in educational campaigns to influence public opinion probably more effectively than other groups. During World War II both the federal and state governments and private business employed advertising to promote the war effort, including enlistment, salvage, and war bond sales. In fact, the use of advertising space to promote public-service campaigns received an impetus during the war which definitely broadened the concept of the function of advertising in society. Today, advertising is used to aid, for example, cancer and heart campaigns, highway, farm, and home safety, and numerous other peacetime crusades in the area of public affairs. Advertising designed to mold opinion in the field of public policy and law requires careful planning and sustained presentation.

---

[1] Fay, S. B., "The Influence of the Pre-War Press in Europe," *Proceedings of Massachusetts Historical Society*, vol. 64, March, 1931.

[2] *International Realities*, 1925, p. 13.

[3] Dr. Chao-Chu Wu, *Editor and Publisher*, May 16, 1931.

EDITORS MAY MISDIRECT THEIR PAPERS' USEFULNESS

There are various factors that tend to defeat the great social values which the press may bring to a democracy.

Publishers Occasionally Corrupt The News. When a publisher or an editor turns politician in his news columns, news may become corrupted. The duty of a newspaper to its immense public is to give all news on all sides of public questions. An editor is expected to have opinions and to take sides in his editorials. An editor without convictions gets little respect. But in his news columns, his duty is clearly to inform, not to influence by suppression, selection, or distortion of the news. In bitter political campaigns the temptation to devote news columns to views rather than news occasionally overcomes publishers and editors with the result that the electorate is denied full and fair information.

Reporters May Succumb To Bias. Reporters have the same duty of impartiality. Their obligation is to report accurately, completely, and without bias what is true in politics and government. Reporters are not deprived of convictions, but they have no value for the reading public unless they can divorce their convictions from their duty to report all the facts. The problem of maintaining the integrity of news columns is an important one for public opinion.

Selfish Groups May Seek Control. When newspaper ownership is acquired by a self-seeking group, the newspaper loses its value as a public-service instrumentality. Such ownership is rare today, however. In the past, powerful interests sought to control public opinion through newspaper ownership. Today such control, if known, would end in failure because the public would not support a newspaper perverted to a private interest.

Propaganda Pressures Threaten. Pressure groups through propagandist techniques attempt to subvert the function of the press. That function is to publish news, opinions, and arguments on all sides of public questions. Propaganda agencies flood newspapers with partisan information, which gives but one side of the story. A counter propaganda agency may serve to complete the story for the public, however. Pressure groups may manufacture "news" and thereby reinforce their arguments. Manufacturing news is done by the device of staging an event which the press cannot ignore as news. The observance of certain holidays and anniversaries may be the result of agitation by self-seeking pressure groups.

Official Secrecy Weakens Democracy. Secrecy in government prevents the press from performing its part effectively in governmental affairs. Such secrecy prevails in every government and in international affairs. What goes on behind the scenes may be difficult to ascertain. Secrecy may be the product of motives which cannot endure publicity. Frequently it results from an official's attitude that the matter is not the public's business. It may be justified if publicity would defeat the attainment of worthy ends, as in the case where the government is opposed by pressure groups or foreign powers who can be outwitted only by secret operations. Such occasions are rare. Government is the public's business and it should be conducted in the public view.

"Handouts" May Hamper Public Enlightenment. Government "handouts" may aid or they may obstruct the press. "Handouts" are information prepared for the press by government departments and handed to reporters, usually in news-story form. They provide information, but frequently they do not tell "the whole story." The press should investigate the facts, and go behind the "handout" to the original source if the occasion warrants. Governmental release of information should be encouraged, but the news sources should be open as far as practicable to the press and public investigating bodies at all times, and a code of honest responsibility for correctly informing public opinion should be adopted by public officials, rather than the code of the partisan propagandizing politician.

Readers Contribute To The Problem. A newspaper's power may be negatived by unintelligent readers. An early Gallup poll cited statistics to show that less than 10 per cent of Washington correspondence or news is read by newspaper subscribers. This figure has been raised in recent years. The public in a democracy has the responsibility of reading the news about government, of correcting the press by criticism or a refusal to support a newspaper when it fails in its mission of fully and impartially reporting such news, and of forming a reasoned judgment upon issues on the basis of the news. Readers' indifference permits the evil of partisanship in the news, which in turn misinforms them, so that a vicious circle is set up. Out of it comes the attitude too frequent among voters: "What's the use?" Democratic government is possible only to the degree that the newspaper reader is supplied with honest news by the press and other agencies so that he may assert himself at the polls intelligently. Too often he cannot so act because of indifference and a perverted supply of political information. Yet compared with the press of the rest of the world, the American press supplies the citizen with more nearly complete and unbiased news about his government than does the press of any other country.

CHAPTER XXXIII

THE WORLD'S PRESS SYSTEMS

The liberty of the Press consists, in my idea, in publishing the truth, from good motives and for justifiable ends, though it reflect on government, on magistrates, or individuals.—ALEXANDER HAMILTON.*

News abroad is controlled, suppressed, and censored to a degree difficult to imagine in the United States. Governments in the dictator-ruled countries, particularly, see in the press chiefly a means by which they can shape and mould public opinion; they have made journalists semi-official workers of the state and have throttled the free flow of news within their countries, and, so far as they are able, news sent abroad.
—EUGENE W. SHARP.**

TWO CLASSIFICATIONS MAY BE MADE

One is based upon the relationship between the press and government; the other upon the primary function assumed by the press.

Systems Reflect Various Relationships To Government. At least four different press systems exist whose types evolved from, and are in large measure dependent upon, the philosophies of governments now controlling the destinies of various world powers. The press in each country varies from that in other nation-states in some measure because of the differences in cultural and political growth patterns, but in general the various press systems, or types of journalistic control, may be classified as: *first,* the free press as exemplified in the United States and the British Commonwealth of Nations; *second,* the semifree press characterized by a precarious freedom of expression in operation in most South American countries and others such as Turkey and Greece; *third,* the communist press system created by Soviet-Russia; and *fourth,* the fascist press system evolved under Hitler in Germany and under Mussolini in Italy, and copied today by a few smaller states.

Systems May Also Be Classified By Functions. Two types of journalism have vied for recognition in the press of the world on the basis of primary function. The older type is the press of opinion, its prime function being the formulation and propagation of opinions, ideas, phi-

---

* From an address by Alexander Hamilton in 1804 to the court in defense of Harry Croswell, who had been indicted for libel of President Jefferson.

** Eugene W. Sharp, *The Censorship and Press Laws of Sixty Countries,* University of Missouri Bulletin, Vol. 37, November 1936, p. 14. Used by permission of the publishers.

losophies. It has flourished in Europe for more than two centuries. The
giving of news is not conceived as its major purpose. The second type is
the press of information or news, best exemplified in the United States.
Its energies are devoted chiefly to factually reporting news rather than to
disseminating opinions.

The American press, which is now pre-eminent in news reporting, began as an opinion press in the colonial period when social, economic,
and political matters were the avowed principal concern of the editors
of pamphlets and newssheets of the day. The rugged nature of later
American development encouraged more factual reporting until "facts"
became almost a fetish of the immense news-gathering machinery of
American journalism. This has continued to be a distinguishing characteristic of the American newspaper. However, as America has emerged
as a world power, the impact of ideas has been felt more in American
newspapers, as well as in other journalistic media. In fact, as the nation
meets political and economic crises, the impact of war, and is obliged to
recognize and deal with other national ideologies, more space and more
credence are being given to interpretations and opinions appearing, and
labeled as such, even in the American press. Thus, once again as need
for interpretation and discussion of the news has become important,
American news columns have made room for articles and columns of
interpretations and opinions which cover the whole field of the day's
factual news.

THE FREE PRESS IS A DEMOCRATIC CONCEPT

A free press is simply the recognized and protected right to gather and
disseminate news according to fact, and views according to conviction,
provided neither libel nor scurrility is involved. Liberty to print "all the
news that's fit to print" is its chief characteristic.

What Is Meant By Freedom Of The Press? The concept of freedom
of the press has evolved to mean an absence of definite restrictions. A
government license or permit to publish a newspaper was employed in
early England to suppress opposition to the government. Only friendly
newspapers were licensed. Today attempts to enforce a government
license upon the press in England or the United States would be, and has
been recognized and fought as, an infringement upon the liberty of the
press. "Previous censorship," by which is meant the requirement that
matter intended for publication be submitted to a government censor
for approval before being published, was once enforced in England. Such
censorship in England or America is today an unconstitutional restriction
upon the freedom of the press except in time of war.[1]

---

[1] Censorship as exercised in World War II was frequently as obnoxious to the
citizenry and to the concept of a free press as it was necessary to the national welfare.

Press freedom means, moreover, that no court or administrative order may be placed against a newspaper to prevent publication of information or opinions even though such publication would be libelous or seditious. Legal action against the newspaper must come after publication of the offending matter.[1] Freedom of the press today also means freedom from arbitrary and excessive taxation aimed to control or injure the press. The struggle over the stamp taxes in England ended in a victory for freedom of the press. In more recent times, when Huey Long attempted to enforce an arbitrary and excessive tax against the daily newspapers in New Orleans, the United States Supreme Court held the taxing law as an unconstitutional infringement of freedom of the press.

Freedom of the press means the freedom to criticize the government, its officials in their conduct of government, and all other persons and organizations whose activities affect the public welfare. The old rule of law of England in the American colonies was that any criticism of government was libelous. The trial of John Peter Zenger[2] in New York in 1735 set a precedent in that the jury freed Zenger for criticizing the governor of New York in his newspaper. The jury said in effect that criticism is not per se a libel. As a practical matter under most circumstances, the principal restriction against freedom accorded the press in England and America is against criticism which is a direct incitement to rebellion or violence against the government. At least in times of peace, in the United States, the press may publish any information about the government which it can obtain. The Official Secrets Act in England was interpreted for a time to mean a prohibition against publishing any information about the government not officially authorized whereas the original intent of that law was that the prohibition applied only to military information. Shortly before World War II Parliament clarified and reinforced the original meaning. In Washington after the war a plan was on foot to bottle up official news and to permit its release only with official sanction. The exposure of this plan by Washington correspondent Nat S. Finney killed it and earned Mr. Finney a Pulitzer award. These attempts to require official sanction for publishing all information about the government again emphasize the vigilance necessary to maintain unimpaired the freedom of the press.

Freedom of the press means the freedom to report and publish news and opinion about public affairs, without the requirement of a government permit, free from previous censorship, exempt from arbitrary and

---

[1] See Chapter XXXIX, *The Law Limits Journalism*.

[2] He was brilliantly defended by Andrew Hamilton, a Philadelphia lawyer of Scotch birth, and his acquittal established the concept that in prosecution for libel the jury is judge of both the law and the facts. Although the point at issue was what constituted libel, the point really gained indirectly was the right to criticize the government.

excessive taxation, and unregulated in the publication of facts and criticism in relation to public affairs. Numerous state constitutions append the
qualification "with good motives and for justifiable ends" and the provision that persons shall be "responsible for the abuse of that freedom,"
which phrases give the courts authority to punish violations of specific
prohibitions described below.

Freedom Of The Press Is Defined.   In the United States, the federal
and state constitutions contain guarantees of the freedom of the press.
Press liberty is further defined in innumerable decisions by federal and
state courts.[1] In England the modern concept of press freedom is obtained
from court decisions, occasional references in the law, and even from the
fact of the absence of law.

There Are Restrictions Imposed.   Except in the abstract, complete freedom of the press can never obtain fully. That is, the freedom of the press
to criticize, to express opinions, and to publish facts is restricted in the
public interest in several ways.[2] The law prohibits the publication of matter which is an incitement to rebellion against the government, to destruction of the government, or to violence which endangers the public
peace and safety. Libel of the individual which is a published defamation
of his character, generally called civil libel, is an offense punishable by the
assessment of damages against the newspapers. Laws are common which
prohibit the publication of obscene matter and of advertisements or information pertaining to certain medical practices. Laws have been enacted
in many states against untruth in advertising. A law common in Europe
and adopted by a few American states prohibits the publication of the
testimony in divorce trials. Lottery laws serve to prevent newspapers from
publishing information in furtherance of lotteries. In every instance, the
newspaper is held responsible for violating these restrictions after the
offending matter has been published. No action can be taken before publication to prevent it.

License May Creep In.   License, or the abuse of liberty, may creep
into a press which enjoys liberty. Antisocial journalistic practices com-
plained of in England and the United States include sensationalism, coloring or distorting the news, propagandizing in the news columns, "trial"
by the newspaper of accused persons, triviality in the news, and "lying"
or falsification, especially in politics. In France, venality or the acceptance
of subsidies from foreign governments and private interests was not uncommon before World War II. A few of these evils have been cured in
press systems in which the government exercises a greater degree of control than it does in a free press system, but more government control has

---

[1] See Hale and Benson, *The Law of the Press,* and F. S. Siebert, *The Rights and
Privileges of the Press;* also in this volume Chapter XXXIX, *The Law Limits Journalism.*

[2] More fully discussed in Chapter XXXIX, *The Law Limits Journalism.*

been accompanied by even greater evils, as will be pointed out later in this chapter.

Under a free press system, few controls can be applied by the government to cure abuses. In England and the United States the high level of professional practice is the result of professional vigilance and professional self-censorship, aided frequently by public opinion and professional critics of the press.

Freedom Of The Press Is Essential To Political Liberty. Freedom of expression contributes to the maintenance and development of a free society in many ways. For example:

1. Freedom to publish news and opinion contributes to an enlightened citizenry in a democracy. It makes for free minds instead of slave minds. It encourages thought and controversy and is an important instrument of communication in a functioning democracy.

2. The right to report and comment freely serves as an essential check upon government which tends to assume more and more authority.

3. A free press combats the development of arbitrary power by the right to criticize freely the conduct of public men. Corruption in public office thrives in secrecy. Publicity is a most effective cauterizing agency.

4. A free press governed by a sense of equity, in the words of Thomas Jefferson, "keeps the waters pure," and is the best defense against streams of calculated misinformation. As such, it can contribute to better international relationships.

THE SEMIFREE SYSTEM IS A COMPROMISE IN PRACTICE

Under this system guarantees of press freedom are negated by provisions for suppression of newspapers.

Fundamental Law Declares For Freedom. The fundamental law in countries with this system of press control generally contains provisions guaranteeing the freedom of the press. This was true in Japan before World War II and it was true under Kaiser Wilhelm II in Germany. The constitutions of most South American nations today contain provisions for freedom of the press.

Freedom Is Negated By Other Provisions Of The Law. Other provisions of the fundamental law authorize invasions of the liberty of the press which practically destroy the grant of such liberty. The common provision, which may be invoked almost at will in most cases, is one which authorizes the head of the state or a minister to set aside the constitutional guarantee of freedom in times of emergency when the public peace and order are threatened. Authority is further granted for the government to suspend and even suppress offending newspapers. Editors may be jailed, fined, and sentenced to penal servitude.

Other Means Of Control Are Used. The government under the semifree system employs other means of control. In Germany government funds were employed under the Kaiser to subsidize newspapers. Another device is to subsidize a single large news-gathering agency which provides national news to the newspapers. A common law in Europe is one prohibiting the publication of "insults" to foreign sovereigns, foreign states, or their emissaries. This law permits a foreign power to register a complaint against a newspaper and thereby to exercise a measure of control of the press of another country. Another device is the employment of government funds for propaganda purposes, chiefly in the setting up of official news bureaus to disseminate information which the press is under duress to print.

Evils Are Offset In Part By Benefits. The semifree system, exemplified, among many other places, in South America, Turkey, and Greece, affords only sporadically the benefits of freedom of the press. In good times, press liberty may be unrestricted. But in times of crisis, when the people need vital information, the government may deny it to them by abolishing or effectively curtailing press freedom. A considerable value of course lies in the fact that the people know what liberty of the press means. Resistance to its suspension or abolition will almost certainly evolve especially where democracy becomes better rooted or public opinion more effective.

THE COMMUNIST PRESS IS AN INSTRUMENT OF SOVIET GOVERNANCE

This system is one of absolute government control, theoretically in the interests of the proletariat, which in Soviet Russia means solely in the interests of the communist system.

In Abstract Theory, It Is Worker-Owned. According to widely propagandized communist doctrine, the Russian press is worker-owned and controlled. Private ownership of newspapers does not exist. In its place is a system of co-operative ownership.

Three Types Of Newspapers Authorized. Soviet-Russian newspapers are generally labelled as government-owned, party-owned, or worker-union-owned. However, all editors of the Soviet press (approximately 7,000 newspapers and 300-odd magazines) are in reality designees of "the party" and as such know their responsibility to the "party line." The government departments issue newspapers designed to keep the masses informed about the government. The leading paper of this type is *Izvestia*, published in Moscow but widely circulated and slavishly quoted throughout the Soviet union and satellite states.[1] The Communist party as such publishes numerous papers, most important of which is *Pravda*,[2]

---

[1] It also serves as an authoritative source of "direction" for such communistic organs as the *Daily Worker* in the United States and *L'Humanité* in France.

[2] National in circulation, and, paradoxically enough, meaning "truth." It is the organ of the central committee of the Communist party.

whose influence and circulation are equally broad and whose columns invariably mirror the current propaganda line of "the party." Its editorial direction is one of the more important party assignments and its editorial and news guidance is an influential deterrent to persons who might be tempted to stray from the "approved" pattern. In addition, worker-unions and co-operative associations publish thousands of newspapers to keep their members informed about affairs within their own field, be it farming or factory work.

Implacable Control Comes From Above. Today, the Russian press is for all practical purposes the carefully guarded property of the Soviet politburo. Thus, through the central government and the Communist party—both effectively led by Stalin—the press of Russia is thoroughly regimented to report news and opinions without important deviation from whatever may be the current Kremlin policy interpretation. Thus, most news and all opinions are colored and slanted. The national news-gathering agency, *Tass,* is likewise government-owned. However, suggestions may, and sometimes do, come from party members and members of worker-unions through their soviets and congresses. Criticisms as to "how" measures may be achieved when divorced from the political issue as to "why" may be made and not infrequently are accepted. Executive control of a newspaper is generally placed in the hands of a committee which is held responsible and accountable for the conduct of the paper. The communist press system differs in control but little from the fascist system. All of the controls employed by Nazi-Germany under Hitler and Fascist-Italy under Mussolini are in force in Soviet Russia and her satellite states today. The one difference is that Russia applies *previous* censorship to what is intended for publication whereas the fascists developed an efficient method of *post* censorship.

"Freedom" Has Its Special Meaning. The *only* freedom of the press in Soviet Russia is the freedom to espouse communism and the communist state and the freedom to criticize not what is done but how it is done. Only loyal communists may write for the press. To advocate any other system of government than communism would mean obliteration of the offender from the ranks of journalists and probably his eventual "liquidation." As previously stated, loyal journalists and even workers themselves may criticize in the press the methods of carrying out communist policies and projects. This criticism is one of the few wholesome elements in Russian journalism.

Newspapers Serve As Agency Of Mass Propaganda. The basic characteristic of the communist press is that it is devoted to the mass indoctrination of the population. This indoctrination is called education. To an extent, it is the dissemination of knowledge and techniques, but more often the "instruction" is not education but communistic indoctrination carried on in a steady, ordered, and repetitive fashion on a gigantic all-inclusive scale.[1]

Some Evils Of The Free Press Avoided. The communist press dedicated to mass education in the communist philosophy has no place for sensationalism, triviality, or venality. On the other hand it follows a policy of propaganda and falsehood concerning all opposition creeds and parties. And, to say that the Russian press is filled with distortions of affairs in capitalistic countries is a gross understatement.

THE FASCIST PRESS SYSTEM IS AUTHORITARIAN

Absolute control by the government of every branch of journalism similarly characterizes the press of other types of dictator states.

The Press Is Considered An Arm Of The State. In fascist totalitarian states like Italy and Germany before World War II, and in small fascist states today, the press is regarded as a semiofficial arm of the all-powerful state to be employed in the influencing of public opinion. In this sense it is not an agency of private initiative, but of government.

Methods Of Control Are All-Embracing. The fascist press has been characterized by a strict organization which extends from the individual journalist through a hierarchy of official agencies to the leader, or dictator, at the top. The journalist has to meet certain qualifications as to race, creed, and competency. Generally, he has to be enrolled upon a government registry which issues him a license or permit to practice journalism. Further, and of special import, he is always a member of the district association, which is a unit of the national body. This national association is a branch of the press chamber in the ministry, which in Germany was called the Ministry of Public Enlightenment and Propaganda. The minister is responsible only to the dictator.

Control is specifically exercised by decrees issued from time to time by the dictator and the minister and by orders from subordinate leaders, which always must have the approval of the minister. The minister's control powers are pretty all-inclusive. For example, he may strike a journalist from the registry without appeal to a judicial body, and he regularly issues instructions to newspapers concerning *what* they shall print and *how* they shall deal with and print important events. An employment contract is enforced which specifies duties and privileges for both the employer and the employee. Special "press courts" try charges of misconduct and disputes under these contracts. The propaganda ministry may also appoint an editor in each newspaper plant to supervise its conduct. Training courses for journalists are given by the state. Further, as would be expected under such circumstances, the schools of journalism are care-

---

[1] No organized group has ever developed the art of propaganda so effectively and with so complete a disregard of truth as has the current Kremlin dictatorship.

fully supervised. A propaganda fund has been utilized by some nations to aid friendly papers both at home and in foreign lands.

The Fascist Compared With The Communist System. Enforced loyalty to a dominant party is required by both the fascist and the communist press systems. In a practical sense, there is no difference. However, the Soviet press is spoken of as a workers' press, designed "to serve the welfare of the masses"; while the fascist press is referred to as a state press, intended to serve the fascist state first, and to serve the masses of the people second. In reality, both serve the purposes of the state first. One contrast though is the almost total lack of opportunity for criticism from the ranks of journalists in the fascist system. And yet, the fascist system permits private ownership, stringently regulated, whereas the communistic press is entirely publicly owned either by worker-associations, divisions of the Communist party, or by the government as such.

The Fascist Concept Of Freedom Is Its Own. As an agency of government control and leadership, a *Staatspresse* or state press, is free in the sense that it is free to serve the welfare of the state and the nation by espousing fascist principles. Loyalty to the dominant creed of government is insisted upon.[1] Criticism is viewed as being obstructive; therefore it is prohibited. The fascist criticism of the free press of America is that it is a press that serves the personal and private interests of individual publishers.[2]

As a concept the principle of serving the public welfare may not be criticized, and is one which some American publications might more firmly grasp. Yet in the fascist state this principle is enforced by methods which make the individual journalist a mere robot. He takes orders from above concerning what he shall print and how he shall print it. The values in individual and group initiative in thinking and especially in criticism and discussion are denied.

Comparison With American Freedom. The first essential difference between the fascist and the American concept of freedom of the press is that the fascist journalist is compelled by the government to serve the public welfare according to the principles of his government, while the American journalist is free to serve the public weal according to democratic and constitutional principles without compulsion except that of his conscience, his profession, and his public. On the other hand, the American journalist is free to commit antisocial acts like coloring, suppression, sensationalism, and even propagandizing in the news without punishment except that which may come from his subscribers. The fascist journalist is prevented from committing certain antisocial acts like sensa-

---

[1] In Germany under Hitler, for example, the journalist was free to serve the public welfare provided he did so in strict accord with National Socialist principles.

[2] According to the fascist view, journalists employed by such publishers have no freedom.

tionalism, "trial" by newspaper, and triviality. But the fascist journalist is compelled to publish news that is colored and propagandized and to suppress information in the interest of the controlling philosophy of government, acts which the fascist defines as patriotic but which free press advocates would define as antisocial because they alter the truth. Thus, the second essential difference is that a fascist press is compelled frequently to mutilate the news, whereas the American press is given the choice of conducting itself uprightly or not.

Another fundamental difference lies in the degree of trust placed in the press. Fascism distrusts the press. Therefore the press is deprived of responsibility. It is controlled in every detail because of fear that it will use its power to destroy the state or to harm the group in power. Newspaper criticism, moreover, is viewed as destructive, not as constructive. In free press countries the press is held in greater respect. It is regarded as an instrument of education and enlightenment of the people and for the formulation by the people of policies for their general welfare. Criticism of government is viewed as helpful and constructive. The evils a free press may commit are less harmful than the evils that would attend the abolition of freedom of expression.

ESSENTIAL DIFFERENCES EXIST BETWEEN OPINION AND INFORMATION PRESS

The opinion press vigorously espouses causes, doctrines, ideas, and points of view as part of its news policy whereas an information press neither propagandizes for good or evil in its news columns on any acknowledged basis nor prints opinion columns or articles as a general rule without disclaiming specific responsibility for the opinions contained therein.[1]

Both Types Have Reader-Appeal. The opinion press has long flourished in Europe. Its earliest beginnings were utilized in pamphleteering for religious and political beliefs in France, Germany, and England. In modern times examples of the opinion press were the *Gruppenpresse* of Germany and the party press of France. In postwar France the revived press is largely a party press, represented by *Le Populaire,* organ of the Socialist party; *L'Humanité,* voice of the Communist party, and *L'Aube,* organ of the Mouvement Republicain Populaire. The opinion press may be the voice of a party, a faction, or a single individual politician or editor.

The information press or news press is best illustrated by American and British papers. America and England are predominantly countries of "news" papers. Continental Europe is a land of "views" papers. France

---

[1] Such *antescript* notations as "The views expressed by the writer are not necessarily those of this newspaper" are common in the information press of America.

today exhibits a few dailies of the information type, notably *France-Soir* and *Ce Soir*. British and American influence is being applied to an extent to the press of postwar Western Germany. Where the Russian influence predominates, the pattern is invariably that of the regimented communist press, which in reality is a giant type of opinion press or party press.

The South American press had its beginnings in the models of the opinion press of the Latin countries of Europe. As a result of American influences, especially of the American press associations, South American newspapers have been transformed during the past thirty years into better-balanced vehicles of news and of opinion.

Both Types Evolve From, And Are Reflections Of, The Society Of Which They Are A Part. In times of emotional, social, or political stress, the opinion press invariably flourishes. A politically mature society which is stable in temper and secure enough to afford objectivity will have. less desire or need for an opinion press.[1] Even the information press adheres more persistently to fact when the pressures within society are well balanced and class is not pitted against class in daily life. An information press can exist only in a free society—not in a totalitarian environment.

---

[1] That America is less secure in its "way of life" than formerly is indicated by the increased reliance of a large segment of the population upon newspaper columnists and radio commentators for their political views.

CHAPTER XXXIV

BUILDING THE MAGAZINE ARTICLE

The writer of an article for a magazine of general circulation is in the position of a man who undertakes to make a speech at a picnic. The people have all gathered around to have a good time, but their attention is vague, wandering and uncertain. It has to be captured on the fly and transformed quickly into definite interest.

—HARVEY V. DEUELL.*

THE ARTICLE DIFFERS FROM THE NEWS STORY

In contrast to the newspaper feature, which depends mainly upon its timeliness and its emotional or entertainment appeal for its success, the magazine article must be anticipative, interpretative, and provocative.

The contents of most magazines are planned weeks, even months, ahead. So the magazine article must be *anticipative:* it must look forward to the time when it will appear in print and must give the reader the feeling that it is up-to-date.

Newspapers chronicle events as they happen, leaving to magazines the task of interpreting them after they have happened. So the magazine article is *interpretative:* it "goes behind the news" and explains the meaning or significance of events.

The magazine article appeals to the intellect, rather than to the emotions, of the reader; and while entertaining him, it satisfies his desire for information. For that reason it must be *provocative* and help him think more clearly on problems and questions of general interest.

THE AUTHOR MUST MEET FOUR BASIC REQUIREMENTS

Although most experts agree that newspaper work is valuable training for magazine writing, at least four basic qualifications are necessary for success in the magazine field.

The Magazine Writer Must Recognize The Larger Audience. The newspaper feature writer ordinarily addresses the people of only one community. But the magazine writer has for his audience the people of many communities with a great diversity of interests. So he needs, first

---

* Harvey V. Deuell, former editor of *Liberty* magazine, "How to Write Articles for Magazines," quoted from *Writing for Profit* by Donald Wilhelm, p. 262. Copyright 1937. Used by permission of the publishers, McGraw-Hill Book Co.

of all, to recognize the existence of this greater reading public and to
become "national-minded" instead of "local-minded."

He Must Have Something To Say. Before you can write for the
magazines, you must "have something to say"—something that will interest the average man or woman. "What interests most people? One thing
only interests all human beings and that is the human being himself.
There you have the gist of the matter. No prescription can beat it—if you
want to know how to get at people and grip their attention." [1]

Obviously, the magazine writer can not write about all readers; but if
he can relate his subject to their needs and their desires and can show
how their interests are affected by the subject he is discussing, he can grip
their attention.

Where can you find such subjects? In conversation with your friends,
in the talk which you overhear on the streets, in trains, in business offices,
and in social gatherings—all will tell you what people are thinking
about. The great variety of news stories in the daily newspaper is also an
accurate index of the present-day interests of mankind.

He Must Say It Simply. The best article is the one which gives the
facts in a simple and direct style that is perfectly clear to every type of
reader. Try to make the average reader see clearly, feel keenly, and understand the things described. "Have something worth while to say. Say it
just as easily as you can and don't be too long-winded about it. Don't try
to copy anybody's style. Study them all and develop one of your own.
Remember grace is ease of motion; style is ease of expression." [2]

He Must Be Accurate. Inadequate information is certain to betray
itself in a magazine article, and some reader among the thousands is sure
to write to the editor about an inaccurate statement or an error of fact.
Since inaccuracy impairs the confidence of readers of a magazine, an
editor hesitates to accept more articles from a writer guilty of careless,
inaccurate work. An error in a newspaper—unfortunate and regrettable
though it is—may be laid to the haste with which most newspaper work
is done. But there is little or no excuse for an error in a magazine article
which often represents weeks, or sometimes months, of preparation. For
this reason the rule of "Accuracy always" is even more binding upon the
magazine writer than upon the newspaper worker.

SYSTEMATIC GATHERING OF MATERIAL IS NECESSARY

Unlike the short newspaper feature, which is often swung around one
incident and can be written rapidly and without extensive advance prepa-

---

[1] From "Where Do I Come In? Asks the Human Being" by John M. Siddall,
former editor of the *American Magazine.*

[2] Arthur T. Vance, former editor of *Pictorial Review*, "Ten Points for a Beginner,"
quoted from *Writing for Profit* by Donald Wilhelm, p. 261. Copyright 1937. Used
by permission of the publishers, McGraw-Hill Book Co.

ration, the magazine or journal article is the result of a thoughtful collection of authentic information.

Some articles may be written from information obtained from only one source—the writer's personal experience. But more frequently they are written from information gleaned in many ways. These include:

PERSONAL INTERVIEWS. When the article is a personality sketch, a "success story," or any other type in which one person is the main theme, obviously the best source of information is the person himself and the material for the article is obtained by an interview with him.[1]

FIRSTHAND INVESTIGATION. This includes visits to persons or places that figure prominently in the article as well as correspondence with authorities on the subject about which one is writing.

PRINTED SOURCES. The thousands of books and files of periodicals in libraries are mines of information for the writer. "A trained writer who knows how to find his way among books can write well on any subject on earth," once declared Frank Ward O'Malley of the *New York Sun.*

PERSONAL REFERENCE LIBRARY. Professional writers find that a personal reference library, or "scraparium," is one of their most valuable pieces of equipment. It usually consists of a filing cabinet filled with newspaper clippings, magazine articles, manuscripts, letters, notes and photographs, filed in envelopes or manila folders and indexed or arranged according to some system which makes the information on various topics readily accessible.

CAREFUL PLANNING AND SKILLFUL WRITING ARE ESSENTIAL

Magazine and journal articles can not be "dashed off" as the result of a sudden inspiration. Just as a thorough and painstaking collection of authentic information is a necessary preliminary to writing, so are intelligent planning, careful writing, and, many times, repeated rewriting essential to an authoritative article.

A free-lance writer once sent an article to *Munsey's Magazine,* explaining apologetically that he had written it in one day. The manuscript came back with this notation from "Bob" Davis, the editor: "It looks like it!"

Forrest Crissey, writer for the *Saturday Evening Post,* once declared, "I wouldn't think of trying to write a *Post* article in less than three weeks."

Irvin S. Cobb in an article on "How to Begin at the Top and Work Down," which appeared in the *American Magazine,* said: "I envy those who dash off those priceless gems. You should see me some morning when I'm in the mood for dashing off the stuff. There I sit, dashing it off at the rate of about an inch and a half an hour, and using sweat for

---

[1] Refer to Chapter XXII, *The Interview and the Interviewer.*

punctuation. I'm the same sort of impetuous dasher that the Muir Glacier is. And so is every other writer I know of who is getting away with it."

So, instead of "dashing it off," most magazine writers follow some such plan as this:

Build The Framework. Before a house is built, an architect draws plans for it. Before an article of any enduring value is written, the writer has in mind what he is going to say and how he is going to say it. He does this by writing the article first in skeleton form—i.e., an outline.[1] In this outline he puts down the main topics he is to discuss and arranges and rearranges them. Under each main topic he jots down briefly examples, incidents, statistics, and other details which may be used in rounding out the article when he writes the first draft of it.

Write The Article. Having an outline which assures the presentation of his subject in a logical order, the writer next proceeds to expand it into the first draft of his article. Rarely is the first draft satisfactory for use as the completed article although it might be. Usually, article writing is a matter of constant rewriting, of two, three, or more revisions. In this revision the material which the article already contains is amplified, the order of presentation is usually rearranged, the errors of fact or interpretation are corrected, and material which is not essential to the expansion of the central idea or which interferes with the smooth flow of the narrative is deleted.

In doing this writing and rewriting, the author of the article keeps his reader constantly in mind and strives to hold his interest by these devices:

1. Addressing him directly and informally and, whenever possible, illustrating the various points in the article by references to similar possible experiences of the reader.

2. Asking him questions so that he will read on to get the answers and then answering those questions in such a way as to raise further questions in the reader's mind.

3. Keeping him anxious to know "what happens next," i.e., making use of "suspense," as does the writer of fiction.

4. Using vivid and sharply-etched figures of speech; making bold, striking, and sometimes paradoxical statements.

5. Sprinkling numerous specific incidents and amusing or exciting anecdotes throughout the article.

6. Giving concrete descriptions of people and quoting them directly; describing people in action with words and phrases that suggest action.

A SALABLE ARTICLE IS ONE DESIGNED FOR ITS MARKET

While a large percentage of the articles which appear in magazines are staff-written or written on order by the editor, the free-lance author

---

[1] Refer to chart on p. 293.

TWO METHODS OF BUILDING
THE MAGAZINE ARTICLE

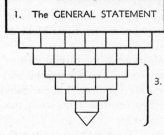

1. The GENERAL STATEMENT

2. WORD PICTURES, Incidents, Examples, which illustrate (1).

3. · MINOR DETAILS which are interesting· but not important to the article.

1. SPECIFIC EXAMPLE or Illustrative Incident.

2. WORD PICTURES, Incidents, Examples, expanding the idea suggested in (1).

3. The GENERAL STATEMENT Summarizing idea of whole article.

METHOD OF OUTLINING
AN ARTICLE

I.   The Topic Stated—i.e., the Lead or Introduction.
   A. By means of a general statement of the subject to be discussed.
   B. By means of a specific example or an illustrative incident.

II. The Topic Defined—i.e., an enlargement of the statement to explain the idea further.
   A. By using repetition to strike the interest in a slightly different expression.
   B. By using contrast, presenting the contrary view, or one allied with the contrary view.

III. The Topic Established—i.e., presenting the logical truth of your subject so that the reader will accept and absorb it easily.
   A. By use of examples or details.
   B. By use of comparison.

IV. The Topic Applied—i.e., showing how the idea fits in with other general truths.
   A. By comparison with similar ideas.
   B. By contrast with different ideas.

can usually find certain moderately profitable "open markets" for his writings.

Study The Markets Thoroughly. "Don't send a bull-fight story to a Sunday-school magazine." "The *Atlantic Monthly* will never publish the best article in the world on how to make toy airplanes."

These two quotations are different ways of stating the same fundamental truth about successful marketing of manuscripts: Make an intelligent study of the markets.

As a preliminary step, read one or more of the several writers' magazines or market guides which report regularly on the general and immediate needs of the various magazines. Having done this, and selected the type of magazine for which you are best fitted to write, study that magazine carefully and analytically in regard to:

THE LENGTH OF ARTICLES IT USES. Some magazines limit them to a maximum of 3,000 words; others print them as long as 8,000 words or more.[1]

THE LITERARY QUALITY AND STYLE OF WRITING. Some editors like breezy informality; others prefer dignified formality. In some magazines the articles are lively and "streamlined"; in others they are profound and academic.

THE POINT OF VIEW. One magazine wants articles written from the "woman's viewpoint"; another prefers the "man's viewpoint." Some magazines are edited for a predominantly youthful reading public; others for an older reading public.

Analyze The Article Prior To Submission. Having decided upon the type of magazine for which you wish to write or to which you wish to offer an article you are ready to prepare, make sure of the following points about your work:

1. That your article does not deal with a subject which has been covered by another article in that magazine within recent years. (It may be advisable to query the editor in regard to this before writing the article.)

2. That it does not deal with a subject which has been covered many times or in many other magazines. If it does, it must have a new approach, fresh data, and a more timely treatment.

3. That the title and lead paragraph are so interesting that they will hold the editor's attention and make him want to read on into the article.

4. That the manuscript is "clean copy," prepared in accordance with the commonly known rules: one side of page only, double-spacing, wide margins, numbered pages, et cetera.

---

[1] Generally, short articles are more in demand.

5. That it is accompanied by clear, interesting photographs (or a suggestion for appropriate illustrative material, if pictures are not available).
6. That it is mailed flat—never rolled—and accompanied by return postage.
7. That you have kept a carbon copy of the article to guard against the lost labor of a lost manuscript.

Chapter XXXV

REVIEWS, COMMENTS, AND OPINIONS

> Surely the complete critical process may include both impressions
> and appeals to the authority of the past, as a basis for judgment,—and
> perhaps more than these. The critic who has espoused one method or
> the other has stopped short at one stage in the process, and has thrown
> undue emphasis on his own preference.—S. STEPHENSON SMITH.*

CRITICAL WRITING IS PROVIDED BY TWO TYPES OF AUTHORS

The critical offerings of a newspaper or magazine are provided by both
professional artists and laymen, and the editor must decide which serves
his readers better.

The Professional Is An Artist. The professional is an artist who writes
upon his art. He has a background of training, knowledge, and practice
which equips him as an expert. His material will be of interest primarily
to those readers who are as well versed as he. He writes for fellow professionals and semiprofessionals, using the language of the craft.

The Layman Is A Writing-Craftsman. The layman is primarily a
writer interested in or assigned to the arts. He lacks the professional's
experience as an artist but possesses sufficient practical knowledge of an
art to write about it in broad fashion and in a manner likely to arouse the
interest of the general reader. He is a writer first and an artist second.
The professional is an artist first and a writer second.

Editors Decide Which Type To Employ. Editors must solve the fundamental problem of which type of critical writer to employ in providing
guidance for their readers. If they engage experts, the majority of their
readers may not understand them. If they use laymen, the specialists
among their readers may receive no benefit from them.

Where feasible, editors employ both, depending upon the interests of
the community or the reader-group. But inasmuch as this is not possible
for the average publication, most journalistic criticism is written by
laymen.

Although this does not increase the amount of expert criticism available
to readers, it does make the critical writing in the press simple and readily understood. The lay critic is not handicapped by the argot of the art

---

* From *The Craft of the Critic* by S. Stephenson Smith, p. 15. Copyright 1931.
Used by permission of the publishers, Thomas Y. Crowell Co.

or by inexperienced readers. The professional often writes only to be ignored by most of the readers.

SUCH WRITING GENERALLY FALLS INTO TWO CLASSES

Journalistic critical writing tends to fall into two generally recognized classes: the impressionistic and the authoritative; but in actual practice critics employ both techniques.

The Authoritative Method Is One.   The authoritative theory derives from the idea that fixed standards may be set up to which all artistic works should conform as closely as possible. To illustrate, the reviewer of a new historical novel might compare it with *Quo Vadis* or *The Last Days of Pompeii* and similar books. The reviewer of a play, under this theory, accepts as final the technique of Aristophanes or Racine and compares all new plays to the works of these older writers. Thus a modern playwright who departs from the rule of the unities is likely to be condemned.

This is the easier way to evaluate a work of art, since it requires mainly a wide familiarity with what has been done in the past and the ability to recognize parallel situations and affinities.

The Impressionistic Method Is Another.   The impressionistic theory of criticism is based on a principle enunciated by Anatole France: "Criticism is the adventure of a great soul among masterpieces." Thus the impressionistic critic cares little if a work of art has been created through the technique or procedure of an early work which may be accepted as classic. This type of critic places greatest emphasis upon impressions. He tells, not how nearly a painting approaches a standard set by some early master's work, but what effect it had upon him and what ideas are aroused in him by viewing the picture.

This critical approach is difficult because it requires more from the critic than does authoritarianism. The critic must have not only more than commonplace knowledge but also keen perceptivity and wide experience for his reactions to possess fullness and sufficient breadth of scope to be of interest to his reader. The impression made upon a shallow, dull mind is not worth recording; the impression made upon a vibrant, eager, questing mind sometimes will exceed in interest the work of art being criticized.

Both Procedures Are Utilized.   In writing criticism, however, it appears that the critic avails himself of both theories and adds to them certain other means of arriving at his conclusions. Listed by Professor S. Stephenson Smith, this way of reaching conclusions employs a particular set of mental processes: impressions, analysis, interpretation, orientation, valuation, and generalization. The impressionist critic will place little emphasis upon orientation; the authoritarian will emphasize orientation heavily.

The great majority of press critics of the drama, literature, the dance, and the other arts are barely cognizant of these schools of criticism and these mental processes. The leading critics on the large newspapers and magazines are aware of them, but most small newspapers and periodicals cannot afford or do not want trained critics and place the burden of such work upon regular staff members or laymen.

Their familiarity with or general historical knowledge of the field wins them the assignments, thus almost certainly assuring that journalistic criticism will in the main be authoritarian.

SUCH WRITING MAY BE EITHER REVIEW OR CRITICISM

Dependent upon the training, facility, or point of departure of the evaluating artist or craftsman the product of the writer may take one of three forms: the review, the criticism, or a combination of these.

A Review Is A Report. When routine newspaper workers are turned loose upon a piece of art, their first impulse is to give a report of it rather than to pass upon it. Their impulse is correct. The two approaches should be kept separate. It should not be supposed that a competent reporter is also a competent critic.

Any general reporter can go to an exhibit of sculpture and write a thousand words upon it. He can say that three figurines by So-and-So are to be seen in the East Wing of the museum or that John Mitchell is represented by a three-foot figure of Ben Jonson and a life-sized copy of some famous statue. He can describe the juxtaposition of the entries, tell how many persons visited the show, who were among the notables on hand, how many pieces are exhibited, and give other data of that nature.

A Criticism Is An Evaluation. It is the expression of opinion on the part of a critic and is more than a report, hence more than a review. A critic visiting the exhibit of sculpture mentioned in the foregoing gives the editor an entirely different type of manuscript than does the reviewer. He discusses in it the effect of the sculpture upon himself (if an impressionist) or the merits of the work when compared with that of earlier artists (if an authoritarian). Presumably the critic is trained in the theory and practice of sculpture, familiar with what old and new sculptors have done, and sensitive to the effect of an artist's work.

A Combination Is A Review Criticism. Actually, most press critics attempt to perform both functions, devoting varying amounts of space to reporting and to evaluating. This explains the general condemnation of press criticism as inexpert, diffuse, and superficial; for neither function is thoroughly performed.

NEWSPAPERS COVER A WIDE SCOPE

Publications of diverse kinds, especially the larger ones, provide critical material on a wide variety of artistic expression.

Large Papers And Magazines Cover The Field. Large publications attempt to cover the entire field of art. They provide special supplements or devote whole regular sections to all artistic expression, and print other articles in addition at other times. But a country weekly cannot afford to do this, and probably does not have many readers who care for more than a brief book column and an occasional article on visiting plays. The small-city daily provides regular space for book, play, music, and motion-picture criticism. Specialized magazines must ignore this field.

Critical Material Is Used When, As, And If Profitable. Whether such critical copy will be prepared depends on three factors. These are the amount of advertising that may be sold as a result of it, the circulation increase that may be expected, and the publishers' or editors' desire to provide coverage for the prestige value regardless of commercial loss or gain. Such material is not always regular in appearance, nor does much of it have a place in the smaller publications.

MANY DIFFERENT DEVELOPMENTS HAVE ARISEN

The main subjects covered by publications in their critical departments are literature, drama, motion pictures, music, art, the dance, and radio-television programs.

Most Papers Have A Literary Department. There is no uniformity in the manner of presenting material for the literary department. There are newspaper book supplements of from twelve to sixteen pages, book sections consisting of from two to eight regular newspaper pages, book pages of an entire page or a portion of a page, and book columns. Most literary departments, however, offer book reviews and criticisms and news of books and authors. In a large literary supplement the readers are presented, in addition to these staples, with poetry, lists of best sellers, correspondence about literary activities, special articles on literary affairs abroad, extensive illustrations of printed matter, and many advertisements. A newspaper book column may be a daily article written on one or a few books by a critic, combined with odds and ends of literary material. In addition, book reviews are sometimes syndicated. Some magazines give much space to book reviews.

The larger literary departments have staffs of several persons to do editorial work and employ professional reviewers. Most papers, however, assign the book department's work to a regular staff member, who receives aid from his colleagues and from outside critics who get books or small payment in return for their manuscripts.

The book department obtains books by asking publishers for review copies or by borrowing them from libraries and from friends of the publication. Records must be kept of the books and their reviewers, and checking copies must be sent to publishers. This requires study of the publishing world and usually entails more work for the book editor than mere preparation of copy and similar aspects of editing his page or writing his column.

The reviews or criticisms cover all types of literature—biography, fiction, poetry, the drama—and are written in scores of ways. The book article is not required, as is the news story, to follow any fixed pattern. It usually is an essay signed by the writer and therefore more flexible and intimate than the ordinary news account. Its length is determined by the literary editor, whose decision is governed by the space available, importance of the book, and quality of the review.

The Drama Department Is Common In Large Cities. The time element enters the dramatic critic's work more than into that of the literary critic. The newspaper drama critic ordinarily reviews a new play the night it opens, and his copy is handled like news matter. He works thus rapidly, not only because the showing of a new play is news, but also because the paper wishes to achieve leadership in giving guidance to its readers promptly.

Publishers send review copies of books well in advance of publication, but even if the journal does not review a book immediately after issue there is little harm done. But the daily newspaper play reviewer does not have this advantage. His readers can see a play in an evening; most of the literary editor's following takes days and usually weeks to read the books he reviews. The drama critic's readers hope to receive, not only an idea of what the play concerns, but also the critic's reactions to the performance, which are important to them since his taste is familiar through other recommendations or disparagements.

Most dramatic departments consist of one person. This may be an outsider, whose reward for covering plays is the tickets, or a regular staff member, who puts his spare time into such activity. On large papers the department may be made up of several full-time workers who review plays almost daily and prepare special articles, such as interviews with actors, little-theater activity news, and descriptions of new techniques, and edit material for a daily page.

The department receives complimentary or press tickets to plays or may purchase them at the expense of the publication if the publisher does not care to receive favors from theaters.

The drama critic's duties require knowledge of the stage as well as of plays. "Not only what the author has written, but what the people of the stage have done with what he has written must concern the reviewer. If he praises the author for triumph of direction, or if he gives the actor credit for beautiful lines, he may 'get by' the casual play-goer, but the practical stage-folk know where to rank him." [1]

---

[1] From *Pathways to Print* by Harrington and Martin, p. 232. Copyright 1931. Used by permission of the publishers, D. Van Nostrand Co.

The Motion-Picture Department Establishes New Precedents. Evaluating the motion picture is relatively new to the field of criticism in the press. Much as it resembles the stage, the motion picture offers somewhat different problems to its critics.

First of all, there are more pictures than plays appearing simultaneously in one city. Few communities are visited by more than one or two theatrical groups at a time and then, usually, at long intervals. Many have no playhouses but even very small villages will have a movie house. But motion pictures change every few days.

The criticism of the cinema is not so well organized as that of most other artistic activities. It is a new form. The stage is centuries old, the movie but a few score years. Also, the play is more costly to attend; the movies are cheaper as well as more common. The motion picture has been of a lower grade, artistically, than that of the stage. It was not considered worthy of critical notice until recently. Drama critics disdained it. But as public demand for guidance arose, large newspapers began giving special attention to the newest screen offerings and many smaller sheets followed suit.

Personnel, copy, editing, and operation problems are about the same for the motion-picture department as for the drama or literary department.

The Music Department Requires Specialists. Music criticism brings greater specialization into service than does literary, dramatic, or motion-picture criticism. Working as they do in the literary form, newspaper critics find it easier to evaluate another literary form than to report upon or give their impressions of an art requiring considerable training, such as music, sculpture, or any of the art forms so far not touched upon.

Music, with literature and the stage, has received criticism at the hands of journalists for many years. Such critics are almost inevitably musicians; even the smallest publication does not often send a general reporter on such an assignment as covering the recital of a visiting musical celebrity or a concert by a symphony orchestra. Music criticism necessarily is the field for the expert, who usually is a practicing musician with a flair for writing.

A concert or recital or opera is covered much in the same way as a play. The newspaper or newsmagazine music critic must work rapidly, so as to continue his function as a guide to his readers and maintain the timeliness of his publication. The music critic almost more than another is called upon for prodigious exercise of memory. Reference books on his art are of greater need to him than to any of his "critic" colleagues, for such facts as the date of an opera première or of a singer's debut or of the first playing of a symphony are important to him.

The Art Department Is Frequently Reportorial. Painting and sculpture usually are thought of together as being the realm of the art department. This division must not be confused with one of the same name which is an adjunct of the editorial department, where cartoonists, retouchers, and other artists produce original work or improve upon photographs, cartoons, and drawings received by the newspaper. The staff now under consideration is made up of critics of the plastic and pictorial arts and persons concerned with art news who provide either a regular series of critical and descriptive articles or occasional evaluations of shows at local galleries.

Here again specialized knowledge is a heavy requirement. Most newspapers giving attention to this department do so in a noncritical way; much of the copy goes to the society and club editors. Only the larger dailies and major cultural magazines in this country concern themselves seriously with art criticism.

The Dance Department Is Reportorial or Specialized. This department is new as an established division of criticism. Evaluation of dance recitals finds its way into the press usually as weekly material in the largest newspapers, with occasional special articles upon a particularly important recital by some famed dancer. Only the latter material is found in the small dailies. The reason for this limited attention is the equally limited interest in this art form. Whole magazines, however, are devoted to it.

The Radio-Television Department Is Increasingly Important. The opinion aspect of the newspaper's radio-television department is coming into increasing prominence. The bulk of its work still has to do with reporting the news of artists, programs, and stations. Extensive space regularly is given to listings of programs, although some publications avoid this practice, since it is thought to be giving advertising space gratis. Brand or trade names are edited out of such listings by many radio editors.

Actual estimating of relative values in programs has been confined largely to certain metropolitan papers and weekly journals of comment.

The professional radio listener's or video viewer's job is unlike that of his fellow critics. He need not leave his office or his home to "cover his story." He has no problems of using or refusing passes—except to studios —or making deadlines on his critical copy. But he must have a wider, although not necessarily more thorough, background than his office companions. For over the air waves go drama and music and other arts— as well as speeches, descriptions of sports events or other spectacles, and the miscellany which all television users and radio listeners recall. The radio-television critic must be catholic in his taste yet cognizant of the mechanical problems behind these newcomers to the field of journalistic criticism.

OTHER DEPARTMENTS MAY PERMIT READER-PARTICIPATION

Aside from such primary opinion outlets as the editorial, the various kinds of columns, the signed article or feature, and others heretofore mentioned in this chapter, there are letters to the editor, special pages, contest departments, and inquiring reporter columns in most newspapers and magazines.

Letters To The Editor Serve As A Forum. The letters-to-the-editor department is a forum and thus a symbol of democracy. It acts as a correcting device for the publication and carries considerable reader-interest, often exceeding that of many paid features. The letters from readers on the larger newspapers and periodicals often require a special editor to handle the mail and prepare the material for publication.

Special Pages Are Sometimes Used. A special page may be composed of critical writing or opinion. Examples of such pages are the amateur, junior or juvenile, and contributors' pages now quite common. The amateur page has cartoons, poems, stories, and articles turned in by non-professionals among the readers.

Great latitude is permitted in these special pages. This is because of the difficulty supervisory editors experience in controlling the unconventional copy submitted by amateurs. The work of tyro poets or fictionizers traditionally is unaltered by editors because it would be impossible to make it conform. The more natural and unchanged the copy the more satisfactory it will be to readers. This has the result of readers finding in the special pages views contrary to those of the publication as an institution.

The Contest Department Serves A Purpose. The contest department permits expression of opinion insofar as such contests are a type that call for it. A contest that asks for essays upon features of the paper or for comments on topics of the day serves such a purpose.

The Inquiring Reporter Is A Popular Device. The inquiring-reporter column is a late development. It has attained greatest popularity among readers of tabloid-size papers but is by no means confined to them. A reporter and cameraman visit employees in an office building or stop pedestrians at a street corner and ask them all the same question, recording their answers and identifications and obtaining their photographs for inserted pictures.

This is not only a device for stimulating direct circulation but also a feature which studies have revealed to be among the most popular in the paper. Typical questions are: "Would you be willing to be shot from a gun?" and "Do you think married women should be allowed to hold positions in the business or industrial world?"

CHAPTER XXXVI

THE ART AND CRAFT OF THE LITERARY JOURNALIST

> We [authors] report the news of the mind and soul of our characters as much as we do the actions and happenings of daily life, which are after all, the material accidents of existence rather than the significant realities of life. There is a disposition in some quarters to call that fiction. But some of it, I insist, is literature. True literature is life translated into letters.—FERENC MOLNAR.*

THE LITERARY JOURNALIST IS CREATIVE

The literary person or author is distinguished from the journalist chiefly in that he writes creatively, in that he makes something where there was nothing before.

Facts May Be The Framework For What He Writes. The ordinary newspaper reporter records what happens in the world around him—a fire, a public meeting, a court trial, a speech. The star reporter or special writer is sometimes allowed to present news from his own particular point of view, with his own comment or interpretation of it. The editorial writer comments upon the events of contemporary life, often explains their meaning or interprets them. The newspaper critic, writing about books, plays, music, or art, offers his comment upon these products; he interprets or evaluates them. Thus, the journalists may be said to record, to comment, and to interpret.

The creative imagination of the literary person may take the same material that appeared as news in a newspaper and reshape it in such fashion that it becomes a novel, a short story, a play, or even a poem. In doing this, he doesn't have to stick to facts as the reporter does; he may use the facts merely as a starting point or as the framework for what he writes.

Insight And Imagination Are Essential. Insofar as the journalist brings to his newspaper writing insight and imagination he approaches literature. When he gets to the point where his desire to express some universal truth carries him beyond the limits of recording, or even of comment, and when he expresses that truth in language so apt and so clear as to make the idea and the expression of it a harmonious whole—

---

* From *The Plays of Ferenc Molnar,* Introduction by Louis Rittenberg, p. xv. Copyright 1929. Used by permission of the publishers, The Vanguard Press.

then he has come close to the creative method we call authorship. Such
a person, writing for a newspaper with creative insight, may be called a
literary journalist. It is the point of view and writing ability that make
this type of newspaperman or -woman. The fact that the staff member
of a newspaper occupies a high position does not mean that he possesses or
uses the ability of the literary journalist. The critic, the editorial writer,
the columnist, the star reporter are not necessarily of this calibre.

Literature Has Been Written For A Deadline. When San Francisco
was devastated by the earthquake of 1906, Will Irwin was a young reporter for the *New York Sun*. Realizing that Irwin had lived in San
Francisco and knew the city well, his editor asked him to write a story
for *Sun* readers about the city that had just fallen in ruins. Irwin sat
down at his typewriter and out of his love for San Francisco and his grief
at its destruction he wrote "The City That Was," a story that told of the
beautiful, gay, picturesque San Francisco he had known so well. That
story, at least in part, is an example of literary journalism.

Seated in the great Protestant Episcopal Cathedral in Washington,
D.C., listening to the solemn funeral ceremonies for Woodrow Wilson,
James O'Donnell Bennett of the *Chicago Tribune* staff felt so deeply the
significance of the occasion, sensed so surely the universal emotion of
the moment, that he wrote for his newspaper a story amply fulfilling the
highest requirements of literary journalism.

Both Irwin and Bennett were acting as star reporters or special writers
for their papers when they turned in their stories. Sometimes it is the
editorial writer who strikes the universal note and does it with true literary skill. William Allen White did it for his paper, the *Emporia
Gazette,* on a number of occasions, but perhaps never so appealingly as
in his simple, moving story on the death of his daughter, Mary White.

Columnists like Don Marquis in the *New York Sun's* "Sun Dial,"
Christopher Morley in the *New York Evening Post,* and Ben Hecht in
the *Chicago Daily News* were literary journalists of distinction.

Writing a simple record of the routine events of everyday life for the
newspaper can be done by anyone with an average education and some
training in journalistic technique. Interpreting the news in an editorial
or signed column requires a broad background in political science, economics, and history, but writing of this sort does not necessarily imply
literary insight. In order to make the reader hear, feel, and see, the newspaper writer must have an approach somewhat similar to that of the
novelist, the short-story writer, and the poet.

THERE HAVE BEEN LITERARY JOURNALISTS IN AMERICA FROM EARLIEST TIMES

From colonial times to the present the writer of literary inclination has
made use of the newspaper as a means of self-expression, as a training

school for writing. The writers who have made such use of newspapers can be divided into five groups: humorists, novelists, short-story writers, poets, essayists, and critics. Humorists, essayists, and critics, and sometimes poets have been able to make direct use of their talents in newspaper columns. Novelists and short-story writers have used newspaper work as an apprenticeship in seeing and evaluating human nature and human relationships.

Newspapers Have Been Receptive To Humorists. Benjamin Franklin put his pungent observations of life and people into his "Silence Dogood" papers, published in his brother's paper, the *New-England Courant*. Later he did humorous sketches for his own newspaper, the *Pennsylvania Gazette*. In his early Nevada days, Mark Twain was the "funny man" of the *Virginia City Enterprise*. Like Franklin, he started at the type case, working first as a young apprentice printer of thirteen for the *Missouri Courier* in the little river town of Hannibal where he set type for five years, working on his brother Orion's *Journal*, in addition to the *Courier*. He contributed to the *Journal*, usually in such hilarious fashion that his Hannibal printer days have become almost a merry legend. When he went to San Francisco he wrote in humorous vein for the *San Francisco Call*, and later still for the *Buffalo* (New York) *Express*. Eugene Field, writing for the *Denver Tribune* and *The Chicago Daily News*, was one of America's first real columnists. Almost the whole of his short life was devoted to writing for newspapers.

Field called his Chicago column "Sharps and Flats." He had an immense amount of sport with it, poking fun at the world in general, and Chicago in particular. His favorite method of attack was to launch a treatise upon an individual or institution with such gravity that the reader would have got well into the article before the accumulation of absurdities warned him that a hoax or clever bit of nonsensical invention was unfolding before his eyes. Finley Peter Dunne wrote his "Mr. Dooley" sketches for a Chicago daily and Ring Lardner acquired fame through his humorous portrayal of baseball players, written as a sports reporter for newspapers.

Novelists Gain Valuable Training On A Newspaper Staff. One of England's first capable journalists, in the modern sense, Daniel Defoe put his observations of English life into the newspapers with which he was connected. Charles Dickens began being interested in people and writing about them as a young London reporter. William Dean Howells grew up in a country print shop and was for several years a member of the staff of the *Ohio State Journal*. Although he found police reporting so distasteful that he abandoned temporarily the idea of newspaper work, referring to this incident many years later, Howells wrote, "I think if I had been wiser than I was then, I would have remained in the employ offered me, and learned in the school of reality the many lessons of hu-

GREAT NAMES IN LITERARY JOURNALISM

Benjamin Franklin, 1706-1790

Wrote his first newspaper sketches, the "Silence Dogood" Papers, for his brother James Franklin's *New England Courant*. Worked as a printer in Philadelphia where he started his own paper, the *Pennsylvania Gazette*.

Philip Freneau, 1752-1832

"The Poet of the Revolution" was a contributor to many newspapers and magazines, and editor of several journalistic publications. Some of his best work was printed in the *Freeman's Journal* in the 1780's.

Walt Whitman, 1819-1892

Beginning as an apprentice printer on the weekly *Long Island Patriot* at the age of thirteen, Whitman later started his own paper, the *Long Islander*. Other papers for which he worked in his journalistic period were the *Brooklyn Eagle*, the *New Orleans Crescent*, and the *Brooklyn Daily Times*.

Mark Twain, 1835-1910

Like Whitman, Twain learned the printer's trade when he was thirteen. For eighteen years, with the exception of brief intervals when he was working as a river pilot or prospector, Twain was associated with newspapers, either as printer, reporter, correspondent, or editor.

Lafcadio Hearn, 1850-1904

Sixteen years of Hearn's American period were spent on the staffs of Cincinnati and New Orleans newspapers. His finest American newspaper sketches were done for the *Item* and the *Times-Democrat* in New Orleans.

Literary Journalism of the Eighteenth Century *

> A RECEIPT TO MAKE A NEW-ENGLAND FUNERAL ELEGY
>
> Having chose the Person, take all his Virtues, Excellencies, &c. and if he have not enough, you may borrow some to make up a sufficient Quantity. To these add his last Words, dying Expressions, &c. if they are to be had; mix all these together, and be sure you strain them well. Then season all with a Handful or two of Melancholy Expressions, such as, Dreadful, Deadly, cruel cold Death, unhappy Fate, weeping Eyes, &c.

Literary Journalism of the Twentieth Century **

> VAGABONDIA
>
> Here they come. Five merry travelers in a snorting, dust-caked automobile. Wanderers, egad! Bowling rakishly across the country. Dusters and goggles and sunburn. Prairie nights have sung to them. Little towns have grinned at them. Mountains, valleys, forests and stars have danced across their windshield.

O. Henry, 1862-1910

Although he was drug clerk, ranch hand, bank teller and short story teller, O. Henry found time to run his own small newspaper, the *Rolling Stone*, to write a column called Postscripts for the *Houston* (Texas) *Post*, and to act as correspondent for the *Cleveland Plain Dealer*. More than sixty of his short stories were first printed in the *New York Evening World*.

Ring W. Lardner, 1885-1933

The greater part of Lardner's writing life was spent in newspaper offices. It was as sports writer for half a dozen large newspapers that he discovered his delectable "lowbrow" types of people whom he put into his short stories.

---

* From one of Benjamin Franklin's "Silence Dogood" papers, printed first in the *New-England Courant* in 1722. This selection may be found in the *Writings of Benjamin Franklin* edited by Albert Henry Smith and published by The Macmillan Company. Copyright 1905. Vol. II, pp. 21–25.

** From the sketch "Vagabondia" in *1001 Afternoons in Chicago* by Ben Hecht, p. 123. Copyright 1927. Used by permission of the publishers, Covici, Chicago. First published in Mr. Hecht's column in the *Chicago Daily News*.

man nature which it could have taught." Richard Harding Davis was a newspaperman until his death. The material for his novels and stories was picked up in his career as a reporter and war correspondent.

Short-Story Writers Gain Technique And Material. Rudyard Kipling wrote his *Barrack-Room Ballads* for a newspaper in India. The first edition of this book was set up and printed in the shop of this newspaper while Kipling was a young reporter on its staff. Bret Harte learned the technique of realistic writing as a reporter for the *Northern Californian,* a country newspaper. A column in the *Houston* (Texas) *Post* was written by O. Henry, who also worked for a Pittsburgh paper and wrote many of his short stories for a New York City newspaper. In his Houston column may be found the germs of two short stories written in later years, "A Poor Rule" (*Options*), and "The Enchanted Profile" (*Roads of Destiny*). As a reporter, special writer, and war correspondent Stephen Crane wrote for New York newspapers, and some of his finest stories grew out of his newspaper experiences. He was a newspaper nonconformist, seeing things in his own way and writing about them, usually, in a manner so original as not to be appreciated by the editors for whom he happened to be working.

Even Poets Profit From Newspaper Experience. Philip Freneau, "the poet of the Revolution," was a newspaperman throughout the greater part of his writing career. Many of his poems dealing with events of contemporary interest were printed in newspapers which he owned or for which he worked. Walt Whitman was connected with a half-dozen newspapers during his life and frequently his poetry made use of themes and material which he had encountered during his journalistic career. For nearly fifty years William Cullen Bryant was on the staff of the *New York Evening Post,* part of the time as editor. As a staff member of the *Chicago Daily News,* Carl Sandburg frequently made use of material gathered as a reporter for his poetry. Sandburg was a first-class reporter. He was always quick to sympathize with the common man, but he saw events through his intellect as well as through his emotions. Sandburg's activities as a newspaperman, in close touch with his city, can be traced throughout many of his poems. He has told interviewers that the *Daily News* office saw the inception of many ideas which later appeared in his writing, and friends on the staff have told of how he used to sit in his small office after the day's work was done, setting down hunches in a few lines on sheets of copy paper and tossing the sheets into a wire basket on his desk for future reference.

Essayists And Critics Have A Place On The Newspaper. Joseph Addison and Richard Steele were newspapermen of the eighteenth century. Their essays in the *Spectator* are excellent examples of early English literary journalism. An American essayist and columnist of the 1840's, Nathaniel Parker Willis, was tremendously popular in his day, although he is little known now. One of the finest examples of the American literary journalist is Lafcadio Hearn. He worked as a special writer for Cincinnati papers, and later, in New Orleans, gained fame as a writer of translations and essays which were first printed in newspapers. Too timid to do regular reporting, Hearn kept his place on the *Cincinnati Enquirer* by writing Sunday feature articles. Later, he was put on night police, but even on that assignment, he continued to be a feature writer. His emotional reactions were too great to enable him to assemble anything but factual material and write it as a straight news story. While in Cincinnati he wrote up the slaughterhouse, the Negro quarter, life on the river levee, and even went so far for a feature as to climb the steeple of a cathedral with a widely-known steeplejack.

Nor is it alone in the field of feature writing that essayists have achieved success. James Gibbons Huneker achieved distinction as a writer of critical articles and sketches for New York newspapers. Edgar Allan Poe wrote some very significant criticism as a newspaper contributor. His critical evaluations were important not only for the age in which he wrote, but they are of value also to the modern student of criticism.

AUTHORS AND LITERARY JOURNALISTS HAVE SIMILAR PROBLEMS

The essentials have been expressed by the novelist Joseph Conrad when he said, "My task which I am trying to achieve, is, by the power of the written word, to make you hear, to make you feel. It is, before all, to make you see." [1] In order to make his readers hear what he is saying, feel what he feels, and see through his eyes, the writer of real literary ability must compel attention through the combination of his subject matter, his point of view, and his style.

There Is No Limitation As To Subject Matter. The material with which the literary journalist works may be news, it may be an offshoot of the news, or it may have no relation at all to any news event, but rather it may be the sort of human-interest story of Ben Hecht in his "1001 Afternoons" column, or it may be the self-revelation of a Heywood Broun. He gives expression to those things which bring about an emotional reaction in him.

Among twentieth-century literary journalists is the writer of what has come to be called reportage, a report that is written for a deadline, the same deadline that the straight news reporter meets, but the writer of reportage must do more than present the facts. He is not merely an observer answering such questions as *who, what, where, why,* and *when;* he must answer these questions . . . plus. In his technique he is not unlike the informal essayist; in his approach to his subject, that is, his re-

---

[1] From *The Nigger of the Narcissus* by Joseph Conrad. Copyright 1897, 1914. Used by permission of the publishers, Doubleday, Doran and Company, Inc.

action to the facts, and his attempt to make readers react in the way he reacted, he is not unlike a novelist or a writer of short stories. His problem is to make people feel . . . to feel through all their senses, to hear, to see, to taste, to smell, to touch. But in his attempt to create an emotional tone, he cannot indulge in any distortion of the facts. Reportage, then, may be defined as the presentation of a particular fact or facts, a specific event, in a setting that aids the reader to experience those facts or that event. Reportage becomes literary journalism when a John Dos Passos writes "Anacostia Flats," or a Ben Field writes "The Grasshopper Is Stirring," although in both cases the events about which they wrote had to do with news occurrences.

Out of news events may come short stories, poems, or even novels. On a newspaper assignment in the district back of the Chicago stockyards, Carl Sandburg was told that seven times as many children die in the stockyards district as in Hyde Park, a little more than a mile away. Out of that assignment came his lines on "The Right to Grief," beginning, "Take your fill of intimate remorse, perfumed sorrow . . . ," and including the defiant declaration, "I shall cry over the dead child of a stockyard's hunky."

Thousands of people must have seen unemployed· men fishing off the breakwater in Chicago, and many of them must have looked without even seeing the men bent over homemade poles, corks bobbing in the water. But Ben Hecht saw the pathos of it, the human interest; what had been meaningless to thousands of people had an emotional appeal for him, and out of that experience he wrote a moving sketch.

The Literary Journalist Is Characterized By His Point Of View. He makes readers feel what he writes because he understands the psychology of human emotion well enough so that he can make what stirs his pity, his love, his fear, stir his readers in a similar manner. He makes readers see, not merely the external fact or event, but what lies beneath it; its significance, its application to universal truth. He makes his readers see in a real sense because he opens their eyes to things they never have seen before, or perceived only dimly. If the news reporter writes a record of reality, the literary journalists may be said to give a pattern to reality through the medium of his imagination.

To do this, the literary journalist personalizes his writing. That is to say, he is more interested in people and their relationship to one another than he is in principles or abstract comment. The newspaperman with the point of view of the political scientist sees news from the angle of its relation to theories and practices of government. The literary journalist sees news in relation to its human quality, its possibilities of showing people in the midst of life, a life that may seem comic, tragic, pathetic, farcical.

If this is to be accomplished, he must achieve a seeming paradox, that is, he must have a perspective that sees things in their entirety, rather than in segments, and at the same time he must take sides in portraying human relationships. The writer must be outside his personal likes and dislikes, but he cannot give the reader the impression that he is looking at the thing about which he writes from the outside. That is, if he sees things in their right perspective, he will not write out of a petty personal bias, but he will know why he is writing that particular thing, what it is he is trying to say, and once he knows what it is he wants to convey to the reader, what his theme is, all that is written is a repetition of that theme. It has been said that life is a comedy to those who think, a tragedy to those who feel. Perhaps that may be all that a writer is trying to convey, but in all that he writes he will express that conviction. The news reporter cannot have a theme, he cannot so color his copy as to make the reader feel that certain things are wrong, but the special writer, the editorial writer, and the columnist can and do. Heywood Broun, for example, frequently gave very vigorous expression to his point of view or attitude toward current, contemporary problems. It is the human element, not the news slant, that concerns the literary journalist, and he writes well because he feels deeply. Emotional depth will make even an inconsequential story important.

The Literary Journalist Is Concerned With His Writing Style. The literary journalist is not bound by the restrictions of straight news coverage imposed on the reporter. His problem is not solely to give people facts, but to make them feel. To do this, he must have the same concern for technique as the literary person who may never have seen the inside of a newspaper office. The problem confronting the literary journalist is one not only of what he says, but also of how he says it.

In literary journalism there are the realists like Ernest Hemingway, John Dos Passos, and James Farrell. There are others who have the biting satire of Sinclair Lewis in such a book as *Main Street*. At the other extreme there are the romanticists, represented by Richard Harding Davis. In order to create their view of life for their readers, such men must give considerable thought to their writing technique. The realist sees certain details which the romanticist overlooks; perhaps he himself does not see the details which impress the realist, but if he did he would have to ignore them in order to give a romantic picture of life. In any form of creative writing the principle of selection is important.

The news writer must stick to one set of facts, to one group of people. The fiction writer and the literary journalist may take more liberties with facts and the people involved. The straight reporter records the facts of a murder. The novelist and literary journalist may be concerned with the motive, the types of people concerned in it, the emotional color in the circumstances surrounding it. But to achieve the effect of dramatic intensity, they must exercise selection in the details included in the story.

Nor can the literary journalist overlook the importance of the manner in which these details are presented. He may adopt an informal style, not unlike that of the informal essayist, a technique that can be applied to the human-interest editorial, and one which is frequently used in the column. On the other hand, Hemingway achieves his effects through the use of short, staccato sentences. There is no one style for the literary journalist, but he must have a style that is his own.

In evolving the manner of presentation then, the problems of the literary journalist are similar to the problems of the novelist, the short-story writer, the poet, and the dramatist.

CHAPTER XXXVII

PUBLISHING THE BUSINESS PRESS

> Business papers are current "textbooks" studiously read by the alert
> man in industry, trade, and profession who never accepted his college
> diploma as the end of his education.—STANLEY A. KNISELY.*

THE BUSINESS PRESS INCLUDES A VARIETY OF NEWS-PAPERS AND MAGAZINES

Among the more important class, trade, and professional journals [1]
are publications devoted to the specialized interests of business. This
group of publications is generally referred to as the business press. Although these publications differ widely as to style and format, they uniformly exist as media for the dissemination of news and views which
have an economic purpose—possibly for the entire business world, or
perhaps for a limited segment thereof, but more often for a restricted
though relatively wide trade area. In effect, whatever the scope of the
trade area covered by any particular business publication, the business
press serves an economic rather than an entertainment purpose.

Business Newspapers Reflect And Interpret Economic Life. The
diverse effects of social and economic factors caused by changing economic, legal, and political aspects of problems affecting business create
the need for a variety of daily business newspapers. A few outstanding
daily business newspapers are well established. Among those that appeal
to specialized groups on a daily presentation basis are the financial and
market dailies, such as the *Wall Street Journal,* the *New York Journal
of Commerce,* and the *Chicago Journal of Commerce.*[2]

The *Wall Street Journal* reports price fluctuations on the New York
Stock Exchange, the New York Curb Exchange, the Chicago Board of
Trade, the New Orleans Cotton Exchange, and other stock and com-
modity exchanges. Price changes on over-the-counter transactions, price

---

* From an address by Stanley A. Knisely, executive vice president, Associated Business Papers, Inc.

[1] The five generally recognized categories of journalism are presented in Chapter I, *The Press as an Institution.*

[2] Indirectly important to the business world but in the legal field, the *Chicago
Daily Law Bulletin* centers its attention on news of courts and legislation. Such news
frequently affects business and consequently this publication also has a certain reader-
group among business and industrial leaders.

ranges on bank, insurance, and unlisted stocks are accurately reported. The *Wall Street Journal* is the voice of the American financial world.

The *Chicago Journal of Commerce,* though concerning itself with finance, reports extensively on commodity markets, transportation, real-estate, insurance, oil, grain, cotton, and other commodity markets. Its policy concentrates on both financial and business news, with interpretations of political, legislative, and judicial decisions and movements. It touches some general news when such may affect the stability of business. World, national, or local spot news of the greatest import is reported briefly.

In the clothing field, the Fairchild Publications publish several daily newspapers, particularly *Women's Wear Daily* and the *Daily News Record,* the latter specializing in the men's clothing market.

The fact that daily newspapers specializing in different fields of business are successful clearly indicates that business is one of the major common denominators of American thinking. Businessmen are interested in the general business situation as affected by many economic, political, and governmental factors; they are interested also in specific factors, both interior and exterior, that affect their judgment in handling their own manufacturing and distribution problems, costs, taxes, consumer-acceptability, and credit.

Business Magazines Serve A Diversity Of Economic Needs. The business press makes extensive use of the magazine format. Such business magazines perform functions necessary to the successful development of business. Many of them, established over a long period, not infrequently exercise considerable direct or indirect influence in their trade areas. The tremendous growth of publications of this character is due to a number of sound reasons.

In the first place, business and industry are highly diversified with special problems demanding constant attention. Geographically, the country naturally creates needs for sectional publications. These are well marked in the agricultural field, such as, for example, the *Washington Farmer,* the *Oregon Farmer,* the *Kansas Farmer,* the *Wisconsin Agriculturalist and Farmer,* and the *Prairie Farmer.* Specialized interests in some fields have created a specialized functional rather than geographical division. There are, for example, specialized agricultural magazines, such as the *American Nurseryman, Hoard's Dairyman,* the *American Fruit Grower,* the *Poultry Tribune,* and the *Turkey World.*

In the second place, businessmen are interested in improving their financial position. They recognize that one way to do this is to increase their service to their customers. This attitude has kept them open-minded to new ideas. The merchant is interested in better store layout, improving methods of taking inventory, increasing the turnover of stock, stimulating sales of slowly moving goods, advertising more effectively at reasonable cost, better window-display techniques, more effective use of personnel, and improved accounting procedure. The manufacturer is interested in the possibilities of increased production, cost studies, plant design, raw-material supply, storage, sales, shipment of goods, credit management, and other administrative problems. The business magazines in the manufacturing and distributive fields cover these various problems with concise, helpful articles, well illustrated. What is true of the better business magazines in the transformative and distributive industrial areas is similarly true for business publications in the extractive and contributive areas.

Third in significance in the development of the business magazine is the need for specialized advertising. The manufacturer of turret lathes would hardly advertise in a daily newspaper, as so few of the readers of the average daily newspaper would be in the market for turret lathes. The manufacturer of such machine tools naturally wishes to reach a particular clientele—those with interest in and capacity to purchase and use such tools. The machine-tool manufacturer, for example, who wishes to reach a definite market in a widely accepted medium usually makes use of the business magazine in his particular field. He knows that the reader of *Iron Age* is interested in knowing more about his special business. He knows that all have confidence in its integrity and policies and that the reader thereof is apt to be in a receptive state of mind.[1]

And finally, business magazines because of the progressive policies followed by the majority of their publishers and editors have grown, prospered, and became influential. In effect, they have been alert to the needs of their respective fields and alertness has paid. That is, business publications which have been established for a long period have been conducted on sound journalistic and business principles. Funds have been expended for improvements and better personnel. Some publishers have even developed supplementary publications to strengthen their financial stability. The railroad field well illustrates how a publishing company can expand its service. The Simmons-Boardman Publishing Corporation, publishers of *Railway Age,* sensing the complexity of reader- and advertiser-demands for specialized service, developed such publications as the *Railway Electrical Engineer, Railway Mechanical Engineer, Railway Signaling,* and *Railway Engineering and Maintenance.* Another major example of this policy is that of the McGraw-Hill Publishing Company, which publishes, besides one general-circulation magazine and industrial catalogs, twenty-five business publications. Five additional business magazines are published by affiliated or subsidiary companies. In

---

[1] Of course, a few such manufacturers use direct-mail booklets, brochures, or folders rather exclusively as advertising media, but most manufacturers recognize that trade-journal advertising is effective and at least supplement their direct-mail programs accordingly.

addition, of course, through its affiliate, the McGraw-Hill Book Company, it ties into the book-publishing field.

BUSINESS MAGAZINES DIVIDE INTO MANY CLASSIFICATION PATTERNS

Diversity of business and industry means that the business-magazine field is rather sharply divided. Accurate classification of the business paper is difficult. Some business magazines overlap in function. Often, there is difficulty in demarcating the limits of publishing functions.

Some Working Standards Of Classification Are Useful. It is useful to distinguish by recognizing that some publications are organized on a horizontal basis and that others are organized on a vertical basis. These bases are primarily interest zones. One publication may cover an entire industry, from the production of raw material, its transportation and fabrication, through the merchandising of the product to the public. It then covers extraction of material, preparation, manufacture, distribution, and sale. Such a publication, like *Coal Age,* is commonly classed as a vertical magazine. *Coal Age* covers all phases of the coal industry, particularly from the viewpoint of management. Mining, shipment, and sale of coal receive attention. Labor conditions and legislation as affecting the coal industry, as well as research, are given consideration. Opinions on various phases of the coal industry are expressed.

The horizontal form of business paper organization embraces one functional activity that may be found in many types of industry. An outstanding example of a publication that cuts across many different industries and business interests is *Printers' Ink.*[1] The advertising managers of a chemical company, a steel manufacturing corporation, or a chain department store, for instance, are all possible subscription possibilities. *Tide* and *Advertising Age* are other publications covering these same general fields.

Illustrative of another form of vertical classification of business publications is the Simmons-Boardman group of railway publications. *Railway Age* is the more general of the four papers in this group, going to railway executives, operating and traffic officers, purchasing officers, and department heads.[2]

---

[1] *Printers' Ink* covers advertising, advertising as related to salesmanship, merchandising, and the general effectiveness of the different advertising media, newspapers, magazines, farm journals, house organs, radio, direct mail, and billboards.

[2] The three other publications are specific in their fields. *Railway Mechanical Engineer* centers its appeal to mechanical-department officers and staffs responsible for locomotives, freight, passenger cars, shops, and shop equipment. *Railway Engineering and Maintenance* bases its coverage on material for engineering and maintenance officers and staffs responsible for roadway, track elevation, building water-supply facilities, and other fixed properties. The fourth publication is *Railway Signaling,* which serves signal and telegraph officers and staffs responsible for signaling and communication facilities.

A Four-Unit Classification Of Business Papers Has Been Used.[1]
Business publications are sometimes classified on the basis of industrial, institutional, professional, and merchandising.[2] Examples of business magazines within these classifications are:

Industrial: *Iron Age, Factory Management,* and *Steel*
Institutional: *Hotel Monthly, Restaurant Management, Hospital Management,* and the *American City*
Professional: *Architectural Forum, Advertising Age, Printers' Ink,* and the *American Bar Association Journal*
Merchandising: *Hardware Age, Chain Store Age,* and *Home Furnishings*

Basic Element Classification Also Is Useful. If the business paper concentrates on producers' goods and services, it may be based either on technical production of the goods or on the distribution of such goods. When the emphasis is on consumers' goods, the emphasis is essentially on the distribution of the goods or services, particularly relating to buying advantages, stock inventories, store layout, display of goods, and advertising; the slant is definitely to those engaged in the distribution of goods, not to the ultimate consumer.

If a business paper is on a paid-circulation basis, it may become a member of the *Audit Bureau of Circulations,* but if it is distributed without charge to persons with certain specialized interests, it may become a member of the *Controlled Circulation Audit Bureau,* in which case the publication is said to be on a controlled-circulation basis. In other words, the publication is distributed as a free paper to those engaged in a well-defined activity. For example, *Burroughs Clearing House* is a controlled-circulation publication distributed largely to banks and financial institutions. Its circulation in 1947 ran to approximately 68,000 copies per month. *Banking,* published by the American Bankers Association, is essentially a membership publication for members of that association; its subscription is based not on an independent subscription to members but

---

[1] A threefold classification of business papers may also be used. This divides them into technical, merchandising, and class publications. *Chemical and Metallurgical Engineering, Construction Methods and Equipment, Railway Engineering and Maintenance,* and *Electronics* are essentially technical magazines. The *Boot and Shoe Recorder, Gift and Art Buyer,* and *Electrical Merchandising* are trade publications. The technical publications cover the techniques of the particular industry, methods of manufacture, equipment, maintenance, plant layout, assembly, and inspection. The merchandising publications confine their contents to the economic phase of distribution, buying, inventory, store layout, sales methods, training of the sales force, accounting, taxation, price regulation, window display, and advertising as applied to volume turnover. It is difficult to set definite limitations on magazines devoted to technical and merchandising fields, for there is some overlapping of content. Class publications might be *Billboard, Editor and Publisher, Etude,* and *Modern Hospital.*

[2] This classification is recommended by Harold Green, associate editor of *Printers' Ink,* who serves as a lecturer for the Associated Business Papers, Inc.

is included in the membership fee of the association. Sucn a publication may sell also subscriptions independently of membership. A membership publication such as *Banking* may take advertising and thus compete with magazines that operate on a subscription basis.

Some magazines operate on a weekly basis, giving particularly news of the industry; others, on a monthly basis, emphasize technical and educational articles, as well as some personnel news. In a survey of specialized publications, it will be observed that the majority of established, widely recognized business publications are produced on a magazine format.[1]

Industrial Classification Is Most Scientific. Probably the most scientific classification of business papers is one that parallels the classification of industry.[2] The basic divisions of this fourfold classification are extractive, transformative, contributive, and distributive.

In the extractive group there may be found industries and publications in such fields as agriculture, forestry, nurseries, fishing, mining, and quarrying; with such publications as *Hoard's Dairyman, Timberman,* the *American Nurseryman, Atlantic Fisherman,* and *Mining and Metallurgy.*

In the transformative division there are such industries as those dealing with food, textiles, furniture, paper, leather, and machinery with such publications as *Food Industries, Textile World, Furniture Index, Paper Industry and Paper World, Shoe and Leather Reporter,* and the *American Machinist.*

In the contributive field there are included such areas as power, insurance, amusement, journalism, architecture, hotels, restaurants, and legal services, with representative publications such as *Power Plant Engineering,* the *Insurance Index, Billboard, Editor and Publisher,* the *Architectural Record, Hotel Management, American Restaurant,* and the *American Bar Association Journal.*

The distributive field embraces such fields as manufacturers' sales, wholesalers, transportation, chain stores, and retailers, with corresponding publications such as *Mill Supplies, Electrical Wholesaling, Corset and Underwear Review, Railway Age, Chain Store Age,* and the *Boot and Shoe Recorder.*

---

[1] If a publication is produced on a newspaper format but uses magazine layout, difficulties are encountered in developing an attractive layout.

[2] This classification of industry and business publications is called by Julien Elfenbein, editorial director of the Haire Publishing Company and author of *Business Journalism,* the most sensible. (Julien Elfenbein, *Business Journalism: Its Function and Future,* Harper & Bros., 1945.) He uses as authority the *Standard Industrial Classification Manual,* prepared by the Bureau of the Budget, Executive Office of the President of the United States, and adopted by the United States Departments of Commerce and Labor, the Federal Trade Commission, and the Federal Reserve System.

PUBLISHING POLICIES ARE GOVERNED BY
SUBSCRIBER NEED

The success of the business paper depends on the economic need which such a publication meets. The prime consideration of the editor and publisher of a business magazine is the subscriber.

The Interests Of Subscribers Must Be Considered. The business paper may be organized on a controlled-circulation basis, going to selected persons without charge, or upon a subscription basis. In the latter case the readers are willing to pay for the publication because they find the publication's service vital to their business interests.

In the early development of specialized business publications, some publishers followed "puffing" tactics. That is, when business firms or corporations contracted for display advertising space, it was understood that they would receive a certain amount of editorial material dealing with the company or the products thereof. These articles were in the main laudatory, irrespective of the merits of the goods or services advertised. The result was that the readers soon realized that the editorial material was not selected on its merit as news or feature articles. However, it wasn't long before the better publishers realized that such a policy was detrimental to the reputation and character of their publications. Hence, today the best business publications do not accept such "puffing" articles.[1] All news is measured on the basis of whether it is real news or fair comment in the particular area of interest served.

Policies In Circulation Management Are Important. Circulation does not parallel the press run. The total number of net-paid subscribers to a magazine may be considerably less than the actual number of copies printed or distributed.

Many publishers believe that the best circulation policy is on a paid-subscription basis. In some fields, however, a business publication may be wholly on a controlled-circulation basis, with distribution to all persons or organizations interested in a certain field of business activity. In any event, to protect the advertisers, the exact amount of the circulation should be definitely known, according to the approved standards of either the Audit Bureau of Circulations or the Controlled Circulation Audit Bureau.

Circulation is an intangible factor. A subscriber contracts to take a certain publication for a period of time, usually for a year. All the issues of the publication for which the subscriber has contracted are not yet in existence. Too, the advertiser is sold space on the ground of the amount and value of the subscription list. The advertisers want to know if the

---

[1] The standards of practice of the Associated Business Papers, Inc., do not authorize its member publications to publish "puffs," free reading notices, or paid "write-ups" presented as legitimate editorial material.

number of subscriptions is authentic, and also to know whether the character of the subscribers is such that they have the need for such a publication and whether they have the purchasing power to buy the goods or services advertised in the publication.

The Value Of A Subscriber Must Be Appreciated. It may be surprising to formulate in dollar value what a subscriber is actually worth to the publication. For example, if the subscription price of a particular business publication is $4, the subscriber is then worth $4 to the publication on the subscription-price standard. On the other hand, if the success of the advertising carried is determined in part by the reaction of subscribers to advertising in the publication, one may develop other formulae for evaluating the subscriber.[1]

Advertising In Business Magazines Centers Its Appeal. Consumer advertising in newspapers or general magazines scatters its appeal. However, advertising pages in specialized publications concentrate upon the special interests of the particular groups of readers served by these publications.

In a business publication, the editorial and news material is presented for the purpose of information, education, and inspiration; it presents articles and news of value to a special field of business, technical, or institutional activity. Editorials as such even create a demand for new ideas and improved methods. In all ways then, there is created a natural desire to read specialized advertising. The reader is in a receptive mood.

Capital and producer-goods manufacturers as well as consumer-goods manufacturers have discovered that they can effectively place advertising in business papers. The use of such trade journals permits the advertiser to stimulate wholesaler preparation for demand from retail merchants. In effect, this is a preconsumer campaign method and helps create consumer demand for any product advertised in business magazines which circulate to the wholesale and retail business fields. It accomplishes a unique selling job.[2]

---

[1] If a publication has 8000 net-paid subscribers at $4 per subscription and if the gross annual volume of advertising totals $120,000, the business volume for both circulation and advertising would be $152,000. On the per-subscriber gross-volume theory the value of the individual subscriber would be $19. Still, another subscriber evaluation method is the net-income theory. If a publication makes a net return of $7 per subscriber a year, before federal income tax, the subscriber might be evaluated at $70, provided the net income were capitalized on a 10 per cent basis. The question is 10 per cent of what equals $7. Naturally, the percentage base could be varied, but for purposes of illustration the 10 per cent base is used.

[2] Should a coffee roaster wish to introduce a new brand of coffee, he might easily err in business judgment if he opened his campaign in the general newspapers; it is true that he might create consumer-demand for the new product, but if the merchants did not have the product on their shelves, the consumer-demand would be wasted; the customers could not purchase the coffee in the retail outlets.

Advertising Ethics Are Important In The Business Magazine. The old principle of *caveat emptor,* or let the buyer beware, no longer obtains in the best business magazines. Once it was considered that the columns of a publication were open to all those who wished to buy. But soon it was realized that questionable advertising injures other advertising by breaking down the faith and confidence of the reader. Accordingly, no misleading advertising is accepted by those adhering to A.B.P. principles.[1]

No publication is legally required to accept advertising that is tendered for publication. The publisher is free to accept whatever advertising he will and there is no penalty if he refuses. Further, post-office regulations are clear in specifying that paid editorial reading notices cannot be published unless it is clearly indicated that such material is an advertisement.

Fraudulent advertising is restricted by such statutes as the *Printers' Ink* statute [2] which is the law in numerous states. When advertising is placed in publications circulating in interstate commerce, the Federal Trade Commission has jurisdiction to investigate and order such advertising stopped.

Another important ethical principle in the business press is that advertising which deprecates the value of a competitor's product is not acceptable. For example, where disputes arise between business concerns in connection with patent infringement, it is not the function of the business press to settle differences in patent rights; the courts are open to try such controversies.[3]

THE HOUSE ORGAN FIELD HAS ITS SPECIAL PROBLEMS

When an institution such as a manufacturing or merchandising company wishes to have its own publication to carry its own story to its own

---

[1] See Chapter 14 of *Legal Control of the Press* by Frank Thayer. Published by Foundation Press, Chicago, 1944.

[2] Any person, firm, corporation or association who with intent to sell or in any wise dispose of merchandise, securities, service, or anything offered by such person, firm, corporation or association, directly or indirectly, to the public for sale or distribution, or with intent to increase the consumption thereof, or to induce the public in any manner to enter into any obligation relating thereto, or to acquire title thereto, or an interest therein, makes, publishes, disseminates, circulates, or places before the public, or causes, directly or indirectly, to be made, published, disseminated, circulated, or placed before the public, in this state, in a newspaper, or other publication, or in the form of a book, notice, handbill, poster, bill, circular, pamphlet, or letter, or in any other way, an advertisement of any sort regarding merchandise, securities, service, or anything so offered to the public, which advertisement contains any assertion, representation or statement of fact which is untrue, deceptive or misleading, shall be guilty of misdemeanor.

[3] If a manufacturer involved in a patent-infringement suit tries to place advertising in a business magazine warning readers that his patent is being infringed and that those using his competitor's product will be subject to damage suits, the best practice is not to accept such advertising.

reader-group, either for the purpose of building good-will among its customers and prospects or to foster a unifying interest among its employees, the house organ is a definite means of achieving its objective. A house organ is a newspaper or magazine published by a firm or corporation, without any price set on its subscription, and distributed to a particularly selected group. Such a publication is designed to build *ésprit de corps* for a product, an institution, or a company.

There Are Various Types Of House Organs. House organs may be either inside or outside house organs.

The employee magazine is an inside house organ, an excellent example of which is the *Baltimore and Ohio Magazine,* published for the employees of the Baltimore and Ohio Railroad Company. This magazine directs its appeal to both the employees and their families.

The outside house organ is designed to increase sales of the company's product. The *Hercules Mixer,* published by the Hercules Powder Company, is an outstanding example of a house organ published for outside circulation.

Thousands of house organs are published in the United States. A house-organ directory published by *Printers' Ink* lists more than 5000 recognized house organs.

For publicity purposes, a trade association may issue a house organ. The American Iron and Steel Institute, for example, publishes *Steelways,* which in reality has all the reader-interest of a general magazine. In character of paper, typography, and illustrations, *Steelways* ranks high.

Employees' Magazines Have An Important Place. The publication of a house organ for employees promotes unity and a sense of team play. Employee house organs are usually published to promote a feeling of "belonging" to a group with common interests, hopes, and ambitions. They serve also to allay fears common to all as to the future by keeping the employee adequately informed of what is happening in his company. They serve a need and show that the employer is interested in the recreation and home life of his employees.

To some degree, the employee's magazine faces the competition of other publications. A poorly edited and printed employee publication cannot expect to hold reader-interest.

As a fundamental policy, it is the best practice not to feature opinion on politics, religion, or other controversial issues. News rather than opinion serves well; pictures possess reader-appeal. By this, it is not meant that if an employee is elected to his community's common town council, to the trusteeship of his church, or to represent his union in a state convention, such news should not be used. Rather, such news should be used, but obvious propaganda should be avoided, particularly when the publication is financed by the company.

To a degree the employee-magazine editor can well appeal to the family as well as the employee. Such magazines may well be mailed to the home of the employee. Generally, this is better practice than to hand the publication to the employee at the door of the plant at the end of a workday. It gives the publication more "position" in the home.

It Is Necessary To Make The House Organ Click. A good house organ is something like a department store. It should contain different types of material so that there may be a breadth of interest. The customer in a department store has a broad possibility in the selection of goods; likewise, the reader of a house organ should have a selection of material, some of which is certain to capture his interest. When the *Benefit News,* the official publication of National Mutual Benefit, a mutual-benefit life-insurance company, was changed in format and character, it was determined to make the magazine of interest to the entire family.[1] It changed its appeal so as to stimulate the reader with interesting material of substantial value attractively presented.

The current success of this publication in reaching the membership of the society is attested to by the fact that shortly after its redesign, the *Benefit News* in a competition for mutual society and fraternal publications won first prize for both improvement and content. Similar contests and affiliation with house-organ editorial associations are doing much to raise the standards of such publications.

---

[1] As this society insures both juveniles and adults, material is planned to reach both classes of readers. Its policy is to reflect human interest, to give information on insurance and family finance, and to report news of the organization. It is a policy to have a picture on each page, or at least a picture or other display on alternate facing pages.

Chapter XXXVIII

RADIO–TELEVISION—A NEW JOURNALISTIC MEDIUM

While the radio is primarily designed for entertainment, . . . radio has . . . advantage in telling a compressed news story quickly. In a few effortless minutes the listener gets, wrapped in one package, the equivalent of the facts of a news dispatch, the editorial comment upon them, and the columnist's personal interpretation. Radio's power is not only in summary but also in synthesis.—Fortune.*

THE DEVELOPMENT OF RADIO JOURNALISM HAS BEEN RAPID

In the autumn of 1920, the first newscast reached listeners from Station KDKA in Pittsburgh, carrying the Harding-Cox presidential election returns; ten years later, in 1930, lowered prices and technical advances had resulted in placing radio sets in thousands of American homes, and the stage was set for real listening; after sixteen years, in December, 1936, millions listened to the dramatic denouement of the abdication of King Edward VIII whereas only a few hundred had heard the first broadcast.

At first, local newspapers and press-association bureaus supplied their news free to radio stations to furnish this new journalistic activity with its raw material. By 1921 and 1922, radio began spot broadcasts of championship boxing matches and football games. A few years later, radio broadcast a solemn account of the funeral of Woodrow Wilson and aired Republican and Democratic national conventions. By 1925, twenty-four stations united in sending to the nation news of Calvin Coolidge's inauguration. When the National Broadcasting Company was founded in 1926 and the Columbia Broadcasting System came into being the next year, national organizations were available to emphasize the importance of radio journalism.

In 1934 newspapers first began to realize that serious competition existed, as radio set up its own network to gather and collect the news. Fear of radio competition brought about a defensive organization in the Press-Radio Bureau, by which the principal news services and two national networks agreed to limit radio newscasts to three daily periods

---

* Reprinted from the *Fortune* Survey April 1938 by special permission of the Editors of *Fortune*. Copyright Time, Inc.

in exchange for free supplies of news by the press associations. But this plan yielded to growing industrial demands and public desire for radio news almost immediately. A special radio news service was set up the same year, and by 1938 the networks and press associations discontinued the agreement.

The United Press led the way in supplying radio stations with news commercially prepared for broadcast purposes, and it was eventually followed by the other two major associations. Coverage by radio's own reporters of World War II familiarized every American listener with radio newscasts and new radio comment programs. Radio journalism had come to stay.

It should be remembered, however, that radio journalism is only half free in the sense that radio broadcasting is operated under government license and thus is potentially subject to political influences. Although the Federal Communications Commission decided in 1949 that a station may express its personal views on current issues, it simultaneously stressed that the station should afford a "reasonably balanced" presentation of contrary opinion. Furthermore, the FCC indicated that the degree of "balance" would be subject to federal appraisal. Therefore, there is no absolute assurance that the doctrine of freedom of expression extends to radio broadcasting. The license of any station may be revoked. Consequently, in America, the important difference between the newspaper press and radio broadcasting is that the former is a free institution and the latter is a licensed medium. This is necessarily so, as radio waves are the property of the nation.

VOCATIONAL OPPORTUNITIES IN RADIO JOURNALISM ARE VARIED

Although get-rich-quick mail-order firms and correspondence houses have overinflated the balloon of vocational opportunity in radio journalism, there is a steady and healthy growth of jobs for trained people in this field. The networks on a national basis, local stations in every medium-sized town and all the larger cities, regional broadcasting systems—all these have opened their doors to radio journalism and created jobs for a new profession. Radio journalism needs continuity and script writers, advertising solicitors, promotion men and women, and television journalists.

Radio Journalism Has Many Facets. The national networks, covering hundreds of stations throughout the country, offer the final accolade of achievement to the radio journalist. In these networks, such as the National Broadcasting Company, Columbia Broadcasting System, Mutual, and American Broadcasting Company, scores of thoroughly trained and experienced men and women operate today in radio journalism. Their fields of activity are many.

Some of them operate as "leg" men, gathering stories on the scene and often broadcasting on-the-spot interviews and descriptions of sporting events, political meetings, and many other activities which may interest the listener.

In addition to the radio leg man or on-the-spot radio reporter, large staffs are employed preparing straight newscasts which are put on the air and fed to member stations of these chains. This job of rewriting and editing news, taken largely from press-association wires, is a major activity.

Besides the radio reporter and rewrite man, experienced reporters with excellent voices have made national names for themselves as analysts, commenting on the news of the day and interpreting it. This sort of top job in radio journalism can be held generally only by a limited few on the national front, although it has its counterpart even in the smaller station.

Finally, the pioneer success of dramatized radio news programs, such as *The March of Time,* has led to a number of similar productions on the air. These shows take the news of the day, surround it with background and sound effects, stage it with professional actors, and create a new field of radio journalism.

The Local-Station Newscast Frequently Requires "Doubling In Brass." Shifting the scenes in radio journalism from the national network to the small local station, there continues to be a demand for trained newsmen—often equipped also with personalities and voices to put their news on the air after it has been written and edited. This double performance, which involves editing wire copy and local news and then presenting it over the microphone to the listener, is the opportunity which the small station offers the beginner to become acquainted with the two most important phases of radio journalism. It is not enough for a man to be able to write or edit news copy, he also must be able to present it clearly, distinctly, and pleasingly to families grouped around the radio sets in their homes. To get started in the radio journalism business, the beginner should plan on breaking in with a small station. That's the sound advice which veterans of this field give. In the small station, the radio journalism cub can get experience which he needs in order to progress to larger stations and the networks.

Continuity And Script Writers Must Be Skilled. Practically every radio show on the air, every broadcast, has a continuity of some kind, which, while it may consist only of an opening and closing announcement, demands handling by skilled writers. Some programs, a very few, are *ad libbed* but most of them depend upon written continuities which are followed by the announcers, the actors, or other participants in the broadcast. These continuities, which may range from a thirty-second spot announcement or commercial to a half-hour or hour radio comedy show or dramatic presentation, generally are prepared by skilled and experienced writers. But the radio profession is constantly seeking new talent because it has a constant and continuous use for such material. Every hour of the broadcast day, continuities are being consumed. Whether it is the interpretation to accompany a symphony program or the gags for a comedy hour, the continuity or script has to be written in advance and often is subject to hasty or last-minute revision. This demands writing skill. While not all radio journalists can hope to have the ability and talent for this type of work, it is a challenge to many interested in radio journalism. Top script writers demand and receive large sums, but even the smaller station has need for the man or woman who can turn out a good commercial between shows and perhaps handle longer continuities also.

Advertising On The Air Is Now Big Business. Radio's share of advertising dollars has been tremendous in recent years. This has meant large advertising staffs who are capable either of soliciting advertising for a local station or of handling advertising accounts for radio in large national agencies. From the solicitor to the advertising copywriter on the air, radio offers practically every variety of advertising work except art, and television has opened that as a field also. Advertising for radio is distinctly different from that prepared for any other medium. It has its own means of expression. The radio *commercial,* the means used for an advertising message over the air, is written to be heard—not read. This conditions the advertising message presented appreciably.

Radio Public Relations Is An Expanding Field. Every radio listener knows that promotion for future shows is a frequent feature of the radio listening day. He also gets acquainted with radio stars and radio performers through features and stories about them in magazines of general circulation, trade journals, and all the varieties of promotion employed by ingenious promotion experts. This means that from the local station on up to the national network, men and women with a talent for public relations and publicity are at work. Again, job opportunities in radio journalism!

Television Occupies An Important Place. By 1948 television was operating on a network basis; already press associations had staffs to prepare special scripts and journalistic material for television shows. Although television's greatest expansion is ahead, it has opened many doors to the radio journalist.

TRAINING IS REQUIRED FOR RADIO JOURNALISM

The Council on Radio Journalism, composed of representatives from the radio industry and from the journalism schools, has indicated that the radio journalist needs to take broad liberal-arts training and then more specialized education in qualified journalism schools. In addition, he should have on-the-job training which he may receive first in a newspaper office and then, later, in the radio station itself.

A Liberal-Arts Educational Background Is Advantageous. Veteran radiomen as well as leading teachers of journalism agree that an aspiring radio journalist should have a broad liberal-arts education in the social sciences, in English, in the arts, and in foreign languages. In effect, they are saying that a useful preparation is a general education as a background for a more detailed specialization in the journalism school or department.

Journalism Schools Provide Technical Training. Certainly, the aspirant to radio journalism should have training in news gathering and news writing. He should be familiar with editing and rewriting copy. If he wants to work on the advertising side, he should prepare himself specifically by taking advertising courses. Following this he should add the curriculum in radio journalism now offered in a number of qualified journalism schools and departments.[1]

The Newspaper Office Serves As A Preliminary Proving Ground. Vital in the training of a radio journalist is the on-the-job experience which he will get working for a newspaper as a reporter or deskman. In newspaper work he forms judgments on news values, learns to collect facts and write them in presentable form, to boil down and edit copy to eliminate excess verbiage. This type of experience, or its full equivalent, is practically essential.

While in the future there may develop a stronger trend towards the employment of radio journalists without preliminary newspaper experience, at the present time work in a newspaper office appears especially desirable as a finishing school. Of course, many of the pioneers in radio journalism learned on the job in radio. Many others had long newspaper training.

On-The-Job Training Provides The Technical Know-How. Finally, the radio journalist will do his learning on his radio job. There is no substitute for the training involved in handling wire copy, preparing local newscasts, writing continuity, going on the air oneself, and observing operations in the control room. It is in the job itself where a man's work is measured on a salary basis and where real specialization begins. For this reason, the newcomer to a radio station without prior experience will do well to keep all his senses alert, observing and absorbing as much as he can of the fascinating but highly technical operations of which he has become a part.

---

[1] The reputable journalism department does not attempt to overspecialize in its radio journalism teaching; it emphasizes the fundamentals of radio news writing, radio newscasts, and the preparation of continuity.

REPORTING AND WRITING MUST BE SLANTED FOR LISTENING

Writing for radio means writing for a medium with its own requisites. Write for the listener's ear, not his eye. Abandon such preconceived ideas of newspaper writing as have to do with summary leads and inverted pyramid structures. Write the news short, simple, and to the point.

The Language Of Radio Writing Is Informal. Radio writing is designed for the home and the home listener. It is designed for millions of listeners whose speaking vocabulary is simple and limited, whose education may not have progressed beyond grammar school. Write "American" as it is spoken on the street, in the stores, in the home. Your stories need to be brief and to the point. Radio time is expensive. Write your stories effectively, playing up feature angles immediately and opening up with your climax to catch the reader's interest. Eliminate all unnecessary identification and excess wordage which merely clutters up the facts. Remember that people hear at an average rate of 160 words a minute, while they may read at a little less than 100 words a minute. If the listener misses a vital point, he can't turn the announcer back and start him off again.

This means radio writing has to be emphatic. Upon occasion, important details may be, and often are, repeated. There are important language considerations to remember. Watch for too many adjectives. Verbs and concrete nouns carry the story of action forward at the necessary pace. Guard against the overuse of sibilants, strings of "s's," and difficult combination of "th" words or repeated consonants. To facilitate oral reading write 25 million dollars, not $25,000,000. But remember that at best numbers are hard to absorb over the air. Write President Truman, not President Harry S. Truman. Eliminate unnecessary and long-drawn-out titles. Sentences don't always need to be complete; descriptive phrases can do a job when spoken, even if a verb or subject may be lacking. Short sentences are desirable but they should be rhythmical and smooth.

Don't be afraid to employ contractions; say "he'll" rather than "he will." Avoid radio vocabularies which misuse the English language; use the short Anglo-Saxon instead of the polysyllabic Latin derivatives. "Build," don't "construct"; "meet," don't "confer"; "send," don't "transmit." Use synonyms to avoid repetition.

Good Taste Is As Essential In Radio Journalism As In The House. Probably radio has received more criticism for its occasional violation of good taste than for any other single error of commission or omission. Stress on intimate physiological functions, in the form of laxative or medical advertising, comes harshly to the ears of men and women seated around a dinner table. Crude or off-color jokes, innuendoes and double meanings, have little place in the family living room. Lack of sensitivity may be responsible for poor manners in referring to solemn or tragic events in a light vein. Profanity is not for the air. Derogatory references to races or creeds are certain to offend. Public hysteria may easily be aroused by unwise or sensational broadcasts: witness Orson Welles' "Invasion from Mars" some years ago. Gory and gruesome details can be overdone, as the newspapers found out when they tried to campaign against highway deaths. Sordid fact is not entertainment for children or teen-age youngsters. Radio has many taboos of its own, many of them foolish, but the ones mentioned in this paragraph make sense and are the fruit of radio's experience.

Preparing A Newscast From Wire Copy Requires Judgment. Having learned how to write simply and directly and in good taste, the radio rewrite man sits down to prepare a newscast from wire copy. Teletypes have poured in a flood of news to him from all over the world, some of it especially for radio station use and sent over radio news wires, some coming over regular press-association wires. In any case, all of this news has to be sorted and much eliminated; the selected stories should be revised, condensed, and rewritten to suit local angles and local interest. The alert radio rewrite man will be quick to seize upon local angles which capitalize on local interest in the wire copy which he edits. There is a knack to expert editing of wire copy, and such proficiency is generally gained only through experience.

Preparing a newscast means balancing the news among all the different reader-interests in the listener-group. It means giving some room to international developments, some to the national political scene, some to disasters and accidents, some to personalities and human interest—a varied menu! Furthermore, one must figure the time element to the second so that the newscast goes into the allotted schedule, with barely a few seconds' leeway at beginning or end.

Local News Is Frequently Handled Poorly. Local news over the air has been badly kicked around for many years by managers of radio stations, primarily because they haven't spent the money to hire reporters who could gather local news and then haven't even used what they do get. The small or local station has a premium in local news which is guaranteed to get the ear of every local listener. The pulling power of local items is tremendous, as the newspaper has known for a century at least. But too many radio stations have ignored this basic principle.

The key to good local news programs is the actual gathering or reporting of such news. However, in many cases, stations are too willing to depend upon pickups from local papers or publicity releases by local organizations. There is a necessity, which radio will realize, for full-time and complete coverage of local events. This reporting can be on-the-spot broadcasts from the scene, it can be the gathering of news for written presentation in newscast form, it can be play-by-play descriptions of local meetings or sports events. It should mean coverage of every community activity.

The journalism-trained man or woman can bring his abilities and knowledge quickly to bear on this field of local news gathering; he can produce results in local coverage. Then it remains for the radio-station management to allot sufficient time for the presentation of such local news on the air. Perhaps the radio reporter also will have to sell his management on the desirability of such broadcasts; if so, he often will have a man-sized job on his hands. In any case, radio journalism will really come of age as it assumes this responsibility and meets the tremendous demand which already exists among local listeners for local news.

CHAPTER XXXIX

THE LAW LIMITS JOURNALISM

> Liberty of the press consists in a right, in the conductor of a news-
> paper, to print whatever he chooses without any previous license, but
> subject to be held responsible therefor to exactly the same extent, that
> anyone else would be responsible for the publication.*

FREEDOM OF THE PRESS EXISTS UNDER LAW

Law affects journalism as it does any other institutional division of life's
activities. In the United States, law guarantees freedom of the press in a
broad, general way but does not permit unlimited publication of news,
comments, or art without regard to certain rights, privileges, and considerations. These definite restrictions and limitations make up that cross
section of several branches of the law which may be properly designated
as the "law of the press."

Publishing Organizations Are Affected By Business Laws. Publications are printed and published by individuals, partnerships, or corporations and are limited by the laws governing these different forms of doing
business. These organizations are affected by the laws of business and
commerce, including especially contracts, negotiable instruments, sales,
and creditor's rights, and the like. A publishing house, newspaper, or
magazine is subject to liability on one of its contracts in the same way as
any other business or individual.

The Law Of The Press Includes Special Phases Of Law. The legal
fields embraced by the law of the press include parts of torts, constitutional and criminal law, procedure, the law of unfair competition and
trade practices, and the law of copyright. These fields deal with the laws
that limit and regulate the press.[1]

**Freedom Of The Press Is Established By Federal And State Constitu-
tions.[2]** Freedom of the press is set forth in the first amendment to the

---

* *Sweeney* v. *Baker,* 13 West Virginia 182.

[1] The law of the press does not embrace all the legal topics of these particular
fields, but rather cuts crosswise, touching and including only definite legal principles as related to the problems of publication.

[2] However, it should be kept in mind that the present comparative liberty or freedom of the press was won after struggle and represents the results of many political and legal battles. Various standard textbooks on the law of libel and on the
history of journalism refer to these important episodes. For example, see Thayer,
Legal Control of the Press, Chapters 1 to 4.

Constitution of the United States as a basic right of the people:

> Congress shall make no law respecting an establishment of
> religion, or prohibiting the free exercise thereof; or abridging
> the freedom of speech, or *of the press;* or the right of the people
> peaceably to assemble, and to petition the government for a re-
> dress of grievances.

The various states likewise have similar provision. For example, the Constitution of the State of Illinois, Article II, Section 4, reads:

> Every person may freely speak, write, and publish on all sub-
> jects, being responsible for the abuse of that liberty; and in all
> trials for libel, both civil and criminal, the truth, when published
> with good motives and for justifiable ends, shall be a sufficient
> defense.

FREEDOM OF THE PRESS MAY BE MISUNDERSTOOD

The term "freedom of the press" is often misunderstood—it does not
include license. Lawyers, jurists, and editors are not yet sure—and probably never will be—of all that such a right means, but it is possible to
approximate its meaning and understand its significance.

Ordinarily There Is No Censorship Prior To Publication. Ordinarily,
freedom of the press in the United States means that there will be no
censorship prior to publication. However, during a period of great national stress as in times of war, a censorship might be enforced, and even
during peace the United States Post Office Department may bar from the
mails distribution of obscene, lewd, or lascivious printing, writing, or
pictures.

Freedom of the press would be a hollow mockery, however, if after
publication, a newspaper or magazine could not be circulated. It was
decided in a case arising in Louisiana that a tax based on the extent of
circulation of daily newspapers fettered the guarantee of freedom of the
press; the Louisiana law was declared unconstitutional.[1]

With Freedom Of The Press Go Obligations And Responsibilities.
While a publication may have freedom to publish news stories, it has a
correlative obligation or responsibility for what it does publish. When
a newspaper publishes a libelous statement, it should be certain it has
legal authority for so doing. In brief, it has full responsibility for having
printed the statement and may have the obligation of justifying it in law.

What Is The Right To Report News? For practical purposes, there
may be said to be such a right, but it is not absolute. Three examples
of certain limitations upon access to news follow:

---

[1] *Grosjean* v. *American Press Co.,* 297 U.S. 233, 56 S. Ct. 444, 80 L. Ed. 660
(1936).

LAW COURTS. There does not seem to be an absolute right for reporters to attend court. The judge exercises authority over his own courtroom and controls the decorum when the court is in session. While reporters are not often barred from the courtroom during a trial, the judge has the power to bar them.

PUBLIC RECORDS. Generally, public records may be inspected and reported by the press. However, the question arises as to what is a public record. The files of the office of the President of the United States are not regarded as public records; neither are certain diplomatic documents in the course of negotiation through the United States Department of State.

FILES OF LAW-ENFORCEMENT AGENCIES. Usually, current files and correspondence of law-enforcement agencies such as the police departments of our cities, particularly the records of current cases concerning the pursuit and arrest of criminals by the Federal Bureau of Investigation of the United States Department of Justice, may not be inspected or reported. For obvious reasons, it is not regarded as within the public interest that such records be generally available.

Journalistic Comment Has Some Limitations. In general, the newspaper is free to comment upon public officers and candidates provided such comment is not defamatory and may be properly regarded as honest comment.

HONEST COMMENT. A newspaper or other journalistic medium may make honest comment upon the government [1] without liability and upon public officers,[2] but even so if the comment is not fair it may be defamatory; and a civil action for libel may be brought, and under certain circumstances the offended party may cause a criminal libel action by the state.

In time of war there are definite limitations upon the right to comment upon the government and its activities. During World War I it was made a criminal offense to oppose by word or deed the cause of the United States.

COMMENT ON PENDING LITIGATION. The right to comment is further limited in the case of litigation pending in the courts.[3] Obviously, the case should not be tried in the newspapers, and the evidence should not be

---

[1] There is no crime of seditious libel at common law in the United States. The Sedition Act of 1798 expired in 1801. The Espionage Act accomplishes somewhat the same purpose as a sedition law, particularly in time of war. The Espionage Act of 1917 remains in force, as amended March 28, 1940. The Alien Registration Act passed by Congress in 1940 and state syndicalism laws serve to control seditious activity.

[2] Under the United States Code, articles tending to incite arson, murder, or assassination are nonmailable.

[3] Comments made adversely against the judge, especially charging judicial corruption or partiality, during the pendency of a suit subject the publisher to contempt of court.

weighed before it has been accepted in court as relevant, material, and competent.

Care must be exercised in commenting upon the result of a case on which a decision has been given, for the case is not concluded legally until the result of an appeal is known, or an appeal is denied, or the opportunity for appeal has expired through lapse of time.

Any publication of news or editorial comment that tends to obstruct justice during the pendency of a trial may be the basis for citation of contempt. If a publication scandalizes a court during the pendency of a trial or publishes a grossly or inaccurate report of a trial, its editor and publisher may be cited for contempt of court.[1]

LIBEL IS A FUNDAMENTAL PHASE OF THE LAW OF THE PRESS

Libel is perhaps the greatest danger for the publisher. If his newspaper, or other publication, oversteps the bounds, defaming person or property, he may be subject to both civil and criminal libel.

Libel Is Written Defamation, And So A Tort. Libel is written defamation. Defamation is a tort. A tort is a civil injury not arising from breach of a contract or from breach of a trust relation, but for which there lies a common-law action for damages.

Sir John Salmond in his notable treatise on *Jurisprudence* defines tort thus: "A tort may be defined as a civil wrong, for which the remedy is an action for damages, and which is not solely the breach of a contract, or the breach of a trust or other merely equitable obligation."[2]

LIBEL DEFINED. A libel may be defined as a malicious publication, expressed either in printing or writing, or by signs, diagrams, cartoons, or pictures, tending to blacken the reputation of a living person so as to expose him to public hatred, contempt, or ridicule.[3]

Such a libel is a civil libel, answerable in damages to the person so libeled. When a libel is published which might tend to incite a riot, the libel could also be a criminal libel punishable by the state in a legal proceeding in its own name for the protection of the public good and public safety. Publication of obscene, seditious, or blasphemous words also is punishable under the criminal law.

TWO TYPES OF LIBEL. Libel *per se* is a libel on its face and requires no proof of special damage; on the contrary, libel *per quod* is a libel not apparent on its face.

---

[1] See *Craig et al.* v. *Harney,* 67 S. Ct. 1249 (1947), in which the clear and present danger test is emphasized.

[2] Sir John Salmond, *Jurisprudence* (7th ed.), p. 486.

[3] Ruling Case Law, Section I, paragraph 2, also *State* v. *Avery,* 7 Conn. 266; 18 *American Decisions* 105; M. L. Newell, *Slander and Libel* (4th ed.), p. 2. It may be criminal libel to blacken the memory of one dead.

To call an attorney a shyster is libelous in itself, for the natural tendency of such an appellation is to degrade one in his profession. If a newspaper publishes that a certain actress is the consort, constant companion, or the like, of a famous prizefighter and that it is understood that they will make a "match," there is libel if it should happen that the actress is married; for in such case she would be held in a contemptuous light by right-thinking individuals. Such a case according to one legal theory would be libel *per quod,* for on its face there would be no libel; it would be necessary to prove surrounding circumstances to show libel—i.e., the woman in question is a married woman.[1] Another theory makes special damages a test.

Libel has been defined as malicious defamation. However, it is not necessary to have an intention to injure or a positive ill-will against the person allegedly libeled; for the injury is done to the person irrespective of whether the publisher intended ill-will, or libel of the person. In this circumstance, the malice is malice in law or constructive malice; it is presumed to exist. If there is actual ill-will, hatred, or intention to do harm, there would be actual malice as distinguished from legal malice. When there is actual malice, the amount of damages for a libelous publication may be increased.

Truth Is A Defense Against Libel. If the publisher publishes a libelous story, the question arises, What defense can be made? The best defense to a civil suit for libel is the truth. Even so, although truth is usually a complete defense in a civil action for damages for libel, certain state laws amend the general rule, and truth becomes a complete defense only when the questioned statement is published with good motives and for justifiable ends.[2]

Truth as a defense is called a justification. Historically, the principle adopted by the courts in handling criminal libel cases is "the greater the truth the greater the libel." However, this principle has no application to civil libel cases. Yet in criminal cases, where, of course, the state is a party,[3] this theory was once the English law. It was believed that the publication of the truth about a person would tend to arouse him to a breach of the peace even more certainly than the publication of an untruth which he could disprove.[4]

Just what constitutes the truth may seem a problem for the news reporter. For example, a well-trained newspaperman realizes that if he is forced to cover an assignment in a hurry his sources of information may not reveal to him the *entire* truth. In fact, his sources of information may

---

[1] See *Sydney* v. *MacFadden Newspaper Publishing Corp.,* 151 N.E. 209.

[2] The Constitution of the State of Illinois, Article II, Section 4, plainly states the amended position, as already noted in the early part of this chapter.

[3] For the protection of the public.

[4] See M. L. Newell, *Slander and Libel* (4th ed.), p. 768.

give contradictory statements or statements that do not agree in every particular. Therefore, his problem is to find out what is the truth *before* he writes the story.[1]

While a story might be accurate, the headline writer could readily commit libel by using a headline which misleads or gives only a half-truth conveying a libelous interpretation to the public.[2]

Privilege Is A Defense Against A Libel. Privilege is either absolute or conditional. Privilege as a defense is permitted on the ground of public policy. If a publication is absolutely privileged, there can be no remedy in a civil action, but the class of articles which are absolutely privileged is indeed a narrow one. On the other hand, conditional or qualified privilege extends to a rather large class of articles.

A publication that is privileged is one which ordinarily might be libelous but which entails the fulfillment of some social, judicial, or political duty. In this instance, actual malice is an element that must be proved in order that the offended party, the plaintiff, may recover.

Ordinarily, the court determines the question of conditional privilege as a matter of law when there is no dispute on the facts; when there is disagreement on the facts the jury decides. In numerous states, the constitutions specify that in libel the jury decides both the law and the fact, though instructions on the law are given by the court.

ABSOLUTE PRIVILEGE. Absolute privilege as one basis for defense arises in part from the Constitution of the United States. Article I, Section VI reads:

> The Senators and Representatives . . . shall, in all cases except treason, felony, and breach of the peace, be privileged from arrest during their attendance at the session of their respective houses; and *for any speech or debate in either house they shall not be questioned in any other place.*

The application here applies to the senators and representatives themselves. There is no reference or application directly to publications, such as newspapers or magazines. For the same reasons, however, there is considerable latitude permitted in reporting official proceedings of Congress and legislative bodies, as well as judicial proceedings.

QUALIFIED PRIVILEGE. The theory of qualified privilege gives the newspaper certain immunity, or freedom from liability, when it publishes the proceedings of a legislative body, even though a libel may be contained therein.

Even so, the doctrine of qualified privilege does not extend complete

---

[1] In writing, the details of the entire story may not be complete. In this case the reporter should report as true only that news he is able to verify.

[2] What the writer meant is not so important as the meaning the word conveyed to those of the community.

freedom in reporting that which takes place in the courtroom. The judge controls his courtroom and may exclude representatives of the press. Yet, in practice, judges permit reporters to attend sessions.[1]

Fair Comment Is Also A Defense. Publications are free to make fair comment on all matters of public concern. The facts on which the comment is based must be essentially true and the comment fair and without malice if the defense of fair comment is to succeed.

Fair comment extends to criticism of the government, quasi-public enterprises, books, magazine articles, plays, motion pictures—in fact, any field in which the public may have an interest.

There is a distinction between qualified privilege and fair comment. In the case of privilege, the person or publication coming within the confines of this qualified privilege possesses a right which others do not enjoy. In the case of fair comment, any person or publication possesses the right of fair comment, so long as the facts on which the comment is based are true. Whether a comment is within the range of public interest is for the judge in a civil libel case to decide; whether the comment is reasonable as based on the facts is a question for the jury; in criminal libel cases particularly, some state constitutions provide that the jury shall be the judge of both the law and facts, though in practice the judge guides technical legal questions through his instructions.

Mitigation Of Damages Is A Defense. A fourth defense is mitigation of damages. This is based upon the theory that there was no malice, or, perhaps, that the acts of the plaintiff merited the statement made. Retraction offered usually lessens the amount of damages—that is, in mitigation of damages. Many papers maintain a "We beg your pardon" section which the editors use to retract statements discovered in error. This retraction does not eliminate the libel, but it tends to prove lack of intent to injure or malice.

PRIVACY IS AN IMPORTANT PHASE OF THE LAW OF THE PRESS

A most important phase of the law of the press is the law of privacy. Privacy may be defined as the inherent right to regulate one's personal affairs.

Private Citizens Are Protected. A tabloid newspaper might publish a candid photograph of a chorus girl taking a sun bath on the roof of a private dwelling. The photographer might violate privacy if he trespassed upon private premises in order to take such a picture as to intrude upon her right to personality;[2] under such conditions there could be liability for damages for the picture's publication.

---

[1] The right to exclude reporters, or any one else for that matter, is well established in law.

[2] Still, in a leading case in the law of privacy the court denied a young woman an

Public Characters Have Less Protection. In case of a public character who has offered his personality to the public, as in the example of an actor or radio singer, more liberality is permitted in discussing the private affairs of that person.

Violation Of Privacy May Involve Suit. In case of a violation of a right of privacy, the publication may be sued at law for damages, and in equity to restrain further publication.

COPYRIGHT IS A VITAL PHASE OF PRESS LAW

Copyright is definitely a part of law of the press. Copyright does not protect the idea or in the case of a newspaper story the news element itself, but rather the literary form of the article, or the identical manner and sequence of statement.

The Constitution Provides for Copyright.[1] The right of copyright is protected by the United States Constitution, Article I, Section VIII, Paragraph 8, as follows:

> "To promote the progress of science and useful arts by securing for limited times to authors and inventors the exclusive right to their respective writings and discoveries."

Copyright May Be Secured Easily. An author or a publisher may secure a copyright by filing an application with the Register of Copyrights, Library of Congress, Washington, D.C., by paying the required fee,[2] by

---

injunction when a company used her photograph without her consent; however, shortly thereafter the legislature of the State of New York passed a statute giving legal protection for certain defined violations of this right, and, to this extent, the right of privacy was upheld.

[1] Under the common law, if an author makes public his work he loses the right to his work or the exclusive benefits thereof, but the constitutional provision gives the legal basis for protection.

[2] Copyright Fees.—The Act of Congress, approved April 27, 1948, amending Title 17 of the United States Code entitled "Copyrights," provides that the following copyright fees shall be payable on and after *May 27, 1948:*

For registration of a claim to copyright in any published or unpublished work (except a print or label used for article of manufacture), including certificate $4.00

For registration of a claim to copyright in a print or label used for article of manufacture, including certificate 6.00

For recording the renewal of copyright, including certificate 2.00

For every additional certificate of registration 1.00

For certifying a copy of an application for registration of copyright, and for all other certifications 2.00

For recording every assignment, agreement, power of attorney, or other paper not exceeding six pages 3.00

(For each additional page or less, 50 cents; for each title over one in the paper recorded, 50 cents additional) [*cont. on p. 340*]

depositing required copies (usually two) of the work desired to be protected, and by carrying on the published article notice of copyright. The copyright protection under the law as in force in 1950 gives protection for a period of twenty-eight years and the right for a renewal of copyright for another period of twenty-eight years.[1]

Trade-Mark Gives Additional Protection. A particular cartoon or column may be copyrighted, that is any day's issue, but the standing title of a cartoon or a column may be given additional protection by having a trade-mark registered. Trade-marks are not mentioned in the United States Constitution, but nevertheless are given statutory protection. Trade-marks are registered in the United States Patent Office.

Use Of Copyrighted Material Subjects One To Damage Suit. Unfair use of a syndicated series, for example, if copyrighted and trade-marked, gives rise to a cause of action for infringement of the copyright and for damages for violation of the trade-mark, as well as an equity action for an injunction to prevent further infringement.

A NEWSPAPER IS NOT A PUBLIC UTILITY

The newspaper, although often termed a "quasi-public" institution, is not regarded in the eyes of the law as a public utility. It is the legal concept that a newspaper publishing business is a private business and as such need not accept advertising or advertising contracts. In one case it was held that if a newspaper were legally compelled to accept advertising for its columns it might also be held liable for its refusal to print a news item; the newspaper was upheld in refusing to accept the advertising.

POST-OFFICE REGULATIONS MUST BE OBSERVED

To take advantage of second-class mailing privileges, a newspaper or magazine must conform to strict regulations set up by the United States Post Office Department.

The publication must be issued from a known office of publication regularly to a legitimate subscription list and must be published for the dissemination of information of a public character, or devoted to the arts, science, or literature, or to some special industry. Matter which tends to incite arson, murder, or assassination is nonmailable, as are also obscene literature or pictures and information on lotteries. For complete information check with the local postmaster or *Postal Laws and Regulations*.

For recording each notice of use containing not more than five titles $2.00
  (For each additional title, 50 cents)
For each hour of time consumed in searching Copyright Office records,
  indexes, or deposits, or services rendered in connection therewith........ 3.00
Remittances are made payable to the REGISTER OF COPYRIGHTS.

[1] A newspaper contribution may be protected as a part of a copyrighted periodical or by special registration as a contribution.

Chapter XL

MAKING JOURNALISM PAY DIVIDENDS

> Publishing a newspaper is a business, similar in many ways to any other type of commercial enterprise. Business is not a benevolence, although motives of generosity and service may enter into a business institution, particularly a publishing business. From this viewpoint, journalism is not play; it is hard work and requires knowledge, vision, and energy to sustain its place in organized society.
> —Grant Milnor Hyde.*

PUBLISHING IS A BUSINESS AS WELL AS A SERVICE

Publishers must see that journalism remains wholesome and that publications maintain their financial independence by serving well their readers and by being solvent through careful management in manufacturing a product to be sold on its merits without servitude or subsidy.

Publication Production Is Costly. As with all other types of publications, the newspaper as an economic good or commodity costs money to produce and distribute. The funds for such manufacture and sale must necessarily come from some source. These funds should come through intelligent publication management, which means fulfilling an existing need or a created want, by making available a good product at a reasonable price, while providing the producers—the publisher and his stockholders—with a fair profit.[1]

To justify their existence newspapers—and almost all other forms of journalism—must be able to pay their way. Of course, a newspaper might pay in dividends of satisfaction, personally or politically, but in the last analysis the publication that does not have an income sufficient to meet its financial obligations and pay some margin of profit will find itself in a wholly unsatisfactory position.

Publications Are No Stronger Than Their Financial Resources. In order to justify its existence a newspaper or magazine must serve. It must do so by its own merits as a publication, by the attraction and retention of readers, by the sale of its advertising space at a profit, by able man-

---

* From an address by Grant Milnor Hyde, professor of Journalism, University of Wisconsin.

[1] In certain instances, losses from unwise publication management or from the founding of poor or unneeded newspapers, or journals, have been paid for by those seeking and receiving political support. Such papers can neither serve well their readers nor be self-respecting institutions.

agement in its original financing, and by capable control of operating expense; in addition, it should have enough funds to meet emergencies, allow for depreciation, and build up a safe reserve fund and surplus. Certainly, a newspaper subsidized by a public utility, even though such utility has millions in resources, is not a satisfactory or strong newspaper. Such a publication is rather a journalistic prostitute.

A Field Must Exist For The Newspaper Or Periodical. Consideration of the economic factors in publication management is essential. To be successful, a newspaper or a magazine must have a field. A town of approximately 5000 population in the middle west which is some considerable distance from a metropolitan area and the center of a fairly prosperous agricultural territory is likely to be a sufficient field for a daily newspaper. It would be better, of course, if the town were the county seat and the trade center of the area in which it is located.[1]

Similarly, a magazine must perform some service. The publication of a magazine for fruit growers might be highly desirable. Such a periodical could serve certain well-defined sections of the country, for example, the citrus fruit districts of California, Florida, and Texas; the apple districts of Oregon, Washington, and certain eastern states; the berry districts of the south; and other fruit-growing areas.

Wherever there are group interests, there are possibilities for such publications,[2] perhaps on the basis of paid circulation, a controlled or free circulation, or, possibly, on the basis of membership in an association such as a lodge, a fraternity, or a trade group.

PUBLISHING NECESSITATES PROPER FINANCING

The financing of a publication is of prime importance. As in other fields of business, the financial problem is twofold: the primary plan concerns the financial structure; the secondary plan concerns the operative functions.

Business Organization May Be Used In Financing. Although practically all of the larger and most of the smaller publications are financed by means of a publishing corporation, there is no fundamental reason for this fact other than the numerous advantages which are associated with this type of business organization. The individual-proprietorship or the partnership organization may be used. Each has certain definite advantages as well as disadvantages.[3]

---

[1] Such a town is Maryville, Missouri, where the *Maryville Daily Forum* has proved a successful daily publication.

[2] See Chapter I, *The Press as an Institution*, for a general classification and Chapter XXXVII, *Publishing the Business Press*, for a description of this field.

[3] INDIVIDUAL PROPRIETORSHIP: *Advantages*—(1) simple organization, (2) few legal restrictions, (3) sole management and control. *Disadvantages*—(1) limited to lifetime of owner, (2) limited to owner's capital, (3) credit of business is credit of owner, (4) business risks high with owner in case of failure. PARTNERSHIP:

Because the publishing corporation [1] is the common form of organization today, it will be discussed in more detail. In general, the problems of publication are the same regardless of the nature or type of business organization.

A Corporation May Be Financed By Stocks Or Bonds. A corporation engaged in the publishing business may be financed by means of stocks or bonds.[2]

COMMON OR PREFERRED STOCK. The common stock is generally regarded as the ownership stock on which dividends may or may not be paid depending upon the earnings of the business. The preferred stock has some of the qualities of common stock and some of the qualities of bonds. Although preferred stockholders may have voting power with the common stockholders, some preferred stock is issued without voting rights, unless certain contingencies arise; but the preferred stock has a fixed rate of return, an advantage over the common stock.

BONDS. Bonds are of various types. A publishing corporation would likely issue a first mortgage on its property against which notes or bonds would be issued. By specifying that the notes would be due on or before a series of expiration dates, the company could lessen its outstanding indebtedness as the returns of the business warrant. Major publishing corporations may issue debenture bonds, or promises to pay, for the safety of which certain collateral may be deposited with the trustees of the bonds.

DANGER OF OVERFINANCING. Some newspaper properties have been overfinanced, and, of course, when a higher price is paid for the property than the returns of the business justify, the additional financial burden must be assumed and eventually made to pay out. Needless to say, this should be avoided, and may be when the appraisal and advice of one experienced in newspaper values are obtained. Obviously, such things as earnings for the five years prior to the purchase of the newspaper property should be ascertained. Likewise, a circulation analysis will determine both the quantity and the quality of the circulation. This type of information is essential in the evaluation of a publication.

Full Attention Should Be Given To Equipment. A prospective publisher, before purchasing a newspaper plant, and an active publisher, at

---

Advantages—(1) combination of abilities of two or more partners, (2) combination of financial resources, (3) better credit obtainable. *Disadvantages*—(1) Each partner liable for all debts, (2) the profits are divided and losses borne by each in accord with articles of copartnership, (4) death or insanity of any partner causes dissolution.

[1] A corporation has been defined as "an association of individuals united for some common purpose and permitted by law to use a common name, and to change its members without dissolution of the association." See any good text on business organization for further explanation.

[2] For temporary financial needs, a line of credit may be obtained through regular commercial bank sources, although, of course, this is not capital financing.

least every few years, should have someone versed in the mechanics of printing machinery inspect the printing plant. This inspection, of course, should include typesetting machines and presses in order to determine not only the value of the machines on the market, but also their efficiency as operating units.

Some publishers in their enthusiasm buy too much or too expensive equipment. Of course, if time or labor can be saved by the use of an improved machine, a publisher can frequently justify the purchase of one more highly improved. Much depends upon the need for the improved service because of competition, waste of time and labor, as well as loss of productive time in operation of the machine due to making repairs and adjustments. When there is any doubt the prospective publisher and the active journalist-publisher should seek advice on the condition of machinery.

Editorial Acceptability Should Be Investigated. Before the purchase of a newspaper, for example, one should ascertain its general standing in the community, its editorial acceptability, and in addition, one should determine the socio-cultural and economic status of the population.

A NEWSPAPER IS A COMMODITY

The newspaper, or other journalistic enterprise, should be regarded from the standpoint of publishing administration as a commodity similar to any other manufactured product.[1] As such, it should be produced at as reasonable a cost as possible commensurate with the quality of the commodity, the service to be given, and the price range which must be met.

Complete News Coverage Expensive. If a newspaper plans to furnish complete news service, costs will be heavy. Especially is this true in the case of metropolitan dailies, using several wire-association news or feature services and maintaining a number of special offices.[2]

On the other hand, a nonmetropolitan daily in a community of 8000 population may have considerable expense with fifty or sixty country correspondents. Although it is expensive to maintain such a staff, even on a space-payment basis, the judgment and experience of enterprising and successful publishers would indicate that it is an unwise policy to neglect such news.

Illustrations And Cartoons Are Costly But Desirable. A paper may coast along without entailing the expense of illustrations, cartoons, and comics, but this is a short-sighted policy. The real value of these as circu-

---

[1] For a discussion of the newspaper as a product, see *Newspaper Management* by Frank Thayer. Copyright 1938. Appleton-Century, N.Y.

[2] For example, a newspaper in Portland, Oregon, may have a special Washington, D.C., correspondent of its own, or it may co-operate with several other dailies in obtaining special Washington news, and in addition subscribe to several special column and feature services. See Chapter XXIV, *News from Near and Far.*

lation builders alone justifies a reasonable allowance to permit their inclusion.

JOURNALISM MUST PAY ON BASIS OF FUNCTIONS

The publisher must bear in mind the specific functions which the newspaper or magazine is to perform and must supervise the departmentalizing and manufacture of the product to meet the necessary specifications.

Publications Perform Basic Functions. For example, the newspaper performs four functions: (1) giving news, (2) commenting and interpreting, (3) entertaining, and (4) merchandising and advertising.[1] The functions should be so controlled that the newspaper meets the needs of a particular community. Similarly, the magazine or trade journal must meet the needs of a reader-class.

In some communities a tabloid newspaper may be a product that will find a ready market. In New York the *Daily News* became a most successful project, despite the fact that New York had such meritorious newspapers as the *New York Times*, the *New York Sun*, the *Wall Street Journal*, the *New York World-Telegram*, and the *New York Herald Tribune*. The publishers of the *New York Daily News* have found a particular newspaper product that meets a public demand. Naturally it has succeeded.

Needless Competition May Well Be Eliminated. In small nonmetropolitan communities the competition between two rival weekly newspapers may be very keen. Perhaps both papers are performing a valuable editorial service to their community, but at excessive cost. To make both papers pay more adequately there are those who advocate that both papers should be published *in the same plant,* as is frequently the case in magazine journalism, despite the fact that the papers are rivals politically. This is reasonable from the standpoint of efficient business administration.

A situation might be found, in numerous small towns and cities, in which a Democratic paper is published in one plant, and a Republican paper in another plant. Where the newspaper press in each plant is used only a few hours a week there is duplication of equipment, fuel, lighting costs, rent charges, and other expense items. These papers might well merge their plants and still maintain their separate political affiliations.[2]

---

[1] The publisher must continually watch his newspaper, magazine, or journal to make certain that his publication is carrying out its functions to the satisfaction of both readers and advertisers.

[2] Those favoring this plan present the argument that attorneys who vigorously oppose each other in the court room may be good friends personally and may be found playing golf together. Their legal interpretations are diametrically opposed, but this fact does not mean that they should be enemies. Thus, it may be argued that it is just as sensible for two publishers, especially in the smaller communities, to merge their noncompetitive interests and so prevent a waste of funds.

Where this plan is followed papers sometimes sell their advertising as a unit and perhaps their subscriptions.[1] In this way, it is argued, two independently operated papers profit by merging their noncompetitive units and are able to give the community a better product, insure sounder income, and yet maintain individual editorial personalities.

WASTE MOTION SHOULD BE AVOIDED

The physical product, the publication—newspaper, magazine, or trade journal—must be produced at some margin of profit. This requirement means that there must be an economy of motion in production.

Producing Too Good A Product Is A Danger. Too good a product might be produced for the community. In other words, a publisher may try to make his paper too much like a metropolitan news organ and, in so doing, may neglect the opportunity he has to stress local news. Those qualified to judge think that the publisher should do the job at hand and not try to compete with the nearest metropolitan newspaper.

The Publisher May Take Too Many Wire Features. When a publisher takes too many wire services, he gets more material than he can use, and the expense is apt to be more than he can afford to bear. Of course, the additional material has some value, but this extra extravagance gives the publisher a product that is too costly. If he can afford to carry the added financial burden, it is probably a good policy.

Equipment Should Be Well Placed. Equipment should be placed in order to facilitate the transition of copy to type placed in the forms, or, in the case of a larger paper, into stereotyped plates placed in the press ready for production. Efficiency engineers have found that generally the movement of a raw product through a plant to the finished stage should be in a straight line. Obviously, this plan is an ideal one. In other words, the movement would be in straight-line effect from function to function.[2] To ascertain if there is a loss of movement, a publisher must study his line of production. When in doubt, he should obtain the advice of a consultant in the printing equipment field.

A similar study should be made of productive and nonproductive time.

---

[1] Where it is desired to make each publication cover the news for the entire week, both advertising and subscriptions may be sold independently. However, it is probably better to sell advertising as a unit, covering like space in both papers, and to plan news coverage for the period of three and one-half days preceding the time of publication of each paper. For protection of subscribers who take only one of the papers, a short news summary should be used covering the news treated more extensively in the other paper.

[2] If the movement of copy to the typesetting machines, the transfer of types to the tables, and the proof to and from the proofreader, passage of corrected type to make-up tables, and hence to the press, on through the intermediate step of stereotyping in the larger offices, is direct and within as short a space as possible without overcrowding of workmen, materials, or equipment, the movement might well be considered as fulfilling the straight-line requirement.

The amount of nonproductive time of compositors and pressmen should be reduced to a minimum. Of course, some nonproductive time is necessary, but it constitutes a charge against operations and reduces the profits of the business.

SALES ARE AN INDEX OF SUCCESS

Salesmanship bespeaks success. The best possible product if unsold indicates a business failure. Likewise, the publication that is unable to sell its products, subscriptions, and advertising space, is running on the shoals of insolvency or bankruptcy unless the publication is subsidized by interests that make up the deficit.[1]

The Publisher Must Determine Advertising And Circulation Policy. After a careful analysis of the field in general and of his product in particular, the publisher must determine and initiate policies that will result in the sale of both subscriptions and advertising space.[2] He must see that these policies are followed. The matter of circulation is a good illustration. Its problems embrace defining the class of readers to whom the publication addresses its appeal, determining a means of reaching that class so that the members thereof know something of the publication, its merits and service, and giving a solicitation that clinches the sale.[3]

Subscription To A Publication Implies Interest. When a person pays for a publication he does so because he values the newspaper or periodical and wants to receive it regularly. At least, this is the justified assumption.

The alert circulation manager divides his time between the efficient operation of his department and the promotion of new subscriptions. There is a continuous flux of circulation. It is for the publisher to check circulation results and to stimulate greater efficiency here as in all other phases of production.

Reader-Interest Surveys May Be Used. Leading newspapers make reader-interest surveys to check whether the material in the editorial and news columns of a newspaper is interesting to a considerable number of subscribers. Checkers visit subscribers, who are asked if they have read the previous day's issue. If the reply is in the affirmative, the practice is

---

[1] Exceptions exist in the case of the free circulation periodical distributed without charge which sells only advertising space, and the house organ distributed to customers or salesmen, or members. However, even in the latter cases, there would be need for salesmanship in that no publication can exist without editorial acceptability and usefulness.

[2] Here we are concerned primarily with these functions of circulation and advertising from the standpoint of the publisher's chair. They are dealt with from other points of view in other chapters of this volume.

[3] The sale cannot be made at too great an expense as it is a United States Post Office rule that a publication accorded second-class mailing privileges must receive not less than 50 per cent of its subscription price, if sold directly by the publisher, or 30 per cent if sold through an agent.

to go over each page and each column, as well as each display advertisement, and ask, "Did you happen to read this?" In this manner a check may be made of the appeal of each class of material. If, for instance, one hundred readers are checked, the number replying that they have read a particular story tends to indicate the percentage of readability. It should be remembered that for larger newspapers the sampling checked ought to be much greater than one hundred in order to give a relatively true picture. Thus it may be determined how well the editors of the newspaper are selecting and editing material for their readers. The question is one of editorial salesmanship.

Market Surveys May Also Be Used. Another method of improving the sales value of the newspaper is the market survey to determine the extent of usage of commodities in the community. By checking approximately from 5 to 8 per cent of the subscribers on their preferences for commodities used, many of which are advertised in the particular newspaper, and through comparisons in light of the number of products advertised, it is possible to determine to some degree the effectiveness of the advertising. It should be realized, however, that advertising alone is not responsible for the large usage of a product in the community. The product must be a good product, it must be well distributed and so available in stores and markets, and merchandising plans must be sufficient to back up consistent linage of advertising space. Through such surveys it is possible for advertising managers and publishers to know more accurately the effectiveness of their efforts.

ACCOUNTING CHECKS ARE ESSENTIAL

The publisher who is not aware of his financial standing is to that extent a poor administrator. It is as necessary to have a periodic financial statement as it is in the banking business to balance the books at the close of each day.

A Good Accounting System Is A Necessity. A good accounting system permits the publisher to know how his business stands at the end of any given period, to prevent unnecessary losses, and to improve departments that are not showing favorable results.

Of course, there are numerous forms of accounting systems and accounting variations from the simplified cost system used by the small weekly paper to the more complex system used by the metropolitan daily, in which its operations are classified into several hundred cost items.

A Detailed Report Should Follow Each Issue. After each week's issue or, in the case of the daily after each day's issue, there should be a report, showing date of publication, number of pages, inches or lines of national advertising, local advertising, classified advertising, legal advertising, and advertising devoted to the promotion of the newspaper itself. In addition, the cash balance of the business should be shown, the total paid circulation stated, and the press run indicated.

Monthly Or Quarterly Reports Are Helpful. Once each month, or at least each quarter, there should be a statement giving advertising volume and net-paid circulation. This statement should be compared with the statement of the preceding period. If, for example, the classified department shows considerably less volume for the last comparative period, the publisher will understand that that department is probably slipping. If so, he should devote some of his time to discovering the cause and to attempting to make up the deficiency.

CHAPTER XLI

ADVERTISING COPY INFORMS, APPEALS, IMPELS

Good copy doesn't *sell*, in the "hard boiled" sense of this word. Its function is to *dispose a person to own*. The only way it can do this is to convince the reader that the act of purchase will help him or her to *live better*—more conveniently, economically, healthfully, comfortably, admirably, hopefully. And to do this, it must breathe the spirit of helpfulness from its first word—if it is to do the best possible job for its sponsor.—MARK HUNTINGTON WISEMAN.*

ADVERTISING IS A TECHNIQUE OF SELLING

Modern society being what it is, the "best mousetrap" would likely rust away unused were it not for a practical means of bringing various producers' goods to the attention of potential consumers. This is generally called selling and its written and pictorial form when published by any one of several kinds of media is called advertising.

Analysis Is Necessary. Simply stated, advertising's purpose is to encourage people to buy goods. Modern advertising recognizes the need for organized planning, which means analysis of prospective markets and of the media most likely to reach customers. Such advertising may be designed: (1) to *create a need* or a desire, (2) to *show advantage* of a given product or service over all other similar products or services, (3) to *retain acceptability* of a given product or service. Most advertising is written to accomplish one or the other of the first two objectives. In any event, advertising copy may not be written until policy and planning have gone before. This requires visualizing the appeal. It also necessitates market analysis. Both require a high degree of professional skill buttressed by imagination on the one hand and intelligent research on the other.

Visualization Creates Ideas Which Produce Advertising. Every advertisement begins with some embryonic idea. The conceptualization of thought which creates the idea makes the end advertisement possible. However, visualizing an idea is not enough. It needs to be crystallized into physical form—written or pictorial or, more generally, both. The end purpose is not "genius at work" but copy and layout which encourage, for example, consumers to want specific kinds of consumer goods.

---

* From *Advertisements: How to Plan Them, Make Them, and Make Them Work,* by Mark Huntington Wiseman, advertising consultant and director of Mark Huntington Wiseman's Advertising Courses, New York, published by Robbins Publishing Co. Used by express permission of the author.

Visualization is sometimes mistakenly confused with layout but, in reality, although somewhat allied to it, the creation of the idea for an advertisement goes before either copy or layout.[1]

Among the more important methods followed to develop ideas for the creation of an advertisement are:

1. Analyzing the product—
   What is the nature of the article?
   What uses has it?
   Why should it be wanted?
   Why is it attractive?
2. Interpreting the market—
   What is the class of potential buyers?
   Where do the buyers live?
   What need exists or may be created?
   How will the buyers react?
3. Defining the objectives—
   What is the primary aim?
   What are subordinate purposes?
   How may they be achieved?
4. Determining the media—
   What media have been, or may be, used?
   Why are certain media most suitable?
5. Determining layout and copy—
   What space is available?
   What should be the relationship of layout to copy?
   What illustrations, ornamentations, and type masses should be used?
   How can the central idea be made easy to grasp?
   How may dramatization be used?
   How may comparison or contrast be used?
   What kinds of typography may be used?

Research Provides Facts Upon Which To Act. Market research is little different from any other fact-gathering, analyzing, and reporting procedure. In advertising, its mission is to determine the answer to the question, "Will money spent on advertising in this way be likely to be profitable?" Like all investigative procedures, advertising research is based in general upon following certain well-recognized steps. This sequence may be stated simply as:

---

[1] Some professional advertising men become so adept that they visualize layout almost simultaneously with the idea for an advertisement. Layout, as such, is discussed in the following chapter.

1. Establishing the purpose and problem areas to be surveyed.
2. Gathering and sifting available data.
3. Tabulating and organizing facts obtained.
4. Review and evaluation of all data.
5. Analysis and appraisal in relation to purpose and problem areas.
6. Conclusions and recommendation of necessary action.

Doing the research job is not so simple. It requires a high degree of professional skill and the employment of many techniques which run the whole gamut of methods developed by researchers.

ADVERTISING IS ONE KIND OF JOURNALISM IN ACTION

Although individual advertisements vary as to their immediate purpose, the ultimate function of all advertising is to sell commodities, services, or beliefs, and while performing these tasks it provides at the same time a revenue for the newspaper, magazine, or other medium in which it appears.

Retail Advertising Furnishes News.   In local newspapers the primary purpose of advertising is to announce such immediate events as sales, receipts of new goods, additions of lines of merchandise, changes in store policy, installation of other departments, and similar news. The advertisements are aimed to make a direct contact between buyer and seller, preferably at the point of sale. Timeliness is an important factor. Retail advertising is highly competitive and succeeds when the buyer is convinced that it is to his interests to buy at one store rather than at the others, whether that conviction has been secured by appeals to economy, sense of good merchandise, or other motivating impulses. As retail advertising gives information as to products which are in immediate need, it stands on its own merits as news. But while performing that function it also brings in much of the revenue and profits of the newspaper or other publication in which it appears.

National Advertising May Also Be News.   When new products are placed on the market or when there are price reductions or increases, changes in models, or similar developments in commodities which have a nation-wide sale, announcements of them have such wide appeal that they are newsworthy. But such news is furnished to the public in the form of national advertising which is paid for by the manufacturer or distributor. Usually national advertising which has an immediacy of purpose faces severe competition with similar advertising of other firms, and, hence, must carry a strong appeal that impels the consumer to buy.

Some Advertisements Have Little Or No News Values.   When manufacturers bring out a new product in a large family of commodities or find a new use for an old product, they may base their advertising plan on such changes which in themselves are news but which are not sufficiently important to carry the whole advertising theme. These developments are used, however, by the manufacturer just as he would use the seasons, the weather, holidays,[1] and other factors as links with his advertising program. Such advertisements serve the dual function of keeping the name of the merchant or manufacturer before the public and at the same time promoting his entire line of products while dealing specifically with only one.

Frequently the theme of national advertising is based on some reason why, or emotional appeal, which has no tie-up with changes in manufacturing or distribution policy. In such cases the advertising may seek to perform such definite purposes as to increase the number of units of purchase or to show additional uses of a product which is already in the good favor of the public. The aim of such national advertising is to increase sales by presenting further argument for the use of the product although there has been no change in the commodities, the price, or distribution.

Advertisements May Seek To Combat Wrong Impressions. When the public has been given the wrong impression of a company or a product, the advertising may have as its sole purpose the correction of this bad impression. Instead of trying to sell goods or services the advertisements put the cause of the attacked company before the public in paid space. A manufacturer may so state his cause in the case of a strike, or a department store or other local outlet may strive to win back public favor when there is dissension between employees and employers. Or when one advertiser by innuendo or statement has attacked another advertiser, either of his own line of products or of another line, the one who has been so reflected upon may reply with a countercharge or defense, having as his purpose not the selling of goods but the correction of a wrong impression.

Advertisements May Sell Services Rather Than Commodities. Associations and professions whose members do not advertise individually appeal to the public in copy which advocates the use of their services, such as dentistry and medicine. In such cases the advertisements explain the value of professional service and the danger of nonprofessional or nonethical aid. Educational and charitable institutions may also sell the idea of the service they render to the public. In this case service is their commodity and the function of the advertising is to secure a wide acceptance of the service. In some cases the advertisements are co-operative, such as by professional associations; or, they may be individually sponsored by educational or charitable institutions. In a similar way, beliefs may be advertised in the hope of gaining public support.

---

[1] The significance of this can be better appreciated by reference to Chapter XIV, *The Calendar as News.*

The
Daily
Telegraph

(LONDON, ENGLAND)

tells the truth about the World to the British—and the truth about the British to the World.

That is why it has the largest circulation of any *quality* newspaper printed in the British Isles.

In a class by itself

Publishers recognize the value of advertising by doing so themselves in their own trade publications. The above is an excellent example of copy appeal. This advertisement appeared in the 1949 Yearbook of *Editor and Publisher*. Used by permission of the *Daily Telegraph*.

Advertisements May Sponsor An Industry. In order to increase the use of a major article of industry in competition with other articles which have gained recent public favor, the trade or industry as a whole may proclaim the superior advantages of its product, as, for instance, copper, in the newspapers and the general and technical press. Sometimes it is expected that the public would buy the articles directly, while in other cases the demand comes indirectly from the consumer to the manufacturer through the dealer.

Some Advertisements Are Noncompetitive. Where a firm has established an excellent reputation, or where it has no serious competition, it may advertise simply to keep its name before the public in order to hold the prestige and trade it has already won. In such advertisements the name of the institution, firm, or product is the central theme, and copy is reduced to a minimum.

GOOD ADVERTISEMENTS CONVINCE THE READER

Regardless of the specific purposes and of the number of elements an advertisement contains, it must have certain attributes if it is to attract attention and convince the reader to the point of purchase or acceptance.

They Should Be Simple And Direct. Advertisements written in simple terms and in a clear, direct style are most apt to convince the reader because they use the language he understands. A further advantage lies in the space saved by simple, rather than verbose, copy and a layout which is so unobtrusive that it calls attention to the advertisement instead of to itself. The sentences are concise and contain no unusual words. The type is not ornate, and the implications of the illustrations are easily understood.

They Are Forceful When Occasion Permits. Because advertisements compete with one another and also with reading matter, the most forceful ones attract the reader's attention. But force which is overdone offends by its very boldness or displeases because of the lack of subtlety. Competition for bold effects has resulted in regulations restricting the means and methods of attracting the reader's attention. Such restrictions apply mainly to the mechanical elements such as typography and illustrations rather than to the central theme as carried out by the copy.

They Must Be Truthful. Copy which makes exaggerated claims, or illustrations which mislead, destroy the confidence the reader has in particular advertisements and in advertising as a whole. Various organizations are co-operating with the reliable advertisers in securing truth in advertising so that advertisements can convince the readers after having attracted their attention. Some firms such as department stores have established rigid codes of ethics in which are listed words and phrases that are barred. Claims for the merchandise of such establishments are understated rather than exaggerated.

The Copy Must Impel The Reader To Act. After the copy and the other elements of the layout have attracted the attention of the reader, held his interest, and secured his conviction, they have the further duty of obtaining action. While all elements contribute to such a result, copy has the best opportunity to so stimulate the reader that he will purchase the goods or services.

Advertising Copy Must Harmonize With The Other Elements. While one of the functions of a layout is to attract attention, the headline and copy, when the two are considered separately, must hold that attention while keeping to the general tone and atmosphere of the entire advertisement. The language and appearance of the descriptive matter in the copy must be in spirit with those sections of the advertisement which first attracted the reader, as otherwise he would feel misled by an attractive promise. The elements, then, must not only harmonize with each other but must also be consistent with the merchandise or event which is seeking public favor.

MANY FACTORS DETERMINE THE APPEAL USED IN THE COPY

The appeals which would best bring together producers and consumers depend upon some minor factors and four major considerations; namely, the nature of the article, the class of potential buyers, the media to be used, and competing advertisements.

The Use Of The Article Determines The Appeal. If the article to be sold is a substantial one of commerce or industry, such as automobile trucks, the appeal used in the copy and the rest of the advertisement is not based on emotion but tends to take its theme from the article itself. The copy may discuss the design of the article, its use, appearance, or durability. If, however, the product to be advertised is one suitable for gifts, such as toys, neckwear, and books, the appeal may be emotional rather than argumentative. The pleasure of giving the article, or the pleasure the recipients would have in its use, could be stressed instead of its practical uses.

The Potential Buyers Influence The Appeal Used. Advertising copy is written for the buyer of the article rather than for the user, for the latter may influence the purchase only indirectly. Children's goods, for instance, are advertised to mothers. On the other hand, men's shoes are purchased by men and so the advertisements are written for them. Appeals are directed to potential buyers, with such other considerations in mind as social class, the purchasing power, age, sex, and race. This involves an understanding of the value of quality and quantity circulation. The former indicates a selected group of potential buyers to whom specific appeals may be made and who are the best possible prospects for any particular commodity. Quantity circulation, on the other hand, describes a reading clientele measured by numbers rather than by purchasing power or their need of the commodities.

The Appeal Varies With The Medium Used.   Advertising copy keeps in tune with the newspaper or magazine in which it appears, as publications differ according to the classes who read them. An advertisement for golf balls written for an architects' magazine could include technical terms of that profession and could be "slanted" in a more professional and formal tone than an advertisement for the same commodity appearing in a low-priced and popular magazine. Likewise newspaper advertisements run in such a paper as the *Christian Science Monitor* would have copy written for a more intellectual class of readers than would advertisements of the same products appearing in sensational newspapers. The character of the advertising is in harmony with that of the newspaper or magazine which carries it.

Competing Advertisements Somewhat Affect The Appeal Used.   The copywriter takes into consideration the position his advertisement is to receive and whether it is to be next to reading matter or competitive advertisements. His layout and copy are affected by discordant surrounding matter, and he must make his own advertising more forceful and eye-attracting if it competes with vital material on either side. He hopes, of course, for sympathetic surroundings of text and advertisements. Sometimes a quiet advertisement set in the midst of blatant, shrieking advertisements or news matter draws attention by its very decorum.

SOME COPY INFORMS

Much advertising copy in newspapers and magazines persuades the reader to purchase an article because it gives the reasons for such purchase in what is usually known as reason-why or argumentative copy.

The Utility Or The Economy Of The Product May Be Cited.   The performance to be expected from a commodity may be the best reason for its purchase, particularly when the product, such as a vacuum cleaner, a washing machine, or a lawn mower, serves a necessary function. Its design may be a weighty argument, or its size, shape, or durability may be the cogent reason to impel the reader to buy. Where the product is not soon outmoded the copy can urge its durability because of its being staunchly built and long-lasting.

Where mass selling and savings in production have contributed to a low initial price, these may be cited as reasons for purchasing that article rather than those of competing firms. Or more powerful reasons may be found in the fact that it consumes less gas or electricity or needs fewer repairs than do the similar products of rival manufacturers. Such copy is most convincing when it includes reports of tests or statements of users, and it is frequently exhibited in advertising of automobiles and electrical and gas appliances.

New Uses Or Improvements May Make Good Sales Points. Changes in the product which permit it to perform additional functions in the home or work of the individuals, or improvements which extend its life or perfect its performance, are powerful sales arguments. These changes may contribute to greater safety, finer operation, or more efficiency. Or they may have minor value but nevertheless be talking points which can be ethically used as a means of competing with inferior products.

Special And Temporary Inducements Are Offered. In retail advertising where timeliness is important the price may be the best argument for immediate purchase. A large percentage of advertisements of department stores is built around sales which in turn are possible because of special purchases, bankrupt stocks, surplus goods. Because of the rapid turnover needed by these larger stores, there are many legitimate occasions when price can be stressed in the advertising. In the retail trade price is the most convincing argument provided it is stressed only when a reason is given for the lower price.

THE COPY MAY MAKE EMOTIONAL APPEALS

Some copy, particularly that in magazines and national advertising, appeals to the reader's instincts, desires, and habits instead of attempting to influence him by arguments.

Self-Preservation Is One Of The Strongest Universal Desires. Where the product is one that is adaptable to the theme, much copy is based on the old adage that "self-preservation is the first law of nature." Copywriters stress this appeal to a basic universal desire in advertisements dealing with food, drink, and safety. Readers are urged to buy revolvers to protect themselves and their families, thus developing the sense of fear. Smokers are urged to buy cigars "not touched by human hands" in order to avoid contamination.

A Second Great Universal Desire Is To Attract The Opposite Sex. On the basis that women dress to please men and that men choose clothing, cars, and other products that will make a favorable impression on women, copywriters stress style, popularity, and any other suggestions which would be buying reasons for one sex in its wish to attract the other. Closely associated with this major universal desire is copy which stresses the undesirability of being behind the times in style or of wearing clothes which fail to bring out one's best appearance. This universal desire is also used in selling cars, gifts, and any products which tend to satisfy that instinct.

The Urge To Be Great Is Another Basic Universal Desire. Copy urging self-improvement is among the most effective, as it deals with a basic desire. Readers are asked to attend college or night school to study languages or to learn to play musical instruments in order to improve their social position and conditions of employment. Particularly potent is copy which convinces the reader that by self-improvement he may receive the adulation of his friends, his associates, and the crowd.

Parental Love Is Instinctive. Copy that deals with parental love has a convincing sales appeal, as the love of a mother for her children is one of the strongest instincts. Based on this original instinct are advertisements which sell products which insure the safety of the child, increase its chances for health, adorn it for personal satisfaction. For birthdays, Christmas, and other gift days much of the copy is based on the instinct of parental love. Even many of the advertisements for such expensive commodities as real estate and insurance endowments are based on the same appeal of love of parent for child.

The Appeal For Escape Is Also A Powerful One. Escape from the humdrum, the regular routine, forms the most effective appeal in advertisements of travel and recreation. Associated closely with this are the opposing instincts of desire to be one of a crowd and the desire to be different. The appeal to be different from the rest is at times as powerful as is the appeal directed to the gregarious instinct. Sometimes the appeal is that of escaping the crowd. Sometimes for the same occasion the appeal is directed to those readers who will follow the crowd because it is instinctive for them to do so or because it is the accepted thing.

The Acquisitive Instinct Is Fostered. Knowing how natural is the acquisitive instinct, copywriters urge a purchase of books, of land, of real estate, and of less worthy articles of commerce and industry. Bank advertisements picture the value of savings and insurance copy agrees. At the same time the opposite of this instinct, namely generosity, is stressed in other advertising. Here the theme is that it is more blessed to give than to receive. The reader finds his instincts being pulled in opposite directions by the powerful sales appeals of able copywriters.

Combative Tendency Is Elemental. The urge to witness struggles prompts the advertising for races, football games, and other contests of strength, speed, and endurance. Some readers are attracted by such appeals while others are motivated because they see in their heroes of the gridiron or boxing ring the fulfillment of their wishes or the chance to be with the crowd when it is most elemental. The instincts of elation and dejection are here closely associated with the appeal to witness the combat.

COPY DIFFERS AS TO STYLE AND FORM

There are as many different kinds of copy as there are different appeals and grammatical forms, as exemplified by styles of copy which may be termed narrative, dramatic, newsy, question and answer.

The Narrative Style Is Popular. When the product lends itself to such treatment, copy which tells the story as a simple narrative is particularly effective. Often this style is used when an incident or historical fact provides the opportunity for the unfolding of a dramatic tale. Copy is the most important element in such an advertisement, although pictures may help to tell the story.

Another Form Is The "How To Use It." This form has psychological effectiveness in that it assumes that the readers need the article and that they are expecting to buy it. The copy and illustration picture the satisfaction of the user of the article and demonstrate how to use it. The emphasis in the copy is not on the excellence of the commodity but on its use after purchase.

Statistical Copy Is Used.   Where figures are impressive, the copy message may be most effectively told by the use of statistics. This may be scare copy such as advertisements of "four out of five" may get it, reason-why copy such as advertisements of gasoline and automobile mileage, or columns of figures briefly explained by accompanying copy which may put over the message of the advertiser.

Some Copy Gives Question And Answer.   By means of dialogue, sales arguments may be advanced that otherwise would be less forceful. Testimonials, tests, and experiences of users may be told with good effect in question and answer or dialogue style. Such copy is simple and easy to read. It depends partly for its effect upon the prestige or interest of those who are the participants in the dialogue.

Copy May Be Humorous.   Humorous advertising copy is enjoying such a vogue that it is now found in comic strips, where it has adopted a medium as well as a form. The success of such copy depends upon its naturalness and upon how harmonious is this style with the product being advertised.

Miscellaneous Styles Are Numerous.   Practically all grammatical forms and their combinations may be used in an attempt to put the producer's goods into the hands of the consumer. The copy and the layout in which it is used may be impressionistic or symbolic, or they may be based on a simple slogan or on weighty reason-why arguments which convince by their solid substance and sincerity. Whether copy informs or appeals, its ultimate purpose is to sell. To perform that function it uses all possible varieties of forms, structures, and styles.

CLASSIFIED COPY IS UNIQUE

Although classified advertising copy is unique, the basic principles of copywriting apply here as elsewhere. However, writing classified copy is more exacting in some respects than writing display copy, as there can be no vitalizing illustrations, hand-lettered headings, or fancy flights of style to get attention.

The success of a classified advertisement depends very largely upon the application of certain copy fundamentals. No classified copy will contain all characteristics of any list of so-called fundamentals but classified copy is likely to "pull" in direct relationship to the extent to which the following considerations are kept in mind:

1. Evaluate your merchandising appeal—notate reasons why your product or service should appeal to a purchaser in order of their probable "pull."

2. Select your first word with care—the first word in any classified copy should be meaningful. It should describe, explain, or impel toward action.

3. Appraise your offering in clear, terse style—though brevity is of the essence, description should be clear and imaginative. In addition it must be complete so that a prospective purchaser understands the offer and how to accept it. All unnecessary words should be avoided.

4. Use the appropriate classification—the classification under which the merchandise or service is offered should be selected with care on the basis of whether or not the heading will automatically attract the kind of prospects interested in the offer.

5. Select the right media—reader-appeal will largely depend upon whether or not there is reader-interest in the publication selected. Advertising farm machinery in the trade journal *Women's Wear Daily* would be obviously stupid.

6. Consider "keying" the advertisement—it is wise to check advertising results. However, in "keying" avoid using obviously fictitious addresses. Hiding behind a post-office box number, for example, is liable to decrease confidence or even to stop the buying impulse at its source.

7. Make use of more than one classification—oftentimes, merchandising results can be doubled or tripled by using several related classification headings.

8. Time your offerings—wherever there is any seasonal consideration, watch your timing.

9. Use only "enough" words—as buying space by the word or the column line is expensive, count your words carefully.

Chapter XLII

ADVERTISING LAYOUT ATTRACTS, DISPLAYS, VITALIZES

> There is a certain quality in practically all great advertising that affects the eye in much the same way that great music affects the ear. It is a quality of splendid harmony—an essential unity that weaves all the elements of an advertisement into one great chorus of selling truth and conviction. It reverberates through the reader's mind. It strikes responsive chords of desire, belief and action.*

THE LAYOUT SPEAKS IN VARIOUS WAYS

The layout is at once a sketch to be followed by the various artisans who contribute to the advertisement, a means by which the merchant may visualize how the advertisement is expected to sell his wares, and a dynamic structural force which attracts attention while it ties the various elements of the advertisement together.

It Determines The Scope Of The Advertisement. What the plan is to a building, the layout is to an advertisement, for it serves as a guide to those who prepare its various parts. By this diagram the various parts are shown in their relation to each other. The sketch indicates by approximate measurements the size and structure accorded to each of the elements and shows where the emphasis is to be placed and how that emphasis is to be secured. Through such a sketch the advertisement is unified and yet particularized. The copy writer, the artist, and the printer can grasp the idea of the entire advertisement and what is their particular task. The layout shows the location, size, and shape of all the elements and at the same time is the framework holding these elements together.

The Layout Sets The Approach. While the layout provides the drawing plan for the advertisement as a whole and performs the above functions, it also sets forth the central theme. It graphically tells what is the approach of the advertisement so that the specific idea and the appeals used to convey that idea can easily be seen and further developed as each division of the layout is prepared and refined. A glance at the layout pictures at once the central theme and the way that theme is to be carried out.

The Layout Aids The Salesman. This preliminary plan aids the solicitor of advertising because through it the manufacturer or merchant can

---

* Lord and Thomas advertisement in *Advertising and Selling,* April 9, 1936.

visualize how the completed advertisement will appear. Or, by this sketch, the division heads in a department store may preview the plans of the advertising manager for selling their goods through the printed word. At this stage the design may be altered until it is acceptable to the maker of the advertisement and the seller of the goods.

Its Ultimate Purpose Is To Attract. The layout, which in its first stages served as a guide and as a means of visualizing the completed advertisement, realizes final value by attracting the attention of the readers of the newspaper or magazine in which it appears. The way in which the layout unifies the advertisement and displays its various elements through emphasis, contrast, and attracting power determines to a great extent the pulling power the advertisement has.

THE LAYOUT HAS MANY ELEMENTS

There are usually four major elements in the layout and there may be several more, most of which are variable and hence make it possible for the layout to be dynamic and interesting in accordance with the way in which the elements of border, copy, headline, white space, illustration, type, trade-mark, trade name, color, artistic devices, and special messages are arranged.[1]

Copy Is A Major Element. Good copy tells a story in itself about the articles or services that the advertisement is expected to sell. The particular appeal of the copy is determined when the layout is made as are also the various sections of copy. The "blocks" of copy may be widely separated in the layout but their essential functions remain the same, namely, to inform, to appeal, to convince. But the layout designer indicates their position within the advertisement and suggests the tone and approach the copy writer should use.

The Headline Attracts Attention. Not all advertisements use headlines, but the majority of layout designers consider them one of the most effective ways of attracting the attention of busy readers. The headline, because it is brief and descriptive, presents a promise as well as a challenge. It is a foretaste of the copy, and as such must sum up in a few words the major purpose of the entire advertisement. It is also a unifying factor when considered as a mechanical device. Subheads break up the type masses and help direct the reader's attention.

White Space Provides Beauty, Adds Contrast. Space left free of type or any illustrative material becomes an element of great value if used as a means to secure brightness and contrast to surrounding matter. It is invaluable when used to secure emphasis by setting apart the leading elements of the advertisement, and it may also be an effective border separat-

---

[1] The character of advertisements changes from year to year. The same forces which influence style in anything affect the seasonal and yearly changes in the appearance of advertising. A new layout *idea* may change the whole trend.

ing one advertisement from others on the page. It clarifies, beautifies, and emphasizes. It may dignify and give the feeling of tone. White space is most effectively used in advertisements dealing with higher-priced articles and when prestige is to be stressed.

Illustrations Tell A Story, Provide Action. The use of pictures, sketches, charts, and other illustrative material gives a dynamic force to the entire layout and offers vital information to the great number of readers who are visual minded. Frequently illustrations inform as well as please, for they picture details which could not be easily described, and they create a general impression, such as the style and lines of the commodities. Especially is this true when illustrations are used with such products as clothes or automobiles. Illustrations must be in harmony with other elements in the layout as to their technical nature and atmosphere.

Type Adds Beauty And Force Of Its Own. While acting as a servant in putting across the copy message, type, considered as an element in relation to the others, adds grace or force or strength or directs the eye-movement. It cannot be all things at one time, but it does provide a distinctive tone to the entire advertisement. Type is a particularly variable unit in the layout because there are so many kinds of type faces and so many sizes as well as shades. The possible arrangements of type are practically unlimited, as the letters can be staggered across the page, can run horizontally or vertically, and can form illustrations in themselves.

The Trade Name Is The Signature. The name of the store or manufacturer who is selling the goods mentioned in the advertisement links the seller with the products he is advertising and acts as the signature and hence a guarantee of the statements. This trade name may appear anywhere in the layout and may vary in appearance with each insertion, but it is customary that the trade name have a distinctive and semi-permanent appearance so that it may indicate stability and become familiar to the reader-customers.

The Trade-Mark Is Also Familiar. The success of a trade-mark or slogan depends upon how immediately it is identified with the product. The trade-mark may be varied in certain characteristics, but enough of its familiar character must be retained in the layout so as to insure its recognition and hence its continued value. Slogans may appear in different type faces and in various forms but the wording is rarely changed so long as they are producing results. When a slogan or trade-mark is particularly well known it may constitute the major element in any layout. Such use lends a continuity and a stability which no other element can so easily provide. The picture of the Smith Brothers is easily recognized as a trade-mark for their cough drops, while everyone knows that "Ask the Man Who Owns One" refers to the Packard automobile.

Color Compels Attention. The layout designer who can use color has available one of the vitalizing elements in any design. When boldly used to attract attention away from competing advertisements or to a particular section of one advertisement, it invariably catches the eye, while suggesting life and action. At other times it may be used mainly for its artistic effect as a means of securing beauty in shade and tone. Or its primary utility may be that of providing contrast. Still another important use of color is that of displaying the exact shades and textures of the products. Color is becoming ever more important as an element in the layout because the improvement in mechanical processes has made color more available to all forms of media.

Special Messages May Constitute An Element. When an advertiser wishes through coupon or some similar means to convey some special message in addition to describing his product, the layout designer separates this special note and makes it an integral unit or element of the layout. But unless the other units of the advertisement have performed their tasks efficiently the coupon may be wasted. For its use must be preceded by the aroused desire to act at once. The advertisement must have attracted and aroused interest, secured conviction, and caused the wish to act through the coupon and perhaps in less direct ways. Any such special message is usually placed in a prominent position in the advertisement, but not in the place of greatest emphasis unless it is used as the chief means of securing action, as in mail orders.

Artistic Devices Aid In Many Ways. Unity and eye-movement are frequently achieved by the effective employment of a number of artistic devices which may simply be rare uses of any of the other elements. The product may be so pictured that it fulfills one of these functions as well as that of giving a picture of the product itself. Or the type may be so arranged in an artistic fashion that it adds beauty while telling its story. Dramatic sketches, attractive symbols, illustrations which fade into backgrounds, symbolic drawings, unusual borders, and the display of ornaments may be used as distinctive elements in effective layouts.

The Border Has Many Possibilities. While the border's chief function is to form a frame for the advertisement, it may actively enter into the working parts of the layout. It may aid in eye-movement and should assist in indicating the nature of the advertisement by its sturdiness, grace and shading of light or black lines and by its width. It may add ornamentation and unity. And even by its absence it may serve to attract attention to the layout.

IN GOOD LAYOUTS THESE ELEMENTS ARE ARRANGED EFFECTIVELY

Whether for newspapers, magazines, or other media the layouts which best serve their purpose are those which are pleasing to the eye, and yet are arresting, and those that suggest action and movement while keeping the reader's attention from other competing advertisements.

The Layout Must Attract Attention.   While a layout must help secure the attention of the reader to the advertisement, it must not call attention to itself. At this point the purpose of the layout is to attract the reader to the advertisement without his awareness of just what it is that is impelling him. Hence the layout is subtly designed to draw the eye to the advertisement in general and to each specific unit. Layouts best perform that function when they are designed for a specific class of readers. As readers and media vary, so must layouts, for some readers prefer a soft artistic effect while others are most easily attracted by bolder lines and more evident action and vigor.

The Elements Must Not Compete.   When there are too many competing elements no one is dominant. The good layout, then, provides that one element be stressed, either the headline, illustration, special message, or some other unit. All others are subordinate in space and value. Some layouts are restricted to only a few elements so that one will stand out clearly and with force. Usually the dominant element is placed in the natural point of interest, namely, the optical center midway of the design, horizontally, but slightly above the center in the vertical direction. All other elements, however, are complementary to the main element.

The Layout Provides Movement Within The Advertisement.   By means of headlines and blocks of copy, pointing devices, illustrations, and other mechanical effects, the readers' eyes are directed from one element to another within the layout. At the same time the layout artist has planned that the eyes stay within the advertisement instead of being taken out into competing advertisements or reading matter. The layout performs this function unobtrusively so that readers are not conscious that their eyes are so directed. This may be done in such ways as facing illustrations toward the advertisement instead of away from it, or having one element end at a point where it leads immediately into another unit of the advertisement.

The Central Idea Is Stressed.   Just as a layout is faulty if it stresses too many mechanical elements, so is it ineffective if it endeavors to present too many ideas of comparable weight and importance. If the advertisement is to tell of a sale, that is the central idea which is stressed. Or if a store is advertising the receipt of new goods, that is the central idea which is given the dominant tone and place. In any one layout, one central idea takes precedence and sets the atmosphere for the whole advertisement. Thus the purpose of the advertisement is best carried out.

Good Layouts Are Simple And Easy To Grasp.   The layout which is too complex bewilders the reader and may furnish so much variety that it becomes monotonous. When it is necessary, as in the case of omnibus advertisements, to present much detail about many things, the layout so groups these minor elements that they are obviously subordinate parts. These may be placed under headings attracting only the readers particularly interested in certain goods. Of such nature are some department store advertisements, especially those announcing a store-wide sale.

THE LAYOUT MAN IS AN ARTIST

While layout must have enough movement and action to attract and hold attention, it must conform to the principles of good art.

The Elements Contrast And Balance Each Other. Because the natural point of interest on a page or within an advertisement is the optical center, the perfectly balanced or bisymmetrical division is seldom used. In preference there is the occult balance, which gives the effect of movement. Such balance is based on a focal point at or near the optical center. Using the principle of the teeter-totter, the lighter elements are placed at a greater distance from the focal point. Weight in this sense is provided by blackness of type or illustration as well as by size and tone. Contrast is effected by using different sizes, shapes, and colors of areas, type, illustrations, and other elements. Further contrast is afforded in type faces and shading color.

Unity Is An Artistic Quality. While the layout divides the advertisement into various sections, at the same time it unites these sections and so performs an artistic function. It provides for an order among the elements and a coherence that is pleasing and unobtrusive. The elements and pointing devices which suggest eye-movement and action also aid in tying the advertisement together to provide unity. Elements are thus brought together in their proper relationship and with emphasis directed to the central idea and its mechanical presentation.

Harmony Is Also Present. Harmony in the layout is achieved by the absence of discordant effects. Not only must the mechanical features of the advertisement harmonize, but also there must be a sympathy of feeling between the subject matter and the mechanics which present it. Bold and strong type faces are not used to announce the sale of organdy dresses; nor are light, graceful type faces used to express the qualities of large tractors. Likewise the illustrations are in tone with the subjects they portray. And the elements must not clash with each other. Type, illustrations, headlines, and the other elements should agree essentially in feeling. Widely variant type faces expressing different moods and attitudes are not used within the same advertisement. Nor do the illustrations differ in character from one another.

Rhythm And Symmetry Add Beauty. When a layout is so designed that its lines either figuratively or actually move into each other in happy proportion, an artistic effect is produced. Such rhythm adds to the symmetry while at the same time it gives the idea of movement. Where this movement is strong, and the rhythmic lines are bold, action is suggested that draws the reader as does a magnet. But whether these lines are in actual evidence or merely suggested, they are artistic in effect, and hence add value to the layout. While giving the feeling of movement, rhythm also provides beauty. In a rhythmic layout the elements move gracefully toward each other and blend rather than exist as separate, disjointed sections. Rhythm is secured in many ways but usually is most happily achieved by a succession or repetition of harmonious shapes, sizes, tones, and directing devices. Dynamic advertisements, those that have movement and force as distinguished from the static layouts, are those that have the quality of rhythm.

Proportion Adds Beauty And Secures Emphasis. The weight or attention value given the various elements is determined by the importance of these elements and by the principle of design that each element must be proportionate to the others and to the layout as a whole. But division of the advertisement into sections or elements must be so accomplished that the general effect is pleasing and yet not noticeable. The principles of proportion are most effective when they are subtly carried out.

LAYOUTS ARE OF SEVERAL KINDS

Layouts vary as to form and content, depending upon the specific purpose of the advertisement and the medium to be used.

They Vary As To Size And As To Shape. Newspaper and magazine layouts may be full-page or any fraction thereof. Or they may run across two full pages in what is known as a "double truck" or center spread. These pages in turn may be considered as two separate layouts or as one single unit. The width of the layouts is figured by columns and may run from one column to eight, with a depth likewise varying. When department stores issue special newspaper sections, each page usually constitutes a separate layout and is classified as one unit. An exception is the center-spread page.

Although most newspaper and magazine advertisements are rectangular in form, there is occasional variance such as is evidenced in the newspaper "stair-step" layout. As the name indicates, the outline of such an advertisement resembles a flight of steps. Of similar unorthodox nature is the layout arranged in the shape of an "L." Newspapers are not regularly accepting such unusual shapes, although advertisers like them because their rarity adds an effective power of attraction.

They Vary As To Content. Layouts differ in that some are designed to express a simple message with only a few elements, while others are of omnibus nature with a consequent need for many elements to help carry out the specific purpose of the advertiser. When the purpose is simply to keep the name before the public, one element may be enough, such as the slogan or the firm's name. But when the product is being pioneered or when competition is severe, several elements may be used within one layout, each assisting in the work of putting over the advertising message. The kinds of layouts according to content include the following:

1. One simple element such as a slogan with a signature or identification.
2. A large element such as an illustration with only a caption and signature.
3. A large element divided into sections, such as several paragraphs of copy, plus the firm's name.
4. One main element which dominates the layout, with a few subordinate and supporting elements.
5. A few elements, each dominating a certain section of the advertisement and constituting a unit in itself. This, in effect, is the layout within a layout such as is used in some of the better department store newspaper advertisements.
6. Several small items grouped in relationship to one or two larger and more dominating elements, each with some copy and perhaps with illustrations such as are used in sale advertisements.
7. The omnibus layout in which numerous items of several classifications must be grouped in one advertisement. The function of such a layout is to try to secure some order out of what would otherwise be chaos.

THE LAYOUT DESIGNER MUST BE VERSATILE

Because of the different important functions of the layout, its designer must have a varied technical knowledge as well as the imagination to conceive the important central theme and to determine how that theme can most effectively be carried out.

He Is A Creator. The layout designer must have the imagination to conceive the advertisement as a whole and to so design it as to embody the best principles of art without calling direct attention to its artistry. He uses his knowledge of accents, contrast, balance, proportion, and rhythm to achieve a unity and force in the layout. Thus he vitalizes it while securing a pleasing artistic effect. He emphasizes the important features of the layout and yet so unifies the elements that the emphasis is not noticeable.

He Is A Technician And An Artisan. To carry out the design he has conceived, the layout maker must know the technique of the various mechanical and artistic processes that are performed in making the different elements. He knows the faces of type and which ones convey the meaning of force, grace, beauty, or other values that harmonize with the product he is advertising. He knows drawing technique and its possibilities just as he understands illustrative composition and the engraving processes. He may not be a technician in all phases, but he understands the possibilities of the mechanics of advertising and can direct the work of the copy writers, the printers, the engravers, and the sketchers.

CHAPTER XLIII

THE VIGOROUS VOICE OF CIRCULATION

There was a time when the ingredients of which newspaper circulation was built were hustle and holler. Today other ingredients are needed. The circulation manager employs all the techniques of modern management in stimulating and making effective the efforts of his staff. But simultaneously he must think of those techniques by which the attention of potential readers can be attracted. For he is the sales manager of the enterprise and upon him rests not only the responsibility of increasing sales, but the larger responsibility of aiding the newspaper to discharge its democratic obligation to present the news of the day to all the people—high and low, rich and poor, those accessible and those unaccessible, and those who are not interested in the affairs of the day as well as those who are.—JOHN J. CORSON *

THE CIRCULATION DEPARTMENT IS IMPORTANT

The importance of the circulation department is such that it is recognized as being on a parity with that of the editorial and advertising departments of the journal. Appropriate distribution is the "life blood" of all media.

A Distributive Agency Is Necessary. Without the functioning of the circulation department as a distributive agency neither the printed word nor the advertisement would have economic value. The business of the circulation department is to sell the commodity of news or views to create advertising value. Indirectly, therefore, circulation is of tremendous importance in producing advertising revenue, and direct revenue from advertising averages four to eight or more times that from circulation.

Only within the last half-century has the importance of circulation been fully recognized as a major phase of nearly all types of journalism. Gradually, it has reached its present high emphasis.

Of particular impetus to the growing significance of circulation was the industrial expansion during the last decade of the nineteenth century. Manufacturers and merchants began to invest more heavily in advertising and to realize that the value of their advertising depended largely upon the extent to which the organ in which they advertised was circulated and paid for. Later, they began to consider the type of reader to

---

* Circulation Director, the *Washington Post*. Written expressly for this book by Mr. Corson.

whom the journalistic medium made its appeal. However, the extent of circulation has been important to the advertiser from the beginning.

With the reduction of competition in "getting the news," as the result of improved press services, greater emphasis was placed upon circulation promotion. Improved mechanical facilities also made it possible to supply easily more papers or magazines than were actually in demand and with little additional cost. Greater distribution thus became essentially a matter of promotion. A keen struggle for circulation became the order of the times and has continued since.

Circulation-Department Organization Varies. Organization of a circulation department varies according to the size and setup of a publication. Headed by a circulation manager, whose duty it is to supervise distribution and promotion methods and policies, the circulation department of a metropolitan newspaper, for example, would be likely to include a city, country, and perhaps a suburban manager, with the latter three directly responsible for distribution methods in their respective areas. Each may also superintend promotion work in his territory. In each of these divisions there may be district managers who carry on the work under the supervision of the city, country, and suburban managers. Throughout the divisions will be numerous carriers and news dealers, and in the office, a clerical and bookkeeping staff. In addition there will be solicitors.

The work of the circulation manager parallels that of a first-class executive whose duties are multiple. He establishes policies, supervises the work of his clerical staff and of the minor executives in his charge, directs promotional activities, and above all helps to create and maintain good-will toward the newspaper and harmony among his staff members and distribution agencies. Only through proper co-operation and thorough harmony can his department function with the greatest efficiency.

DISTRIBUTION—STREET, CITY, MAIL, AND COUNTRY— IS A MAIN ACTIVITY

Distribution, one of the two vital activities of the circulation department, involves, in the case of newspapers of general circulation, street, city, mail, and country circulation. Although street sales are sometimes considered part of city circulating activity, and mail as part of country activity, the larger the publication the more necessary it is to separate each from the other.

Street Sales May Be Handled Differently. Street sales may be handled in a variety of ways, depending upon the size of the city and the efficiency of particular methods with respect to each publication. In some cases newspapers sell their street-sale copies to a wholesaler who then undertakes the distribution, either somewhat under the supervision and suggestion of the circulation department or largely independent of it. In other instances newspapers handle the street sales directly through the circulation department, usually under the direction of the city circulator whose duty it is to secure able street sellers and allot them papers according to their needs. In addition, of course, newsstand distribution is important as an outlet agency. Although it usually plays a somewhat limited role in the distribution of newspapers,[1] it frequently plays a major part in the distribution of other types of journalism.

City Subscribers Present Special Problems. Delivering newspapers to city subscribers presents many complicated problems of administration in efficient handling from the standpoint of speed, economy, and subscriber-satisfaction. A newspaper may hire carriers to distribute papers and undertake its own collections; or it may hire carriers with the understanding that they both distribute and collect for papers; or the newspaper may adopt the "little merchant" plan. Under this last plan the newspapers are sold to the carrier, and the difference between what the boy pays for the papers and the monthly delivery or daily street-sale price which he collects is his profit. In large metropolitan centers it has been found efficient to distribute papers through a carrier in each district who handles all newspapers being delivered in that district. This has proved to be both efficient and practicable. The plan eliminates duplication of routes which exists under a system in which as many boys travel the same route as there are newspapers in the city.

Meeting Time Schedules Is Vital For Mail Subscribers. Distribution by mail involves careful attention to mail schedules, folding, wrapping, addressing, sorting, and delivering publications to trains with the precision which makes for placing them into the hands of subscribers with the greatest speed and economy. Costly but efficient mailing equipment is now obtainable to fold, address, and prepare all types of printed material for mailing. Because timeliness of news is essential and newspapers can no longer safely force ahead too far the predate, many newspapers prepare a special mail edition to catch the most important trains.

Country Circulation Includes Outside Areas. Country newspaper circulation includes that outside the city or suburban areas. Papers for distribution in the country area may be carried to their points of destination by trains or buses, and frequently they are delivered by conveyances owned and operated by the newspaper itself. When the papers reach a designated town, they may then be distributed through a newspaper agency which undertakes its own methods of delivery and collection, or the newspaper may employ a system of hiring carriers to deliver papers and make collections as it does in the city. Then, also, the "little merchant" plan may be used in country circulation.

---

[1] However, in metropolitan centers where there is a large body of commuters newsstand sales are correspondingly greater.

CIRCULATION PROMOTION IS A MAIN ACTIVITY

Circulation promotion, the second main activity of the circulation department, requires attention to every factor influencing circulation volume since such knowledge is necessary both for securing and retaining readers.

The Circulation Manager Has Large Responsibility. The circulation manager must understand all the factors directly affecting circulation and its promotion. Efficient administration of the detailed work is but half his duty. Carrying out the other half of his duty requires not only study, planning, and intimate knowledge of the factors affecting the circulation of his publication but also the complete co-operation of the producers of the vehicle which he is to deliver and promote. Any change in the policy or mechanics of the publication is of vital concern to him, and while he may not be able to alter policies detrimental to circulation, his knowledge of them will enable him to make the best possible adjustments.

Many Factors Affect Circulation Volume. While every phase of a publication's organization and activity has an indirect relation to the other, there are certain elements which have an especially direct bearing upon circulation volume. These include those more readily recognized, such as: *competition,* a problem which may be met by improving the commodity or its distribution; *selling price of the newspaper or magazine,* which should preferably be determined by cost analysis; *location and density of population* (in the case of newspapers), since a densely populated area provides greater circulation possibilities than does a thinly settled area, under average circumstances at least; *territory to be covered,* inasmuch as some arbitrary limit must be placed upon the point at which efforts to secure subscribers should be discontinued. Other equally important, but somewhat less appreciated, factors are: *peculiarities of the consumer-group,* for the publication must be consistent in its appeal to the particular type of readers and the community or area for which it is designed, depending somewhat upon the racial, social, educational, political, and vocational factors involved; and the *personality* of the newspaper or of the magazine, which encompasses its treatment of news or other content, its typography, and its editorial policy.

Competition among magazine publishers for circulation is generally acute. This may be the better understood when one realizes that a magazine rarely has a field to itself for long. Most magazine publishers have devoted much time, energy, and money to analyzing the distribution, scope, and nature of their publication reader-group in order to accomplish the dual purpose of building editorial and advertising prestige through circulation.

Insofar as newspapers are concerned, the peculiarities of the community and the type of reader are somewhat closely associated with the personality of the newspaper. For instance, a newspaper located in a church town would be unwise not to give prominence to church activities in its news treatment, even though it might maintain a neutral attitude in its editorial columns. Unless party affiliations are about evenly balanced, an independent paper, politically speaking, is not likely to flourish, nor would a Democratic newspaper long survive in a wholly Republican community. The personality of a newspaper depends upon treatment of news in a conservative or sensational fashion, choice of features, emphasis upon news values, type, headlines, make-up, and quality and color of paper. The circulation manager's concern is that of determining just how these factors are adapted to his class of readers and how, if necessary and possible, they may be altered if they are a hindrance to increasing circulation.

Efficient Service Must Be Maintained. One of the first essentials in promoting circulation is the maintenance of efficient service. Effort spent on good-will promotion is seldom unrewarded. Careful attention must be given to delivery and to the wishes of subscribers relative to place of delivery and method of collecting for subscriptions. For example, many a faithful newspaper subscriber has been lost by careless delivery or failure of a carrier to regard the subscriber's wish about placing a paper inside a door or out of the rain. Courtesy and accommodation are necessary to insure the best results. Treating complaints with courtesy and making an effort to remedy the causes of the complaints are profitable policies.

SPECIFIC FORMS OF CIRCULATION PROMOTION ARE NUMEROUS

Mail and personal solicitation; contests; premiums; advertising through billboards, electric signs, posters, other publications, and radio; and special services are specific forms of circulation promotion.

Campaign Methods May Be Used In Various Ways. Campaign methods may be used singly or in various combinations, continuously or in intensive drives. The question naturally arises whether circulation campaigns should be handled within the department or by outside circulation builders. Although there is the difficulty that the outside specialists may not understand local conditions, they are often valuable in revitalizing a lagging publication. Which method or methods a publication employs should be determined by the results desired and the type of the reader-group to which the method is to be applied.

Personal And Mail Solicitation Are Given Chief Emphasis. Mail solicitation and personal solicitation are points of chief emphasis in circulation promotion. Mail solicitation, as well as personal solicitation, is frequently employed both in an attempt to secure new subscribers and in an effort to bring about renewals of expiring subscriptions. Often a close tie-up between mail solicitation and personal solicitation proves extremely effective.

On larger papers it is customary to have some form of personal solicitation in force fairly continuously both in the city and in the country. Personal solicitation may be carried on by full-time solicitors, part-time solicitors, and carriers. Full-time workers are usually supervised by the city and country circulation managers or by district circulation-department men and are directed and instructed by them. Many news organs, as well as other forms of journalism, handle direct solicitation through a series of crew managers who move from section to section, or town to town, with their crews. When the crew manager is employed, he works directly under the circulation manager or one of his assistants, and the solicitors themselves are either wholly or partially responsible to him. Special care is necessary in selecting solicitors and crew managers who, among other qualifications, must have a belief in their ability to sell. Circulation authorities make every effort to obtain honest, dependable, courteous, and persistent persons who realize that the good-will toward the publication which they represent is of prime importance.

In any community part-time solicitors may be recruited from persons who are anxious to earn a little extra money. They may be employed as auxiliary agents to full-time solicitors, who for the most part move from one town to another as suggested previously. Although school-age carriers may seem too young to solicit subscriptions, they can, with training, become the best solicitors possible, for youth can gain entrance and attention where age cannot.

Various methods of payment have been devised for the services of personal solicitors. There are disadvantages, in one way or another, to most of them from the point of view of both the solicitors and press authorities. However, the combination of commission and salary is used advantageously by many publications, whereas in other instances commission is the only type of payment.

Several Types Of Contests Are Employed. Several types of contests may be employed in circulation promotion, but no publisher can afford to utilize a contest which arouses discontent among the readers or contestants or which results in unstable circulation. The most effective type of contest is the one that interests the carriers. Prizes, awarded on the basis of a certain number of subscriptions secured, should be something coveted by the carrier and something which he would not otherwise be likely to obtain. Cash prizes are usually less desirable than are merchandise rewards. Another type of contest is the subscriber contest, but in order to arouse initial interest the rewards have to be greater than those offered carriers. Likewise the number of subscriptions required in order to qualify in the contest must be greater. Popularity or beautiful-girl contests are sometimes used, but strict rules are necessary to avoid jealousy and discontent.

Premiums Are Often Used Effectively. There are also several methods of promoting circulation by premiums such as the straight premium and the coupon method. The straight premium involves giving an article with each subscription, whereas the coupon method requires the clipping of a specific number of coupons in order to secure a premium. Frequently a premium is offered with a subscription plus the payment of a small amount in addition. It should be noted that a publisher is limited by the United States postal regulations to premiums that cost not more than fifty per cent of the price of the subscription.

Insurance Has Helped Build Circulation. In recent years, insurance has played an important and a successful part in building newspaper circulation. By contracting with an insurance company, a newspaper is able to supply accident policies to its readers at slight cost.

Advertising Is Frequently Used. Advertising also has become a recognized method of circulation promotion. No longer do publications consider their own columns sufficient to reach the public; they are now advertising in other newspapers and magazines. In addition to this display type of advertising, posters, cards, and radio have become increasingly effective agencies. Many newspapers have found it profitable to own and to operate their own radio stations. Many of the best stations today are newspaper controlled.

Other Promotion Plans Often Developed By Newspapers. Other promotion plans include trial subscriptions at a reduced rate for a trial period, sample copies, the delivery of two papers to a home for a slight increase in regular subscription price, localized news, special editions, and feature services. By localized news is meant the printing of local news concerning the areas served outside the city. A staff of country correspondents supplies the news and special feature articles from the areas without the city and thus unifies the entire territory covered by the newspaper. Although feature services may be considered the primary concern of the editorial department, they are also important circulation builders. They may be informative articles of general or specialized interest, opinions and comments, or comics. Other good-will promotion services include the sponsoring of cooking schools, charity funds, civic improvements, and the like. Special departmentalization of a newspaper into automobile, financial, dramatic, book, women's, children's, society, real-estate, radio, magazine, sports, and other sections is useful for the purposes of increasing both circulation and advertising possibilities.

Magazines Use Various Promotion Devices. Besides using most of the newspaper promotion schemes, magazines also employ certain merchandising service devices. For example, the publishers of *Good Housekeeping* and *Parents' Magazine* have worked out services by creating the Good Housekeeping Institute and the Consumer Service Bureau, respectively. These test for consumer-value products submitted to them and then award a seal of approval to such items as come up to the standards established. *Vogue* and *McCall's* publish their own dress patterns and gain promotion by co-operating specifically with retail merchants in various ways.

CIRCULATION MEASUREMENT IS STANDARDIZED

Since circulation without verification is an unsatisfactory commodity from the advertiser's point of view, there have come into existence the Audit Bureau of Circulations and the Controlled Circulation Audit Bureau, Inc., the former serving to audit paid circulation.

Organization Of A.B.C. Was Important Step Forward. Prior to 1914 several unsuccessful efforts had been made to collect circulation data, but not until the establishment of the Audit Bureau of Circulations was a sound and standardized method devised for verification of circulation. The Audit Bureau of Circulations [1] (known in the profession as the A.B.C.) is a mutual organization composed of national and local advertisers, advertising agencies, and publishers who share in the control of the organization. The buyers (advertisers and advertising agencies) are in a majority on the board of directors.[2]

Not until A.B.C.'s advent was it possible for buyers of advertising to select media as applied to markets and to purchase space on the basis of facts rather than wishful thinking. Similarly, it was not until the organization of A.B.C. that full credit for factual circulation statements could be assured the publisher. This was an important and necessary step forward from the advertiser's point of view. As stated in the "Foreword" of its own explanatory brochure entitled *A.B.C.—Self-Regulation in the Advertising and Publishing Industry:*

> The objectives of the founders of the Bureau were to define and provide standards of definition for paid circulations, establish uniform methods of auditing paid circulations and an organization to furnish accurate reports of publication circulation, the lack of which had threatened to wreck the whole structure of advertising.

---

[1] The headquarters of the association, as well as the managing director's office, is located at 165 W. Wacker Drive, Chicago, and serves newspapers and periodicals in the United States, Canada, and Mexico. It also has a New York office at 330 W. Forty-Second Street.

[2] Article IV of the *By-Laws and Rules,* January, 1947, provides for a board of directors consisting of twelve advertiser, three advertising-agency, six newspaper-publisher, two magazine-publisher, two farm-paper-publisher, and two business-paper-publisher members. Article V provides that "no person shall be elected president of the Bureau who is not an advertiser or advertising agency member or the registered agent of an advertiser or advertising agency."

The A.B.C. Is Maintained By Dues And Services Provisions. The Bureau is maintained by charging each class of membership according to a definite plan of assessment in relationship to the service rendered by the Bureau as provided for in the by-laws. Each publisher is required to give a sworn statement of circulation every six months on A.B.C. blanks, and an annual audit is made by the Bureau of each publication. At the close of each statement period the statements released are bound in a volume or volumes entitled *A.B.C. Blue Book for Period Ending. . . .* Copies of this are given to certain classes of members and may be purchased by others. Through the reports of the Bureau, based on the publisher's statements and the actual audits made by the Bureau itself, the buyer of the advertising space learns the number of copies printed by a publication, how many are paid and how many unpaid,[1] where these copies are distributed, and how the distribution was obtained. Definite standards, audits, reaudits, limitations, and other detailed provisions are provided by the Bureau in by-laws and rules to protect its membership and the public at large from misstatement of fact and misinformation.

The board of directors has the power to discipline members for infraction of the by-laws and rules, even to suspension and expulsion. These latter penalties, which have very serious consequences for the offenders, are imposed only for fraud and, to the credit of the industry, they have been necessary in comparatively few cases.

Development Of C.C.A. Widened Audit Field. The Controlled Circulation Audit Bureau, Inc. (known in the profession as the C.C.A.) serves *business publications*[2] which are distributed without charge to persons or organizations *bona fide* interested in a field of business activity. Until January, 1948, Controlled Circulation Audit, Inc., maintained during its seventeen years of existence that no controlled circulation publication could become a member if more than 50 per cent of its total distribution had been paid for by the recipients at a rate of more than half the published subscription price. Today, C.C.A. serves the same purpose as in the past but the membership rules are now broadened so as to simply require that a publication be sent periodically and confined to a specific industry, business, trade, or profession and that it has operated as a controlled-circulation publication for six months or more. C.C.A. does not now audit circulation as "paid" and "unpaid" but rather merely audits as to a publication's *bona fide* distribution.

Circulation Measurement And Advertising Are Inseparable. Circulation measurement is of the utmost importance as it relates to advertising.

---

[1] The Audit Bureau of Circulations does not generally audit *unpaid* circulation in any detail—A.B.C. rules provide that unpaid distribution may not exceed 30 per cent of paid distribution.

[2] If a trade journal is on a paid circulation basis, and about 350 are considered to be, it may become a member of A.B.C.

When an advertiser buys space he is interested in knowing the character of the circulation of the publication in which his advertising is to appear. To the advertiser circulation is important not only in its length, which is known as the number of copies circulated to net-paid subscribers, but also in its breadth and thickness. Breadth represents the geographical territory in which the publication is circulated. Thickness applies to the quality of the circulation as it depends upon the methods used in obtaining that circulation. For instance, an advertiser is interested in knowing whether circulation was secured on the basis of regular rates or as the result of offering premiums or reduced rates. Circulation measurement is not an end in itself but rather is a guide to advertisers and a means by which publications obtain advertising which is directly their most tangible life line.

Chapter XLIV

MECHANICS OF PUBLICATION

Modern newspapers could not exist if it were not for the developments of the mechanical side of their business, the composing machines,
the improvements in stereotyping, the marvelous presses, almost human
in their performance. The advertiser has at his command today, ready
made for his purpose, typographic tools, types that can express the most
varied appeals, opportunities for printed salesmanship that have become
the most important factor in turning the wheels of modern business.
—Kenneth E. Olson.*

MACHINES MAKE LARGE CIRCULATION POSSIBLE

Mass production of newspapers and magazines was facilitated by the
invention of intricate machines and the development of technical processes
which changed small shops into delicately adjusted industrial plants.

Editorial Departments Are Linked With Mechanical Divisions. Systematic production of newspaper editions in the mechanical departments
demands that editors understand the requirements imposed by machines
in the composing and press rooms. With a working knowledge of typography and the mechanical processes involved in publishing, the editorial
department contributes to accuracy, speed, and efficiency of the whole
plant. Specifically, the editorial division supplies instructions which the
mechanical departments follow for setting the type, laying out the pages,
and constructing a uniform and attractive publication. In fact, in all
types of journalism there is an interdependence between editorial and
mechanical functions.

Successful Mechanical Departments Are Carefully Managed. Machines in publishing plants represent costly investments. Careful management, close supervision over costs of production, and maintenance of an
effective division of labor are essential.

In newspaper plants a dual problem involves setting the news matter
in type and building up the advertising, partly by using composing machines and partly by setting type by hand.

Machines used in composing rooms are operated by fallible human
beings, and consequently specialists called proofreaders are employed in
the mechanical departments to facilitate speed and assure accuracy. Their

---

* From *Typography and Mechanics of the Newspaper* by Kenneth E. Olson, p. 430.
Copyright 1930. Used by permission of the publishers, D. Appleton-Century Co.

work is essentially different from that of the editors or copyreaders and their place is with the printers.

Printers and operators of composing machines are required to set in type the material sent to them by the editorial department exactly in the form in which they receive it. That is to say, the copy should require no changes or corrections after it leaves the hands of the editors and copyreaders. When the copy is set in type, however, mechanical errors often result. Wrong letters, misspelled words, errors in spacing, punctuation, capitalization, serious omissions, variations in type and many other inaccuracies may occur and must be corrected. Therefore, after the type has been set up an impression or proof is taken. The proofreaders compare the original copy with the proof and mark for correction [1] by the printers any errors which have resulted during the printing process.

TYPOGRAPHY CARRIES THE MESSAGE EFFECTIVELY TO THE READER

Type is used and selected primarily to transmit messages clearly, simply, and attractively to the readers, without interfering with the purposes of the publication.

Editors Familiarize Themselves With Basic Printing Terms. Editors need not be practical printers, but they must know something of printers' terms in order to co-operate effectively with the composing room.

Whether type is hand-set or machine-set, its size is designated in units of $\frac{1}{72}$ inch, or points. The point size applies to the height of the type, measured from the front to the back of the metal shaft bearing the letter. The width of the type line, column or page, is expressed in terms of ems. The standard or 12-point em is $\frac{1}{6}$ inch, and consequently a column of type set three inches wide is referred to as an 18-em column.

Type faces are classified in accordance with certain basic characteristics which they possess. Familiar *groups* are roman, gothic, script, and text, although newspapers and magazines are concerned largely with the familiar roman types. Reading matter is usually set in small sizes of body type. Headlines and titles are set in display type. The following are illustrative:

This line is set in 12-point Script.

𝕿𝖍𝖎𝖘 𝖑𝖎𝖓𝖊 𝖎𝖘 𝖘𝖊𝖙 𝖎𝖓 12-point Text.

This line is set in 12-point Roman.

THIS LINE IS SET IN 12-POINT GOTHIC.

A large number of *families* is included in the roman race, each identified by certain distinctive features in the letters and elements which set

---

[1] For a list of proofreaders' marks, refer to chart on page 382.

PROOFREADERS' MARKS

Marks	Explanation
⊙	Insert period at point indicated by caret.
⌃	Insert comma at point indicated by caret.
⊙	Insert colon at point indicated by caret.
⌃	Insert semicolon at point indicated by caret.
/=/	Insert hyphen at point indicated by caret.
/ēm/	Insert 1-em dash at point indicated by caret.
?/	Insert question mark at point indicated by caret.
!/	Insert exclamation mark at point indicated by caret.
⌄	Insert apostrophe at point indicated by caret.
⌄⌄	Enclose in quotation marks as indicated by carets.
rom	Reset encircled matter in roman (regular) type.
lc	Reset crossed-out letter or encircled matter in lower-case type.
ital	Reset underscored matter in *italic* type.
sm caps	Reset double-underscored matter in SMALL CAPITALS.
caps	Reset triple-underscored matter in CAPITALS.
bf	**Reset** matter thus underscored in **boldfaced** type.
⌀	Delete letter, letters, or words which are crossed out.
∧	Insert the marginal addition at point indicated by caret.
#	Insert space where indicated by caret.
⌒	Delete space. Draw the word together.
⑨	Turn inverted letter which is encircled.
X	Broken letter. Encircled letter must be replaced.
wf	Wrong font.
tr	Transpose letters or words as indicated.
stet	Let it stand as it is. Disregard all marks above the dots.
eq #	Equalize spacing where indicated by carets.
⌞	Move left to point indicated.
⌟	Move right to point indicated.
⌐⌐	Lower to point indicated.
⌐⌐	Raise to point indicated.
⊥	Push down space which is showing up.
ⓢⓟ	Spell out all encircled words.
¶	Start a new paragraph at point indicated by caret.
No ¶	Should not be a separate paragraph. Run in.
▢	Indent 1 em.
=	Out of alignment. Straighten.
Out, see copy	Set from copy the words which were left out and insert as indicated.
⑦	Query to author. (Encircled in red.)

it apart from other families. Roman families commonly used in newspaper headlines are, for example, Bodoni, Cheltenham, Caslon, and Century old style. Variations in proportions and general appearance within each family account for *series* of type, such as condensed, expanded, boldface, and medium. Most of the roman types can also be obtained in *italics*. Following are examples of four roman families of type:

This line is set in 8-point Bodoni.

This line is set in 10-point Caslon.

This line is set in 10-point Century old style.

This line is set in 14-point Cheltenham.

Type Faces Have Different Appeals And Personalities. Much progress has been made in recent years in the study of typographic appeals. Advertisements and magazine pages show more careful choice of type faces and a more discriminating study of type effects than do newspaper columns. Nevertheless, newspaper editors and publishers are aware today that type faces differ widely in distinctiveness and in the uses to which they can be put. Some types have a feminine appeal, some are rough and blatant, others are refined, colorful, informal, businesslike, soft, conservative, or full of individuality. These characteristics often vary among the series of a given type family. The best type face is the one which best expresses the appeal and best fulfills the purpose of the message. Notice the variations in appeal of the following examples:

Garamond is a refined, beautiful, very legible, classic type face.

Caslon is a versatile and extremely useful type family.

Bookman is a simple, uniform, useful, relatively undistinguished face.

Century is a very legible type, lacking grace except in old-style series.

Cheltenham is rugged, masculine, honest, commonplace.

Bodoni is a vigorous, clean, dignified, conservative, businesslike face.

Goudy is informal, free, colorful, and distinguished.

Eve is exotic, original, smart, restricted in utility.

Cloister is an interesting, informal type, suggesting hand-drawn letters.

Kabel is a modern sans serif, flat, simple and unaffected.

Stymie is flat-serif type, crisp, straightforward.

Type Users Must Have A Good Sense Of Design. Legibility is usually the first consideration in the choice of type faces. This factor, together with the desirability of attracting attention to the page and of presenting an orderly design to the reader, requires consideration of proper type sizes, spacing, leading,[1] length of line and judicious use of white space.

---

[1] By leading is meant the practice of widening the space between lines of type. In hand-set type this is done by inserting strips of metal or "leads," varying in thickness, between type lines.

Good contrast and proportion among the type masses and harmony in the families, the series, and the sizes of type serve to promote the function and purpose of the publication. Finally, the arrangement of the various elements which go to make up a page, including illustrations, rules, boxes, and other devices, contributes to the success of the typographic plan.

Experience And Experimentation Develop New Ways Of Using Type. Typography has few, if any, absolute laws. Still, experience has developed a number of practices, considered standards of good usage, which prevent the user of type from going astray. Constant experimentation serves to prevent these rules from becoming frozen into dogmatic systems. Students of the press watch new trends constantly, observing, for example, the new forms of headlines [1] and page designs which forward-looking editors and publishers are using.

TYPESETTING IS DONE LARGELY BY MACHINES

The demands for speed, economy of production, large circulation, and facilities to meet sharp competition have virtually eliminated hand composition in the publishing business.

Line-Casting Machines Revolutionized Publishing. Most of the reading matter today is set by mechanical composing machines. The *Linotype* and the *Intertype,* based on inventions of the late nineteenth century, are used to set body type, headlines, and titles, and with the development of new models the amount of composition which each operator can turn out is steadily increasing.

These intricate and costly machines are operated by a keyboard resembling that of a typewriter. Pressure on the keys releases brass matrices, carried in magazines on top of the machine. These matrices, each containing a letter mold, are arranged automatically into lines of the required column widths. Space bands slip into position, and the line of matrices moves in front of a casting device where molten metal is forced against the line of letter molds, forming a solid line of type. The metal line or slug is automatically trimmed and placed in position with the slugs which have previously been cast. The matrices are returned to their places in the magazine while new lines of type are being cast. Detachable magazines, containing matrices bearing selected type faces and sizes, are available for some machines. While one operator is setting straight reading matter in 8-point type, another may be turning out headlines in 18- and 24-point.

The Monotype Sets Single Type Pieces Or Letters. The *Monotype,* an elaborate machine which involves a longer operation than the line-casting machines, is used more generally for tasks other than those required in newspaper plants. The keyboard unit perforates a paper roll,

---

[1] Reference should be made to Chapter XXVII, *Headlining the News.*

various sets of perforations representing letters. The roll is fed into a second unit, the caster, in which compressed air brings into position the correct letter molds in a special casting box. Separate pieces of type of the desired face and size are the result.

Many newspaper plants use the caster alone to produce hand-set type, leads, rules,[1] and other metal printing materials. The type is used in place of foundry type, and the advantage is largely that fresh pieces can be produced and old type melted down for recasting.

Other machines, such as the *Elrod,* are also used to supply composing-room materials, such as rules and slugs.

The Ludlow Typograph Supplements The Typesetting Machines. For setting display headlines and titles many publishing plants are equipped with a *Ludlow* machine, which, instead of operating by keyboard and automatically placing brass matrices or letter molds in position for producing a metal line of type like the *Linotype* or *Intertype,* furnishes matrices which are set by hand in a special composing stick. The line is then cast in the Typograph unit.

The advantage of the *Ludlow* process over hand-setting is that the equipment takes up little space in the composing room and always assures a fresh supply of type. A space of six feet square will hold the equipment and cabinets for casting type lines of from 12- to 60-point in size, whereas many cabinets are required for a good assortment of hand-set type.

Recent Inventions Contribute Further Changes In Publishing. The *Teletypesetter* is a machine which sets automatically news matter brought by wire into composing rooms. Electrical impulses representing letters and words are transmitted directly into a composing machine which reproduces the message in type, ready for the printing process. An operator at a master keyboard hundreds of miles away can set the type in printing plants throughout the country. This remarkable invention should not be confused with the printer-telegraph machines or *Morkrums* which produce typewritten articles directly from electrical impulses transmitted by wires from distant cities. The latter, in widespread use for distributing news gathered by the press associations, are adjuncts of the editorial or news departments.

Successful experiments have been made in transmitting by electrical impulses whole facsimile pages of reading matter exactly as they are made up in page forms at the distributing point. Extensive use of this innovation awaits further development of the process. Once perfected, a complete newspaper could be made up at a central point and distributed to branches throughout the country, eliminating completely the operations and costs involved in maintaining separate composing rooms.

---

[1] Rules are strips of metal, type high, which produce lines between columns and at the end of printed articles.

Varitype Printing Permits By-Passing Standard Linotype. Although not entirely a new machine, the *varityper,* which is really a glorified type-writer, recently brought about a new technique in printing when walk-outs by Linotype operators forced publishers to discover some way of preventing their newspaper plants from being paralyzed. The principal obstacle in the use of varitype printing is the relatively high cost of photo-engraving the varityped pages. What effect development of this new technique in printing will eventually have is hard to foresee, but if the engraving cost can be cut and other obstacles to its use be overcome it may well be adopted by smaller publications which are not fully equipped with the traditional costly printing equipment. At the present time vari-type printing is slow in that photoengraving alone takes a considerable period of time. In addition, varitype cannot print headlines.

ENGRAVING PROCESSES MADE PICTORIAL JOURNALISM POSSIBLE

Reproduction of photographs and drawings in newspapers and maga-zines, made possible by the invention of innumerable engraving processes, has resulted in the era of the picture press.

Good Illustrations Tell The Story Better Than Words. Ever since newspapers and magazines first used woodcuts, they have turned in-creasingly to pictures to help tell the story. The assertion is often made that pictures create interest even better than words because of their direct appeal to the eye. The demand for illustrations resulted in the develop-ment of many processes for reproducing pictures in the press. Today the possibilities supplied by technical improvements in publishing methods and the various kinds of paper stocks and printing presses have resulted in the widespread use of many kinds of illustrations, each suited to a particular purpose.

There Is An Engraving Process For Every Need. Illustrations suitable for various published media range from woodcuts and chalkplates to high-light halftones, quartertones, and cuts of wash and crayon drawings. Line engravings, halftones, and rotogravure are common means of presenting pictures.

LINE CUTS. Line engravings, used largely to reproduce pen-and-ink sketches, maps, or any other illustration made up of black lines on a white background, are a simple and useful form of cuts. Shading can be added by using Ben Day [1] patterns in the process leading up to the engraving.

HALFTONES. Most of the illustrations used by the press involve the use of halftone engravings for reproducing photographs. The cut usually bears tiny dots, rather than lines, which are distributed on the engraving

---

[1] The artist can select any of a number of Ben Day screens to produce the desired kind of shading for a line cut. Various patterns of dots, grain, stipple, lines, heavy or light backgrounds can thereby be added to a drawing.

to present the various degrees of black, gray, and white represented on the photograph. The optimum size of the dots or fineness of the screen used in producing the halftone is affected by the quality of the paper and the nature of the printing process. Newspapers use coarse screen cuts because of the rough print paper which is used and the speed which is required in the pressroom.

ROTOGRAVURE. Halftones are relief plates. That is to say, the printing surface which is inked and which leaves an impression on paper during the printing process stands out in relief. In rotogravure the parts of the cut which are to be printed are sunken below the surface of the plate. The ink fills these wells of various shapes and is absorbed by the paper when it rolls over the plate in the printing process. This is called "intaglio" printing, to distinguish it from relief or letterpress printing. Color printing is done in both processes.

PHOTOLITHOGRAPHY. In this process reproductions of drawings or designs are prepared for printing on flat or level surfaces. In recent years a considerable amount of commercial printing is being done by planographic or offset printing in which the impression is taken from a plane surface. Offset is a speedy and economical process in which an impression from the printing surface is first transferred to rollers which in turn transmit the printed and illustrated message to the paper.

STEREOTYPING MADE POSSIBLE SPEEDY ROTARY PRINTING

Means for transforming the flat printing surface of page forms made up in the composing room to the semicylindrical plates required by rotary presses are provided by the stereotyping process, used almost universally in daily newspaper plants.

Stereotyping Duplicates Type Forms, Cuts, And Page Forms. Small newspapers and many commercial jobs are printed directly from type and original engravings. The production of large newspapers demands the intermediate process of stereotyping, in which a special paper is pressed down on the type form, resulting in a paper mold of the page. The paper mat is then shaped in semicylindrical form, corresponding to the curvature of the press cylinders, and placed in a casting machine where molten metal is poured into a form containing the paper mat. The result is a curved metal plate, bearing the reproduction of the page form, which is clamped on the cylinders of the rotary press.

Small casting boxes are available for printing plants which have only a limited use for stereotype mats. Any number of reproductions of cuts or type forms can be produced cheaply by this process in the form of flat plates.

I AM THE
PRINTING PRESS

BY ROBERT H. DAVIS

I AM the printing press, born of the mother earth. My heart is of steel, my limbs are of iron, and my fingers are of brass.

I sing the songs of the world, the oratorios of history, the symphonies of all time.

I am the voice of to-day, the herald of to-morrow. I weave into the warp of the past the woof of the future. I tell the stories of peace and war alike.

I make the human heart beat with passion or tenderness. I stir the pulse of nations, and make brave men do braver deeds, and soldiers die.

I inspire the midnight toiler, weary at his loom, to lift his head again and gaze, with fearlessness, into the vast beyond, seeking the consolation of a hope eternal.

When I speak, a myriad people listen to my voice. The Saxon, the Latin, the Celt, the Hun, the Slav, the Hindu, all comprehend me.

I am the tireless clarion of the news. I cry your joys and sorrows every hour. I fill the dullard's mind with thoughts uplifting. I am light, knowledge, power. I epitomize the conquests of mind over matter.

I am the record of all things mankind has achieved. My offspring comes to you in the candle's glow, amid the dim lamps of poverty, the splendor of riches; at sunrise, at high noon, and in the waning evening.

I am the laughter and tears of the world, and I shall never die until all things return to the immutable dust.

I am the printing press.

The poem reprinted above appeared on a bronze plaque in the reception room of the *New York Sun*.

"I AM THE PRINTING PRESS" [1]

A poem, dedicated to the printing press and mounted on a bronze plaque in the offices of a New York newspaper, is one of many testimonials to the enormous consequences of the inventions which produced the modern presses.

The Presses Complete The Pattern Of Speedy Production. [2] Modern presses are symbolic of the widespread distribution of printed materials and diversified literature which today meets the needs and interests of the world's millions. Innumerable models are available to satisfy the specific requirements of printers and publishers.

FLAT-BED PRESSES. Flat-bed presses, used largely for printing small publications, range from small and crude hand presses to the flat-bed cylinder and web perfecting flat-bed presses. These presses print directly from the type forms. The advantage of the "web" presses is derived from the use of rolls or webs of paper which feed the paper in a continuous stream to the press.

ROTARY PRESSES. Following the development of presses which printed from cylinders and rollers and which used continuous webs of paper, the size and capacity of rotary presses were increased to meet new demands by adding set upon set of printing cylinders. The multiple and the unit rotary presses of today, built to suit the needs and the space requirements of publishers, and speeded up decade by decade to keep up with mounting circulations of newspapers, are almost complete factories for turning out huge editions. Printing, color work, cutting, folding, and counting the output are among the operations performed by these modern machines. Units can be supplied and added in vertical or horizontal tiers to increase the capacity of the plants.

A description of the mechanical processes involved in the publishing of newspapers and magazines is inadequate without a visit to publishing plants. Each machine should be observed firsthand in operation.

---

[1] Reproduced on page 388.

[2] See *Typography and Mechanics of the Newspaper* by Kenneth E. Olson, referred to in the bibliography.

CHAPTER XLV

TERMINOLOGY AND PRESS JARGON

Newspapermen, like other craftsmen, have a language of their own which is quite unintelligible to the outsider. It consists mostly of technical terms of the editorial rooms, the print shop, and the pressroom, with some of the characteristic abbreviations and contractions that have been found useful.—GEORGE C. BASTIAN.*

TECHNICAL TERMS USED BY MOST JOURNALISTS

The journalistic world is colored, as are all specialized fields, with its own peculiar terminology of slang, abbreviations, and technical terms with which the layman is not familiar. The following list includes and defines those terms most widely used:

A.A.A.A. American Association of Advertising Agencies. Referred to as the "4 A's."

A.B.C. Audit Bureau of Circulations.

A.B.P. Associated Business Papers, an organization of trade papers.

ACCOUNT. Advertising-agency terminology for all matters pertaining to a client's advertising.

ACCOUNT EXECUTIVE. Advertising-agency staff member who has charge of accounts.

AD. Advertisement.

ADD. Additional news material to be appended to a story.

AD-SIDE. The part of the composing room where advertisements are set.

ADVANCE. A story concerning a future event.

ADVERTISING PROMOTION. Publisher's efforts to sell advertising, increase it, or make it effective.

ADVERTISING RATES. Set charges for advertising space.

A.F.A. Advertising Federation of America, the senior organization consisting of member divisions representing different advertising activities.

AGATE. Type measuring 5½ points in depth. Newspaper columns and advertisements are measured by agate lines, fourteen of which equal one column inch.

AGONY COLUMN. Column of personal want ads.

ALIBI COPY. News-story duplicates placed in the morgue.

ALLEY. Print-shop aisle.

ALL IN HAND. Copy is said to be "all in hand" when it has been distributed to the compositors.

---

* From *Editing the Day's News* by G. C. Bastian and L. D. Case, p. 265. Copyright 1932. Used by permission of the publishers, The Macmillan Co., New York.

ALL UP. Copy is said to be "all up" when it is all set.

A.M. A newspaper appearing in the morning.

A.N.A. Association of National Advertisers.

ANGLE. Aspect of a news story.

ANGLE BARS. Press devices for turning paper into folder or in new direction.

A.N.P.A. American Newspaper Publishers' Association.

A.P. Associated Press.

ART. Newspaper illustrations.

A.S.C.A.P. American Society of Composers, Authors, and Publishers. A group which protects the copyright rights of its members and collects royalties in their behalf.

ASSIGNMENT. A reporter's designated task.

ASSIGNMENT BOOK. Record of assignments.

ASSIGNMENT MAN. A newsman usable for general commissions.

ASTONISHER. Slang for exclamation point.

BACKING UP. A printer's term to indicate that one side of a sheet has been printed and that its reverse side is now being printed.

BACK OFFICE or BACK ROOM. Mechanical department.

BAD BREAK. Awkward typographical appearance resulting when body type begins a new column or new page with a short line; also when a story ends a column with a paragraph but continues elsewhere.

BALANCE. Headlines of the same length and type face placed on opposite sides of a page and in the same position are considered "balanced."

BALLOON. First used extensively in reference to comics and cartoons. A visual device showing words issuing from a character's mouth.

BANK. Lower section of a headline; a table on which set type is placed.

BANNER or BANNER LINE. A page-wide head in large type.

BARLINE. *See* Crossline.

BASIC WEIGHT. The weight of a ream of paper if cut to the basic or standard size for its class. The basic sizes in inches are: writing papers, 17×22; book papers, 25×38; cover stocks, 20×26.

BASTARD TYPE. Type not conforming to the standard point system.

BEARERS. Strips of metal placed at the sides of a type form for protection during electrotyping. Also, excess metal left on an engraving to protect and strengthen it during the process of electrotyping.

BEAT. A reporter's regular territory for news coverages. Also, a story published solely by one newspaper.

BEN DAY. Term referring to mechanical process for shading line engravings.

B.F. Bold or black-faced type. *See* Bold Face.

BINDER LINE. One line of large type, on an inside page, over an especially lengthy story or a number of stories on one general topic.

BITE. Used in engraving to indicate the etching action of acid on metal. A deep bite gives a sharper engraving reproduction than does a shallow bite.

BLANKET HEAD. A headline across all the columns above a story or department.

BLEED. A cut is said to "bleed" when it runs to the edge of the page. To "bleed" a cut is a common artistic device in magazines.

BLIND INTERVIEW. An interview which does not reveal the name of the interviewed person—e.g., "a government spokesman said."

BLIND QUERY. A query not giving definite information. *See* Query.

BLOTTER. Records of arrests made by police.

BLOWUP. An enlargement—e.g., of an advertisement for display purposes.

BLUEPRINT. A quick, low-priced photographic print, in white on dark blue background. (Not infrequently used by an advertiser to prepare type layout while the engraving is still being made, as it can be available several hours before the completion of a plate.)

BLURB. A short description of a book; a story, or an article designed to advertise it.

BODY TYPE. Type in which the major part of a publication is set. Contrasts with display type.

BOIL DOWN. To shorten a story.

BOILER PLATE. Syndicate materials in metal-plate form.

BOLD FACE. Bold or black-faced type, as agate B.F., or minion B.F.

B.O. MUST. "Business-office must" notation signifying that an item must be printed.

BORDER. Type-metal strips used to box a story or head.

BOX. Type bordered by rules.

BOX HEAD. A headline enclosed by a border.

BOX STORY. A story enclosed in a box.

BREAK. The point at which a story goes from one page or one column to another. A story "breaks" when it is available for publication.

BREAKOVER. *See* Jump.

BROMIDE. A trite expression; a stereotype.

BUG. A type ornament, now out of style, used in a headline or beside a cut.

BULLDOG. Early edition.

BULLETIN. Significant last-minute news.

BULLPUP. First mail edition of Sunday newspapers.

BUREAU. News-gathering body organized in a center of importance.

BURNISHING. A process of smudging the dots in a halftone to make them darker.

BY-LINE. Signature above a story.

BY-LINE STORY. A signed story.

CABLESE. Abbreviations and codes used in cable copy.

C. AND L.C. Capital and lower-case letters.

CANNED COPY. Material received from publicity offices or press agents.

CAPS. Contraction for "capitals."

CAPTION. Explanation of a photograph, illustration, or diagram.

CARRIER. Person who delivers papers.

CASE. Cabinet of type where printer works.

CASTING OFF. Estimating the amount of space a piece of copy will occupy when set in any given size of type.

CATCH LINE. *Same as* Guideline.

C.C.A. Controlled Circulation Audit Bureau, Inc.

CENTER SPREAD. *Same as* Double Truck.

C.G.O. "Can go over," meaning that the story is such that it can be printed at any time.

CHASE. Metal frame used for holding, in page form, type and cuts ready for printing.

CHECKING COPY. A copy of a newspaper or magazine submitted to an advertiser so that he may check his own advertisement.

CHECK UP. To verify information.

CHEESECAKE. Slang for pictures in which feminine legs are generously revealed.

CIRCULATION PROMOTION. Publisher's efforts to increase or maintain circulation.

CIRCUS MAKE-UP. The use of many headlines of various sizes and many kinds of type to create a bizarre effect.

CITY EDITOR. Head of a local newsroom.

CITY ROOM. Workshop for handling local news.

CLASSIFIED ADVERTISING or WANT ADS. Advertising appearing under classified headings, such as "For Rent," "Help Wanted," etc.

CLEAN COPY. Copy needing little or no revision.

CLEAN PROOF. Proof with few errors.

CLIPS. Clippings from newspapers or morgue files.

CLIPSHEET. Publicity prepared in sheet form for easy use.

CLUBBING OFFER. An arrangement whereby subscriptions to two or more different publications are offered at a reduced combination price.

COARSE-SCREEN HALFTONE. A halftone with a comparatively low, or coarse, screen.

COL. Column.

COLOROTO. Colored rotogravure.

COLUMN. A department regularly published. Also a row of type.

COLUMN INCH. Measure by which advertising is sold, one inch in length and two and one-sixth inches in width.

COLUMN RULE. A thin metal plate, which is type high and is used to divide one column from another.

COMBINATION PLATE. The joining of halftone and line plate in one engraving.

COMPOSING ROOM. Department where type is set.

COMPOSITE STORY. A story containing numerous angles.

COMPOSITION. Operations incident to preparation of forms for press.

COMPOSITOR. Person who sets type.

COMPOSOGRAPH. Picture of the face of one person pasted on the picture or the body of another person.

CONDENSED TYPE. Type which is narrower than standard width; other widths include standard, extended, and extra-condensed.

CONTRAST. Placement of different style headings in such a way as to bring out each to the best advantage.

COPY. Matter to be printed; that is, news manuscript, advertising text, pictures or illustrations.

COPY BOY. Boy who carries copy or performs errands in an editorial room.

COPYCUTTER. Employee of the composing room who cuts up manuscript for rapid setting and who distributes copy among typesetters.

COPY DESK. Desk where copy is edited and headlined.

COPY EDITOR. *See* Copyreader.

COPYHOLDER. Proofroom employee who reads aloud to the proofreader from manuscript.

COPYREADER. Newsroom employee who reads, edits, and headlines manuscript.

COPY WRITER. A person who writes advertising copy.

CORRESPONDENT. Out-of-town reporter.

COVER. In magazines, the front cover of a publication is known as the "first cover"; the inside of the front cover is the "second cover"; the inside of the back cover is the "third cover"; the outside of the back cover is the "fourth cover." The verb "to cover" means to get the facts or be responsible for a story.

COVERAGE. Covering or completing a story. Also, approaching the saturation point in circulation.

CREDIT LINE. Line acknowledging the source of a story or cut.

CROSSBARS. Press device to guide or turn print paper.

CROSSLINE. Portion of a headline differentiated from the top and banks.

CRUSADE. A newspaper campaign for reform or improvement.

CUB. An unseasoned reporter.

CUT. A newspaper engraving. "To cut" is to shorten a story.

CUT-IN LETTER. A large initial letter which begins a paragraph and protrudes above the usual type line.

CUTLINE. Caption for a cut.

CUTOFF. A rule across a column or columns to separate one part of the page from the rest of it.

DASHES. Short lines which separate parts of a headline, headlines and stories, and stories from each other. Normally, dashes separating parts of a headline are short and those separating stories somewhat longer.

DATE LINE. Place of origin and date put at the beginning of nonlocal news. Also, the top line of a page giving the publication date.

DAY SIDE. The newspaper personnel working during the daytime.

DEAD. News material, especially type, that is no longer usable.

DEAD BANK. Composing-room rack for holding type no longer available for use.

DEADLINE. The time when a story must be completed or an edition go to press.

DEAL. The copy-desk head distributes or "deals" copy to copyreaders.

DECK. Part of a headline.

DEPTH OF COLUMNS. The number of inches or agate lines in a column measured from top to bottom.

DESK. The copy desk, where stories are edited and headlined.

DESK EDITOR. Editor having charge of assignments for reporters.

DINGBAT. Headline or cut ornament. Also, a boxed story.

DINKY DASH. A special dash used as a substitute for subheads or as a separation between short items.

DIRECT HALFTONE. A halftone made by photographing an object itself instead of a picture of it.

DIRTY COPY. Copy containing many corrections.

DISPLAY TYPE. Large, prominent, or ornamental type used to make headlines or advertisements conspicuous.

DISTRICT MAN. A reporter assigned to a particular district.

DOGWATCH. *Same as* Lobster Shift or Trick.

DOPE. Advance news information, frequently rumor.

DOPE STORY. A story, commonly by-lined, explaining a situation and giving the opinions of others as well as those of the writer.

DOUBLE LEADING. Spacing out a story in type by placing two thin strips of metal between the Linotype slugs.

DOUBLET. Material set twice and repeated in the same paper.

DOUBLE TRUCK. An editorial or advertising layout covering two pages and made up as a single unit.

DOWN STYLE. Use of small or lower-case initial letters in words whose first letters are often capitalized; minimum use of capital letters.

DRESS. Make-up of paper, involving styles and sizes of type and headlines.

DROP HEAD. A headline which accompanies a streamer.

DROP LINES. Lines that are stepped; for instance, if the first line is indented two spaces, the second is indented four spaces, the third, six, etc.

DUMMY. Diagram showing the layout of a page.

DUMP. To place type in galleys.

DUOTONE. Two-color illustration.

DUPE. Inadvertent repetition of a news item. Also, carbon copies of a story.

EARS. Small boxes appearing in the upper corners of any page.

E.D. Advertiser's instruction, meaning "run every day."

EDITION. Newspaper copies printed during one press run, such as "Mail," "Home," "Final."

EDITORIALIZE. To include opinion in a news story or headline.

ELECTROTYPE. A facsimile plate for printing, made by electroplating a wax impression; also, a print from such a plate.

EM. A measure of type width corresponding to the point size of the type in use; e.g., in 6 point an em is six points. It is the square of any given size of type.

EN. One-half em.

ETAOINSHRDLU. An unusable line of type made by a typesetter's running his fingers down a row of keys on a typesetting machine.

EXCHANGES. Copies of other newspapers received on an exchange basis.

EXCLUSIVE. A story published by only one newspaper.

EXTRA. A newspaper edition other than a regular one.

FACE. The printing surface of type or of a plate.

FAKE. A fraudulent, invented story.

FAT HEAD or FAT LINE. A headline or line which is too large for the space available for it. *See also* Phat.

FEATURE. A story which, though timely and interesting, is not exactly news. Also, the significant fact of a story. "To feature" a story is to give prominence to it.

FILE. To dispatch a story by cable or telegraph.

FILE A STORY OVERHEAD. To send a story by wire.

FILLER. Material that can be used at any time or to fill space.

FINGERNAILS. Slang for parentheses.

FIRST-DAY STORY. A current story; one published for the first time.

FIVE W'S. Who? What? When? Where? Why?

FLAG. The newspaper title appearing on the first page. Also, a lead sticking up in type as a warning to the printer that correction or addition is to be made.

FLASH. A message giving the first brief news of an event.

FLAT PROOFS. Rough proofs, or stone proofs, taken of type when it is on the compositor's workbench; in contrast to "press proofs," the latter made after the type has been adjusted to give a finished impression.

FLAT RATE. In advertising, a uniform charge for space in a medium, without regard to the amount of space used or the frequency of insertion. (When flat rates do not prevail, time discounts or quantity discounts are available.)

FLIMSY. Thin carbon copy of a manuscript.

FLOP. When an illustration is reversed in an engraving, it is said to be "flopped."

FLUSH AND HANG. First line set even with left margin and subsequent lines indented one em or more.

FLUSH AND INDENT. *Same as* Flush and Hang.

FLUSH HEAD. A headline with lines set flush to the left but ending raggedly at the right.

FOLD. Place where the half-fold is made in a newspaper.

FOLIO. A page; a page number.

FOLLOW or FOLLOW-UP. A story giving later developments of one printed earlier.

FOLLOW COPY. Instruction to compositor to set the copy precisely as it is written.

FOLLOWING, or NEXT TO, READING MATTER. In advertising, the specification of a position for an advertisement to appear in a publication. Sometimes known as "full position"—a preferred position usually costing more than run-of-paper position.

FOLO. Follow; instruction to reporter to obtain new developments of a story.

FONT. A complete assortment of type of one style and size.

FOOTSTICK. The bottom heavy metal bar of a chase used in locking it.

FOREIGN ADVERTISING. Advertising of an organization which is outside the city where the newspaper is published.

FORM. A page of type locked in a chase and ready for the press.

FORMAT. The size, shape, style, and appearance of a book or publication.

FORMS CLOSE. The deadline date on which all copy and plates must be available.

FOTOG. Photographer.

FOUNDRY PROOFS. The proofs of a typographical setup just before the material is sent to the foundry for electrotyping; identified by the heavy funeral-black border (the foundry rules).

FREE LANCE. Writer or artist not attached to any publication or organization.

FRONT OFFICE. The office of the publisher, the editor, or the business manager—any one, or all three.

FUDGE COLUMN. A first-page column for last-minute news.

FULL POSITION. A preferred position of an advertisement in a newspaper. *See* Following, or Next To, Reading Matter.

FURNITURE. Wood or metal pieces, less high than type, used for packing type in order that a form may be locked.

FUTURE. Memorandum of a future event.

F.Y.I. For your information.

GALLEY. An oblong metal tray for holding type; approximately a newspaper column, or twenty inches, of type.

GALLEY PROOF. An imprint of type on a strip of paper made while the type is being held in the galley for corrections.

GHOST WRITER. An unknown writer who produces copy to be signed by persons of prominence.

GIVE-AWAYS. Premiums which are given away.

GOODNIGHT. Closing of the news division after the final edition.

GRAPEVINE. Set copy which may be used at any time as filler.

GREEN PROOF. Uncorrected proof.

GUIDELINE. A word or words placed at the top of copy to identify it; slug line.

HACK. A writer available for hire for any sort of writing.

HAIRLINE BOXES. Thin-line boxes.

HALF STICK. Type set in half-column width.

HALFTONE. A picture that is photographed on metal through a screen and chemically or electrolytically etched.

HAND COMPOSITION. Type set up by hand in contrast to type set up by machine.

HAND LETTERING. Any lettering that is drawn by hand—e.g., in a name plate —as distinguished from type regularly set.

HANDOUT. Statement prepared for publication.

HAND-SET. Type set by hand.

HAND TOOLING. Handwork on an engraving or plate to improve its reproducing qualities.

HANGER. Headline which appears below banner head and belongs to the same story.

HANGING INDENT. Type set with the first line flush and with the remainder indented at the left.

HEAD. Short for headline. Also, the headings of several news stories.

HEAD OF DESK. Employee having charge of copy desk.

HELLBOX. Container for discarded type and furniture.

HIGH LEADS. Leads which stick up in the columns and print undesirably.

HIGH LINES. Lines of irregular depth resulting from a faulty Linotype.

HOLD FOR RELEASE. Instruction placed upon copy to be set, but not printed until the editor in charge so orders.

HOLDING. "Holding" a paper is delaying the deadline for a news story of importance.

HOLD PRESSES. If important news breaks, the presses are held until such news can be set in type and included in the paper.

HOLE. Vacancy on a page.

HOME PRINT. Material set and printed in a newspaper's own shop.

HOT NEWS. Up-to-the-minute and important news.

H.T.C. or H.T.K. "Head to come," used when a story is rushed to the composing room before the head is written.

HUMAN INTEREST. A story or phase of the news appealing emotionally.

INDENT. Instruction to compositor to start a line a specified distance in from the margin.

INDEX. A listing of the day's news, usually on the first page.

INITIAL LETTER. The first letter in a piece of copy, set in a size of type larger than that of the rest of the copy.

I.N.S. International News Service.

INSERT. New copy to be incorporated in a story that has gone to the composing room.

INTAGLIO PRINTING. Printing from the depressed surface of a copper or steel plate. Rotogravure is a form of intaglio printing.

INTERTYPE. Trade name for typesetting machine.

INTERVIEW. A conference for the purpose of obtaining news.

INVERTED PYRAMID. A head in which each successive line is shorter than the preceding one and is centered in the column.

ISLAND POSITION. Position of an advertisement, in a newspaper, which is entirely surrounded by reading matter.

ITALS. Italics.

JOB PRESS. A press which prints pages up to 25 × 38 inches. Often used by a small publication and for "job printing."

JOB PROMOTION. Effort to promote new job-printing business.

JOB TICKET. A sheet or an envelope which accompanies a printing job through the various departments, bearing all the instructions and all records showing the progress of the work.

JUMP. The carrying of a story from one page to another.

JUMP HEAD. A headline identifying a continued story.

JUMP LINES. Lines indicating continuation of a story from one page to another.

JUSTIFYING or JUSTIFICATION. Spacing out a line to fill a column or type to fill a form.

KEEP STANDING. Instruction to printer to hold type for possible additional use after it has been used.

KEYING AN ADVERTISEMENT. Giving an advertisement a code number or letter so that when people respond, the source of the inquiry can be traced. May be a variation in the address, or a letter or number printed in the corner of a return coupon.

KILL. To exclude from copy; to destroy a story in type.

LABEL or LABEL HEAD. A colorless headline.

LAMPPOST INTERVIEW. *Same as* Blind Interview.

LATE WATCH. The reduced staff which stays to handle late stories and late editions after the greater part of the editing and printing is complete and most of the staff has been released. The late watch on a morning paper is from one o'clock to four o'clock.

LAYOUT. A sheet ruled into columns representing a page on which the positions of stories or of stories and advertisements are indicated.

L.C. Lower-case or small letters as distinguished from capital letters.

LEAD. (Pronounced *leed*.) The introduction (sentence or paragraph) of a news story; the chief story of the day; a hint which may lead to a story.

LEAD. (Pronounced *led*.) Thin metal pieces for spacing out lines of type; "to lead" is to space out.

LEAD ALL. A lead that replaces all previous leads of a news story.

LEADERS or LEADERS OUT. Instruction to printer to run a row of dots to the matter at the end of the line.

LEG MAN or LEGGER. One who gathers news but does not write it.

LETTERPRESS PRINTING. Printing from a raised or relief surface.

LIBEL. A false or defamatory presentation.

LIBRARY. Files of newspaper clippings and other reference material.

LINE. A unit of measuring space, $\frac{1}{14}$ of a column inch.

LINE ENGRAVING. A photoengraving made without photographing it through a screen.

LINE OVER THE TOP. A banner or streamer at the top of page one above the newspaper's name plate.

LINO. Linotype, a machine for setting type.

LOBSTER SHIFT or TRICK. The late watch; on an evening paper, the early watch.

LOCAL. News story occurring in the territory covered by the paper.

LOCAL ADVERTISING. Advertising of a local organization—that is, one within the city where the newspaper is published.

LOCAL ITEMS. Short stories about local people and events.

LOCALIZE. To emphasize a story's local aspects.

LOCAL NEWSROOM. The working quarters of the city news staff.

LOCKING UP. Tightening up the type matter put into a chase (an iron frame used by printers) preparatory to going to press.

LOG. Book of assignments.

LOGOTYPE. A single type which contains two or more letters; a small reproduction of a name plate or signature.

LUDLOW. A machine which casts slugs from hand-set matrices.

MAGAZINE. Section of a Linotype machine containing matrices.

MAKE OVER. To rearrange a page or pages of type to accommodate new stories or to better the appearance.

MAKE-READY. Getting a job (forms which have been set) ready for printing.

MAKE-UP. The placement of stories, pictures, and advertisements on a page.

MAKE-UP EDITOR. Editor, often called the "news" or "night" editor, who plans the make-up.

MAKE-UP MAN. Printer having charge of assembling one or more pages.

MARKETS. Section for financial, grain, livestock, and produce market news.

MASTHEAD. The editorial-page heading that supplies information about the newspaper. Such information includes the publishing company, some officers thereof, the names of some of the officials of the publication, place of business and editorial offices, subscription rates and similar ownership, editorship, and distribution facts.

MAT. Matrix; the papier-mâché mold of a page of type used for making a stereotype plate; the Linotype brass mold for casting type.

M.E. Abbreviation for managing editor.

MERG. Abbreviation for Mergenthaler, inventor of the Linotype machine; a Linotype machine.

MILL. Reporter's typewriter.

MILLINE. An agate line of advertising appearing in one million copies of a publication.

MILLINE RATE. Advertising charge per agate line per million copies circulated.

MINION. Seven-point type.

MISCELLANY. Plate matter consisting of filler material.

MONOTYPE. A machine which casts a single character at a time rather than a full line of type as does a Linotype machine.

MORE. Word written at the end of each page of copy, except the last, as an indication that more material follows.

MORGUE. A reference file of newspaper clippings and other useful information.

MORTISE. Section of a photoengraving which is cut away and into which type can be inserted.

MUST. Instruction on copy meaning that it must be printed without fail.

NAME PLATE. Newspaper's name as carried on page one.

NEWSHAWK. A reporter.

NEWSROOM. Place where all the news is handled.

NEWS SUMMARY. Summary of the day's news, usually on the first page.

NEXT TO READING MATTER or N.R. The location of an advertisement immediately adjacent to reading matter.

NICKELTYPE. A nickel-faced electrotype; more durable than one of copper.

NIGHT SIDE. The division of the staff that works at night.

NONPAREIL. Six-point type; a measurement of type widths.

NOSE FOR NEWS. Aptness in sensing news.

OBIT. Obituary; general biographical information, not necessarily pertaining to a deceased person.

OFF REGISTER. A plate which fails to register in the right position is said to be "off register."

OFFSET. Process of photographing copy and transferring the negative to a zinc plate for printing from an inked rubber roller.

OFF THE RECORD. Not to be printed.

ON SPECULATION. In advertising—an offer to create an idea which is to be paid for if used, but which is not to be paid for if not used.

O.S. Old-style type.

OUTLINED CUT. A halftone with the background cut away.

OVERLINE. Caption appearing over a cut.

OVERNIGHT. An assignment for the following day.

OVERRUN. The number of pieces of matter printed in excess of the specified quantity.

OVERS or OVERSET. Type set in excess of that needed to fill the paper.

PAD. To elaborate and include more details than those necessary to make the story clear.

PAGE OPP. Page opposite, meaning page opposite the editorial page.

PAGE PROOF. Proof of the whole page.

PATENT INSIDES. Metal plates bought from syndicates and service agencies and ready to use as inside pages.

PERSONAL. A brief news item concerning one or more persons.

PHAT or FAT. To hold type for possible repetition is "to phat" it. A "fat take" or "page" is one of many cuts or other matter not requiring setting. "Fat type" is extended type; and a "fat line" is one that cannot be set in the space available.

PHOTOENGRAVING. A picture photographed on metal and chemically or electrolytically etched. *See* Halftone; Zinc.

PHOTOSTAT. A photographic reproduction.

PI. Mixed and disordered type which cannot be used.

PICA. Twelve-point type (⅙ inch high).

PICKUP. Standing type that is to be included with new copy; an instruction to the composing room to include such type with that which is being set.

PIED. Said of type that is in disorder and unusable.

PIG IRON. Copy that is heavy, serious.

PIX. Pictures.

PLANER. Printer's wooden block used to even the type surface of a form ready for locking.

PLATE. A page of type which is cast in metal and is ready for locking on the press; a reproduction used in printing.

PLAY UP. To display a story prominently.

PLEASE USE. Instruction to use the copy if possible.

P.M. A newspaper appearing in the afternoon.

POINT. Measurement for type sizes, a point being 1/72 of an inch.

POLICE BLOTTER. Police record from which reporter secures news.

POLICY. A newspaper's stand on a public issue.

POLICY STORY. Story designed to serve the policy of the publisher.

PONY SERVICE. A brief telephone report from a press association's central bureau of the important news of the day.

PORK. Reprint or Time Copy.

POSTSCRIPT. A page rearranged between editions for corrections or the accommodation of new and important stories.

P.P.A. Periodical Publishers' Association.

PRECEDE. Material that is to precede a news story.

PREDATE. To date in advance of publication time.

PRESS AGENT. Publicity person employed by private interest.

PRESS ASSOCIATION. An organization for gathering news for distribution to many papers.

PRESS RUN. Total number of printed sheets.

PRINTERS. Employees of the composing room who correct type and assemble it in the chases as directed.

PRINTER'S DEVIL. Printer's apprentice.

PROGRESSIVE PROOF. Series of proofs from the various plates in a color-plate process.

PROOF. An imprint of type on paper taken so that errors may be corrected.

PROOFREADER. One who corrects proof against the copy.

PUFF. Publicity story that is personal.

PULL IN. Printing matter without waiting for proofroom corrections.

PULLING A PROOF. Obtaining an impression of type.

PUNCH. A vigorous, snappy quality in words, stories, and headlines.

PUT TO BED. To lock up the forms in preparation for printing an edition.

Q. AND A. MATTER. "Question and answer" material, testimony often being printed verbatim.

QUAD. A blank space or type character with a width equaling its height.

QUERY. Correspondent's written or telegraphic synopsis, indicating existence and nature of a story. On the basis of the summary the news executive designates the number of words desired.

QUOIN. Device used for locking type in a form.

QUOTE. Quotation.

RACK. Cabinet containing galleys of type.

RAILROAD. To rush copy in an emergency to the composing room without careful editing.

READY PRINT. Newsprint paper printed on one side with syndicated material.

RELEASE. An instruction to print a story set earlier and held for later disposition.

RELEASE COPY. Copy to be published at a specified time.

REPLATE. Postscript.

REPRINT. Material printed first in late editions which is thus usable in the following issue of the early editions.

REVISE. Proof taken after type has been corrected.

REWRITE. To write a story again in order to improve, lengthen, or shorten it.

REWRITE MAN. One who writes stories from facts taken over the telephone; one who revises other reporters' copy or clipped stories.

RIBBON. A headline stretching across the top of a page beneath a streamer set in larger type.

RIM. The outer edge of the desk, usually in the shape of a horseshoe, where copy is edited and copy editors sit.

RING. To draw a ring around a symbol or word in manuscript indicates spelling out or abbreviating.

RING BANK. Composing-room stands where type is corrected.

RING MACHINE. Linotype machine devoted to making type corrections.

RING MAN. Printer correcting type.

RIPPED OPEN. If important news comes in after the paper is already in press the front page must be "ripped open" to permit inclusion of the story.

ROTARY PRESS. A press which prints from curved plates.

Roto. Rotogravure or printing process in which an impression is made from a copper cylinder on which an etching has been made.

Rule. A metal strip which is the height of the type and prints as a line. "Column rules" make the printed lines separating the columns of a paper.

Rule For Insert or For Pickup. Instruction to printer to turn a type rule to indicate the place for an insert in the body of a story or to show that type already set is to be incorporated in the story.

Run. A reporter's regular territory. "To run" a story is to print a story.

Run-Around. Type to be set around a cut of odd measure.

Run Flat. To set the manuscript without revision.

Run In. To make into one paragraph a series of paragraphs or names. Also, to combine sentences.

Running Story. A news story that continues over a period of time; a story sent to the composing room in sections.

Rush. Instruction on copy to insure rapid handling in the composing room.

Sacred Cow. Slang for material of interest to the publisher or superior editors which must be printed.

Schedule. A list of assignments kept by the city editor; a list of stories edited and headed by a copy editor; a dummy page.

Scoop. An exclusive story printed by only one paper.

Second Day. Story developing out of one printed previously.

Second Front. The first page of a newspaper's second section.

Sectional Story. A big news story with different aspects appearing under two or more separate headings; a story sent in takes to the printer.

See Copy. Order to the composing room to consult copy and verify.

Set and Hold. Instruction to set type and hold it for release.

Set Flush. Instruction to set without paragraph indentation or margin.

Shank. Main body of a type unit.

Sheet. Vernacular for newspaper.

Shorts. Relatively unimportant brief stories.

Shoulder. Top surface of type upon which the character is made.

Shouts. Exclamation points.

Sit-In Man. Substitute for head of the copy desk.

Sked. Schedule.

Skeletonize. To frame a cabled story so as to omit unimportant words. Code words are frequently used.

Slant. Emphasis placed on a particular aspect of a policy or other story.

Sleuth. Term for reporter specializing in stories involving extensive investigations.

Slip-Sheeting. Where a sheet of tissue, or cheap porous stock, paper is placed so as to prevent the sheets of a printing job from offsetting or smudging as they come from the press.

Slot. Position where the copy-desk editor sits.

Slotman. Copy-desk head who sits within the slot of the horseshoe-shaped copy desk.

Slug. Notation placed on copy to identify the story; a guideline in type; a Linotype line.

SLUG LINE. Same as Guide Line.

SMALL CAPS. Small capital letters.

SMASH. A sensational story which dominates a page.

SOB-SISTER. Reporter who writes sob stories.

SOB STUFF. Stories that are sentimental and designed to appeal to the sympathy of the reader.

Soc. Society; used to indicate copy for society columns.

SOLID. Type set without leads separating the lines.

SPACE. Blank type unit for spacing between words. Also, commodity that is bought by an advertiser and sold by a publisher for advertising display purposes.

SPIKE or HOOK. To reject copy by "spiking" it.

SPLIT PAGE. First page of second section.

SPOT NEWS. Unexpected, live, important news.

SPREAD. A chief story and its auxiliary stories; a story requiring a head at the top of a column; also used at times to indicate the head itself.

SQUIB. A brief news item.

STANDING ADS, HEADS, or TABLES. Type kept on hand for repetition.

STANDING BOXES. Type boxes which are kept as framework for future use.

STAR EDITION. Refers to order of editions—"one-star" being the first, "two-star" being the second, "four-" or "five-star" being the final edition.

STEAM TABLE. Mechanical device at which matrices of page forms are made.

STEP LINES. See Drop Lines.

STET. Let it stand.

STICK. A measuring unit for type equaling two inches; a typeholder.

STICK-UP INITIAL. See Cut-In Letter.

STONE. A stone- or metal-topped bench or table upon which a page is assembled.

STORY. An article written by a reporter.

STRAIGHT NEWS. An unembellished account of news facts.

STREAMER. Same as Banner.

STREET JOB. The reporter's job of gathering news.

STRING. Newspaper clippings pasted together in a strip or scrapbook.

STUFF. Raw news material.

STYLEBOOK or STYLE SHEET. Rules of style governing a paper.

SUBHEAD. A line of type differing from body type and used to break up a long story.

SUMMARY. A brief statement of a news story.

SUMMARY LEAD. A lead incorporating answers to the five W's.

SUNRISE WATCH. Lobster Shift or Trick.

SUSPENDED INTEREST. A story whose feature or climax appears near the end.

SYNDICATE. An association which, in conjunction with or apart from a newspaper, buys or sells news stories, features, and other material for newspaper use.

TABLE. Tabulated statement.

TABLOID. A small-sized newspaper (generally half the size of a seven-column newspaper), which is usually illustrated.

TAKE. A section of a story sent to the composing room by the copy editor or given to an operator by the copycutter.

TELEGRAPHIC NEWS. Stories received by telegraph.

TELEPHOTO. Photograph received by wire.

T.F. (1) "Till forbid." (2) "To fill." (3) Copy is "to follow."

THIN LINE. A line too scant for the space allotted for it.

THIRD STICK. Instruction for setting type one-third of a column wide.

THIRTY. The end.

TIE-BACK or TIE-IN. Inclusion of previously printed information in a later story to refresh the reader's mind.

TIGHT PAPER. A paper so filled with advertisements that a reduction of news space is necessary.

TIME COPY. Copy held for later use after it has been set.

TIP. Information suggesting a news story.

TITLE LINE. By-line.

TOENAILS. Parentheses.

TOMBSTONE. Effect produced when two headlines in capital letters and the same size and kind of type appear side by side giving the effect of one head instead of two.

TOP HEADS. Top-column headlines.

TOP LINES. Lines of type which form the top of a headline.

TR. Transpose.

TRIM. To shorten a story.

TURN. A story running from the bottom of the last (right-hand) column of the first page to the top of the second-page first column is said "to turn."

TURN RULE. Instruction for printer to turn up the broad edge of a rule, thus indicating a place for correction. A rule has both a broad and a thin edge. The common position of the metal strip is with the thin edge up.

TURN STORY. A story running from the first-page last (right-hand) column to the second-page first column and requiring no jump head.

TWO-LINE INITIAL, TWO-LINE FIGURE. Initial and figure two lines in depth.

TYPE HIGH. Printing height, .918 inch.

TYPO. Typographical mistake.

U. AND L.C. Upper and lower case.

U-DESK. Copy desk in the shape of a horseshoe.

UNDERLINE. Explanation under a cut.

UNDERSET. A paper is said to be underset when there is an insufficient amount of matter set in type.

UNQUOTE. Indication of the end of a direct quotation.

U.P. United Press.

UP STYLE. Opposite of Down Style, in that initial letters of words are capitalized.

VERSE STYLE. Instruction to set in the manner of poetry.

VIGNETTE. *See* Outlined Cut.

WHEN ROOM. Story may be used at any time.

WHIFF. Publicity of small news value.

WIDE-OPEN PAPER. The opposite of a Tight Paper.

WIDOW. A short word or part of a word which stands alone on the last line of a paragraph of body type.

WIREPHOTO. Trade name for a newsphoto transferred by telephone wires.

WOODEN HEAD. Meaningless headline.

WRONG FACE or WRONG FONT. Type differing in style or size from that specified.

YELLOW or YELLOW JOURNALISM. Sensational.

ZERO HOUR. Last minute for receiving news before the paper goes to press.

ZINC. Zinc etching or photoengraving made without photographing it through a screen.

TECHNICAL TERMS PECULIAR TO RADIO JOURNALISM

The coming of radio journalism has brought with it additional technical jargon which is used by journalists in this field. The following list includes and defines the more generally useful of these new additions to the vocabulary of practicing journalists.

AD LIB. To extemporize lines or music not included in the script, or in the score.

ALLOCATION. The assignment of frequency and power to a broadcasting station by the Federal Communications Commission.

ANNOUNCEMENTS. Short commercial statements interspersed between programs on the air.

ANNOUNCER. Radio-station staff member assigned to be master of ceremonies to the radio audience.

AUDITION. An over the mike test of prospective artists or musicians.

BACKGROUND. Sound effect used behind program elements.

BRIDGE. Sound effects or music used to indicate transition from one scene to another.

BROADCASTING. Distribution of sound programs by means of radio-telephone transmission.

BROADCAST SPECTRUM. That part of the range of electromagnetic wave frequencies used by broadcasting stations.

C.A.B. RATING. Co-operative Analysis of Broadcasting Rating. Purports to show the comparative popularity of certain sponsored radio programs. It is called *Crossley Rating.*

CALL LETTERS. A combination of assigned letters which serves as the official designation for a radio station, such as WINX, WJZ, KFI.

CHAINS. An established system of interconnected broadcasting stations.

CLASS A (CLASS B) RATES. Rates for radio time depending upon the hour of the day that the time is used.

CLEAR-CHANNEL STATION. A station that is allowed the maximum power and is given a channel on a frequency band of its own.

COMMERCIAL PROGRAM. A sponsored radio program providing broadcasting stations revenue.

CONTINUITY. Written action script, including lines, music, sound effects, commercials, and cues.

COVERAGE MAP. A map giving the territory regularly covered by a radio station—sometimes divided into "primary coverage" and "secondary coverage."

CROSSLEY RATING. *See* C.A.B. Rating.

CUE. A phrase designating the transfer of the point of program origin; or, as in network identification, a statement such as, "This is the National Broadcasting Company" to serve as a signal for the switching of channels. Also, the last few words of an actor's speech which serves as a signal for another actor to enter, or a musical or other sound, or a manual, action signal.

CUT. Deletion of material to fit a prescribed period of program time, or stopping the transmission of a program abruptly.

DEFINITION. Clean-cut transmission and reception, providing identification of musical or other sounds.

DISC JOCKEY. Master of ceremonies for a sponsored program of transcriptions.

DUBBING. The playing on a transcription of a program from another transcription.

FADING. The variation in the intensity of a radio signal from a distance.

FADING AREA. The area in which a broadcasting station suffers from the greatest variation in fading.

F.C.C. Federal Communications Commission.

FILM TRANSMISSION. Transmission by means of television.

F.M. Frequency modulation.

FREQUENCY. The frequency of broadcasting stations is defined in kilocycles or thousands of alternations per second.

GROUP DISCOUNT. A discount in station rates when certain groups of stations are used by an advertiser.

HOOPERATING. The relative rating of any given radio program for listener appeal as shown by the Hooper method of program grading.

HOUR. A scheduled radio feature—ordinarily refers to sixty-minute programs, but may refer to shorter periods.

ICONOSCOPE. Television camera which picks up the image to be sent.

INTERFERENCE. An extraneous electrical noise or program interfering with the receipt of a desired program.

LIMITED-TIME STATION. A station which shares its channel with other stations.

LIVE. A broadcast by actual speakers and musicians rather than a transcribed or recorded broadcast.

LOCAL-CHANNEL STATION. A station only permitted enough power to be heard near its point of transmission.

LOG. An accurate journal record of broadcasting which is required by law.

M.C. Master of ceremonies.

MICROPHONE. An instrument used in broadcasting for "picking up" programs.

NETWORK. A permanent setup of wire telephone lines interconnecting radio broadcasting stations to provide simultaneous distribution of radio programs.

ORIGINATION POINT. The actual place at which the artist performs.

PARTICIPATION SHOW. A show conducted by a station which provides a number of advertisers an opportunity to have their products featured.

PICTURE RESOLUTION. The clarity with which the image appears on the television screen.

PRIMARY SERVICE AREA. The primary broadcasting-station area served—that is, the area where sufficient volume exists to override noise levels both day and night.

PRODUCER. The individual or the broadcasting company that presents a program.

PRODUCTION. The development, organization, and presentation of a radio program.

PROGRAM FOLLOWING. The radio program which follows any given program.

PROGRAM OPPOSITE. The radio program on other stations at the same time and reaching the same territory.

PROGRAM PRECEDING. The program which is on directly before any given program.

REBROADCAST. A radio program repeated at a later time—it may be either live or transcribed.

RECORDED PROGRAM. Any radio program consisting entirely of phonograph records or electrical transcriptions.

REGIONAL-CHANNEL STATION. A station that has more power than a local station but less than a clear-channel station.

REMOTE CONTROL. The operation of a radio program at a place other than the regular studios of the station.

SCRIPT SHOW. A serial program (often fifteen minutes) on the air several times a week at the same hour and station.

SEGUE. Translated from the Italian meaning "it follows." Used to describe the transition from one musical number to another without a break or announcements.

SIGNATURE. The musical number or sound effect which is used to identify a radio program.

SOUND EFFECTS. Devices or recordings used to produce lifelike imitations of sound; e.g., ocean waves, auto horns, shutting and opening of doors, crackling fire.

SPLIT CHANNEL. Two or more network sections working simultaneously with different programs.

SPONSOR. The individual or company that pays for talent and broadcasting station time for a radio feature.

SPOT BROADCAST. A program issued directly from a station for a national advertiser.

STATION ANNOUNCEMENT. The identification announcement.

STUDIO. A room provided with acoustic treatment, microphones and associated equipment, signaling lights, and other necessaries for broadcasting purposes.

SUSTAINING PROGRAM. Program of any type produced as a service feature by a broadcasting station or network—frequently has an educational appeal.

TELECAST. A sound and pictorial image sent by television.

TELEVISION. The method of broadcasting sound and pictorial effects.

TRANSCRIPTION PROGRAM LIBRARY. A collection of transcription records—various standard transcription libraries exist and an advertiser may select by numbers from the library.

VISUAL SHOW. A radio program which is also given before a studio audience.

APPENDIX

A MODEL STYLE GUIDE *

This guide is of average length. It could be followed by a publication which does not wish to be either ultramodern or ultraconservative. It includes the principal divisions offered in typical style books and sheets and is to be considered a set of instructions about style in general as well as a satisfactory model for editorial office use. Emphasis has been placed upon points frequently misunderstood or violated.

GENERAL INSTRUCTIONS

Use a typewriter in preparing all copy.

Write on copy paper size 8 × 11 inches.

Begin every story in the middle of the sheet, numbering each page at the top.

Write on one side of a sheet only.

Keep a one-inch margin on all sides of the page except on the first sheet, as noted in the third line of these instructions.

Double-space all copy to provide room for guide lines, corrections, and other markings by the editor.

Write the reporter's name in the upper left-hand corner of the first page.

Write a word, or phrase, symbolic of the story in the upper left-hand corner of each page, above or below the reporter's name.

Place the word "more" at the end of each page if there is more than one page.

Use the symbol "#" at the end of the story to signify the conclusion.

Avoid long paragraphs, unnecessary words, and choppy sentences. Four typewritten lines generally make a satisfactory length for a paragraph.

Do not begin succeeding paragraphs with the same word.

Avoid the use of the same sentence structure continually—vary it.

Do not overwork any writing device, such as the practice of beginning a paragraph with a direct quotation.

Hackneyed words and expressions, "fine" writing, and sensational phrases are to be avoided as much as possible.

---

* Style books and newspapers were consulted in compiling this model, including those of the *New York Times, Baltimore Sun, Reading* (Pa.) *Tribune, Evanston* (Ill.) *Daily News-Index,* and *Chicago Tribune;* also the guides compiled by the Medill School of Journalism, Northwestern University; Institute for Journalistic Studies, Stanford University; School of Journalism, University of Wisconsin; School of Journalism, University of Iowa; Ripon College; and Lewis and Clark High School, Spokane, Washington.

Complete a paragraph on the last line of a page.

Always read a story over before turning it in to the editor—unless time prohibits.

Read the story in the paper and note the changes.

Never write more than one story on a sheet.

Make copy conform to the authorized style sheet.

Use the most reliable sources of information, such as city directory, almanac, dictionary, telephone directories, the Bible, a concordance, and an encyclopedia.

ABBREVIATIONS

(When In Doubt Spell It Out)

Abbreviate:

Names of states only when they follow names of cities: *Rockford, Ill.*

Names of months that contain more than five letters, but only in dates: *Dec. 20.*

The phrases *master of arts, doctor of philosophy,* etc.: *M.A., Ph.D.*

Hours of the day: *7 p.m.*

Railway and railroad, when initials are used for the name of the railroad: *C.M.St.P. & P. Ry.*

The titles *Dr., Mr., Mrs., the Rev., M., Mme., and Mlle.*

All other titles only when the first name or initials are used: *Gov. E. B. Jones.*

Nouns expressed in figures: *No. 3,469.*

Saint, Mount, and *Fort* before names: *Ft. Wayne.*

The word *and* to *&* only in business titles: *John Jones & Co.*

Common designations of weights and measures when occurring several times in a story: *1 yd. by 15 yds.*

Books of the Bible when the name of the book contains more than one syllable.

Names of political parties when used in statistics or parenthetically.

Senior and *Junior* when used after names.

Do Not Abbreviate:

Auxiliary nouns when used as parts of names: Harvard *college,* Central *street.*

The word *Christmas.*

The word *per cent,* except in tabulations.

The word *cents,* except in tabulations.

Christian names.

Names of centuries.

Points of the compass, except with figures.

Years, except in referring to college classes.

Names of cities.

Days of the week.

Professor to *prof.* and other colloquialisms, except before a full name.

Et cetera to *&c.* Use *etc.*

ADDRESSES

Spell out numbered streets up to *Tenth,* inclusive.
Write it *John D. Jones, 932 Pilmant street.*
If there is no street address, make it *John D. Jones, East Orange.*

CAPITALIZATION

(When In Doubt Do Not Capitalize)

Capitalize:

Names of political parties, religious denominations, and religious orders.
Names of races and nationalities, athletic teams and clubs.
Horses' and dogs' names, but do not use quotation marks also.
Seasons of the year, months, days.
Directions when used to denote national subdivisions.
Political and geographical divisions and regions when used as nouns.
Titles when they precede proper nouns.
First and principal words when in titles of plays, books, etc.
Abbreviations of college degrees.
Names of varieties of flowers, fruits, etc., when derived from names of persons or places: *Herefords, American beauty roses.*
Names of companies, except words denoting form: *First National bank.*
Names of legislative acts: *Volstead act.*
All cabinet officers: *Secretary of Labor.*
All proper nouns.
Nicknames of cities, states, nations: *Wolverine, Windy City.*
Words signifying divisions of real estate or documents: *Room 43.*
Names of places or official residences: *Vatican.*

Do Not Capitalize:

Points of the compass: *northeast.*
College degrees when spelled out.
Auxiliary nouns.
The word *former* when it precedes a title.
Names of national, state, and city bodies.
The abbreviations *a.m.* and *p.m.*
Names of studies, except languages.
Scientific names of plants and animals.
Titles when they follow a name: *John Jones, chief botanist.*
Names of college classes.
Titles in lists of officers.
Common nouns that originally were proper nouns.
Debate questions, except first word.
Adjectives derived from proper nouns which have lost their original association.
Such words as gulf, island, lake, county, district, and ward when used singly.

FIGURES

Numbers from *one* to *ten,* inclusive, should be spelled out; *eleven* and higher should be written as digits.

Use *10 p.m.*

Write it *March 15, 1950* and *Sept. 15, 1951.* Omit *st, rd, th,* after dates.

Use figures for all sums of money, scores, telephone numbers, street numbers, degrees of temperature, times in races, automobile numbers, latitudes and longitudes, distances, votes, betting odds, ages, percentages, and dimensions. Certain phrases involving the use of figures should be spelled out: *one case in a hundred.*

If a sentence begins with a number, spell the number out.

In sentences requiring more than one numeral, one below and the other above *ten,* spell out both, except in tabulations of such material.

Write it *50th.*

All numbers in statistical material should be written in figures.

Avoid unnecessary ciphers: *9 a.m.,* not *9:00 a.m.; $10,000* not *$10,000.00.*

Spell out fractions, except after figures.

Spell out ordinal names of streets.

PUNCTUATION

Apostrophe

Use an apostrophe to make clear the omission of a letter: *can't, it's.*

Use it to indicate possession except in pronouns: *John's* but not *their's.*

Use it in making plurals of letters, but not of figures: *four A's, early '90s.*

Use but one to indicate common possession: *John and Mary's car.*

Omit before common contractions like *varsity, bus, phone, plane, possum.*

Use it in unusual plurals: *Co.'s, D.A.R.'s.*

Omit in *Lawyers association, Fencers club.*

Use with year of college classes: *'40.*

Colon And Semicolon

Use a colon after a statement introducing a direct quotation of one or more sentences.

Use the colon to introduce a series: *Those elected are: president, etc.*

Use the colon to introduce a resolution: *Resolved:*

Use the colon between chapter and verse in scripture references: *John 3:16–18.*

Use it in giving the time of day: *7:35 a.m.*

Use the semicolon to separate co-ordinate clauses of the same sentence when they are not separated by a co-ordinate conjunction: *There are the Indians; we should have taken the other trail.*

A semicolon should be used to separate a series of names and addresses.

It should be used in giving election results: *Johnson, 4,657; Jamestown, 2,390.*

Comma

Use a comma whenever the meaning is doubtful and a comma will make it clear.

Use the comma to set off appositives.

When an adverbial clause begins a sentence, separate it from what follows by a comma.

When a clause ending in a verb is immediately followed by another verb, a comma should separate the verbs: *Whatever is, is right.*

A nonrestrictive adjective clause should be set off by commas.

A comma should be used to separate the parts of a compound sentence.

Separate the parts of a date by commas: *Thursday, Feb. 2, 1950.*

Use commas to set off parenthetical matter.

Set off by commas a noun used in direct address: *John, when did you arrive?*

Adjectives modifying the same noun should be separated by commas.

Omit the commas before *of* in such a construction as *Mary Brown of Chicago.*

Use the comma in scores: *Juniors, 2; Freshmen, 2.*

Dash

Use a dash after a man's name placed at the beginning of a series of interviews: *Henry Keith—I have nothing to say.* (Quotation marks are omitted with this form.)

Use dashes to indicate broken speech.

Use a dash to indicate a sudden breaking off in a direct quotation.

Use a dash to set off a parenthetical expression.

Use it to indicate omission of letters.

Hyphen

Use the hyphen with prefixes joined to proper names: *un-American.*

Use it in measures only if employed as an adjective: *3-in. valve.*

Use it in titles that begin with the word *vice.*

Compound numbers and fractions take it: *two-thirds.*

In compound adjectives use the hyphen.

Between a prefix and a proper noun it is to be used.

Use no hyphen in *today, tonight,* etc.

Leave it out of civil and military titles: *attorney general.*

Omit it from Latin forms: *ex officio member.*

Omit it from such phrases as *newly married couple, widely known person.*

Write the following as shown: *anybody, everybody, nobody, somebody, anyone, everyone, no one, someone* (but *some one* when a single specific thing or person is meant).

When two words are united to express a new meaning they should be either printed as one word or hyphenated.

When each of the words of which a compound is formed retains its original accent, they should be united by a hyphen.

Parentheses And Brackets

Avoid parentheses as much as possible. When parentheses are used, punctuate the remainder of the sentence as if the parentheses and the inclosed words were not there.

When the name of the state, though not a part of the title of a newspaper, is given with the title, use this form: *Mankato (Minn.) Free Press*.

Brackets should be used to inclose a phrase already marked by parentheses.

Use parentheses to inclose figures that indicate subject divisions: *Five points were raised: (1) cost of construction, etc.*

When a legislator's political party and state are to be indicated in short: *Sen. John Jones (Dem., N.Y.)*, use parentheses.

Use brackets to inclose matter inserted by someone other than the author: *They [the Jesuits] are expected to take action.*

Period

Omit the period after headings, captions, subheads, figures, paragraph numbers, single-line heads, Roman numerals, letters used in formulas, the words *per cent* and *pro tem.*

Use a period with all abbreviations except government agencies like *SEC*.

Use a series of three or four periods to indicate omission of quoted matter: . . .

Use periods with the abbreviation of a college degree: *B.A.*

Use a period before the last parenthesis mark when an entire sentence is enclosed: *(See other story on Page 4.)*.

Use a period after the last mark if final words of a sentence are parenthetical: *Once the book was stolen (at least so they said).*

Omit the period after nicknames.

Never use it after *Miss* but always after *Mr.* and *Mrs.*

Quotation Marks

Use quotation marks when naming books, paintings, operas, magazine articles, songs, dramas, subjects of lectures, and topics of sermons.

Use them at the beginning of each paragraph of a continuous quotation of several paragraphs, but at the end of only the last paragraph.

Use quotation marks outside periods and commas, but put them inside question marks, exclamation points, colons, and semicolons, except in cases where the punctuation is part of the quotation.

When quoting a quotation: A quotation within a quotation requires single quotation marks, but a third quotation reverts to double quotation marks. Use them to set off a word of unusual meaning or an unfamiliar, excessively slangy, or coined word the first time it is used. Quotes are unnecessary thereafter.

Use them when quoting all direct testimony, conversation, and interviews given in direct form, except when the name of the speaker or the Q. and A. (question and answer form) with a dash precedes.

Use quotation marks for all quotations when they are to be set in the same type and measure as the context, but not when they are in narrower measure or smaller type.

Avoid quotation marks when naming characters in plays or novels, with names of newspapers or other periodicals, with common nicknames except when used with the full name, and with names of vessels, animals, and sleeping cars.

TITLES

Always give initials or first names of persons the first time they appear; use either initials or first names; never say *Mr. William H. Conley,* or *Mr. Wm. Conley;* make it *William H. Conley* and, for second reference, *Mr. Conley,* unless the person is a criminal or a juvenile.

Give first names of unmarried women, not initials only: *Miss Mary Carney.*

Put *the Rev.* before a minister's full or last name: *The Rev. John Jones* and *The Rev. Mr. Jones.* Priests, on second reference, are called Father.

A Catholic sister's rank is given but not her last name, unless in exceptional cases or in case of death.

Never write it *Mrs. Doctor* or *Mrs. Professor.*

Avoid long and awkward titles before a proper name: *Joseph V. Jones, superintendent of public works.*

Write it *Mr. and Mrs. John Jones,* not *John Jones and wife.*

Use *Miss* before an unmarried woman's name.

Avoid *Mesdames* and *Messrs.* before groups of names.

SELECTED SPECIAL BOOKS *

For key to numbers listed below, see pages 419 to 431. The note below explains use of this table.

* Table numbers refer to selected books following designated code number: e.g., 66 after Chapter I refers to Ernst, M. L., *The First Freedom*.

KEY TO BOOK CODE NUMBERS *

1. Adams, S. H., *A. Woollcott*. Reynal & Hitchcock, N.Y., 1945.
   Entertaining but detailed biography of the famed raconteur, journalist, and author.

2. Albig, W., *Public Opinion*. McGraw-Hill, N.Y., 1939.
   The most comprehensive treatment of public opinion.

3. Allan, D. *How to Write for Television*. Dutton, N.Y., 1946.
   Although journalism plays little part, the general explanation of techniques is helpful.

4. Allen, C. L., *Country Journalism*. Nelson, N.Y., 1928.
   Old, but in many ways still practical.

5. Allen, E. W., *Printing for the Journalist*. Knopf, N.Y., 1928.
   Brief, exceedingly useful in its time, but neglectful of the editor's viewpoint.

6. Allen, J. E., *The Modern Newspaper*. Harper, N.Y., 1940.
   This typographer's second book explaining and illustrating page design, make-up, and headlines.

7. Allen, J. E., *Newspaper Makeup*. Harper, N.Y., 1936.
   The only modern book on this subject, it is invaluable; typography is emphasized at the expense of dealing with certain make-up problems.

8. Arthur, W. R., and Crossman, R. L., *The Law of Newspapers*. McGraw-Hill, N.Y. Revised, 1940.
   A widely-used text for college journalism classes.

9. Bailey, R., *Techniques in Article-Writing*. Appleton-Century, N.Y., 1947.
   A dozen newspaper and magazine articles are reprinted with commentaries by authors of the originals and by Mr. Bailey; useful as a supplement to a main text.

10. Bakeless, J., *Magazine Making*. Viking, N.Y., 1931.
    A comprehensive book, in view of the barren condition of magazine text material, but outdated at important points.

11. Barnhart, T. F., *Newspaper Sales Promotion*. Burgess, Minneapolis, 1939.
    A useful manual in a neglected area.

12. Barnhart, T. F., *Weekly Newspaper Management*. Appleton-Century, N.Y., 1935.
    Commends itself to the newspaper owner, no matter how experienced, as well as to teacher and student.

13. Barrett, J. W., *The End of "The World."* Harper, N.Y., 1931.
    Reactions of various staff writers who were on the *New York World* at its death; a poignant commentary on American journalism.

14. Bastian, G. C., Case, L. D., and Wolseley, R. E., *Around the Copydesk*. Macmillan, N.Y., 1946.
    The revised edition of a workbook on all phases of newspaper editing.

15. Beckman, F. W., O'Brien, H. R., and Converse, B. *Technical Writing*. Iowa State College, Ames, 1947.
    The third edition of a text originally for farm writers; it has been so improved that it can serve as a guide for writers on any technical topic.

---

* These books are in addition to those in Tabulated Bibliographies I and II.

419

16. Bent, S., *Ballyhoo*. Boni & Liveright, N.Y., 1927.
Trenchant criticism of U.S. newspapers, particularly the New York tabloids of its day.

17. Bent, S., *Newspaper Crusaders*. Whittlesey House, N.Y., 1939.
A usually adverse critic of newspapers here points to the good they have done.

18. Bent, S., *Buchanan of "The Press."* Vanguard, N.Y., 1932.
A mature novel of life on medium-sized dailies.

19. Bentley, G., *How to Edit an Employee Publication*. Harper, N.Y., 1944.
An internal house publication editor provides simple guidance for one new to the job.

20. Bernays, E. L., *Crystallizing Public Opinion*. Boni & Liveright, N.Y., 1924.
An expert in publicity applies mass psychology to his job.

21. Bernays, E. L., *Propaganda*. Liveright, N.Y., 1928.
Further analysis of propaganda and publicity from the standpoint of the social psychologist.

22. Bessie, S. M., *Jazz Journalism*. Dutton, N.Y., 1938.
A superficial but highly readable history of the tabloids; important in the absence of more probing work.

23. Biklen, P. F., and Breth, R. D., *The Successful Employee Publication*. McGraw-Hill, N.Y., 1945.
Covers the internal house publication and offers tested advice and methods.

24. Bird, G. L., *Article Writing and Marketing*. Rinehart, N.Y., 1948.
Combining newspaper and magazine feature and article writing and selling, this teachable text contains a logical plan for developing writing skill.

25. Bird, G. L., and Merwin, F. E., *The Newspaper and Society*. Prentice-Hall, N.Y., 1942.
An anthology on newspaper influence; many valuable bibliographies are under each heading, with integrating essays uniting the whole.

26. Bleyer, W. G., *Main Currents in the History of American Journalism*. Houghton Mifflin, Boston, 1927.
Commonly considered this journalism educator's major contribution to the literature of journalism, it is his most readable book and long one of the few fine historical works in the field.

27. Bleyer, W. G., *Special Feature Articles*. Houghton Mifflin, Boston, 1919.
Although one of the earliest books on the subject, little is outdated except the illustrations.

28. Bond, F. F., *How to Write and Sell Non-fiction*. Whittlesey House, N.Y., 1938.
Professor Bond's reader-interest theories as applied to free-lance writing.

29. Boughner, G. J., *Women in Journalism*. Appleton, N.Y., 1926.
One of the few texts about women's newspaper and magazine work, it covers many phases but needs drastic revision.

30. Britt, G., *Forty Years—Forty Millions*. Farrar & Rinehart, N.Y., 1935.
A fair, exceedingly well-written evaluation of Frank Munsey, New York publisher who merged or abolished many papers and periodicals.

31. Brucker, H., *Freedom of Information*. Macmillan, N.Y., 1949.
A defense of traditional freedom of the press as understood in the United States but an acknowledgment of the economic forces that affect the press.

32. Brucker, H., *The Changing American Newspaper*. Columbia, N.Y., 1937.
An intelligent and forward-looking discussion of the mutations of newspapers, in methods as well as typography and make-up.

33. Burack, A. S., Editor, *The Writer's Handbook*. Writer Magazine, Boston, 1946.
Articles by numerous contributors to *The Writer* give advice on the preparation and sale of most types of material; a useful market guide is included.

34. Bush, C. R., *Editorial Thinking and Writing.* Appleton, N.Y., 1932.
Broad treatment of editorial writing, with concern for techniques of presentation as well as content.

35. Bush, C. R., *Newspaper Reporting of Public Affairs.* Appleton, N.Y., 1940.
Detailed guidance to the coverage of municipal, county, state and national bodies, as of the time of publication.

36. Campbell, L. R., and Jones, J. P., *News Beat.* Macmillan, N.Y., 1949.
A storehouse of tests, exercises, study blanks, and other materials for class use, as well as concise summaries of standard principles.

37. Campbell, W. S., *Writing Non-Fiction.* Writer Magazine, Boston, 1944.
Types and production problems of writing articles and books.

38. Carlson, O., *Brisbane.* Stackpole, N.Y., 1937.
A cold dissection of an influential American journalist.

39. Charnley, M. V., *News by Radio.* Macmillan, N.Y., 1948.
To the time of publication, late in 1948, this was the most precise analysis and description, with many suitable examples of news on the air; more suitable as a text than other recent books covering the subject.

40. Charnley, M. V., and Converse, B., *Magazine Writing and Editing.* Cordon, N.Y., 1938.
An explanation of how it's done in the magazine offices, with a home and garden periodical as the central example.

41. Commission on Freedom of the Press, *A Free and Responsible Press.* University of Chicago Press, Chicago, 1947.
Although uninformed on journalism education, the report (a summary of the findings in six other volumes) accompanies adverse criticism of the press with constructive suggestions for making it socially more responsible and useful.

42. *Continuing Study of Newspaper Reading.* Advertising Research Foundation, N.Y., 1946.
An assembly of the findings from 100 individual studies made widely over the U.S.; an invaluable guide to advertisers and editors.

43. Corbin, C. R., *Why News Is News.* Ronald, N.Y., 1928.
A study of news as a commodity.

44. Cortissoz, R., *The Life of Whitelaw Reid.* Scribner, N.Y., 1921.
A precise biography of the successor to Greeley as editor of the *New York Tribune,* by the *Herald Tribune's* long revered art critic.

45. Crawford, N. A., *The Ethics of Journalism.* Knopf, N.Y., 1924.
A high-minded discussion of journalistic ethics, with emphasis on codes and resolutions.

46. Crawford, R. P., *The Magazine Article.* McGraw-Hill, N.Y., 1931.
A helpful guidebook for the beginner.

47. Crews, A. R., *Professional Radio Writing.* Houghton Mifflin, Boston, 1946.
Survey of the different types, with a little attention to the journalistic angle, but not enough; excellent as a general treatment, however.

48. Dabney, T. E., *One Hundred Great Years.* Louisiana State University Press, Baton Rouge, La., 1944.
History of the *New Orleans Times-Picayune.*

49. Dale, E., *How to Read a Newspaper.* Scott, Foresman, Chicago, 1941.
Well-organized, pleasantly illustrated and printed, and accurate, this makes easy and attractive reading for high-school or college students.

50. Dana, C. A., *The Art of Newspaper Making.* Appleton, N.Y., 1895.
Three of the famed editor's speeches, revealing him as dogmatic and wise.

51. Davis, C. B., *"The Great American Novel—."* Farrar & Rinehart, N.Y., 1938.
An ironical novel of the newsman beset by frustration, chiefly professional.

52. Davis, E., *History of the New York Times,* Times, N.Y., 1921.
Tightly packed with facts, this account is ready for "Add 1."

53. Davis, H. W., *The Column.* Knopf, N.Y., 1926.
Old examples and unawareness of what was to occur in the next two decades gives this only limited usefulness today.

54. Davis, R. H., *From "Gallegher" to "The Deserter."* Scribner's, N.Y., 1927.
The war correspondent's short stories about journalism and other subjects.

55. Dennis, C. H., *Victor Lawson.* University of Chicago Press, Chicago, 1935.
A full, somewhat labored, but needed biography of the one-time publisher of the *Chicago Daily News.*

56. Desmond, R. W., *Newspaper Reference Methods.* University of Minnesota Press, Minneapolis, 1933.
Precious to all who have to do with the newspaper library.

57. Desmond, R. W., *The Press and World Affairs.* Appleton-Century, N.Y., 1937.
A thorough explanation of how the news throughout the world is gathered by co-operative agencies and valuable comments on many papers of the globe; pre-war.

58. Doherty, E., *Gall and Honey.* Sheed & Ward, N.Y., 1941.
One of the country's best reporters and feature writers, with long experience in metropolitan journalism and other writing areas, tells the story of his unusual career.

59. Doob, L. W., *Propaganda.* Holt, N.Y., 1936.
A broadminded, calm social psychologist restates the best views on this disputed subject.

60. Downey, F., *Richard Harding Davis—His Day.* Scribner, N.Y., 1933.
An artistically-written biography that tends to debunk Davis; the only book available on him.

61. Drewry, J. E., *Book Reviewing.* Writer Magazine, Boston, 1945.
Systematic presentation of the mechanics of reviewing and types of reviews; useful appendices.

62. Drewry, J. E., Editor, *Post Biographies of Famous Journalists.* Random House, N.Y., 1944. Another volume issued by University of Georgia Press, Athens, 1946.
About 50 biographical articles reprinted from the *Saturday Evening Post,* some by leading journalists, and on widely-known editors, publishers, writers.

63. Dyar, E., *Newspaper Promotion and Research.* Harper, N.Y., 1942.
An explanation of newspaper promotion activities, describing the planning of cooking schools, store promotion, and other devices.

64. Edson, C. L., *The Gentle Art of Columning.* Brentano, N.Y., 1920.
Little about columning; much about what goes into columns.

65. Elfenbein, J., *Business Journalism.* Harper, N.Y., 1947.
For editors and publishers of business publications, covering the history, departmental operations, and other helpful material about this main member of the specialized press.

66. Ernst, M. L., *The First Freedom.* Macmillan, N.Y., 1946.
A lawyer for journalistic groups contends that the real danger to freedom of the press is the monopolistic situation existing in the newspaper, magazine, and radio fields.

67. Essary, J. F., *Covering Washington.* Houghton Mifflin, Boston, 1927.
A combination guide for Washington correspondents and a record of experiences; historical in value only.

68. Ferber, N., *I Found Out*. Dial, N.Y., 1939.
Required reading for all would-be "star" reporters; it is the cynical autobiography of a crusading newsman.

69. Field, M., *Freedom Is More than a Word*. University of Chicago Press, Chicago, 1945.
The credo of the publisher of the *Chicago Sun-Times* and owner of radio stations; a document remarkable for its liberalism.

70. Fisher, C., *The Columnists: A Surgical Survey*. Howell, Soskin, N.Y., 1944.
A columnist pokes fun at some of the leaders of his profession; a breezy combination of biography and evaluation.

71. Flint, L. N., *Conscience of the Newspaper*. Appleton, N.Y., 1925.
The case method used to advantage in consideration of the ethics of journalism.

72. Flint, L. N., *The Editorial*. Appleton, N.Y., 1928.
This and an older edition were warhorses among journalism texts; certain chapters still valuable.

73. Ford, E. H., *A Bibliography of Literary Journalism in America*. Burgess, Minneapolis, 1937.
A useful list for a field where confusion frequently occurs and where little reading matter exists.

74. Fowler, G., *Timber Line*. Blue Ribbon, N.Y., 1933.
One of the most entertaining and readable books in journalism; although useless to careful scholars, it provides biographies of the *Denver Post* and its notorious owners, Bonfils and Tammen.

75. Gard, W., *Book Reviewing*. Knopf, N.Y., 1927.
Guide book offering the authoritarian point of view.

76. Gardner, G., *Lusty Scripps*. Vanguard, N.Y., 1932.
A vigorously-written and fair evaluation of E. W. Scripps.

77. Garst, R. E., Editor, *The Newspaper—Its Making and Its Meaning*. Scribner, N.Y., 1945.
Twelve addresses on basic newspaper operations by prominent *New York Times* staff writers and executives.

78. Gauvreau, E., *Hot News*. Macaulay, N.Y., 1931.
A sensational, exaggerated novel of early New York tabloid journalism; but no more sensational than that journalism.

79. Goddard, M., *What Interests People*. American Weekly, N.Y., 1935.
The philosophy behind the huge Sunday supplement of the Hearst papers; views that must be examined for basic understanding of reader-interests.

80. Goldberg, I., *Major Noah*. Jewish Publication Society of America, Philadelphia, 1936.
An appreciation of the picturesque editor of the *New York Courier* and *Evening Star*.

81. Gramling, O., *A.P.—The Story of the News*. Farrar & Rinehart, N.Y., 1940.
A popular history of the press association.

82. Greene, T. M., *The Arts and the Art of Criticism*. Princeton University Press, Princeton, N.J., 1940.
The arts are analyzed philosophically and examined from the standpoint of the principles of criticism.

83. Hale, W. G., *The Law of the Press*. West, St. Paul, 1948.
The revised edition of a long used, basic text using the case method.

84. Harrington, H. F., and Martin, L., *Pathways to Print*. Van Nostrand, N.Y., 1931.
Most short forms of journalistic writing are explained in neat chapters.

85. Harrington, H. F., and Watson, E. S., *Modern Feature Writing*. Harper, N.Y., 1935.
The revised, shortened, brightened and generally improved edition of Harrington's earlier *Chats on Feature Writing,* which itself was widely used.

86. Harrington, H. F., and Wolseley, R. E., *The Copyreader's Workshop*. Heath, Boston, 1934.
A combination text and workbook covering all desk duties.

87. Hecht, B., *1001 Afternoons in Chicago*. Covici Friede, N.Y., 1922.
Sketches from the *Chicago Daily News;* excellent examples of literary journalism.

88. Hecht, B. and MacArthur, C., *The Front Page*. Covici Friede, N.Y., 1928.
Good drama, but typical only of newspaper life in Chicago during a certain period.

89. Hepner, H. W., *Effective Advertising*. McGraw-Hill, N.Y., 1949.
The psychology of advertising, with some social analysis, presented in an unusually effective format.

90. Hoffman, F. J., Allen, C., and Ulrich, C. F., *The Little Magazine*. Princeton University Press, Princeton, N.J., 1946.
A careful check list and a sensitive history of the "little literary" magazines by appreciative, meticulous scholars working in a new field.

91. Holt, H., *Commercialism and Journalism*. Houghton Mifflin, Boston, 1909.
Briefly presented adverse criticism of the American newspaper; the charges still apply in some quarters.

92. Hotaling, B. L., *A Manual of Radio News Writing*. Journal, Milwaukee, 1947.
This slender book is highly realistic and tested.

93. Hotchkiss, G. B., *Advertising Copy*. Harper, N.Y., 1936.
Expert methods of preparing advertising messages; a book used widely in school and office.

94. Hotchkiss, G. B., *An Outline of Advertising*. Macmillan, N.Y., 1940.
Analysis of the objectives of advertising and practical treatment of problems in production, copy testing, legal aspects, and other phases.

95. Hudson, F., *Journalism in the United States from 1680 to 1872*. Harper, N.Y., 1872.
A rare volume by a pioneer historian who was managing editor of the *New York Herald;* includes many famous documents and quotations.

96. Hunt, L. W., *Displaying the News*. Harper, N.Y., 1934.
An all too brief but useful combination text and workbook on newspaper editing, prepared for university laboratory use.

97. Hutchinson, T. H., *Here Is Television*. Hastings House, N.Y., 1946.
A leading executive in this new field describes the procedures, mechanisms, and possibilities in a realistic fashion, resisting the usual glamorizing.

98. Hyde, G. M., *Journalistic Writing*. Appleton-Century, N.Y., 1946.
The latest edition of a text especially adaptable to high-school journalism classes and staffs of student publications; also a guide for the faculty adviser of limited experience.

99. Ickes, H., *America's House of Lords*. Harcourt, Brace, N.Y., 1939.
A pungent attack on the U.S. press by a former Cabinet member and ex-reporter; not without its constructive sections.

100. Irwin, W., *Propaganda and the News*. McGraw-Hill, N.Y., 1936.
Although sound analysis of news presentation in the mid-thirties with emphasis on the effect of propaganda on the newspaper and radio, it covers old ground.

101. Johns, O., *Time of Our Lives*. Stackpole, N.Y., 1937.
Stories of reporting feats and escapades by the author or his father (the latter was editor of the *St. Louis Post-Dispatch*).

102. Johnson, B., *As Much as I Dare*. Washburn, N.Y., 1944.

Burges Johnson was a newspaperman under Steffens, a Harper's book editor, a magazine editor, a journalism and English teacher; his autobiography is winningly written.

103. Johnson, G. W., *An Honorable Titan*. Harper, N.Y., 1946.

A biography of Adolph S. Ochs of the *New York Times;* thoroughly appreciative and in a period setting.

104. Johnson, G. W., *What Is News?* Knopf, N.Y., 1926.

A spirited analysis of a still unsolved problem, its definition came closer to reality than any prepared earlier.

105. Johnson, G. W., Kent, F. R., Mencken, H. L., and Owens, H., *The Sunpapers of Baltimore*. Knopf, N.Y., 1937.

The history of two famous American dailies by distinguished authors.

106. Jones, L., *How to Criticize Books*. Norton, N.Y., 1928.

A summary and discussion of techniques from an impressionistic critic, then in newspaper work.

107. Jones, R. W., *The Editorial Page*. Crowell, N.Y., 1930.

Still useful, but many changes have occurred, especially in format, that leave behind this somewhat routine treatment.

108. Jones, R. W., *Journalism in the United States*. Dutton, N.Y., 1947.

The newest history, it is most readable in its coverage of the early years; it carries the chronology to the post-war period; badly indexed.

109. Kelly, F. F., *Flowing Stream*. Dutton, N.Y., 1939.

Autobiography of an outstanding American woman journalist, long connected with the *New York Times;* it is worth consulting for data on women in news work and historical material on the U.S. Press.

110. Kinsley, P., *The Chicago Tribune*. Knopf, New York, 1943. Vols. II and III, Tribune, Chicago, 1945, 1947.

The first volume of the *Tribune's* 100 years of life is integrated; the remaining two are merely rehashes; so many interesting events occurred in the period so far treated (1847–1900) that the summarizing is useful.

111. Kleppner, O., *Advertising Procedure*. Prentice-Hall, N.Y., 1941.

The magnum opus of advertising books, it is simple in its treatment but encyclopedic in scope, considering, in detail, technique, handling, departmental organization, media, and copy.

112. Kobre, S., *Backgrounding the News*. Twentieth Century, Baltimore, Md., 1939.

A pioneering and significant application of sociological ideas to news handling; gradually news publications are adopting the author's suggestions.

113. Lasky, J., *Proofreading and Copy-preparation*. Mentor, N.Y., 1941.

The most detailed and thorough-going treatment available on these two subjects, it has become a standard in shop and school.

114. Lasswell, H. D., *Propaganda Technique in the World War*. Knopf, N.Y., 1937.

Important when first issued, this book had double importance during World War II; it is an impartial summary.

115. Leach, H., and Carroll, J. C., *What's the News?* Covici, Chicago, 1926.

Philosophizings upon the news, with the conclusion that the newspaper can be no better than its readers.

116. Lee, A. Mc., *The Daily Newspaper in America*. Macmillan, N.Y., 1937.

The first social analysis of the metropolitan newspaper, this is a broadly challenging volume which must be included in any study of the history of journalism.

117. Lee, J. M., *History of American Journalism*. Houghton Mifflin, Boston, 1923.

One of the modern histories, wide in scope, it rightly places emphasis on trends rather than dates and names; it tends to dismiss some subjects too briefly and its accuracy has been challenged.

118. Lippmann, W., *Public Opinion*. Harcourt, Brace, N.Y., 1922. Also Penguin Books, N.Y., 1946.

Produced when the author was in his most liberal and original frame of mind, it is to be used in study of reader-interest, publicity, and propaganda in relation to the journalist.

119. Logie, I. R., *Careers for Women in Journalism*. International Textbook, Scranton, Pa., 1938.

A study of vocational aspects usually left to guesswork; many helpful case histories, although somewhat dated.

120. Lumley, F. E., *The Propaganda Menace*. Century, N.Y., 1933.

A lengthy study, marred by its author's inability to maintain objectivity.

121. Lundberg, F., *Imperial Hearst*. Equinox Cooperative Press, N.Y., 1936. Also Modern Library, N.Y., 1937.

An indictment of the publisher, it is at the same time a powerful criticism of the U.S. press; the author weakens his case by sometimes unwarranted conclusions.

122. MacDougall, C. D., *Covering the Courts*. Prentice-Hall, N.Y., 1946.

A genuine reporting text for its subject, it tells the newsman what he must know to cover the court beat; not a news writing text on court stories but a more valuable source of facts about various court systems, procedures, etc.

123. MacDougall, C. D., *Newsroom Problems and Policies*. Macmillan, N.Y., 1941.

An objective and scholarly presentation of the major social problems confronting the press, such as treatment of crime news.

124. Mansfield, F. J., *The Complete Journalist*. Pitman, N.Y., 1936.

An omnibus volume by a leading British journalist, who mixes his experiences with instruction in technique; American methods are considered.

125. Maulsby, W. S., *Getting the News*. Harcourt, Brace, N.Y., 1925.

A skimpy book on reporting, presented in colorless language, but an improvement in certain respects over earlier volumes.

126. Maverick, A., *Henry J. Raymond and the New York Press for 30 Years*. Hale, Hartford, Conn., 1870.

Covering U.S. journalism from 1840 to 1870, with special attention to the career of Raymond, the *New York Times'* publisher.

127. McClure, S. S., *My Autobiography*. Stokes, N.Y., 1914.

This is the McClure whose name still clings to a large syndicate and who, with his magazine publishing policies, gave space and encouragement to the muckrakers (Steffens, Tarbell, Russell, etc.).

128. McKelway, St. C., *Gossip*. Viking, N.Y., 1940.

An acid biographette of Walter Winchell; also an excellent example of literary journalism.

129. McKenzie, V., *Behind the Headlines*. Cape & Smith, N.Y., 1931.

A dozen stories of reporters' exploits; entertaining reading.

130. McRae, M. A., *Forty Years in Newspaperdom*. Brentano, N.Y., 1924.

Pen portraits of journalists in the days of E. W. Scripps, with whom the author was associated; also McRae's autobiography.

131. Mencken, H. L., *Happy Days*. Knopf, N.Y., 1940.

The first of several in a series of autobiographical volumes; this and the second (*Newspaper Days*) tell some of his journalistic experience and views, all in bristling Menckenian style not without sentimentalism.

132. Mich, D. D., and Eberman, E., *The Technique of the Picture Story*. McGraw-Hill, N.Y., 1945.

An illustrated description of picture story production, useful to the editor of large magazines chiefly.

133. Miller, D. W., *Practical Exercises in News Writing*. Heath, Boston, 1933.

Style exercises, materials for news stories, problems in rewriting, and faulty stories for rewriting and criticism, all based on actual news accounts.

134. Miller, D. W., *Practical Exercises in Newspaper Copyreading, Proofreading and Make-up*. Heath, Boston, 1935.
Intended for university courses in editing, it offers workable exercises.

135. Mitchell, D. E., *Journalism and Life*. Little, Brown, Boston, 1939.
A social approach to journalism, ideal for teaching it in high school as a social science; in addition an excellent technical book for journalism courses or production of high school publications.

136. Morley, C., *Religio Journalistici*. Doubleday, Page, N.Y., 1924.
A pleasant essay to the point that religion and journalism can benefit society.

137. Mott, F. L., *American Journalism*. Macmillan, N.Y., 1941.
The foremost history, it covers interestingly and informatively the development of newspaper and magazine, with some attention to radio, journalism education, and related subjects; too detailed for easy use as a text.

138. Mott, F. L., *History of American Magazines*. Harvard, Cambridge, 1938.
The outstanding piece of scholarship in journalism, this 3-volume work, still incomplete, won the Pulitzer Prize in 1939 and is the standard source on U.S. magazine history.

139. Mott, F. L., and Casey, R. D., *Interpretations of Journalism*. Crofts, N.Y., 1937.
This anthology contains many of the most famous speeches and writings upon journalism.

140. Mowrer, P. S., *The House of Europe*. Houghton Mifflin, Boston, 1945.
A top foreign correspondent and editor tells his personal story as well as that of the inter-war years abroad.

141. Nixon, R. B., *Henry W. Grady*. Knopf, N.Y., 1943.
A long-needed study of the Southern editor, orator, and political leader.

142. O'Brien, F. M., *The Story of "The Sun."* Appleton, N.Y., 1928.
A classic in journalistic history and literature, it deals with a proud paper and a vital period in U.S. history.

143. Older, F., *My Own Story*. Call, San Francisco, 1919. Also Macmillan, N.Y., 1926.
One of the two or three major autobiographies of U.S. journalism; like Steffens', it is part of journalistic and general history.

144. Olson, K. E., *Typography and Mechanics of the Newspaper*. Appleton, N.Y., 1930.
Marked by comprehensiveness, this has been the authoritative book in its field.

145. Pattee, F. L., *The New American Literature*. Century, N.Y., 1930.
Discusses twentieth century American literature, with all the journalistic forces that have impinged upon it.

146. Payne, G. H., *History of Journalism in the United States*. Appleton, N.Y., 1920.
Lacks both popular appeal and scholarly approach, but still useful for general trends.

147. Pollard, J. E., *The Presidents and the Press*. Macmillan, N.Y., 1947.
A major work of scholarship in journalism and political and governmental history; a thorough description of the press relationships from Washington to Truman.

148. Pollard, J. E., *Principles of Newspaper Management*. McGraw-Hill, N.Y., 1937.
On the metropolitan level, it is thorough and useful for the professional as well as the student.

149. Powell, J. B., *My Twenty-Five Years in China*. Macmillan, N.Y., 1945.
The story of a heroic editor who practiced journalism many years in the Orient; an amazing story calmly told.

150. Presbry, F., *History and Development of Advertising*. Doubleday, N.Y., 1929.
For the period covered it is a standard, often used work, long considered the leading history.

151. Price, J., *News Photography*. Industries, N.Y., 1935.
Instructive and at one time widely-used, but written down and superficial, emphasizing glamour over-much; technological changes have left it far behind.

152. Radder, N., *Newspapers in Community Service*. McGraw-Hill, N.Y., 1926.
Helpful to the crusading editor and a record of good deeds.

153. Rae, W., *Editing Small Newspapers*. Mill, N.Y., 1943.
A supplementary book on editorial and newsroom procedures, aimed at scholastic journalists but helpful to others.

154. Redmond, P. and W., *Business Paper Writing*. Pitman, N.Y., 1939.
Limited in scope, but helpful in an area where little assistance is available.

155. Reed, P. I., *Writing Journalistic Features*. McGraw-Hill, N.Y., 1931.
Mainly of interest to creative writing classes, but useful to students of the feature for any purpose.

156. Rich, E., *William Allen White*. Farrar & Rinehart, N.Y., 1941.
After the Emporia editor's autobiography, this is the basic work on White.

157. Robertson, S., *Introduction to Modern Journalism*. Prentice-Hall, N.Y., 1930.
Emphasizing the editorial side of newspapers, it was thoroughgoing for its period.

158. Rogers, C. E., *Journalistic Vocations*. Appleton-Century, N.Y., 1937.
The only general book in the field; fundamentally excellent but should be brought up to date.

159. Rosewater, V., *The History of Cooperative Newsgathering in the United States*. Appleton, N.Y., 1930.
Valuable, especially because there is no other as broad or detailed.

160. Ross, I., *Ladies of the Press*. Harper, N.Y., 1936.
A record of woman's contribution to American journalism; comprehensive but somewhat indiscriminate in its praise.

161. Rosten, L. C., *The Washington Correspondents*. Harcourt, Brace, N.Y., 1937.
Sample of a type of journalistic study needed for many phases; this one proves that newspapers too often are policy-ridden and gives data on the correspondents' procedures and views.

162. Safely, J. C., *The Country Newspaper and Its Operation*. Appleton, N.Y., 1930.
Because changes have occurred with least rapidity in the community field, this thorough book still has much valuable material to offer.

163. Sedgwick, E., *The Happy Profession*. Little, Brown, Boston, 1946.
An autobiographical fragment, not a full story, it tells much about the famed *Atlantic* editor's early struggle with that magazine and others.

164. Seitz, D. C., *Horace Greeley*. Bobbs-Merrill, Indianapolis, 1926.
Of the many biographies of the great liberal editor, this is one of the best balanced.

165. Seitz, D. C., *The James Gordon Bennetts*. Bobbs-Merrill, Indianapolis, 1928.
The biographies of two potent editors, with greater justice done the younger of these dictators of the *New York Herald*.

166. Seitz, D. C., *Joseph Pulitzer*. Garden City, Long Island, N.Y., 1924.
Long used as the definitive biography of the dynamic editor of the *New York World*.

167. Seldes, G., *Freedom of the Press*. Bobbs-Merrill, Indianapolis, 1935.
Sweeping criticism of the U.S. press, not always proved; several chapters of positive suggestions for solutions and ways of improvement are its chief value.

168. Seldes, G., *Lords of the Press*. Messner, N.Y., 1938.
A repetition of the author's charges against newspapers, it is wound around personalities.

169. Sevareid, E., *Not So Wild a Dream*. Knopf, N.Y., 1946.
A radio war correspondent's thoughtful and graciously written autobiography; one of the best of the many war books.

170. Shuler, M., Knight, R. A., and Fuller, M., *Lady Editor*. Dutton, N.Y., 1941.
Three women journalists or publicists give vocational guidance to young girls interested in magazine, newspaper writing, or book publishing careers.

171. Siebert, F. S., *The Rights and Privileges of the Press*. Appleton-Century, N.Y., 1934.
Well-organized and a favorite with students because it was written for them rather than for lawyers; the subject is treated positively.

172. Sinclair, U., *The Brass Check*. Author, Pasadena, Calif., 1919. Also, Boni, N.Y., 1936.
Exposé of a prostituted press by a major social critic and writer; the generalizations are not always warranted; a lack of understanding of newspaper operations weakens some accusations.

173. Smith, H. J., *Extra! Extra!* North, Chicago, 1934.
Two newspaper novels, *Deadlines* and *Josslyn,* by a literary and beloved Chicago editor.

174. Sontheimer, M., *Newspaperman*. Whittlesey, N.Y., 1941.
Anecdotal, chip-on-the-shoulder comment and advice on newspaper life as a vocation.

175. Spencer, M. L., *Editorial Writing*. Houghton Mifflin, Boston, 1924.
An inclusive presentation of editorial writing methods; despite its age a remarkably timely volume.

176. Stanley, T. B., *The Technique of Advertising Production*. Prentice-Hall, N.Y., 1940.
Analysis of the typographical aspects of advertising, with instruction in planning and carrying out many forms of printed advertising material.

177. Staudenmayer, M. S., *Reading and Writing the News*. Harcourt, Brace, N.Y., 1941.
Combination newswriting workbook and a high-school manual in newspaper reading; rich in content and original in concept.

178. Steffens, L., *The Autobiography of Lincoln Steffens*. Harcourt, Brace, N.Y., 1931.
A distinguished book, among the very best in the literature of journalism as well as social history, by a great journalist.

179. Stewart, K., *News Is What We Make It*. Houghton Mifflin, Boston, 1943.
A liberal, widely-experienced newsman, now a journalism professor, describes journalism in the inter-war years as well as his own life story.

180. Stoddard, H. L., *Horace Greeley*. Putnam, N.Y., 1946.
A journalist's biography, it emphasizes Greeley's newspaper work rather than his political activity.

181. Stone, M. E., *Fifty Years a Journalist*. Doubleday, N.Y., 1921.
The life story of a leader in Chicago and press association journalism.

182. Sutton, A. A., *Design and Makeup of the Newspaper*. Prentice-Hall, N.Y., 1948.
Prepared as a successor to Olson's text, it presents the newspaper practices of the day as well as background suitable for a newspaper typography course.

183. Tebbel, J., *An American Dynasty*. Doubleday, N.Y., 1947.
The Medill-McCormick-Patterson family is the dynasty; it is the history of a journalistic group much in controversy over the years.

184. Tebbel, J., *George Horace Lorimer and the Saturday Evening Post*. Doubleday, N.Y., 1948.
An admiring biography of the editor who made the *Post* a leading magazine.

185. Thayer, F., *Legal Control of the Press*. Foundation Press, Chicago, 1944.
The most recent book on law of the press, it is encyclopedic and organized for easy use.

186. Thayer, F. B., *Newspaper Management*. Appleton-Century, N.Y., 1938.
The revision of a text that has been a standard since it first was published in 1926; the new version overcomes the narrowness of the old editions.

187. Van Deusen, G. G., *Thurlow Weed*. Little, Brown, Boston, 1946.
First genuine biography of the Albany editor and Whig and Republican leader.

188. Van Doren, C., *Benjamin Franklin*. Viking, N.Y., 1938.
Accepted as the definitive biography, this won the Pulitzer Prize.

189. Villard, O. G., *The Disappearing Daily*. Knopf, N.Y., 1945.
A new version of a book called *Some Newspapers and Newspapermen,* this is penetrating criticism and praise of the U.S. press by a level-headed editor of long experience.

190. Villard, O. G., *Fighting Years*. Harcourt, Brace, N.Y., 1939.
In a class with Steffens' autobiography, although not as well written or as detailed, this is the unusual story of a noted and courageous editor and publisher.

191. Vitray, L., Mills, J., Jr., and Ellard, R. B., *Pictorial Journalism*. McGraw-Hill, N.Y., 1939.
One of the few texts in photo-journalism, it is excellent for picture editing courses preparing students for big-city work.

192. Waldrop, A. G., *Editor and Editorial Writer*. Rinehart, N.Y., 1948.
Appealingly written, it quickly became the standard book on editorial writing, for it is rich with background and examples as well as incisive analysis of practices and possibilities.

193. Walker, S., *City Editor*. Stokes, N.Y., 1934.
Favorite reading of many journalism students, it is a stimulating set of essays on various aspects of journalism by a blasé New York editor and writer.

194. Waller, J. C., *Radio: The Fifth Estate*. Houghton Mifflin, Boston, 1946.
A description of the institution in the United States; an authoritative general presentation by a widely-experienced radio executive.

195. Warren, C. N., *Modern News Reporting*. Harper, N. Y., 1934.
The later edition of a book popular for its pioneering and successful use of geometric patterns for news; now dated and narrow in scope.

196. Watterson, H., *"Marse" Henry*. Doran, N.Y., 1919.
The autobiography of the so-called last individualist among U.S. newspapermen; an invaluable chronicle of Southern journalism.

197. Whipple, J., *How to Write for Radio*. Whittlesey, N.Y., 1938.
Originally one of the three or four most useful manuals in the field, it still is widely consulted.

198. White, Paul W., *News on the Air*. Harcourt, Brace, N.Y., 1947.
The first full-length treatment of radio news preparation; the 20 chapters cover all phases and are well illustrated with scripts.

199. White, W. A., *The Autobiography of William Allen White*. Macmillan, N.Y., 1946.
A major book in journalism's literature, it is the story of a great journalist's thoughts and actions as well as a description of political activity in the author's state and in the nation.

200. White, W. A., *The Editor and His People*. Macmillan, N.Y., 1924.
A collection of editorials representative of this noted editorialist of contemporary U.S. journalism.

201. White, W. A., *In Our Town*. Macmillan, N.Y., 1925.
A book by the *Emporia Gazette* editor which is not appreciated; it consists of semi-fictionized accounts of newspaper personalities and other citizens in small towns.

202. Williams, B. A., *Splendor*. Dutton, N.Y., 1927.
A novel of a newspaperman's life, achieving the scope but hardly the quality of an American *Forsyte Saga*.

203. Williams, J. L., *The Stolen Story*. Scribner, N.Y., 1906.
Romantic short stories of the journalism of the turn of the century.

204. Williams, T., *The Newspaperman*. Scribner, N.Y., 1922.
Guidance and evaluation, in compact form and valid for a by-gone day, by a famed teacher.

205. Wolseley, R. E., *The Journalist's Bookshelf*. Quill & Scroll Foundation, Chicago, 1946.
Most recent and comprehensive bibliography of U.S. journalism; annual supplements are issued.

206. Wood, J. P., *Magazines in the United States*. Ronald, N.Y., 1949.
A brief history, more up-to-date than any other available, as well as evaluative chapters.

207. Wylie, M., *Radio Writing*. Farrar & Rinehart, N.Y., 1939.
Generally accepted as one of the best books in the field; thorough and based on first-hand experience.

208. Yost, C. S., *The Principles of Journalism*. Appleton, N.Y., 1924.
An explanation of the import of the Canons of Journalism of the American Society of Newspaper Editors, by a *St. Louis Globe-Democrat* editor and ASNE officer.

INDEX

For technical terms not listed in this index, see Chapter XLV, "Terminology and Press Jargon," pp. 390–410.

433